W9-AFD-843

THE ESSAYS OF HENRY D. THOREAU

SELECTED AND EDITED

BY LEWIS HYDE

NORTH POINT PRESS

A DIVISION OF FARRAR, STRAUS AND GIROUX

NEW YORK

THE ESSAYS OF HENRY D. THOREAU

North Point Press
A division of Farrar, Straus and Giroux
19 Union Square West, New York 10003

Distributed in Canada by Douglas & McIntyre Ltd.
Printed in the United States of America
First edition, 2002

Grateful acknowledgment is made to the following for permission to reproduce images on the essay title pages in this book:

To the Thoreau Institute for pages from *The Dial*, July 1842, preceding "Natural History of Massachusetts," and October 1843, preceding "A Winter Walk"; for the page from the *Democratic Review*, November 1843, preceding "Paradise (To Be) Regained"; for the page from *The Union Magazine*, November 1848, preceding "Ktaadn"; for the title page from *Aesthetic Papers*, 1849, preceding "Civil Disobedience"; for the leaf cut from *The Atlantic Monthly*, October 1862, preceding "Autumnal Tints"; for the page from *Echoes of Harper's Ferry*, ed. James Redpath (Boston: Thayer and Eldridge, 1860), preceding "A Plea for Captain John Brown"; and for the page from *The Atlantic Monthly*, November 1862, preceding "Wild Apples."

To the Houghton Library at Harvard University for the manuscript page from 1851, preceding "Walking"; for excerpts from *The Liberator*, July 21, 1854, preceding "Slavery in Massachusetts," and July 27, 1860, preceding "The Last Days of John Brown"; and for the advertisement from *The Liberator*, December 1, 1854, preceding "Life without Principle."

And to the Concord Free Public Library for the page from *Transactions of the Middlesex Agricultural Society*, 1860, preceding "The Succession of Forest Trees."

Library of Congress Cataloging-in-Publication Data
Thoreau, Henry David, 1817–1862.
[Essays. Selections]
The essays of Henry D. Thoreau / selected and edited by Lewis Hyde. — 1st ed.
p. cm.
Includes bibliographical references and index.
ISBN 0-86547-585-7 (alk. paper) —ISBN 0-86547-646-2 (pbk. : alk. paper)
I. Hyde, Lewis, 1945– II. Title.

PS3042 .H93 2002
814'.3—dc21

2001054600

Designed by Jonathan D. Lippincott

www.fsgbooks.com

1 3 5 7 9 10 8 6 4 2

CONTENTS

THE ESSAYS

INTRODUCTION: PROPHETIC EXCURSIONS

LEWIS HYDE

I. A TALL WHITE PINE

When I was young and longed to write, I was much in love with Henry D. Thoreau. I loved the plain declarative sentences and flat statements of belief from which he built his work: "Surely joy is the condition of life." "We must look a long time before we can see." "What is time but the stuff delay is made of?" "The blue-bird carries the sky on his back." "They are lovers of law and order who observe the law when the government breaks it." "It is not indifferent to us which way we walk. There is a right way."

I liked it that Thoreau sorted life into the sacred and the profane, the true and the trivial, the living and the dead. Take the opening paragraphs of his essay "Walking":

> I wish to speak a word for Nature, for absolute freedom and wildness, as contrasted with a freedom and culture merely civil,—to regard man as an inhabitant, or a part and parcel of Nature, rather than a member of society. I wish to make an extreme statement, if so I may make an emphatic one, for there are enough champions of civilization: the minister and the school committee and every one of you will take care of that.
>
> I have met with but one or two persons in the course of my life who understood the art of Walking, that is, of taking walks,—who had a genius, so to speak, for *sauntering*, which word is beau-

> tifully derived "from idle people who roved about the country, in the Middle Ages, and asked charity, under pretense of going *à la Sainte Terre*," to the Holy Land, till the children exclaimed, "There goes a *Sainte-Terrer*," a Saunterer, a Holy-Lander. They who never go to the Holy Land in their walks, as they pretend, are indeed mere idlers and vagabonds; but they who do go there are saunterers in the good sense, such as I mean.

The man draws the line and makes a choice. The "merely civil," "mere idlers": lowlife surrounds us, but we needn't be a part of it. That elevated tone I loved, and I loved the demands that followed on it:

> We should go forth on the shortest walk . . . in the spirit of undying adventure, never to return,—prepared to send back our embalmed hearts only as relics to our desolate kingdoms. If you are ready to leave father and mother, and brother and sister, and wife and child and friends, and never see them again,—if you have paid your debts, and made your will, and settled all your affairs, and are a free man, then you are ready for a walk.

I was in my early twenties when I read these essays, and I longed for someone to tell me what to do. My life was not what I wanted. I had quit graduate school in a late-adolescent huff. I wished to be a writer, but I wasn't a writer. The country was at war; my best friend in jail. I was stuck in a bad marriage, having neither the wisdom to improve it nor the courage to leave. I was terrified of death, convinced my heart might stop at any minute. I lay in bed unable to sleep, rebuilding in fantasy a stone wall I had once built in childhood.

And I loitered near the café tables where old men were saying, "I believe," and "We must look," and "There is a right way." "Believe," "must," "is": what simple, beautiful verbs! I wanted to talk like that.

I did not know it then, but the voice that attracted me to these essays is rightly called prophetic. We have a tradition of prophetic literature that goes back to the Old Testament, of course, and though it is hardly the modern style, prophetic poems, even prophetic novels, can sometimes still be found. Whitman has this voice: he invites us to feel we are among the immortals, large-mannered, spanning continents. As for novels, E. M. Forster once gave a lecture on prophetic fiction, and his examples were Dostoyevsky, Melville, Emily Brontë, and D. H. Lawrence. I would add Flannery O'Connor: prophets offer revelation, and so did O'Connor; she designed her tales to induce in us that second sight by which we see the workings of an invisible world.

Poems and novels are not what concern me here, however. Here I want to offer a point of entry into Thoreau's essays, and reflecting on how he pitches his voice—especially in "Walking"—seems a good way to start. Before I begin, I should say that by "prophetic" I do not mean "telling the future." The prophetic voice has a relationship to time, but telling the future is the least of it. The prophet does not say that the price of oil will go up in October, or that a comet will strike the earth in twenty years. Rather, *the prophet speaks of things that will be true in the future because they are true in all time.* In 1963, when Martin Luther King, Jr., said that if the "repressed emotions [of African-Americans] are not released in nonviolent ways, they will seek expression through violence," he was not predicting the race riots of the later 1960s; he was describing the nature of things no matter the decade. Sometimes a prophet's words do come true, of course, but that may have more to do with whether or not people are paying attention than with any prescience on the prophet's part.

The prophetic essay has several distinguishing marks. To begin with, it always has a person in it. The mock-modest demand that Thoreau makes at the beginning of *Walden* states the case well:

> In most books, the *I*, or first person, is omitted; in this it will be retained. . . . [I]t is, after all, always the first person that is speaking. I should not talk so much about myself if there were any body else whom I knew as well. Unfortunately, I am confined to this theme by the narrowness of my experience. Moreover, I, on my side, require of every writer, first or last, a simple and sincere account of his own life . . . ; some such account as he would send to his kindred from a distant land.

In the prophetic essay, a person comes forward and addresses us.* This person is not, however, the self-involved, moody, or obsessed first person who carries on in the journals we keep or the letters we address to estranged lovers. The prophetic first person speaks at the point where the personal touches what is in no way personal. When Dante says, "In the middle of the journey of our life, I found myself in a dark wood," the shift in pronoun lets us know, if we needed the hint, that he is talking both about himself and about every human being. "In Dostoevsky," says Forster, "the characters and situations always stand for more than themselves; infinity attends them. . . . Mitya is—all of us. So is Alyosha, so is Smerdyakov." Similarly, in *Walden* and in the essays Thoreau implicitly claims he's writing not about *his* life but about *the* life, the life each of us would lead were we communicants in the church of Nature. The prophetic voice may give a "simple and sincere account" of its story, but it does so in a way that makes us feel we are reading the story of the race, not the story of one man or woman.

The second thing about the prophetic voice is that it asks us to imagine being free of the usual bonds of time and space. In regard to time, the rhetoric of prophecy typically invokes daily and seasonal cycles rather than the straight arrow of chronology. "We had a remarkable sunset one day last November," Thoreau tells us toward the end of "Walking":

> It was such a light as we could not have imagined a moment before, and . . . [w]hen we reflected that this was not a solitary phenomenon, never to happen again, but that it would happen forever and ever, an infinite number of evenings, . . . it was more glorious still.

The conceit is typical: the prophet pushes off with a particular day and a particular year, only to swamp them both in eternity, wiping out large sections of history; one November is all Novembers, each evening all evenings.

*I should here mark the fact that I am deriving my portrait of prophecy from Thoreau's practice rather than beginning with an image and seeing if the practice matches. There are different styles of prophecy. In the Hebrew Bible, for example, prophets do not speak in the first person; God speaks through them. Self-abnegation was the precondition of their utterance, not self-reliant individualism. In Thoreau we find the prophetic voice in its American, Protestant mode.

The prophetic voice alters space as well as time, though here the technique is slightly different. An unobtrusive description at the beginning of Isak Dinesen's *Out of Africa* sets a tone for the whole book: "The farm lay at an altitude of over six thousand feet. In the day-time you felt that you had got high up, near to the sun." Dinesen has a touch of the prophet, and these phrases should alert us to that fact, for the prophetic voice is spoken from high ground. Nothing in Concord stands at six thousand feet, but in "Walking" we find Thoreau climbing up whenever he can. He climbs a tall white pine and finds a flower his townsmen never saw. He climbs a hill and looks down on civilization in miniature:

> The farmers and their works are scarcely more obvious than woodchucks and their burrows. Man and his affairs, church and state and school, trade and commerce, and manufactures and agriculture, even politics, . . . I am pleased to see how little space they occupy in the landscape. Politics is but a narrow field. . . . I pass from it as from a bean-field into the forest, and it is forgotten. In one half-hour I can walk off to some portion of the earth's surface where a man does not stand from one year's end to another, and there, consequently, politics are not, for they are but as the cigar-smoke of a man.

Spoken from on high, the prophetic voice strips the lowlands of their detail. Democrat and Whig, Sunday and Monday, Concord and Charleston—distinctions that preoccupy us in the valley are flattened out as if drawn on a commemorative plate. From Thoreau's hill the woodchuck and the first selectman may as well occupy the same lodgings.

This does not mean, however, that the prophet is above it all. He may not be constrained by the place of his birth, but the high altitudes have their own, subtler constraints. Thoreau always liked to include a little fantasy about the solar system in his work ("the sun is but a morning star"), and "Walking" is no exception, for at one point he imagines himself higher even than that hill: "The outline which would bound my walks," he says, "would be . . . one of those cometary orbits which have been thought to be non-returning curves, . . . in which my house occupies the place of the sun." We are so high up now that Earth's gravity itself has been canceled. And yet the sun's remains. Solar gravity may be thinner or more delicate, but it still exerts its pull. "There is a subtle magnetism in Nature," Thoreau says, and we cannot feel it until we get up high. There we drop the accidents of time and place and feel only the constraints of what it is to be human. From high up, everything seems less personal and therefore less of a burden. To achieve the voice he wants, Thoreau ignores or erases his own particular sufferings. The sentence "Surely joy is the condition of life" was written three months after Thoreau's brother, John, had died of tetanus, and that death had thrown Thoreau into a depression, during which he suffered a full hysterical psychosomatic imitation of the symptoms of tetanus. No "sincere account" with details such as these is ever reported in the work, however; Thoreau pitches his voice above it. He had his familial losses and his disappointments in love, as we all do, but the house he offers in the work is a dwelling for those who wish to live deliberately, and serves to focus cometary orbits.

Extended thus in space and time, the prophetic voice speaks in declarative sentences. It does not debate or analyze. It does not say "several options face us" or "studies must be done." The prophetic voice dwells in the verb "to be," from which it draws the simple syntax of belief. "This is the case," it declares, or "I am I," or "I am the Way." Thoreau's sentences are long and shapely, but they are grounded in such simplicity. "Morning is when I am awake and there is a dawn in me." "Every walk is a sort of crusade." "In Wildness is the preservation of the World."

In the prophetic essay, declarations of belief appear in the foreground, and this alone makes it different from most essays we now read in magazines. The television show *Dragnet* used to feature a cop named Joe Friday, whose interrogations were punctuated with the phrase "Just the facts, ma'am; just the facts." Joe Friday is the ghostwriter of most of the essays written in my lifetime. The prophetic essay would never make it through the fact-checking departments of our finer magazines. "In Wildness is the preservation of the World": There is no way to check that. It certainly does not follow from evidence the way conclusions in an analytic essay do. And yet that does not mean it is not true. Students are often disappointed to discover that when he lived at Walden Pond, Thoreau would go into town to eat meals with his family or the Emersons. It's a fact: Thoreau was not a hermit. But the facts of the case are not the spirit of the case, and sometimes the spirit is primary.

Thoreau did not need pure isolation to describe the solitude of our lives.

The prophet does not stoop to argue or to concede belief to the so-called facts, and these refusals bring us to the dangers, or at least the limitations, of this voice. All the marks of prophecy that I have touched on so far—the extended first person, the lifting of the particular into the eternal, the declarations of simple belief—imply that the divisions, confusions, and ambiguities marking our lives are illusory. Under the spell of the prophetic voice, we are led to believe that there is a simple unity toward which each of us might travel. But there are times we cannot or should not make the move toward unity, either in the self or in society.

To begin with the social example: to the degree that the prophetic voice flattens out diversity, it is at odds with pluralist politics, for it has no model of contention. Or, to say this another way, it has its politics, but they are not presented as such. "Walking" is a political essay (most patently in the way it endorses the westward expansion of the American empire), but Thoreau claims that is not so (the woodland dwellers he eulogizes "are of no politics"). And he seals his claim with a self-protecting rhetoric, saying that he is describing nature, not culture (thus Columbus discovered America with an instinct "akin to the migratory instinct in birds"), asserting that the territory under review is sacred ("the backwoodsman" in America is better situated than "Adam in paradise"), and subordinating all empirical evidence to the insights of sympathy and sempiternal memory. In these and other ways the prophetic voice puts the opposition beyond the pale of speech, or, should oppositional voices arise, it makes it seem as if they were opposed to nature, the sacred, and the wisdom of the ages.

To recast all this in terms of the self: the prophetic voice has little to say about those parts of our lives that are messy or prone to depression. At home on the mountaintop, it is silent about those valleys that are, by definition, "long depressions." A Thoreauvian prophetic essay leads us on a redemptive journey—about which I shall say more below—but there is a redemption of the valley as well, one that comes from abandoning all hope of getting it together. If you need to come apart, you do not need to listen to the prophetic voice. Stop trying to be a hero. There is a time to fall to pieces, to identify with the confusion of your life as it is, confined absolutely to the present November sunset and your present apartment.

Finally, the prophetic voice lacks humor. Things in the valley may be more confusing than prophecy allows, but they are also funnier. E. M. Forster contrasts prophecy with fantasy, and the novel that is his prime example, *Tristram Shandy*, reminds us that the comedy of the valley includes digression, coincidence, and muddle. Thoreau has humor to be sure. (I have always wanted to hear the opening of *Walden* read with a laugh track, especially the bit about how his neighbors torture themselves as if they were penitential Brahmins "measuring with their bodies, like caterpillars, the breadth of vast empires.") But Thoreau's jokes typically have an upward thrust. We laugh at the mundane so as to move toward the eternal. We're not talking about Lenny Bruce or Richard Pryor here. Thoreau never jokes about sex, or about race relations, or about Christians and Jews. He lacks, in short, the humor of pluralism, of the particular, ambiguous, and tattered world—all those jokes that help us live our inexorable divisions in this body, time, and place.

Be this as it may, I listen up sharply when I hear the prophetic voice, for it offers something we cannot get from humor, analysis, or party politics. As I said above, there is a sort of redemptive journey in "Walking," an "excursion" Thoreau would call it, and it has several stages. At the beginning, as in fairy tales that open with a wicked king and a famine in the land, all is not well in Concord. "Every walk is a sort of crusade," Thoreau says, "to go forth and reconquer this Holy Land from the hands of the Infidels." Evil days are upon us. A saunterer's requisite leisure "comes only by the grace of God," and few now have such grace. "Some of my townsmen . . . have described to me . . . walks which they took ten years ago, in which they were so blessed as to lose themselves for half an hour in the woods; but I know very well that they have confined themselves to the highway ever since." Thoreau himself sometimes "walk[s] a mile into the woods bodily, without getting there in spirit . . . , [t]he thought of some work" running constantly through his head.

The essay begins, then, reminding us of our "quiet desperation" in the fallen present. Thoreau wakes our dissatisfaction and uses it to lever us out of the present and into the heights, the second stage of this journey. Here, we see the world below with new eyes. The historian of religion

Mircea Eliade once suggested that when evil days are upon us, the sacred survives by camouflaging itself within the profane. To recover it, we must develop the eyes—some sort of night vision or hunter's attentiveness—that can discover the shapes of the sacred despite its camouflage. Prophets speak to us at the intersection of time and eternity, and if we join them there, we are given that vision, that sight. "It is much easier to discover than to see when the cover is off," says Thoreau, but that is the job at hand. He means, I think, that it is one thing to disclose the world, quite another to see what it means. The prophetic voice is apocalyptic: it doesn't just uncover the world; it uncovers the eyes. Then, as we walk, we see blossoms that we never saw before, though they were always there.

I have suggested that the prophetic voice is spoken in the extended first person. When we identify with such a speaker, we are led to imagine our lives differently. We have, for a moment, two lives, the one we actually lead and a concurrent imaginary one. The second is not imaginary in the sense of "invented," however. If the prophet is speaking of things that will be true tomorrow because they are true in all time, then that second life is real even if it isn't realized. The prophetic voice juxtaposes today and eternity to make it clear that the latter may inform the former. It sets the mundane against the imaginary so that we might see whether or not they match up. Where they are congruent, we discover the true value hidden in the everyday; where they are incongruent, we discover what we may abandon. In either case there is a reevaluation, a redemption. You look at your work, your loves, your children, parents, politicians, and, as at a funeral or birth, you see what matters and what does not.

In the final stage of his essay, Thoreau returns to home ground. He claims at the outset that the walker must be ready to leave home never to return, but nonetheless, in his final pages we find him sauntering home with the sun "like a gentle herdsman" at his back. A true walk changes the walker, not the walker's hometown. We read in books of some distant past when there were giants on the earth, or of some future when they will return. The prophetic voice seeks to have us see that the golden age is not in the past or the future. It is here. We who have been "saunterers in the good sense" return to find the Holy Land in the Concord we left behind. Where before we and all our townspeople looked like infidels, now we see that each might be a hero. "This [is] the heroic age itself, though we know it not."

There is yet another stage to the prophetic excursion, though it takes place after the prophet falls silent. The prophetic voice doesn't necessarily push us into action. It is more declarative than imperative, more revelatory than moralizing. And yet where revelation succeeds, we suddenly see paths that were obscure before. "It is not indifferent to us which way we walk. There is a right way." Most of us live in a world of almost paralyzing free choice. In America at least, it is difficult to buy the right brand of cell phone, let alone find the right way. But under the spell of the prophetic voice, we can, sometimes, sort the true from the false and begin to move. We find ourselves in a story that makes sense, and such stories engender action.

You quit graduate school, rent a room somewhere, and start to read in earnest. You hunker down in your pointless job and paint at night. You go back to the family farm and begin the fifty-year job of reclaiming the spent land. You leave a hopeless marriage or rededicate yourself to a good one. You resist an immoral war and go to jail. The heroic age will not be with us unless we will be its heroes. Great cold air masses gather over the North Atlantic and slide slowly toward the shores of America. Sometimes late at night you get an unexpected whiff of that salt air. You had forgotten that you live in a city by the sea, and now you remember.

II. IGNORANCE

If the prophetic voice is apocalyptic, if it uncovers and opens the eyes, then what exactly is revealed? What do we see once the cover is off?

Just southwest of Walden Pond the Sudbury River widens to form Fair Haven Pond. In February 1851 Thoreau recorded in his journal a memory of things seen there:

> One afternoon in the fall . . . , I saw Fair Haven Pond with its island and meadow; between the island and the shore, a strip of perfectly smooth water in the lee of the island; and two hawks sailing over it—(and something more I saw which cannot easily be described, which made me say to myself that the landscape could not be improved). . . .
>
> Yet I do not know what these things can be; I begin to see such

> objects only when I leave off understanding them. . . . But I get no further than this.
>
> How adapted these forms and colors to our eyes, a meadow and its islands! What are these things? Yet the hawks and the ducks keep so aloof, and nature is so reserved! We are made to love the river and the meadow, as the wind to ripple the water.

There is observation here, and description of things, and then some limit where description fails and, oddly, seeing begins.

Thoreau had a recurrent interest in such moments or, more globally, a concern with what might be perceived should we ever get beyond understanding and utterance. His first book, *A Week on the Concord and Merrimack Rivers*, ends with an ode to silence (a book, he says, being but a rock "whereon the waves of Silence may break"), and in "Walking" he urges us to learn the value of "ignorance" ("We have heard of a Society for the Diffusion of Useful Knowledge. . . . Methinks there is equal need of a Society for the Diffusion of Useful Ignorance"). This is a theme Thoreau also addresses in the opening pages of *Walden*, where he says that his neighbors are so busy that the laboring man "has no time to be any thing but a machine. How can he remember well his ignorance—which his growth requires—who has so often to use his knowledge?" A few pages later, he cites Confucius to the effect that true knowledge amounts to knowing what we do not know, then remarks, "When one man has reduced a fact of the imagination to be a fact to his understanding, I foresee that all men will at length establish their lives on that basis."

That is an enigmatic declaration, I suspect, unless one has had a chance to learn the terms by which the American Romantics imagined human consciousness. In 1690 John Locke had published *An Essay concerning Human Understanding*, arguing that all we know comes ultimately from the senses, from contact with the world, and not from any innate ideas, inborn intuition, or Platonic memory. The mind at birth is a blank slate that maturation slowly fills with the script of experience. A century later, in Germany, Immanuel Kant had replied to Locke, arguing that the mind must bring certain things to experience (a sense of time, for example, or of cause and effect). In his ethics, Kant added "conscience" to his list: the feeling of right and wrong is a law of the heart, not something learned at school.

Kant's portion of this philosophical argument eventually reached

New England by way of an 1813 book on German culture by Madame de Staël and an 1829 American edition of Samuel Taylor Coleridge's *Aids to Reflection.* Responding to Locke and following a somewhat muddled version of Kant, these writers imagined the mind as composed of two primary faculties, Reason and Understanding. Here is how Ralph Waldo Emerson explains the distinction in an 1834 letter to his brother:

> Reason is the highest faculty of the soul—what we mean often by the soul itself; it never *reasons*, never proves, it simply perceives; it is vision. The Understanding toils all the time, compares, contrives, adds, argues, near-sighted but strong-sighted, dwelling in the present the expedient the customary.

Reason is spontaneous rather than willed, imaginative rather than empirical, poetic rather than practical. Intuitive and supersensuous, it transcends the senses so as to apprehend larger patterns and unities (it transcends the senses; thus those who value it are transcendentalists). "The senses give us representations of things," Emerson elsewhere says, "but what are the things themselves, they cannot tell." If one wishes to know what are those hawks at Fair Haven Pond, or to know the spiritual world, the purposes of life, the larger meaning of things, then one must nurture Reason.

In Thoreau's version of this psychology, "Reason" does not much appear (happily so to the modern ear, for if "Reason . . . never *reasons*" it should have some other name). He speaks instead of "genius," or of a demoniacal "wisdom," or, most often, of "imagination":

> My genius makes distinctions which my understanding cannot—and which my senses do not report.

> It is much easier to discover than to see when the cover is off. . . . Wisdom does not inspect, but behold. . . . He has something demoniacal in him, who can discern a law or couple two facts.

> I witness a beauty in the form or coloring of the clouds which addresses itself to my imagination—for which you account scientifically to my understanding. . . . What sort of science is that which enriches the understanding but robs the imagination?

Such are the terms Thoreau prefers, at any rate, but it was always part of his artistry to go beyond the inherited nomenclature and evoke these things descriptively. It is in his imagistic elaborations of our faculties of mind that we shall get a fuller sense of what they were for him, and come back to what he means by "ignorance." In "Walking," having praised ignorance for both its use and its beauty, Thoreau writes:

> The highest that we can attain to is not Knowledge, but Sympathy with Intelligence. I do not know that this higher knowledge amounts to anything more definite than a novel and grand surprise on a sudden revelation of the insufficiency of all that we called Knowledge before. . . . It is the lighting up of the mist by the sun.

Though this last image has its corollaries in mystic literature, Thoreau draws it from his own experience. When a young man, he once spent a night alone on top of Saddle-back Mountain, near Williamstown, Massachusetts. He woke early to see the sun rise, but as the day came on, he discovered himself to be above the clouds. The entire valley below was brimmed with mist, which, as the sun crossed the hidden horizon, slowly filled with light. "There was not a crevice left through which the trivial places we name Massachusetts or Vermont or New York could be seen. . . . I found myself a dweller in the dazzling halls of Aurora."

Thoreau usually becomes aware of the insufficiency of knowledge by way of unusual kinds of light. In this case it is sunlight caught in a mist sufficient to erase the sun itself and all the "trivial" things that light would usually reveal. In other cases it is the light of the moon. For many years, whenever there was a full moon—especially in summer—Thoreau would walk for several hours at night, recording his impressions in his journal the next day. Here is an entry that follows the full moon of June 13, 1851:

> After walking by night several times I now walk by day, but I am not aware of any crowning advantage in it. I see small objects better, but it does not enlighten me any.

And early in August of the same year:

> As the twilight deepens and the moonlight is more & more bright, I begin to distinguish myself, who I am & where. . . . The intense light of the sun unfits me for meditation, makes me wander in my thought—my life is too diffuse & dissipated—routine succeeds & prevails over us—the trivial has greater power. . . .
>
> I am sobered by the moon light—I bethink myself. . . . Nature broods us, and has not left our germs of thought to be hatched by the sun.

I introduce this image of Moonlit Knowing not so much for the ways it can be matched with Imagination or Reason but because Thoreau's night walks are so suggestive of what may lie beyond such categories. If Sunlit Knowing encompasses the received conventions by which we understand our lives (all the social knowledge that is, in "Walking," "an excess . . . of informing light"), then going out by moonlight is an exercise in quitting those conventions so as to recover sight again.

There is a long tradition of seekers after knowledge who begin with exactly such refusals of the accepted sense of things. The anonymous fourteenth-century English author of *The Cloud of Unknowing* was one such, his advice being to do what Thoreau had done on Saddle-back Mountain, that is, to get yourself into a mist sufficiently thick to obscure the things you thought you knew. A century later, in Germany, Nicholas of Cusa suggested that those who wish to know God should give up seeking Him directly and take instead the *via negativa*, the path by which one refuses, item by item, all the categories and ideas the Church has employed to describe the divine. Grace, predestination, original sin, omnipotence—drop all of it, forget it; it only makes you think you know something when in fact you don't. As Cusa wrote:

> We may be compared to owls trying to look at the sun; but since the natural desire in us for knowledge is not without a purpose, its immediate object is our own ignorance. Nothing could be more beneficial for even the most zealous searchers for knowledge than this being in fact most learned in that very ignorance which is peculiarly his own.

But once we have become learned in this ignorance, what should we do? How shall we poor owl-eyed beasts come to see more fully? It would seem, to follow out the image, that we have several choices. We might try to improve the eyes we have or try to acquire new ones better fitted to their objects. Or perhaps we already have such eyes, which is to say we might search out some as yet undiscovered organ of sense or faculty of mind. Finally, if none of this will do, if there is no way to improve the dazzled owl, and if no better eyes are yet to be unlidded, then perhaps we can learn to look by indirection, as viewers of a solar eclipse look not directly at the sun but at its reflection in a pail of water.

My suggestion, in any event, is that it helps to read Thoreau under the assumption that his interest in ignorance draws him toward experiments such as these. He regularly gets himself into positions where he might see by indirection (lit mist and the moon both offer sunlight dilute enough for human eyes). He has a genius for perspective, for getting or imagining himself into situations where common things can be seen from uncommon angles.

In the first chapter of *A Week on the Concord and Merrimack Rivers*, for example, he comes upon a dam across the Concord River and immediately assumes the fish's-eye view, considering how the thing must appear to the salmon, shad, and alewives that formerly migrated up that stream. ("Poor shad! where is thy redress? Still wandering the sea in thy scaly armor to inquire humbly at the mouths of rivers if man has perchance left them free for thee to enter.") Or, to give a second instance, what interested him in retrospect about his night in the Concord jail was the novel view it offered of his home ground. ("It was like traveling into a far country . . . , to lie there for one night. It seemed to me that I never had heard the town clock strike before, nor the evening sounds of the village.")

This urge to get outside the ordinary marks a large portion of Thoreau's pursuits. We see it in his endless reading of travel books, his interest in Native Americans, his temporal and spatial fantasies (imagining Concord by way of Rome, for example, or from some distant star), and above all in his going to nature, as this collection testifies from the first essay, where nature is salutary because it lies beyond "religion, literature, and philosophy," to the last, where we cannot *know* wild apples until we have eaten them in the fields and in the wind.*

*As might be expected, Thoreau's talent for perspective fails him sometimes. He seemed mostly unable to imagine what it must have been like to be an Irish immigrant to America in the 1840s; he never takes the woman's-eye view of things; public lectures especially seemed to draw his voice back to the community's underlying way of thinking ("Walking" is, among other things, a patriotic ode to manifest destiny, and in the John Brown essays he falls willy-nilly into stock comparisons of Brown and Christ).

If such experiments with altered perspective do not help us see what lies beyond our ignorance, then perhaps we must attend to the organs of perception themselves, purifying them or waking them up. Thoreau's walking by moonlight was, in addition to all the rest, an experiment in the renewal of sensation: "In the night the eyes are partly closed or retire into the head. Other senses take the lead. . . . The senses both of hearing and smelling are more alert." Despite his fabled bachelorhood, Thoreau was a great sensualist (note how, in "Ktaadn," he picks up the scent of a cornfield a third of a mile away), but his was a sensuality with a future tense, one that leaned on the promise of perception rather than its limitations. The five senses "are but the rudiments of what they are destined to become," he once wrote. They are "divine germs" that we must "educate and develop."

And should the education fail, should we be unable to purify the senses we have, then all that's left is to become learned in our ignorance, front the world with it, and wait. Wait under the assumption that there are things to be known if we have cleared a space for knowing and that there are faculties of mind beyond understanding and imagination, ones that exist potentially, though we do not have them in fact.

One of Thoreau's journal entries will help me explain what I mean. On October 26, 1851, Thoreau wrote out a long and complicated dream that ends with him walking in a meadow and meeting his friend Bronson Alcott. They fall to speaking lines of poetry to each other:

> I quoted one which in my waking hours I have no knowledge of, but in my dream it was familiar enough. I only know that those which I quoted expressed regret, and were like the following, though they were not these, *viz.*:
>
> "The short parenthesis of life was sweet,"
>
> "The remembrance of youth is a sigh," etc.
>
> It had the word "memory" in it!! And then again the instant that I awoke, methought I was a musical instrument from which I heard a strain die out—a bugle, or a clarionet, or a flute. My body was the organ and channel of melody, as a flute is of the music that is breathed through it. . . . I awoke, therefore, to an infinite regret—to find myself, not the thoroughfare of glorious and world-stirring inspirations, but a scuttle full of dirt.

Thinking back on what might have induced this dream, Thoreau remembers that he had been reading a book about the Northmen the night before and that as he read he felt "a fertile regret" and derived "an inexpressible satisfaction" from that feeling.

Here "memory" seems to be the name of the faculty of mind that, if purified, might know what we do not know and express itself in poetry or music. But it is not quite available, at least not in daylight. Each of us has had the experience of being on the verge of uttering a thought, then being distracted and forgetting what we had to say, then being madly haunted by the ghost of what was so clearly present a moment ago. Imagine living a life suffused with that feeling. Imagine having the sense that you have come here to say something only to find it has slipped your mind. Worse yet, imagine such is the case but that you do not even feel the loss. Thoreau finds his regret satisfying and fertile because it indicates some loss is felt and thus implies there was something to be lost. This "fertile sadness," as he elsewhere calls it, contains a sort of backward promise, a hope that arises because something has been taken away. The literary critic Barbara Johnson writes that it was Thoreau's great gift to wake us to "our own lost losses." Not losses simply—we all have those—but the losses we do not even remember. This prophet speaks to wake his neighbors but not, once they are awake, to tell them any assertable truth. Wakefulness in Thoreau is not a perception of truth; it is a perception of ignorance and comes suffused with promising regret.

III. SIGNING OFF

Thoreau's politics may be described as an experiment in seeing how far the *via negativa* might be extended to social life. In *Walden*, remembering the one time he thought of buying a farm, he writes: "My imagination carried me so far that I even had the refusal of several farms,—the refusal was all I wanted,—but I never got my fingers burned by actual possession." This is a wry assertion of his creed, his constant questions being, How much of what the world expects might we simply refuse to do? How many obligations and inherited institutions might we drop so as to clear the field (for what?—well, for what has yet to be imagined)?

In public refusal, Thoreau exercises the political version of his talent for perspective, for finding a place to stand outside the common frame. His critique of professional politicians is that they rarely think of quitting their jobs, which is the only way they could get in a position to imagine a fundamentally new world. Instead, they dwell inside their own assumptions and run in circles. As he writes in "Civil Disobedience":

> Statesmen and legislators, standing so completely within the institution, never distinctly and nakedly behold it. They speak of moving society, but have no resting-place without it. . . . [Daniel] Webster never goes behind government, and so cannot speak with authority about it.

Nature had early become Thoreau's own favored "resting-place without." Going to the woods was an experiment in removing himself from institutions so as to see them freshly and speak "with authority." This is why, by the way, the present collection presents Thoreau's essays in the order of their creation, abandoning the long-standing editorial practice of separating the political work from the natural history. That conventional division has always muted one of the things that makes Thoreau interesting: the way in which his various passions inform and influence one another. Thoreau's "reform papers" are "excursions" and vice versa.

Thoreau's earliest concrete political refusals can be dated to the early 1840s. He had graduated from Harvard College in 1837 and moved back to his family's home in Concord; he had tried his hand at teaching in the local schools; he had developed a close friendship with his mentor Ralph Waldo Emerson and in 1841 had begun living in the Emerson household. Then, in 1842, when he was twenty-four years old, he stopped paying his taxes. Four years later—in 1846, the second year of his stay at Walden Pond—he was arrested for his continued tax refusal and spent a night in jail. That case has become the most famous example of Thoreau's trying to get "behind government" by refusing to act, but a lesser-known case from 1841, mentioned in passing in "Civil Disobedience," is in some ways more telling:

> Some years ago, the State met me in behalf of the Church, and commanded me to pay a certain sum toward the support of a clergyman whose preaching my father attended, but never I myself. . . . I declined to pay.

We are now so used to the idea of the division of church and state that we forget it took decades to build the wall between them and that federal practice was distinct from the practice in individual states. Massachusetts in fact had an established church for many years after the Revolution, the state constitution of 1780 having authorized towns to support by taxation a "public protestant teacher of piety, religion, and morality." The First Parish Church of Concord was supported in this way during most of Thoreau's life. In 1834 the state moved to disestablish Massachusetts churches. By state law, however, citizens were still considered members of their parish church unless they formally resigned, and First Parish thus remained the Concord town church for decades after disestablishment. The town maintained the church building, it supplied the pastor with firewood, and it collected the parish tax. Only in 1855 did a town meeting formally declare that the "municipal corporation" would no longer do any "parochial business."

Around the time Thoreau turned twenty-one, First Parish added his name to its rolls. A few years later, when the town sent him a church tax bill, Thoreau went to the town clerk and "signed off," a common practice at the time. Thoreau's mother and aunts had signed off when they had changed churches years earlier; many more had done so in 1834 when the church was disestablished. By the time Thoreau signed off, only a third of the town's taxpayers were paying the ministerial tax.

While he may not have known it, signing off from First Parish made Thoreau part of one of the key social movements of nineteenth-century America, denominational Protestantism. The essence of denominationalism is voluntary association. In older church practice, men and women were simply born into a church and inherited its creed, rituals, and tradition. If they wished to leave, their family, their community, and oftentimes the state would make sure they did not. In nineteenth-century America, however, it became more and more important that a member of a church had chosen to belong, had at best undergone a conscious conversion to a particular way of knowing and worshiping the divine, and then joined a community as the outward expression of this inner, and individual, experience.

Actually, it overstates the case to say that by signing off Thoreau became part of this movement, for the true denominationalist signs off, then signs on somewhere else, and Thoreau never took the second step. And yet in another sense it doesn't overstate the case, for there is no voluntary association without voluntary disassociation, and in the latter Thoreau is our patron saint. He keeps denominationalism alive by keeping himself ready for a church that does not yet exist. He is the great refuser by whose actions the rest of us know that we are choosing to do what we do. If just one family in town teaches its children at home, and the state allows it, then all who use the public schools are more clearly making a free choice; if just one draftee is allowed to be a conscientious objector, then all others must be conscientious assentors. In like manner, when Thoreau conducts the ritual of not joining, those of us who do join can rest assured we are not slaves to convention but masters of choice. Voluntary association does well to have one man or woman out there vigilantly exercising the right of refusal.

Paradoxes such as these imply that Thoreau's nay-saying may offer more aid to conformity than is usually thought. That is probably the case, at least in the sense that American ideology never objects too much to the kind of dissent that keeps us all talking of free choice even as we all do exactly as our neighbors do. Stepping outside the frame sometimes only serves to polish it up.

But that line of thought speaks more to the uses that might be made of Thoreau than to Thoreau himself. He never used refusal to burnish conformity. He never signed on to some other church in Concord, or to any political party (he never voted), or to any abolitionist committee, or to any of his friends' utopian communities. There was a great flurry of socialist experiments in the 1840s—more than forty communities founded in that decade alone—and Thoreau, who had been raised in a boardinghouse, was never inclined to join: "As for these communities—I think I had rather keep bachelor's hall in hell than go to board in heaven." Most reformers, he thought, "want faith, and mistake their private ail for an infected atmosphere." So doing, they set out to heal the world before they have healed themselves, like men crusading against the national debt when they themselves are bankrupt ("Paradise (To Be) Regained," the third essay in this collection, is Thoreau's amusing critique of one such reformer).

If reform has a positive meaning for Thoreau, it means the cure of the soul, not the cure of social ills. It means a practice like that of Christian monks in late antiquity who isolated themselves on bare and empty islands off Scotland, trying to see how far they could turn away from their own culture so as to face themselves and God. Reform by such enacted refusal is not necessarily antisocial; turning away from one's culture is a cultural act—especially if you publish your results—one whose goal, in

Thoreau's case, is an exemplary accounting of whatever "ails" you have and, if possible, the healing, even the ripening, of the self.

But to do all that, one must live in a world that accepts the *via negativa*; politically speaking, one needs a government that will let you sign off and then leave you alone. At the end of "Civil Disobedience," Thoreau tries to imagine such a state. He recalls the historical progression from an "absolute to a limited monarchy, from a limited monarchy to a democracy," and calls it "a progress toward a true respect for the individual." His own experience with democracy, we gather, indicates that such progress had not come to an end. Beyond the democracy he knew he thus imagines a state that "would not think it inconsistent with its own repose if a few were to live aloof from it" (for example, not to pay their taxes). He pictures these men and women as a "kind of fruit" that the state would let "drop off as fast as it ripened." Set apart from the state but nonetheless fulfilling "all the duties of neighbors and fellow-men," these ripened souls, or rather the state that sanctioned them, "would prepare the way for a still more perfect and glorious State, which also I have imagined, but not yet anywhere seen."

This conclusion is admittedly a little vague and faraway, meaning we have come now to the public form of fertile regret. We are in an eschatological politics—not "the art of the possible," as politics is sometimes said to be, but the imagining of what has never been seen before. But unseen ends are well fitted to the faith we are examining. After all, we *do not* know what lies beyond the known; we are ignorant of what we might become if we stopped being the things we are. Thoreau is arguably the original American ecologist, but he is original exactly because there was no ecology when he went walking in the Concord woods, or went to Maine (the terms didn't even exist until a decade after his death). His day saw an aggressive cutting of the four-hundred-year-old white pines of Maine, and it disturbed him deeply, as he explained after the second of his trips into those woods:

> A pine cut down, a dead pine, is no more a pine than a dead human carcass is a man. Can he who has discovered only some of the values of whalebone and whale oil be said to have discovered the true use of the whale . . . ? I have been into the lumber-yard, and the carpenter's shop, and the tannery . . . ; but when at length I saw the tops of the pines waving and reflecting the light at a dis-

> tance high over all the rest of the forest, I realized that the former were not the highest uses of the pine. It is not their bones or hide or tallow that I love most. It is the living spirit of the tree. . . . It is as immortal as I am, and perchance will go to as high a heaven, there to tower above me still.

It is sometimes hard to know when one is outside the frame of the community, but in this case we have a nice proof, for when *The Atlantic Monthly* printed these remarks in 1858, the editor cut the final sentence (against Thoreau's express wishes) as being too pantheistic or, as we might say now, as perceiving too well the interdependence of the species.

By moving from Thoreau's fantasy of a state whose "aloof" citizens drop like ripe fruits to his legacy for environmentalists, I mean to indicate that while he never signed on to one of the town churches, his refusals nonetheless gave rise to a world of action. As with my model of the "prophetic excursion," turning away may be followed by return. Thoreau was so clear about his nay-saying that his social side usually goes unnoticed, but it is there. He was an individualist, yes, but he also believed in public life, the unit of which was the town. In "Civil Disobedience" he says that there was one tax he was happy to pay: "I have never declined paying the highway tax, because I am as desirous of being a good neighbor as I am of being a bad subject." What it means to be a neighbor is one of the great puzzles Thoreau poses for his readers; here we have a hint at the answer: it means chipping in to make the town work. This is in accord with one of the several ways in which Thoreau did in fact "sign on"—his lifelong involvement in the Concord Lyceum.

The lyceum movement was a nineteenth-century experiment in popular adult education, town lyceums being established throughout the Northeast to spread useful information by way of lectures and debates. The citizens of Concord started theirs in 1829, and twelve-year-old Thoreau joined immediately. When he was twenty, he gave his first lecture there. Shortly thereafter, for two years he served as the lyceum curator, arranging the lecture series and managing the details—the hall, the fuel, the lights, the fees. It was a central part of his life for decades. Ten of the essays collected here were first given as public lectures; two of them, "Walking" and "Life without Principle," were given many times over many years. One of the last lectures he ever gave was a version of "Wild Apples" delivered to the Concord Lyceum in 1860.

In this and other ways Thoreau was a communitarian. He was active in the group that produced the journal *The Dial* and edited one issue; almost against his own will, he constantly addressed himself to the fight against slavery; in his essays and journal he imagined and wrote stirringly of the possibility of national parks—so much so that we have them today in part because people like John Muir read Thoreau and took him seriously. Which is to say that, above all, we find Thoreau "signing on" by writing books and essays. Thoreau was an individualist, to be sure, but the complaint that he was antisocial has always seemed odd to me when publication is one of the most deliberate social acts we have.

IV. SLAVERY IN MASSACHUSETTS

The most important social movement of the nineteenth century was the fight against slavery, and four of the essays here testify to Thoreau's involvement in that struggle. Behind all of these lie what was then a national debate about whether slavery would be extended into the territories being settled in the West. In 1817, the year Thoreau was born, the Union consisted of twenty-two states, half of them prohibiting and half allowing slavery. Thereafter, however, this balance of power was regularly threatened, mostly because the Louisiana Purchase had opened vast new areas to settlement. Over the ensuing decades, each time one of the western territories applied for statehood the same questions would arise: Would this state be "Free-Soil" or not, and what then would happen to the balance of power in Congress?

The first of such debates resulted in the Missouri Compromise of 1820. When the slaveholding Missouri Territory applied to enter the Union in 1818, Northern lawmakers insisted that its admission be contingent on its abolition of slavery. Southerners refused, and the petition stalled. A year later, when Maine applied for statehood, a compromise allowed Missouri to enter as a slave state and Maine as a Free State. Moreover, and most important for the decades that followed, the compromise prohibited future slavery in any part of the Louisiana Purchase north of latitude 36°30'. Almost all of Missouri lies north of this line. So does what are now Kansas and Nebraska—though why that mattered would not become apparent for thirty-four years.

This compromise quieted things for many years, but the power struggle resurfaced as soon as new land was opened for settlement beyond the Louisiana Purchase. This territory became one focus of Thoreau's most famous political essay, "Civil Disobedience," first delivered as a lecture in 1848, his question there being why a citizen of Massachusetts should, in any way, help the government acquire the land in question. Thoreau's opening paragraph speaks of "the present Mexican war," a conflict whose roots went back to 1836, when Texas seceded from Mexico and declared itself an independent (and slaveholding) republic. In 1845 Congress annexed the territory as a new state, and in the spring of the next year the Mexican army attacked American troops on the Texas border, Mexico never having accepted Texas's independence in the first place. The subsequent war lasted a year and a half, and by the end of it Mexico had lost not only Texas but California and all of what are now the states of the Southwest.

When Texas had first been considered for admission to the Union, abolitionists blocked the proposal, fearing that several new slave states might be created from the territory. When Texas was finally admitted and fighting broke out, Thoreau and other abolitionists opposed the war on the same ground: winning would be a victory for slavery, not for freedom.

At the close of the Mexican War, American holdings finally reached to the Pacific, and the struggle over slavery in the West played out its final acts. In 1849 California sought to join the Union. If it was to enter as a Free State, the slave states wanted something in return, and what they got was another series of torturous trade-offs. Under the Compromise of 1850, California entered as a Free State, but slavery was allowed to continue in the District of Columbia (though the slave trade itself was outlawed there), and the South got a new Fugitive Slave Law lending increased federal power to the capture and return of slaves seeking freedom in the North.

Nor was this the last attempt to legislate a balance of power before the Civil War. By the time we get to Thoreau's 1854 essay "Slavery in Massachusetts," we find him speaking of the repudiation of "the compromise compact of 1820" and the North's concern for "the destiny of Nebraska." In the spring of 1854 Congress had broken the promise of the Missouri Compromise by passing the Kansas-Nebraska Act, which turned the question of slavery in those territories over to the settlers themselves. Rather than quieting the issue, this "popular sovereignty" provision prompted each side to send armed settlers west, and before long "border ruffians" from Missouri and Free-Soilers from the North were fighting a civil war in Kansas. One of those Free-Soilers was a man named John Brown, recently emigrated with his sons from Ohio.

In sum, every decade of Thoreau's adult life saw westward expansion exacerbating the division between North and South and rekindling the slavery debate. Moreover, by the mid-1850s it seemed to New Englanders that every case had ended in a compromise with slavery (always in the name of saving the Union), so that compromise itself appeared less and less like wise statecraft and more and more like dealing with the devil.

Still, as long as the devil in question did his dealing several thousand miles away, many in New England were content to leave him be. It wasn't just that the Union should be preserved; New England textile factories depended on Southern cotton, and many merchants saw no need to pick a fight with their suppliers. When the Compromise of 1850 was passed, nine hundred wealthy Bostonians signed a public letter praising Massachusetts senator Daniel Webster for his eloquent support of the measure.

Soon, however, a key part of the compromise that Webster helped negotiate brought the distant devil to the streets of Boston (and goaded Thoreau, who had been polite about Webster before the compromise, into calling him a "dirt-bug"). Since the first days of the Republic, there had been no good resolution to the problem of how the Free States should deal with escaped slaves. In this regard, in fact, the U.S. Constitution itself might well be called the Compromise of 1787, for its promise of liberty was regularly cut with concessions to slavery. The delegates had agreed, for example, to count each slave as three-fifths of a free person and to let the slave trade continue for at least twenty years. More important for the Compromise of 1850, they had agreed that fugitive slaves must be returned to their masters, even if they had managed to get themselves to the North. A paragraph in Article IV spelled this out in euphemistic language, allowing that any person "held to service or labor in one State . . . , escaping into another, shall . . . be delivered up on claim of the party, to whom such service or labor may be due." In 1793, shortly after the Constitution was ratified, an early Fugitive Slave Law had fleshed out this clause by articulating the procedure for seizing and returning escaped slaves.

Northern states bridled at the way this law took judicial matters out of their hands, and consequently many of them enacted "personal liberty laws" meant to limit the federal law. (These laws gave slaves the right to a jury trial, for example, which the federal law denied.) The result was fifty years of dissatisfaction on both sides. In some cases escaped slaves were captured and returned to slavery, angering the North; in others they found safe haven, angering the South. It was at the insistence of the South, then, that the Compromise of 1850 included a new and more stringent Fugitive Slave Law, one that not only denied jury trials to runaways but prohibited them from testifying on their own behalf, levied heavy penalties against anyone who came to their aid, and allowed for enforcement by federal troops and marshals.

In the short term the law was often effective, but in the long term it backfired, for in response to each slave captured and returned, a thousand Northern hearts were hardened against slavery, the South, and the North's complicit public servants. Just as in the Vietnam era, when the military draft forced young men to make personal decisions about a distant conflict, in the early 1850s the Fugitive Slave Law forced local functionaries in New England to make personal—and public—decisions about what had recently been a hateful but distant practice. Before the 1850s Boston's Cotton Whigs—those conservative merchants who praised Webster's acceptance of the Fugitive Slave Law—had the luxury of saying that while they personally opposed slavery, it was more important to preserve the Union than to solve a problem that didn't exist at home. But then came a series of cases in which local blacks—men and women with families, with jobs, with ministers who cared about them—were being captured by slave hunters and held at the Boston Court House, their faces staring through the bars at citizens passing on the street. Under these conditions, more and more Boston Brahmins found themselves able to imagine joining their abolitionist neighbors and breaking the federal law.

The first of the fugitive slave cases that caught Thoreau's attention was that of Thomas Sims. Having fled from Georgia, Sims was captured on April 3, 1851, in Boston and sent back to his master on April 12. Thoreau filled pages of his journal with scornful complaint about the servility of the newspapers and the complicity of the state. As for how the law itself should be tested, the journal entries express his doubt that any court was in a position to decide the case:

> It has come to this, that the friends of liberty, the friends of the slave, have shuddered when they have understood that [Sims's] fate has been left to the legal tribunals, so-called. . . . The people have no faith that justice will be awarded in such a case. The judge may decide this way or that; it is a kind of accident at best. It is evident that he is not a competent authority in so important a case. I would not trust the life of my friend to the judges of all the Supreme Courts in the world put together, to be sacrificed or saved by precedent.

Ideally, in American jurisprudence grave legislative attacks on liberty could be blocked by appeals to the Constitution, and it is likely that Thoreau is thinking of the history of such appeals when he doubts the power of "precedent" to save poor Sims.

The problem was that legislation involving slavery was a special case in constitutional law. The Sims case proved the point, for those who appealed to the law to stop his return to Georgia found themselves met and turned back exactly on constitutional grounds. Lemuel Shaw, chief justice of the Massachusetts Supreme Court (and, by the way, Herman Melville's father-in-law), ruled not only that the Fugitive Slave Law was constitutional but that the United States itself would never have come into existence had the Constitution not allowed for slavery. In a decision that let Sims be sent back to Georgia, Shaw wrote:

> Slavery was not created . . . by the Constitution; it existed before; it would have existed if the Constitution had not been made. The framers of the Constitution could not abrogate Slavery, or the rights claimed under it. They took it as they found it, and regulated it to a limited extent.
>
> The Constitution . . . was the best adjustment which could be made of conflicting rights and claims, and was absolutely necessary to effect . . . the general pacification, by which harmony and peace should take the place of violence and war.

Similar decisions came down from the U.S. Supreme Court whenever it was faced with questions about slavery. In the 1857 Dred Scott case, for example, the Court found that it had no legal obligation toward slaves because they were not actually citizens, having been viewed as belonging to an inferior order when the Constitution was written.

For many in the North such legal sophistry did nothing but reduce respect for law itself and give new currency to the transcendentalist creed that written law should always be held accountable to the higher law inscribed in human conscience. Thoreau's aphoristic assertion "They are the lovers of law and order, who observe the law when the government breaks it" comes from "Slavery in Massachusetts," his published attack on the Fugitive Slave Law, where we also find what must be his answer to Shaw's ruling in the Sims case:

> The question is not whether you or your grandfather, seventy years ago, did not enter into an agreement to serve the devil, . . . but whether you will not now, for once and at last, serve God . . . by obeying that eternal and only just CONSTITUTION, which He, and not any Jefferson or Adams, has written in your being.

In the course of denying slaves any constitutional refuge, Justice Shaw had tried to highlight the virtues of compromise, speaking grandly of "harmony and peace" replacing "violence and war." Within a few years, however, his ruling proved instrumental in a reversal of that logic. In May 1854 an escaped slave named Anthony Burns was arrested in Boston, and his master began the proceedings to return him to Virginia. The hearing to determine if Burns was in fact the man his master said he was (the only question open to review under the Fugitive Slave Law) threw the city into turmoil. Abolitionists, having learned from Shaw that legal arguments would not help their cause, resolved to rescue Burns from the Boston Court House, where he was being held, and speed him off to Canada. Thus two days after Burns was arrested, and following an inflammatory rally at Boston's Faneuil Hall, a woefully disorganized mob attacked the courthouse, battering down the door and killing a deputy U.S. marshal before being beaten back.

If the object was to rescue Burns, the attack was a grave mistake, for by morning an overwhelming force of federal troops and state militia had secured the building. A week later, when Burns was finally remanded to Virginia, he was led to a ship in Boston Harbor surrounded by a guard of U.S. marshals carrying pistols and drawn cutlasses. In front of these guards marched a company of U.S. Marines, a company of U.S. infantry, and—on horseback—a company of Boston's National Lancers. Behind the marshals marched another company of marines, followed by artillery officers with a horse-drawn cannon. In short, for a week in the spring of 1854 Boston—which had long imagined itself the cradle of liberty—was an occupied city, with local law suspended and federal law carried out by force of arms. Harmony and peace seemed then quite distant, and even Thoreau, whose earlier essay on disobedience was a model of civility, found himself imagining violence and war: "My thoughts are murder to the State."

V. "SUPPOSE BLOOD SHOULD FLOW"

Because "Civil Disobedience" so deeply influenced both Mohandas Gandhi and Martin Luther King, Jr., the impression has arisen that Thoreau himself was an advocate of nonviolent resistance. That is, in fact, a plausible reading of "Civil Disobedience," for Thoreau's action in the instance he describes was almost wholly passive. He simply didn't pay his taxes. He did not announce his case beforehand and force the state to act; he did not organize fellow tax resisters; he did not lie in the streets to interfere with the business of the town. Though his position on taxation was considered and deliberate, his actual arrest arose because he was simply going about his business when the state stood in his way. Nor was Thoreau himself a violent man. There are no famous stories of his prowess with a gun.

Still, "Civil Disobedience" contains hints of Thoreau's more aggressive side, one that would become patently evident a few years later. The essay's original title, "Resistance to Civil Government," is one indication. At the time he wrote, Thoreau was well aware of a national debate between resisters and nonresisters, the latter being the ardent Christian pacifists of the nineteenth century. Men like William Lloyd Garrison and Adin Ballou called themselves nonresisters because they believed, as Ballou wrote, in the "non-resistance of injury with injury—evil with evil." A declaration that Garrison wrote in 1839 spelled out the consequent positions: nonresisters refused all physical force and coercion; they would submit passively to enemies and thieves and forgive rather than punish them; they would countenance no prisons, no retaliation, no retribution, no revenge; they would suffer "insult, outrage . . . , even death," for after all "so they treated the Messiah."

As early as 1841 Thoreau had apparently dissented from such sweeping pacifism, for in a debate at the Concord Lyceum he had taken the affirmative on the question "Is it ever proper to offer forcible resistance?" The later essay takes the affirmative again, though mutedly. Other than the title, the only passage where we find a brief flash of the possibility of confronting injury with injury is this:

> When the subject has refused allegiance, and the officer has resigned his office, then the revolution is accomplished. But even suppose blood should flow. Is there not a sort of blood shed when the conscience is wounded? Through this wound a man's real manhood and immortality flow out, and he bleeds to an everlasting death. I see this blood flowing now.

Thoreau begins here with his preferred politics, revolution by signing off, and when he turns to an imagined alternative, it is not a little figurative, but nonetheless there it is: it would be better to shed blood than to compromise a matter of conscience.

This metaphoric blood has become literal by the time of Thoreau's next overtly political essay, "Slavery in Massachusetts." There we find a reference to the "heroic attack on the Boston Court-House," a phrase that deserves to be underlined so as to see the progression of Thoreau's thought. "Slavery in Massachusetts" is primarily a response to the Fugitive Slave Act of 1850 and to the Anthony Burns affair, which, as I have said, included the storming of the courthouse where Burns was being held and the death of a deputy U.S. marshal. That assault, that political murder, is the "heroic attack" to which Thoreau refers.

Thoreau and his fellow transcendentalists had always had an interest in heroes and bravery. Thoreau's earliest journal contains long entries on bravery ("We do all stand in the front ranks of the battle . . . ; where there is a brave man there is the thickest of the fight"), and a youthful essay, "The Service: Qualities of the Recruit," is an ode to the martial spirit. One gathers that this side of Thoreau came forward most fully in debate and argument. As Emerson said at Thoreau's funeral:

> There was somewhat military in his nature not to be subdued, always manly and able, but rarely tender, as if he did not feel himself except in opposition. . . . He . . . required . . . a roll of the drum to call his powers into full exercise.

Every greeting-card shop in America now has something to remind us of that line from *Walden* about marching to "a different drummer," but as a recent biographer points out, it is mostly soldiers who march to drums.

Again, the military side of Thoreau is spiritual rather than physical, but his metaphors predispose him to assent when anyone appears actually willing to join heroic conscience with physical action. Such, he thought, were the men who attacked the courthouse trying to free Anthony Burns (the fact that in doing so they killed a man is not mentioned in the essay, only the "heroic attack"). Such, above all, was John Brown, who later led an attack on the federal arsenal at Harpers Ferry, Virginia.

I shall have more to say about Brown below, but for now I want simply to mark the last phase in the evolution of Thoreau's relationship to violence. In his lectures on John Brown, Thoreau clearly is a resister, not a nonresister. It was John Brown's position, he says, "that a man has a perfect right to interfere by force with the slaveholder, in order to rescue the slave. I agree with him." "[F]or once the Sharps' rifles and the revolvers were employed in a righteous cause. The tools were in the hands of one who could use them." This from a man who worried all his life about a culture dedicated to producing "improved means to unimproved ends." Here the improved end is the abolition of slavery, and the old means—rifles and revolvers—serve very well.

What had changed in the decade between "Civil Disobedience" and the John Brown essays such that bloodshed and armed insurrection would replace passive resistance and simple signing off? The pivotal moment is recorded toward the end of "Slavery in Massachusetts." I earlier mentioned Thoreau's genius for perspective, his great ability to get himself outside the common frame of reference. On that ground, as I noted, "Civil Disobedience" contained his critique of traditional politicians who "speak of moving society, but have no resting-place without," who "never [go] behind government, and so cannot speak with authority about it." But once the Fugitive Slave Law began to be enforced in Massachusetts, Thoreau found that he himself no longer had a "resting-place without"; not even nature allowed him to get "behind." Thus he writes in "Slavery in Massachusetts": "I walk toward one of our ponds, but what signifies the beauty of nature when men are base? . . . The remembrance of my country spoils my walks." There was a time when he had imagined that his life might be conducted in a space between heaven and hell, but now he found that no matter where he went he was "*wholly within* hell." "My old and worthiest pursuits have lost I cannot say how much of their attraction . . . since Massachusetts last deliberately sent back an innocent man, Anthony Burns, to slavery."

It wasn't just that the politics of slavery had penetrated to "our ponds," either; it was the humiliation that went along with it. For years the slaveholders had managed to draw the line against Northern abolitionists, and to do so with physical force and violence. In 1844, when Thoreau's neighbor the former congressman Samuel Hoar was sent to South Carolina to advocate for free Massachusetts blacks who were being jailed in Charleston without cause, a mob unceremoniously rode him out of the city. In 1851 several hundred federal troops helped ship Sims back to Georgia, and there his master had him publicly whipped almost to death. This display of cruelty was meant more for Yankee eyes than for the poor remanded slave, a point made clear by the date chosen for the whipping: the anniversary of the Battles of Lexington and Concord.

Men in the North took each of these events as a blow not just to their self-esteem but to their manhood. When Thoreau read the news account of those who tried to prevent Sims from being carried back to the South, he was proud to find a citizen of Concord "represented in that tea-party," but then his feelings turned to doubt and shame because the man in question was a relative newcomer and "because the *men* of Concord in recent times have done nothing to entitle them to the honor of having their town named in such a connexion." The emphasis on men here is a sign that Thoreau counted himself as a grandson of the men who wrote the Constitution, a patriot in a revolutionary patriarchy on guard lest the nation's store of manhood run out. Those early notes on "bravery" equate manhood with virtue, noting the "virility" that is the etymological link between the two.

An easy way to mark the virile strain in Thoreau's work is to contrast his slavery essays with another work written as a consequence of the Fugitive Slave Law, Harriet Beecher Stowe's *Uncle Tom's Cabin.* The characters in Stowe's novel weep on almost every page (and the author constantly urges the reader to join them); at the end, in answer to the question what must be done to rid the world of slavery, Stowe asks her audience *to feel* and *to pray.* Thoreau would not necessarily argue with Stowe, but his methods are not hers. Surely there are few who weep while reading Henry Thoreau. In writing about Anthony Burns, Thoreau would never think to wring our hearts with images of what young Burns's mother must be feeling. There is feeling in Thoreau, yes, but it springs more from conscience than from sympathy, and it moves toward direct action, not prayer. He is out to stiffen the back and draw the line, not to evangelize for a religion of the heart. Like Frederick Douglass, Thoreau takes resistance to be an exercise in recovering manhood. Responding to the murder of the U.S. marshal in Boston, Douglass had written: "Every slavehunter who meets a bloody death in his infernal business, is an argument in favor of the manhood of the race." Such was Thoreau's position for white manhood, too, at the end of the 1850s. What he liked about John Brown was that the man did what men should do. Faced with years of humiliation at the hands of slaveholders, he didn't go to law; he bought weapons and attacked the enemy.

VI. A LITERAL GIDEON

In October 1859 John Brown and twenty-one men attacked the federal arsenal at Harpers Ferry, Virginia, hoping to incite a slave insurrection and start a guerrilla war against the South. Though the raid revealed that the South was deeply anxious about possible slave revolts, and though it so polarized the nation that it arguably helped spark the Civil War, in the short term it was an utter failure. Although five escaped, Brown and the rest of his men were all killed or captured within forty-eight hours. Brown himself was hanged six weeks later.

After Brown was captured, and again after he died, Thoreau spoke out in defense of his actions. He had met Brown twice in Concord in the years just before the raid. In each case Brown had recently come from Kansas, where he and his sons were involved in the civil war brought on by the Compromise of 1850. Before immigrating to Kansas in 1855, Brown had been involved in a series of business ventures in New England and Ohio; he had been a tanner, a land speculator, a wool grower, and a wool merchant. Each of these enterprises had failed, most of them ending in lawsuits and bankruptcy. Brown had married twice (his first wife having died) and fathered twenty children. By the time he moved to Kansas, he had seen nine of these children die and fifteen businesses ruined. He was an unlucky man, but also stubborn, private, and self-involved, refusing to take advice from anyone and more willing to join himself to a scheme or grievance than to give one up.

Two things ran parallel in Brown's life during his years of hapless struggle: a devout Christianity and a hatred of slavery. Brown was an old-school Calvinist of the sort who believes not just that we are "sinners in the hands of an angry God," as Jonathan Edwards put it, but that we have an obligation to bring that wrath to bear against the sin, which in practice can mean against ourselves and our loved ones. When Brown was a small boy, his father whipped him for the most minor of crimes (for stealing three pins, for example). Brown used this style of discipline on his own children (once beating his three-year-old son, Jason, for "lying" when the boy insisted that a dream he'd had was real). It wasn't so much about particular transgressions as about the sin each of us inherits; one time while beating another son, he astonished the boy by handing him the switch and having himself beaten until the blood began to show on his back. Severity was the mark, from first to last, of John Brown's religion. His final communication to the world was a note handed to a jailer on his way to the scaffold: "I, John Brown, am now quite certain that the crimes of this guilty land will never be purged away but with Blood." He was fond of a verse from Hebrews: "Without the shedding of blood there is no remission of sins."

From his youth onward, Brown joined his Calvinism to a conviction that slavery was a sin against God, a position he had inherited from his father and from the sermons of Jonathan Edwards, Jr. At a prayer meeting in Ohio he had publicly vowed to consecrate his life to the abolition of slavery; once he had been expelled from a church for insisting on sharing his pew with black families. Many abolitionists were themselves racists, hoping to end slavery by returning American blacks to Africa, but not John Brown. He had many black friends, he treated them as equals, he called them by their surnames, and he shared his table with them. Five of the raiders on Harpers Ferry were black.

These and other parts of John Brown's mind and method are well illustrated by his organizing a group called the United States League of Gileadites. This was early in 1851, in Springfield, Massachusetts; the Fugitive Slave Law had recently been passed, and Brown and his friends in the black community were exceedingly anxious that slave hunters would come to town and carry fugitives away. Brown thus gathered his friends and urged them to join together in a league pledged to mutual armed resistance. Forty-four men and women signed on.

Brown had taken his inspiration from a story in the Bible. In the Book of Judges we read that in the generation after Joshua, the Israelites had forsaken God, who therefore gave them over into the hands of the Midianites for seven years. At the end of these years God called on Gideon to redeem His people. Gideon at first protested ("How can I deliver Israel? Behold, my clan is the weakest . . . , and I am the least in my family"), but God prevailed and soon Gideon had gathered an army of more than thirty thousand men. God then announced that the army was too large; if the Israelites were to win, they might praise themselves and not the Lord. So Gideon thinned his troops until only three hundred remained. These then scattered the Midian armies, many thousands strong: "When they blew the three hundred trumpets, the Lord set every man's sword against his fellow and against all the army; and the army fled."

In Springfield, the League of Gileadites never set its swords against an enemy—slave hunters did not in fact arrive—but its formation was an uncanny foreshadowing of Harpers Ferry and offers a glimpse of how Brown imagined himself. To begin with, Brown thought he saw providential purpose even in such apparent evils as the Fugitive Slave Law ("It really looks as if God had his hand in this wickedness," he wrote to his wife). And why might God have allowed an unjust majority to pass evil laws against the will of a righteous minority? To punish the faithless, first of all, but also, come the turning point, because God does not work by the carnal arithmetic of majority rule. He prefers small numbers so that His hand might be all the more evident.

In the Calvinist reading, apparently, God's favorite number is one: one righteous man. This had been Thoreau's position in "Civil Disobedience": "if one honest man" resisted slavery and got locked up in jail, "it would be the abolition of slavery in America." John Brown said the same thing to the gathered Gileadites, only Brown's position was a touch more resistant and a touch more violent. He imagined "one bold and to some extent successful man . . . , defending his rights in good earnest," then being put on "trial for life," finally to be "hanged, if [he] must," all of which would "arouse . . . sympathy throughout the nation," for "nothing so charms the American people as personal bravery."

We have here not just the literalizing of prophecy; we have also one nineteenth-century political form—or rather an apolitical form, for the final thing to note about how Brown imagines his world is that it centers on a small, unaffiliated group or, even better, on a single hero. Brown himself never joined any of the antislavery societies. There is no politics in the story of the League of Gileadites, just good against evil, a threat of violence, and the hope of heroic charm. Similarly, Brown's style, once he had arrived in Kansas, was to work alone and in secret, never showing any interest, for example, in working with others involved in the struggle to make Kansas a Free-Soil state. In fact, by the time he went west in the spring of 1856, he had become what we would now call a terrorist.

The initial and most striking case of John Brown at work in Kansas has come to be known as the massacre at Pottawatomie Creek. Tensions were high in southeastern Kansas in the early months of 1856. Pro-slavery settlers had murdered six Free-Soil settlers in a variety of confusing situations. A pro-slavery army had attacked Lawrence, Kansas, burning the governor's house and destroying the presses at Free-Soil newspapers. In this context, Brown and four men (two of them his sons) took it upon themselves to murder five pro-slavery settlers near their cabins along Pottawatomie Creek, about thirty-five miles south of Lawrence.

One victim was James Doyle, a poor white farmer who had left Tennessee because he'd decided that slavery was "ruinous to white labor" but had staunchly defended the pro-slavery faction once he got to Kansas. Brown's band came to Doyle's cabin about eleven o'clock at night and—with Mrs. Doyle weeping in the door—took the man and his two older sons out onto the road, where Brown's sons hacked them to death with broadswords. One of Doyle's sons had his arms cut off. Brown himself shot Doyle in the forehead to make sure he was dead. He later declared the killings to be "decreed by Almighty God, ordained from eternity." If so, God wanted war, for soon southeastern Kansas, "Bleeding Kansas," was plunged into chaos; armed bands roamed the countryside, one of them led by Brown. More than two hundred died before the fighting abated.

Not much detail about these matters, or about Brown's early days, reached Concord. Thoreau knew nothing of all those disappointments in business (his "Plea for Captain John Brown" makes the baseless claim that the man had "great common sense"). As for the terror on Pottawatomie Creek, Thoreau had heard of it but had no reason to believe the story: exaggerated claims were being made on all sides, Brown himself lied about his actions, and the two New York newspapermen who had actually met Brown in Kansas got the story wrong. Beyond this, as Robert Penn Warren has argued, Brown had a gift for creating compelling stories after the fact. From all accounts, he was a persuasive and charismatic man. He stood only five feet nine inches, but everyone in Boston called him tall. People who knew him ended up speaking of him in the terms he himself had invented: his first biographer, James Redpath, happily called him one of the Gideons; after his death, so did the pacifist William Lloyd Garrison!

It was more than the old man's fire and fabulations that fed Thoreau's enthusiasm, however. Beyond all that, and beyond the arch individualism, there was John Brown's impatience with words and his drive toward action. By 1859 many abolitionists had tired of talk and were ready for a fight. They had been humiliated too long. Most recently, a few days before the Pottawatomie massacre in fact, a senator from Massachusetts, Charles Sumner, had been beaten on the floor of the U.S. Senate by Representative Preston Brooks of South Carolina. Objecting to a Free-Soil speech by Sumner, Brooks had approached Sumner at his Senate desk and thrashed him with a cane so furiously that the cane shattered and Sumner, blinded by his own blood and trying to rise, ripped the bolted desk from the floor.

The beating of Sumner was merely the latest in a decades-old string of insults. As I've mentioned, there had been the bullying of Thoreau's neighbor Samuel Hoar in South Carolina; there had been the removal from Boston and the public whipping of Thomas Sims; there had been the occupation of Boston for the remanding of Anthony Burns. Some eight months after the beating of Sumner, John Brown visited the recuperating senator in Boston and asked to see the coat he had been wearing when attacked. Sumner limped to the closet and brought out the garment, stiff with blood. Brown held it silently, Sumner reported, his eyes shining "like polished steel." No wonder they loved him in Concord. Whoever was casting this melodrama had at last found someone who would stop arguing about the Constitution and arm himself.

Unfortunately, the ensuing events never rose to the restorative ending we expect from melodrama, at least not on the carnal plane. Even this, however, the proximate failure of the Harpers Ferry raid, appealed to Thoreau. To see why, let's go back to the story of Gideon and the Midianites, where weakness and small numbers signified the Lord's presence and the warriors' virtue. Gideon did not fail, of course, so here we must turn from the Book of Judges and concentrate on Brown's retelling of the tale, for note that the solitary hero he conjured up for his friends was not a "bold and successful man" but, oddly, a "bold and to some extent successful man." In retrospect, the fable Brown spun the day he gathered his league nicely prefigured what was to happen at Harpers Ferry eight years later: a tiny army, sure they were summoned by God, were "to some extent successful" in their enterprise, though hanged in the end. That, at any rate, gives it the kind of literal-prophetic reading Brown himself preferred. A more temporal reading of that modifying clause, "to some extent," would take it as an echo of Brown's actual fortunes at the time and a suggestion that apparent failure might be a sign of virtue yet to be disclosed.

Regardless of how we understand what Brown does with Gideon, Thoreau was quick to assert the promise hidden in the Harpers Ferry fiasco. Reversals of this sort were Thoreau's stock-in-trade—we travel by staying home, heaven is beneath our feet, poverty makes us rich—and for similar reasons: figuratively they point to the spiritual world (by jerking the mind away from the literal), and literally they help assuage whatever limits and losses he himself had suffered. In Brown's case, then, Thoreau is quickly scornful of the newspapers that "talk as if a man's death were a failure" and scornful too of a neighbor who asks ("Yankee-like") what Brown hoped to gain by his action:

> Such a one has no idea of gain but in this worldly sense. . . . [I]f he does not get a new pair of boots . . . it must be a failure. "But he won't gain any thing by it." Well, no, I don't suppose he could get four-and-sixpence a day for being hung . . . ; but then he stands a chance to save a considerable part of his soul.

Thus in addition to weakness and small numbers, failure in this world becomes a sign of virtue, for it implies a relative lack of self-interest. Surely the motive must be high when a man acts with no idea of gain. Such, at any rate, was not only how Thoreau cast Brown but how Brown presented himself to the world after his capture. If he couldn't be one of the triumphant Gideons of this world, then he would be one of the dying Christs who show us all that failure in one world is high success in another. In this way did the state of Virginia, by its sentence of death, get old Brown out of the Hebrew Bible and into the New Testament at last. The Lord once saw fit to send him into battle armed; now, Brown wrote from his jail cell, "Christ . . . saw fit to take from me a sword of steel . . . , but he has put another in my hand ('The sword of the Spirit')." Brown had a sense of narrative, and if he had to die, he knew what the form required. Before his hanging, he wrote consolingly to his family: "Remember, dear wife and children all, that Jesus of Nazareth suffered a most excruciating death on the cross as a felon."

The story itself demanded this Christlike death. Without it, how could steel be converted into spirit? How could the seed of virtue be winnowed from the husk of failure? At his trial Brown declared, "If it is deemed necessary that I should forfeit my life for the furtherance of the ends of justice . . . , I say let it be done," and after his conviction, when friends plotted to free him, he told them not to: "I am worth inconceivably more to *hang* than for any other purpose." Nor was Brown the only one who felt the plot must end in death. The journalist James Redpath said as much; so did Henry Ward Beecher, and so did Thoreau, making his plea for the still-living Brown in a rather chilling past tense: "I see now that it was necessary that . . . [he] be hung. . . . I *almost fear* that I may yet hear of his deliverance, doubting if a prolonged life . . . can do as much good as his death."

The fear Thoreau articulates here belongs to democracy in its American, Protestant form. Thoreau had spent a good deal of his intellectual energy trying to escape the fences of his Christian town, but when the fight against slavery drew him to the ground of actual politics, and especially when he was speaking to his actual Christian neighbors, he reverted to the local type, for whom the martyrdom of Christ is the greatest story told, now in its New World version, which promises that a majority of one might stake a transcendental claim, and then triumph by dying. That is to say, the John Brown story points toward otherwise obscure connections among the mathematics of majority rule, acts of conscience, and failure. Democratic practice has long been haunted by the fear that majority rule might bring a new form of despotism, kingship replaced by the mob. As Thoreau puts it in "Civil Disobedience," "A wise man will not . . . wish [the right] to prevail through the power of the majority. There is but little virtue in the action of masses of men." The warning to Gideon—that large numbers will obscure the hand of the Lord—is God's version of this point. Useful, then, is the trick of spiritual reversal by which the weak are strong and the finest proof of good conscience is that the crowd will not believe in it. Thus when some fundamental change is needed, some change that the majority by its very nature cannot see, the spiritual politics of Christian democracy must call out a martyr, one whose death becomes the symbolic event by which the dissident position acquires its political life. That is why Thoreau can say, in the speech read over the dead man's grave, that John Brown "is more alive than ever he was," that he "*had not died.*"

VII. THE NICK OF TIME

I myself part company with Thoreau when he gets to John Brown. Except for the clarity of Brown's stand against slavery, and for his ability to form friendships in the black community, I find little to recommend him. I don't like the willful violence. I don't like the refusal of organized politics and collective action. I am put off by what a friend of his called "his God idea," especially when joined to his "imperial egotism."

And because Thoreau seems not to feel, or at least never expresses, any such reservations, I find that I hear a number of things differently when I turn back to the earlier essays with the Brown case echoing in my ears. When first describing the prophetic voice, I mentioned in passing that it has its dangers, and the difference I now speak of is probably best described as another version of that point. I pause more now when Thoreau proclaims his love of heroes. I am cautious before his grandiosity, his mythmaking, his manliness. His solitude and his refusals still stir me, but I am more aware of the political registers that they exclude. Moreover, as one born in a century that brought both the horrors of ethnic cleansing and the insights of psychoanalysis, I can no longer hear Thoreau's longing for "purity" without hearing as well an undertone of potential cruelty, the threat, that is, to whatever the purist hopes to purge, be it (in Thoreau's case) the appetites of his own body and the imperfections of his friends or (in Brown's case) the sins of unwitting children and the imperfections of "this guilty land." (Perhaps it is exactly this—the potential cruelty of good conscience—that led Gandhi and King to insist on nonviolent action, a tactic that is latent in the early Thoreau but then abandoned, not developed.)

It often turns out, once we get some specific cases before us, to be difficult to translate prophetic idealism into actual practice. At the close of the first section of this essay, I made it sound simple: "You resist an immoral war and go to jail." You quit, you hunker down, you go back, you leave: it seems so easy when put so briefly. And I meant it to seem easy:

Thoreau is a master at calling out our optimism, and I was there happily joining my voice to his in hopes of casting the old spell. In that can-do mode, one might similarly have said, in 1859, "You see the wrong of slavery, attack the slaveholder, and put an end to it." But at this distance in time at least, the turmoil and carnage that followed John Brown should make us pause to reflect on the territory between seeing the wrong and putting it right.

Not all slaveholding societies, after all, resorted to violence to bring an end to slavery. None, I think, had to suffer the kind of civil war we had to suffer. The British, for example, slowly ended slavery in the West Indies by converting slaves into "apprentice laborers" who had to give a good portion of their income to their masters for four years before becoming fully free. The British also reimbursed West Indian planters for the capital they had invested in slaves; the government essentially bought the slaves to free them. They spent twenty million pounds to do so, a significant sum of money in 1834, the year of West Indian emancipation.

Similarly, in the United States several Northern states ended slavery by slow and compromising measures. In 1804 New Jersey passed an act for gradual abolition. As of July 4 of that year, the children of slaves were born free, though they had to remain servants of their mother's owner until they came of age. In 1846 the state abolished slavery entirely, though again by a gradualist formula: the children of slaves were now wholly free at birth, but slaves themselves were converted to "apprentices" whose condition combined continued involuntary servitude with legal rights that slaves had never had before. In 1850 there were 236 such apprentices in New Jersey; in 1860 there were 2.

Such pragmatic and middling solutions would be unthinkable to all-or-nothing men like Thoreau and Brown. For one thing, they require accepting that there might be such a thing as property in persons (the British, that is, could not buy West Indian slaves without recognizing slavery as a legal fact). Gradualist solutions require dealing with the devil and staining the conscience, and purity of conscience is Thoreau's point of departure, the ground on which he stands. But, the pragmatist might ask, what exactly is the alternative? Refusing to work with slavery as it in fact existed meant inviting a conflict that only war could settle, and war surely is the devil's playground. Might not a man also stain his conscience by insisting that its price can only be reckoned in the currency of Union dead? Emerson once called John Brown "a pure idealist" and, noting that

Brown believed above all in the Golden Rule and the Declaration of Independence, recalled that he had once said, in regard to these: "Better that a whole generation of men, women and children should pass away by a violent death, than that one word of either should be violated in this country." As others have pointed out, there is a grim confusion here between figurative eloquence and literal statement. A whole generation? By violent death? Really?

Ah, but Emerson did not speak of Brown on some infinitely recurring November evening. He spoke on November 18, 1859. John Brown was two weeks away from the scaffold, and the failed fight against the Fugitive Slave Law was a decade old. Northerners had found all the avenues of compromise to be dead ends. There is an earlier, more pragmatic Emerson (who in 1844 offered the British in the West Indies as a model for how America might abolish slavery), as there is an earlier Thoreau whose image of disobedience was more "civil." Which is to say that there is no point reading the late political essays the way I read "Walking." The prophetic voice, as I said, erases history, and we are emphatically in history now.

That "prophetic excursion" I outlined earlier ends with the prophet falling silent, leaving the rest of us to figure out how best to turn vision into fact. In the 1850s we have Thoreau embarking on that last phase, letting himself be drawn into the most temporal of matters and, with John Brown, attaching himself to an actor and an action. It is a shift that requires Thoreau to forget his ignorance, of course, for remembering ignorance, and cultivating it in a spirit of fertile regret, are conditions of refusal and retreat, not of consent and public engagement. The late political essays are the fruit of a prophetic temperament, but they themselves are not prophetic; they are time-bound, and they need to be read, first of all, with as much sense of the historical moment as possible.

Thus, though it is the case that I do not follow Thoreau in his praise for John Brown, it also feels quite churlish to be recalling gradualist solutions to slavery at this late date. The more I try to imagine what it was like to live in Concord in the fall of 1859, the more I know that my reservations are born and bred in a luxury of time. I not only have a century-and-a-half distance from the events that gripped Thoreau; I know more than he did about Brown, and I know about the Civil War. With such a large remove in time it is not hard to be dispassionate about strategy, and not hard to find the fault in every action. But these are the privileges of the noncombatant, and few who take their own times seriously can have them.

At the close of *Walden*, Thoreau suggests how varied might be the pitches of his voice, saying that the poems of Kabir were supposed to have four different senses—illusory, spiritual, intellectual, and esoteric—and complaining of readers who hope to settle on a single one of these. In speaking of Kabir, he may have been teasing Christian readers more familiar with the medieval system by which the Bible was read at four levels—the literal, the allegorical, the moral, and the anagogical. The terms are not the point, however; the point is that much of Thoreau's art lies in his ability to move (gracefully, annoyingly) among the several kinds of sense. If you think *Walden*'s story about the bean field is there as a practical lesson, you are wrong: he means it as a parable. But if you think it's a parable, you are wrong: it's the literal truth; he really did plant those beans.

I have been coming back to Thoreau's essays regularly for more than thirty years, and something different happens each time I pick them up. I cannot now read him without marking the history in his words, the degree to which the ideals he calls us toward belong to the common rhetoric of the mid-nineteenth century and to his own lived life. But cleaving to a historical reading of Thoreau does not account for his persistence and appeal. For that we need to open our ears to other levels of meaning. We must allow his erasures of chronology if we are to sense how, yes, a snowstorm in Concord is like the snowstorm in Book XII of *The Iliad*. We must allow his attack on Understanding if we ever hope to feel how large our ignorance is. We must take seriously his claim that the divine was at work in John Brown if we are to feel how pitched the forces were that fed the Civil War. These essays are now five or six generations behind us, but that does not mean they cannot come quickly back to life for any reader with ears to hear the many registers of their author's voice.

A NOTE ON THE SELECTION

An industry sprang up around Thoreau's essays shortly after he died in 1862, and it continues to this day. He himself set it in motion: when he knew he was dying, he converted some of his lyceum lectures into essays for posthumous publication. These had not been published during his lifetime because, as lectures, they were his bread and butter, or perhaps only his bread, for Thoreau never made much money lecturing, nor did he lecture widely (one scholar estimates that over a twenty-three-year career Thoreau earned an annual twenty-seven dollars for public speaking). Thoreau first delivered "Life without Principle" in 1854, and then repeated it many times over the years; "Walking" began in 1851 and was delivered at least eight times; "Autumnal Tints" he gave three times in 1859 and once the next year. These three, and the later "Wild Apples," he readied for publication in the last year of his life, and they subsequently appeared in *The Atlantic Monthly* between 1862 and 1863.

Then in November 1863 the *Atlantic* printed something called "Night and Moonlight," unsigned, though clearly from Thoreau's hand (parts of it coming directly from his journal). Thoreau had in fact given a lecture on the topic once, shortly after *Walden* was published, but as far as anyone knows, he never repeated it and certainly never turned it into an essay. All he left was a stack of notes, which his sister Sophia probably assembled as an essay and sold to the *Atlantic*. In 1927 someone at Houghton Mifflin with access to the journal manuscripts found "a sheaf of notes" on moonlight and published them as a little book, *The Moon*.

These are typical of the ways in which essays that Thoreau never wrote have become essays by Thoreau. They are also a betrayal of Thoreau's method of composition. In one journal entry he writes: "I would rather write books than lectures. That is fine, this coarse." As the "Reading" chapter of *Walden* makes clear, Thoreau did not think a lecture was an essay:

> [T]here is a memorable interval between the spoken and the written language, the language heard and the language read. The one is commonly transitory, a sound, a tongue, a dialect merely, almost brutish, and we learn it unconsciously, like the brutes, of our mothers. The other is the maturity and experience of that; if that is our mother tongue, this is our father tongue, a reserved and select expression, too significant to be heard by the ear, which we must be born again in order to speak.

Thoreau's own method of traveling this familial landscape was to begin taking notes by pencil in a little notebook as he walked, then to transcribe and expand these notes in his journal, then from the journal to assemble topics on a theme, then to offer these as lectures, and finally to revise the lectures into essays or books for publication. That is how *Walden* was made (parts of it being spoken as lectures long before the book appeared), and with *Walden* the written version went through seven drafts before Thoreau was ready to publish. As he once said in a letter to Emerson, "In writing, conversation should be folded many times thick." *Walden* was folded seven times.

The industry that has been producing essays by Thoreau that Thoreau never wrote operates by traveling backward across the territory of his method until something is found that never made it to reserved and select expression. Thus we have an essay called "Love" culled from a letter Thoreau wrote to a friend, an essay on Sir Walter Raleigh published in 1905 from notes for an 1843 lecture, an essay called "Huckleberries" made from lecture notes and published in 1970, and in one of the early posthumous volumes an essay called "Prayers," which later scholars have decided was written by Emerson, though it is adorned with poems by Thoreau. More recently we have the book-length *Faith in a Seed* ("the first publication of Thoreau's last manuscript") and *Wild Fruits* ("Thoreau's rediscovered last manuscript"), and there will be more to follow.

All this is to the good. We are lucky to have Thoreau's notes on moonlight, his reflections on huckleberries, and especially all his late work in botany, as we are lucky to have his journals. But in selecting "Thoreau's essays," I have felt obliged to honor his own method and pass over things that he did not himself prepare for publication. Each of the thirteen pieces gathered here was either printed during his lifetime or edited by him for publication in the last year of his life. That said, I should add that a number of essays that Thoreau published, or prepared for publication, are not included here. Some are not accomplished enough to include ("The Service," for example, which was rejected by *The Dial* and not printed until 1902), many are occasional, and a few made their way into longer books (remarks on Homer, for example, that appeared in *The Dial* but were then included in *A Week on the Concord and Merrimack Rivers*). Texts of all these may be found in *Early Essays and Miscellanies* and the other volumes of the Princeton University Press series, *The Writings of Henry D. Thoreau*.

The thirteen essays in this collection are presented in the approximate order of their composition rather than thematically. As I mentioned earlier, ever since Thoreau died it has been the custom to separate his natural history ("excursions") from his politics ("reform papers"), but doing so obscures the ways in which these two are constantly entwined. What he calls Nature is, after all, the constant "outside" to the "inside" of public life, and each invariably shadows the other. The first essay here is a review of books about the flora and fauna of Massachusetts, but we find Thoreau unable to address himself to his topic without clearing his throat by dismissing politics. "Slavery in Massachusetts" would seem to be a fully political essay, but it ends with an invocation of the white water lily, whose bloom is proof that purity can be extracted from "slime and muck." In a journal entry on the meaning of "wild" Thoreau noted that "a wild man is a *willed* man," one "who does what he wills," and that, therefore, "the Almighty is wild above all" because he *wills*—all of which points to the ways in which an "excursion" like "Walking" is inexorably connected to "reform papers" like the essays on that most willful of men, John Brown.

I have taken the texts from two sources. Princeton University Press has been issuing carefully edited versions of all of Thoreau's work, and, with two exceptions, where Princeton has printed a rectified text, I have used it. I am grateful to Princeton for permission to reprint the following:

"Ktaadn," "Slavery in Massachusetts," "Life without Principle," "A Plea for Captain John Brown," and "The Last Days of John Brown."

Two of the essays that have appeared in the Princeton series present special cases. First, "Paradise (To Be) Regained" was originally printed in the *United States Magazine, and Democratic Review*, November 1843. After Thoreau died, a shorter and in many ways better-made version of the essay appeared in a volume called *A Yankee in Canada, with Anti-Slavery and Reform Papers* (1866). Similarly, "Civil Disobedience" was printed first in 1849 (under the title "Resistance to Civil Government") and again—slightly revised and with the title changed—after Thoreau's death. Absent any clear indication of an author's intent, it is the Princeton policy to publish the earlier version of a work, and the editors therefore reproduce the first version in each of these cases. It seems most likely to me, however, that Thoreau himself edited the later versions, so they are the ones I have chosen. For their texts, and for all the other essays collected here, the versions I reproduce appear in the "Walden Edition" of *The Writings of Henry David Thoreau* (Boston: Houghton Mifflin, 1906).

ACKNOWLEDGMENTS

This collection began as a result of a Thoreau seminar I taught at Kenyon College in which my students and I struggled with the odd fact that there was, in the late 1990s, no easily available edition of Thoreau's essays. To the degree that this volume solves that problem I am first of all indebted to those students, especially to the many who, as I was putting the book together, helped me learn what details in Thoreau need annotation for modern readers. Two students, Burke Hilsabeck and Abbi Russal, also signed on as research assistants to help me outside the classroom; several of their discoveries are preserved here.

Once I got going, I discovered that Bradley P. Dean, then working at the Thoreau Institute in Lincoln, Massachusetts, had done considerable work toward a similar collection. Rather than duplicate my efforts, Brad kindly decided to concentrate his energies on an edition of Thoreau's "Indian Notebooks" and to share with me the work he had done on the essays. I am deeply grateful for that collaboration; Brad helped me fill in many gaps and saved me from many errors.

Robert D. Richardson's intellectual biography of Thoreau and Stephen B. Oates's biography of John Brown were key sources throughout my project. Larry Rosenwald clarified many of the obscurities in "Civil Disobedience" and led me into the scholarship. Albert Von Frank's *The Trials of Anthony Burns* was an immense help in illuminating the background of "Slavery in Massachusetts," and Dr. Von Frank himself cordially responded to a draft of my notes on that essay.

I'm grateful to the Henry Luce Foundation, which supported my position at Kenyon College for many years, and to the MacDowell Colony where I spent a happy month writing the early drafts of the introduction.

I am indebted as well to Jeffrey Cramer, the librarian at the Thoreau Institute, and to Leslie Wilson, the curator of special collections at the Concord Free Public Library. The classicist Danielle Freedman helped me check some of Thoreau's Greek and Latin sources. Both Brian Donahue and David Foster took a crack at a few of Thoreau's more obscure remarks about New England farming. J. Parker Huber and Joseph Moldenhauer each solved some puzzles pertaining to "Ktaadn." Larry Rosenwald, Taylor Stoehr, Sacvan Bercovitch, Larry Buell, and Ethan Nosowsky read drafts of my introduction, and the final version benefits greatly from their comments. Once that version was done, Patsy Vigderman told me just what I needed to hear.

NATURAL HISTORY OF MASSACHUSETTS

NATURAL HISTORY OF MASSACHUSETTS.

Reports — on the Fishes, Reptiles, and Birds; the Herbaceous Plants and Quadrupeds; the Insects Injurious to Vegetation; and the Invertebrate Animals — of Massachusetts. Published agreeably to an Order of the Legislature, by the Commissioners on the Zoological and Botanical Survey of the State.

PRELIMINARY NOTE.

We were thinking how we might best celebrate the good deed which the State of Massachusetts has done, in procuring the Scientific Survey of the Commonwealth, whose result is recorded in these volumes, when we found a near neighbor and friend of ours, dear also to the Muses, a native and an inhabitant of the town of Concord, who readily undertook to give us such comments as he had made on these books, and, better still, notes of his own conversation with nature in the woods and waters of this town. With all thankfulness we begged our friend to lay down the oar and fishing line, which none can handle better, and assume the pen, that Isaak Walton and White of Selborne might not want a successor, nor the fair meadows, to which we also have owed a home and the happiness of many years, their poet.

Editor of the Dial.

Concord, Mass.

Books of natural history make the most cheerful winter reading. I read in Audubon with a thrill of delight, when the snow covers the ground, of the magnolia, and the Florida keys, and their warm sea breezes; of the fence-rail, and the cotton-tree, and the migrations of the rice-bird; of the breaking up of winter in Labrador, and the melting of the snow on the forks of the Missouri; and owe an accession of health to these reminiscences of luxuriant nature.

Within the circuit of this plodding life
There enter moments of an azure hue,
Untarnished fair as is the violet
Or anemone, when the spring strews them
By some meandering rivulet, which make
The best philosophy untrue that aims
But to console man for his grievances.
I have remembered when the winter came,
High in my chamber in the frosty nights,
When in the still light of the cheerful moon,

The Dial, July 1842. The preliminary note is by Ralph Waldo Emerson.

*NATURAL HISTORY OF MASSACHUSETTS**

Books of natural history make the most cheerful winter reading. I read in Audubon with a thrill of delight, when the snow covers the ground, of the magnolia, and the Florida keys, and their warm sea-breezes; of the fence-rail, and the cotton-tree, and the migrations of the rice-bird; of the breaking up of winter in Labrador, and the melting of the snow on the forks of the Missouri; and owe an accession of health to these reminiscences of luxuriant nature.

Within the circuit of this plodding life,
There enter moments of an azure hue,
Untarnished fair as is the violet
Or anemone, when the spring strews them
By some meandering rivulet, which make
The best philosophy untrue that aims
But to console man for his grievances.
I have remembered, when the winter came,
High in my chamber in the frosty nights,
When in the still light of the cheerful moon,

**Reports—on the Fishes, Reptiles, and Birds; the Herbaceous Plants and Quadrupeds; the Insects Injurious to Vegetation; and the Invertebrate Animals of Massachusetts.* Published agreeably to an Order of the Legislature, by the Commissioners on the Zoölogical and Botanical Survey of the State.

On every twig and rail and jutting spout,
The icy spears were adding to their length
Against the arrows of the coming sun,
How in the shimmering noon of summer past
Some unrecorded beam slanted across
The upland pastures where the Johnswort grew;
Or heard, amid the verdure of my mind,
The bee's long smothered hum, on the blue flag
Loitering amidst the mead; or busy rill,
Which now through all its course stands still and dumb,
Its own memorial,—purling at its play
Along the slopes, and through the meadows next,
Until its youthful sound was hushed at last
In the staid current of the lowland stream;
Or seen the furrows shine but late upturned,
And where the fieldfare followed in the rear,
When all the fields around lay bound and hoar
Beneath a thick integument of snow.
So by God's cheap economy made rich
To go upon my winter's task again.

I am singularly refreshed in winter when I hear of service-berries, poke-weed, juniper. Is not heaven made up of these cheap summer glories? There is a singular health in those words, Labrador and East Main, which no desponding creed recognizes. How much more than Federal are these States! If there were no other vicissitudes than the seasons, our interest would never tire. Much more is adoing than Congress wots of. What journal do the persimmon and the buckeye keep, and the sharp-shinned hawk? What is transpiring from summer to winter in the Carolinas, and the Great Pine Forest, and the Valley of the Mohawk? The merely political aspect of the land is never very cheering; men are degraded when considered as the members of a political organization. On this side all lands present only the symptoms of decay. I see but Bunker Hill and Sing-Sing, the District of Columbia and Sullivan's Island, with a few avenues connecting them. But paltry are they all beside one blast of the east or the south wind which blows over them.

In society you will not find health, but in nature. Unless our feet at least stood in the midst of nature, all our faces would be pale and livid.

Society is always diseased, and the best is the most so. There is no scent in it so wholesome as that of the pines, nor any fragrance so penetrating and restorative as the life-everlasting in high pastures. I would keep some book of natural history always by me as a sort of elixir, the reading of which should restore the tone of the system. To the sick, indeed, nature is sick, but to the well, a fountain of health. To him who contemplates a trait of natural beauty no harm nor disappointment can come. The doctrines of despair, of spiritual or political tyranny or servitude, were never taught by such as shared the serenity of nature. Surely good courage will not flag here on the Atlantic border, as long as we are flanked by the Fur Countries. There is enough in that sound to cheer one under any circumstances. The spruce, the hemlock, and the pine will not countenance despair. Methinks some creeds in vestries and churches do forget the hunter wrapped in furs by the Great Slave Lake, and that the Esquimaux sledges are drawn by dogs, and in the twilight of the northern night the hunter does not give over to follow the seal and walrus on the ice. They are of sick and diseased imaginations who would toll the world's knell so soon. Cannot these sedentary sects do better than prepare the shrouds and write the epitaphs of those other busy living men? The practical faith of all men belies the preacher's consolation. What is any man's discourse to me, if I am not sensible of something in it as steady and cheery as the creak of crickets? In it the woods must be relieved against the sky. Men tire me when I am not constantly greeted and refreshed as by the flux of sparkling streams. Surely joy is the condition of life. Think of the young fry that leap in ponds, the myriads of insects ushered into being on a summer evening, the incessant note of the hyla with which the woods ring in the spring, the nonchalance of the butterfly carrying accident and change painted in a thousand hues upon its wings, or the brook minnow stoutly stemming the current, the lustre of whose scales, worn bright by the attrition, is reflected upon the bank!

We fancy that this din of religion, literature, and philosophy, which is heard in pulpits, lyceums, and parlors, vibrates through the universe, and is as catholic a sound as the creaking of the earth's axle; but if a man sleep soundly, he will forget it all between sunset and dawn. It is the three-inch swing of a pendulum in a cupboard, which the great pulse of nature vibrates by and through each instant. When we lift our eyelids and open our ears, it disappears with smoke and rattle like the cars on a railroad. When I detect a beauty in any of the recesses of nature, I am reminded, by the serene and retired spirit in which it requires to be contemplated, of the inexpressible privacy of a life,—how silent and unambitious it is. The beauty there is in mosses must be considered from the holiest, quietest nook. What an admirable training is science for the more active warfare of life! Indeed, the unchallenged bravery which these studies imply, is far more impressive than the trumpeted valor of the warrior. I am pleased to learn that Thales was up and stirring by night not unfrequently, as his astronomical discoveries prove. Linnæus, setting out for Lapland, surveys his "comb" and "spare shirt," "leathern breeches" and "gauze cap to keep off gnats," with as much complacency as Bonaparte a park of artillery for the Russian campaign. The quiet bravery of the man is admirable. His eye is to take in fish, flower, and bird, quadruped and biped. Science is always brave; for to know is to know good; doubt and danger quail before her eye. What the coward overlooks in his hurry, she calmly scrutinizes, breaking ground like a pioneer for the array of arts that follow in her train. But cowardice is unscientific; for there cannot be a science of ignorance. There may be a science of bravery, for that advances; but a retreat is rarely well conducted; if it is, then is it an orderly advance in the face of circumstances.

But to draw a little nearer to our promised topics. Entomology extends the limits of being in a new direction, so that I walk in nature with a sense of greater space and freedom. It suggests besides, that the universe is not rough-hewn, but perfect in its details. Nature will bear the closest inspection; she invites us to lay our eye level with the smallest leaf, and take an insect view of its plain. She has no interstices; every part is full of life. I explore, too, with pleasure, the sources of the myriad sounds which crowd the summer noon, and which seem the very grain and stuff of which eternity is made. Who does not remember the shrill roll-call of the harvest-fly? There were ears for these sounds in Greece long ago, as Anacreon's ode will show.

"We pronounce thee happy, Cicada,
For on the tops of the trees,
Drinking a little dew,
Like any king thou singest,
For thine are they all,
Whatever thou seest in the fields,
And whatever the woods bear.

Thou art the friend of the husbandmen,
In no respect injuring any one;
And thou art honored among men,
Sweet prophet of summer.
The Muses love thee,
And Phœbus himself loves thee,
And has given thee a shrill song;
Age does not wrack thee,
Thou skillful, earthborn, song-loving,
Unsuffering, bloodless one;
Almost thou art like the gods."

In the autumn days, the creaking of crickets is heard at noon over all the land, and as in summer they are heard chiefly at nightfall, so then by their incessant chirp they usher in the evening of the year. Nor can all the vanities that vex the world alter one whit the measure that night has chosen. Every pulse-beat is in exact time with the cricket's chant and the tickings of the death-watch in the wall. Alternate with these if you can.

About two hundred and eighty birds either reside permanently in the State, or spend the summer only, or make us a passing visit. Those which spend the winter with us have obtained our warmest sympathy. The nuthatch and chickadee flitting in company through the dells of the wood, the one harshly scolding at the intruder, the other with a faint lisping note enticing him on; the jay screaming in the orchard; the crow cawing in unison with the storm; the partridge, like a russet link extended over from autumn to spring, preserving unbroken the chain of summers; the hawk with warrior-like firmness abiding the blasts of winter; the robin* and lark lurking by warm springs in the woods; the familiar snowbird culling a few seeds in the garden or a few crumbs in the yard; and occasionally the shrike, with heedless and unfrozen melody bringing back summer again:—

*A white robin and a white quail have occasionally been seen. It is mentioned in Audubon as remarkable that the nest of a robin should be found on the ground; but this bird seems to be less particular than most in the choice of a building-spot. I have seen its nest placed under the thatched roof of a deserted barn, and in one instance, where the adjacent country was nearly destitute of trees, together with two of the phœbe, upon the end of a board in the loft of a sawmill, but a few feet from the saw, which vibrated several inches with the motion of the machinery.

His steady sails he never furls
At any time o' year.
And perching now on Winter's curls,
He whistles in his ear.

As the spring advances, and the ice is melting in the river, our earliest and straggling visitors make their appearance. Again does the old Teian poet sing as well for New England as for Greece, in the

RETURN OF SPRING

"Behold, how, Spring appearing,
The Graces send forth roses;
Behold, how the wave of the sea
Is made smooth by the calm;
Behold, how the duck dives;
Behold, how the crane travels;
And Titan shines constantly bright.
The shadows of the clouds are moving;
The works of man shine;
The earth puts forth fruits;
The fruit of the olive puts forth.
The cup of Bacchus is crowned,
Along the leaves, along the branches,
The fruit, bending them down, flourishes."

The ducks alight at this season in the still water, in company with the gulls, which do not fail to improve an east wind to visit our meadows, and swim about by twos and threes, pluming themselves, and diving to peck at the root of the lily, and the cranberries which the frost has not loosened. The first flock of geese is seen beating to north, in long harrows and waving lines; the jingle of the song sparrow salutes us from the shrubs and fences; the plaintive note of the lark comes clear and sweet from the meadow; and the bluebird, like an azure ray, glances past us in our walk. The fish hawk, too, is occasionally seen at this season sailing majestically over the water, and he who has once observed it will not soon forget the majesty of its flight. It sails the air like a ship of the line, worthy to struggle with the elements, falling back from time to time like a ship on its beam ends, and holding its talons up as if ready for the arrows, in the attitude of the national bird. It is a great presence, as of the master of river and forest. Its eye would not quail before the owner of the soil, but make him feel like an intruder on its domains. And then its retreat, sailing so steadily away, is a kind of advance. I have by me one of a pair of ospreys, which have for some years fished in this vicinity, shot by a neighboring pond, measuring more than two feet in length, and six in the stretch of its wings. Nuttall mentions that "the ancients, particularly Aristotle, pretended that the ospreys taught their young to gaze at the sun, and those who were unable to do so were destroyed. Linnæus even believed, on ancient authority, that one of the feet of this bird had all the toes divided, while the other was partly webbed, so that it could swim with one foot, and grasp a fish with the other." But that educated eye is now dim, and those talons are nerveless. Its shrill scream seems yet to linger in its throat, and the roar of the sea in its wings. There is the tyranny of Jove in its claws, and his wrath in the erectile feathers of the head and neck. It reminds me of the Argonautic expedition, and would inspire the dullest to take flight over Parnassus.

The booming of the bittern, described by Goldsmith and Nuttall, is frequently heard in our fens, in the morning and evening, sounding like a pump, or the chopping of wood in a frosty morning in some distant farm-yard. The manner in which this sound is produced I have not seen anywhere described. On one occasion, the bird has been seen by one of my neighbors to thrust its bill into the water, and suck up as much as it could hold, then, raising its head, it pumped it out again with four or five heaves of the neck, throwing it two or three feet, and making the sound each time.

At length the summer's eternity is ushered in by the cackle of the flicker among the oaks on the hillside, and a new dynasty begins with calm security.

In May and June the woodland quire is in full tune, and, given the immense spaces of hollow air, and this curious human ear, one does not see how the void could be better filled.

Each summer sound
Is a summer round.

As the season advances, and those birds which make us but a passing visit depart, the woods become silent again, and but few feathers ruffle the drowsy air. But the solitary rambler may still find a response and expression for every mood in the depths of the wood.

> Sometimes I hear the veery's* clarion,
> Or brazen trump of the impatient jay,
> And in secluded woods the chickadee
> Doles out her scanty notes, which sing the praise
> Of heroes, and set forth the loveliness
> Of virtue evermore.

The phœbe still sings in harmony with the sultry weather by the brink of the pond, nor are the desultory hours of noon in the midst of the village without their minstrel.

> Upon the lofty elm-tree sprays
> The vireo rings the changes sweet,
> During the trivial summer days,
> Striving to lift our thoughts above the street.

With the autumn begins in some measure a new spring. The plover is heard whistling high in the air over the dry pastures, the finches flit from tree to tree, the bobolinks and flickers fly in flocks, and the goldfinch rides on the earliest blast, like a winged hyla peeping amid the rustle of the leaves. The crows, too, begin now to congregate; you may stand and count them as they fly low and straggling over the landscape, singly or by twos and threes, at intervals of half a mile, until a hundred have passed.

I have seen it suggested somewhere that the crow was brought to this country by the white man; but I shall as soon believe that the white man planted these pines and hemlocks. He is no spaniel to follow our steps; but rather flits about the clearings like the dusky spirit of the Indian, reminding me oftener of Philip and Powhatan than of Winthrop and Smith. He is a relic of the dark ages. By just so slight, by just so lasting a

*This bird, which is so well described by Nuttall, but is apparently unknown by the author of the Report, is one of the most common in the woods in this vicinity, and in Cambridge I have heard the college yard ring with its trill. The boys call it "yorrick," from the sound of its querulous and chiding note, as it flits near the traveler through the underwood. The cowbird's egg is occasionally found in its nest, as mentioned by Audubon.

tenure does superstition hold the world ever; there is the rook in England, and the crow in New England.

> Thou dusky spirit of the wood,
> Bird of an ancient brood,
> Flitting thy lonely way,
> A meteor in the summer's day,
> From wood to wood, from hill to hill,
> Low over forest, field, and rill,
> What wouldst thou say?
> Why shouldst thou haunt the day?
> What makes thy melancholy float?
> What bravery inspires thy throat,
> And bears thee up above the clouds,
> Over desponding human crowds,
> Which far below
> Lay thy haunts low?

The late walker or sailor, in the October evenings, may hear the murmurings of the snipe, circling over the meadows, the most spirit-like sound in nature; and still later in the autumn, when the frosts have tinged the leaves, a solitary loon pays a visit to our retired ponds, where he may lurk undisturbed till the season of moulting is passed, making the woods ring with his wild laughter. This bird, the Great Northern Diver, well deserves its name; for when pursued with a boat, it will dive, and swim like a fish under water, for sixty rods or more, as fast as a boat can be paddled, and its pursuer, if he would discover his game again, must put his ear to the surface to hear where it comes up. When it comes to the surface, it throws the water off with one shake of its wings, and calmly swims about until again disturbed.

These are the sights and sounds which reach our senses oftenest during the year. But sometimes one hears a quite new note, which has for background other Carolinas and Mexicos than the books describe, and learns that his ornithology has done him no service.

It appears from the Report that there are about forty quadrupeds belonging to the State, and among these one is glad to hear of a few bears, wolves, lynxes, and wildcats.

When our river overflows its banks in the spring, the wind from the meadows is laden with a strong scent of musk, and by its freshness advertises me of an unexplored wildness. Those backwoods are not far off then. I am affected by the sight of the cabins of the muskrat, made of mud and grass, and raised three or four feet along the river, as when I read of the barrows of Asia. The muskrat is the beaver of the settled States. Their number has even increased within a few years in this vicinity. Among the rivers which empty into the Merrimack, the Concord is known to the boatmen as a dead stream. The Indians are said to have called it Musketaquid, or Prairie River. Its current being much more sluggish and its water more muddy than the rest, it abounds more in fish and game of every kind. According to the History of the town, "The fur-trade was here once very important. As early as 1641, a company was formed in the colony, of which Major Willard of Concord was superintendent, and had the exclusive right to trade with the Indians in furs and other articles; and for this right they were obliged to pay into the public treasury one twentieth of all the furs they obtained." There are trappers in our midst still, as well as on the streams of the far West, who night and morning go the round of their traps, without fear of the Indian. One of these takes from one hundred and fifty to two hundred muskrats in a year, and even thirty-six have been shot by one man in a day. Their fur, which is not nearly as valuable as formerly, is in good condition in the winter and spring only; and upon the breaking up of the ice, when they are driven out of their holes by the water, the greatest number is shot from boats, either swimming or resting on their stools, or slight supports of grass and reeds, by the side of the stream. Though they exhibit considerable cunning at other times, they are easily taken in a trap, which has only to be placed in their holes, or wherever they frequent, without any bait being used, though it is sometimes rubbed with their musk. In the winter the hunter cuts holes in the ice, and shoots them when they come to the surface. Their burrows are usually in the high banks of the river, with the entrance under water, and rising within to above the level of high water. Sometimes their nests, composed of dried meadow-grass and flags, may be discovered where the bank is low and spongy, by the yielding of the ground under the feet. They have from three to seven or eight young in the spring.

Frequently, in the morning or evening, a long ripple is seen in the still water, where a muskrat is crossing the stream, with only its nose above the surface, and sometimes a green bough in its mouth to build its house with. When it finds itself observed, it will dive and swim five or six rods under water, and at length conceal itself in its hole, or the weeds. It will remain under water for ten minutes at a time, and on one occasion has been seen, when undisturbed, to form an air-bubble under the ice, which contracted and expanded as it breathed at leisure. When it suspects danger on shore, it will stand erect like a squirrel, and survey its neighborhood for several minutes, without moving.

In the fall, if a meadow intervene between their burrows and the stream, they erect cabins of mud and grass, three or four feet high, near its edge. These are not their breeding-places, though young are sometimes found in them in late freshets, but rather their hunting-lodges, to which they resort in the winter with their food, and for shelter. Their food consists chiefly of flags and fresh-water mussels, the shells of the latter being left in large quantities around their lodges in the spring.

The Penobscot Indian wears the entire skin of a muskrat, with the legs and tail dangling, and the head caught under his girdle, for a pouch, into which he puts his fishing-tackle, and essences to scent his traps with.

The bear, wolf, lynx, wildcat, deer, beaver, and marten have disappeared; the otter is rarely if ever seen here at present; and the mink is less common than formerly.

Perhaps of all our untamed quadrupeds, the fox has obtained the widest and most familiar reputation, from the time of Pilpay and Æsop to the present day. His recent tracks still give variety to a winter's walk. I tread in the steps of the fox that has gone before me by some hours, or which perhaps I have started, with such a tiptoe of expectation as if I were on the trail of the Spirit itself which resides in the wood, and expected soon to catch it in its lair. I am curious to know what has determined its graceful curvatures, and how surely they were coincident with the fluctuations of some mind. I know which way a mind wended, what horizon it faced, by the setting of these tracks, and whether it moved slowly or rapidly, by their greater or less intervals and distinctness; for the swiftest step leaves yet a lasting trace. Sometimes you will see the trails of many together, and where they have gamboled and gone through a hundred evolutions, which testify to a singular listlessness and leisure in nature.

When I see a fox run across the pond on the snow, with the carelessness of freedom, or at intervals trace his course in the sunshine along the ridge of a hill, I give up to him sun and earth as to their true proprietor. He does not go in the sun, but it seems to follow him, and there is a visible sympathy between him and it. Sometimes, when the snow lies light and but five or six inches deep, you may give chase and come up with one on foot. In such a case he will show a remarkable presence of mind, choosing only the safest direction, though he may lose ground by it. Notwithstanding his fright, he will take no step which is not beautiful. His pace is a sort of leopard canter, as if he were in no wise impeded by the snow, but were husbanding his strength all the while. When the ground is uneven, the course is a series of graceful curves, conforming to the shape of the surface. He runs as though there were not a bone in his back. Occasionally dropping his muzzle to the ground for a rod or two, and then tossing his head aloft, when satisfied of his course. When he comes to a declivity, he will put his fore feet together, and slide swiftly down it, shoving the snow before him. He treads so softly that you would hardly hear it from any nearness, and yet with such expression that it would not be quite inaudible at any distance.

Of fishes, seventy-five genera and one hundred and seven species are described in the Report. The fisherman will be startled to learn that there are but about a dozen kinds in the ponds and streams of any inland town; and almost nothing is known of their habits. Only their names and residence make one love fishes. I would know even the number of their fin-rays, and how many scales compose the lateral line. I am the wiser in respect to all knowledges, and the better qualified for all fortunes, for knowing that there is a minnow in the brook. Methinks I have need even of his sympathy, and to be his fellow in a degree.

I have experienced such simple delight in the trivial matters of fishing and sporting, formerly, as might have inspired the muse of Homer or Shakespeare; and now, when I turn the pages and ponder the plates of the Angler's Souvenir, I am fain to exclaim,—

> "Can such things be,
> And overcome us like a summer's cloud?"

Next to nature, it seems as if man's actions were the most natural, they so gently accord with her. The small seines of flax stretched across the shallow and transparent parts of our river are no more intrusion than the cobweb in the sun. I stay my boat in mid-current, and look down in the sunny water to see the civil meshes of his nets, and wonder how the blustering people of the town could have done this elvish work. The twine looks like a new river-weed, and is to the river as a beautiful memento of man's presence in nature, discovered as silently and delicately as a footprint in the sand.

When the ice is covered with snow, I do not suspect the wealth under my feet; that there is as good as a mine under me wherever I go. How many pickerel are poised on easy fin fathoms below the loaded wain! The revolution of the seasons must be a curious phenomenon to them. At length the sun and wind brush aside their curtain, and they see the heavens again.

Early in the spring, after the ice has melted, is the time for spearing fish. Suddenly the wind shifts from north-east and east to west and south, and every icicle, which has tinkled on the meadow grass so long, trickles down its stem, and seeks its level unerringly with a million comrades. The steam curls up from every roof and fence.

I see the civil sun drying earth's tears,
Her tears of joy, which only faster flow.

In the brooks is heard the slight grating sound of small cakes of ice, floating with various speed, full of content and promise, and where the water gurgles under a natural bridge, you may hear these hasty rafts hold conversation in an undertone. Every rill is a channel for the juices of the meadow. In the ponds the ice cracks with a merry and inspiriting din, and down the larger streams is whirled grating hoarsely, and crashing its way along, which was so lately a highway for the woodman's team and the fox, sometimes with the tracks of the skaters still fresh upon it, and the holes cut for pickerel. Town committees anxiously inspect the bridges and causeways, as if by mere eye-force to intercede with the ice and save the treasury.

The river swelleth more and more,
Like some sweet influence stealing o'er
The passive town; and for a while
Each tussock makes a tiny isle,
Where, on some friendly Ararat,
Resteth the weary water-rat.

No ripple shows Musketaquid,
Her very current e'en is bid,
As deepest souls do calmest rest
When thoughts are swelling in the breast,
And she that in the summer's drought
Doth make a rippling and a rout,
Sleeps from Nahshawtuck to the Cliff,
Unruffled by a single skiff.
But by a thousand distant hills
The louder roar a thousand rills,
And many a spring which now is dumb,
And many a stream with smothered hum,
Doth swifter well and faster glide,
Though buried deep beneath the tide.
Our village shows a rural Venice,
Its broud lagoons where yonder fen is;
As lovely as the Bay of Naples
Yon placid cove amid the maples;
And in my neighbor's field of corn
I recognize the Golden Horn.

Here Nature taught from year to year,
When only red men came to hear,—
Methinks 't was in this school of art
Venice and Naples learned their part;
But still their mistress, to my mind,
Her young disciples leaves behind.

The fisherman now repairs and launches his boat. The best time for spearing is at this season, before the weeds have begun to grow, and while the fishes lie in the shallow water, for in summer they prefer the cool depths, and in the autumn they are still more or less concealed by the grass. The first requisite is fuel for your crate; and for this purpose the roots of the pitch pine are commonly used, found under decayed stumps, where the trees have been felled eight or ten years.

With a crate, or jack, made of iron hoops, to contain your fire, and attached to the bow of your boat about three feet from the water, a fish-spear with seven tines and fourteen feet long, a large basket or barrow to carry your fuel and bring back your fish, and a thick outer garment, you are equipped for a cruise. It should be a warm and still evening; and then, with a fire crackling merrily at the prow, you may launch forth like a cucullo into the night. The dullest soul cannot go upon such an expedition without some of the spirit of adventure; as if he had stolen the boat of Charon and gone down the Styx on a midnight expedition into the realms of Pluto. And much speculation does this wandering star afford to the musing night-walker, leading him on and on, jack-o'-lantern-like, over the meadows; or, if he is wiser, he amuses himself with imagining what of human life, far in the silent night, is flitting moth-like round its candle. The silent navigator shoves his craft gently over the water, with a smothered pride and sense of benefaction, as if he were the phosphor, or light-bringer, to these dusky realms, or some sister moon, blessing the spaces with her light. The waters, for a rod or two on either hand and several feet in depth, are lit up with more than noonday distinctness, and he enjoys the opportunity which so many have desired, for the roofs of a city are indeed raised, and he surveys the midnight economy of the fishes. There they lie in every variety of posture; some on their backs, with their white bellies uppermost, some suspended in mid-water, some sculling gently along with a dreamy motion of the fins, and others quite active and wide awake,—a scene not unlike what the human city would present. Occasionally he will encounter a turtle selecting the choicest morsels, or a muskrat resting on a tussock. He may exercise his dexterity, if he sees fit, on the more distant and active fish, or fork the nearer into his boat, as potatoes out of a pot, or even take the sound sleepers with his hands. But these last accomplishments he will soon learn to dispense with, distinguishing the real object of his pursuit, and find compensation in the beauty and never-ending novelty of his position. The pines growing down to the water's edge will show newly as in the glare of a conflagration; and as he floats under the willows with his light, the song sparrow will often wake on her perch, and sing that strain at midnight which she had meditated for the morning. And when he has done, he may have to steer his way home through the dark by the north star, and he will feel himself some degrees nearer to it for having lost his way on the earth.

The fishes commonly taken in this way are pickerel, suckers, perch, eels, pouts, breams, and shiners,—from thirty to sixty weight in a night. Some are hard to be recognized in the unnatural light, especially the perch, which, his dark bands being exaggerated, acquires a ferocious aspect. The number of these transverse bands, which the Report states to be seven, is, however, very variable, for in some of our ponds they have nine and ten even.

It appears that we have eight kinds of tortoises, twelve snakes,—but one of which is venomous,—nine frogs and toads, nine salamanders, and one lizard, for our neighbors.

I am particularly attracted by the motions of the serpent tribe. They make our hands and feet, the wings of the bird, and the fins of the fish seem very superfluous, as if Nature had only indulged her fancy in making them. The black snake will dart into a bush when pursued, and circle round and round with an easy and graceful motion, amid the thin and bare twigs, five or six feet from the ground, as a bird flits from bough to bough, or hang in festoons between the forks. Elasticity and flexibleness in the simpler forms of animal life are equivalent to a complex system of limbs in the higher; and we have only to be as wise and wily as the serpent, to perform as difficult feats without the vulgar assistance of hands and feet.

In May, the snapping turtle (*Emysaurus serpentina*) is frequently taken on the meadows and in the river. The fisherman, taking sight over the calm surface, discovers its snout projecting above the water, at the distance of many rods, and easily secures his prey through its unwillingness to disturb the water by swimming hastily away, for, gradually drawing its head under, it remains resting on some limb or clump of grass. Its eggs, which are buried at a distance from the water, in some soft place, as a pigeon-bed, are frequently devoured by the skunk. It will catch fish by daylight, as a toad catches flies, and is said to emit a transparent fluid from its mouth to attract them.

Nature has taken more care than the fondest parent for the education and refinement of her children. Consider the silent influence which flowers exert, no less upon the ditcher in the meadow than the lady in the bower. When I walk in the woods, I am reminded that a wise purveyor has been there before me; my most delicate experience is typified there. I am struck with the pleasing friendships and unanimities of nature, as when the lichen on the trees takes the form of their leaves. In the most stupendous scenes you will see delicate and fragile features, as slight wreaths of vapor, dew-lines, feathery sprays, which suggest a high refinement, a noble blood and breeding, as it were. It is not hard to account for elves and fairies; they represent this light grace, this ethereal gentility. Bring a spray from the wood, or a crystal from the brook, and place it on your mantel, and your household ornaments will seem plebeian beside its nobler fashion and bearing. It will wave superior there, as if used to a more refined and polished circle. It has a salute and a response to all your enthusiasm and heroism.

In the winter, I stop short in the path to admire how the trees grow up without forethought, regardless of the time and circumstances. They do not wait as man does, but now is the golden age of the sapling. Earth, air, sun, and rain are occasion enough; they were no better in primeval centuries. The "winter of *their* discontent" never comes. Witness the buds of the native poplar standing gayly out to the frost on the sides of its bare switches. They express a naked confidence. With cheerful heart one could be a sojourner in the wilderness, if he were sure to find there the catkins of the willow or the alder. When I read of them in the accounts of northern adventurers, by Baffin's Bay or Mackenzie's River, I see how even there, too, I could dwell. They are our little vegetable redeemers. Methinks our virtue will hold out till they come again. They are worthy to have had a greater than Minerva or Ceres for their inventor. Who was the benignant goddess that bestowed them on mankind?

Nature is mythical and mystical always, and works with the license and extravagance of genius. She has her luxurious and florid style as well as art. Having a pilgrim's cup to make, she gives to the whole—stem, bowl, handle, and nose—some fantastic shape, as if it were to be the car of some fabulous marine deity, a Nereus or Triton.

In the winter, the botanist need not confine himself to his books and herbarium, and give over his outdoor pursuits, but may study a new department of vegetable physiology, what may be called crystalline botany, then. The winter of 1837 was unusually favorable for this. In December of that year, the Genius of vegetation seemed to hover by night over its summer haunts with unusual persistency. Such a hoar-frost as is very uncommon here or anywhere, and whose full effects can never be witnessed after sunrise, occurred several times. As I went forth early on a still and frosty morning, the trees looked like airy creatures of darkness caught napping; on this side huddled together, with their gray hairs streaming, in a secluded valley which the sun had not penetrated; on that, hurrying off in Indian file along some watercourse, while the shrubs and grasses, like elves and fairies of the night, sought to hide their diminished heads in the snow. The river, viewed from the high bank, appeared of a yellowish-green color, though all the landscape was white. Every tree, shrub, and spire of grass, that could raise its head above the snow, was covered with a dense ice-foliage, answering, as it were, leaf for leaf to its summer dress. Even the fences had put forth leaves in the night. The centre, diverging, and more minute fibres were perfectly distinct, and the edges regularly indented. These leaves were on the side of the twig or stubble opposite to the sun, meeting it for the most part at right angles, and there were others standing out at all possible angles upon these and upon one another, with no twig or stubble supporting them. When the first rays of the sun slanted over the scene, the grasses seemed hung with innumerable jewels, which jingled merrily as they were brushed by the foot of the traveler, and reflected all the hues of the rainbow, as he moved from side to side. It struck me that these ghost leaves, and the green ones whose forms they assume, were the creatures of but one law; that in obedience to the same law the vegetable juices swell gradually into the perfect leaf, on the one hand, and the crystalline particles troop to their standard in the same order, on the other. As if the material were indifferent, but the law one and invariable, and every plant in the spring but pushed up into and filled a permanent and eternal mould, which, summer and winter forever, is waiting to be filled.

This foliate structure is common to the coral and the plumage of birds, and to how large a part of animate and inanimate nature. The same independence of law on matter is observable in many other instances, as in the natural rhymes, when some animal form, color, or odor has its counterpart in some vegetable. As, indeed, all rhymes imply an eternal melody, independent of any particular sense.

As confirmation of the fact that vegetation is but a kind of crystallization, every one may observe how, upon the edge of the melting frost on the window, the needle-shaped particles are bundled together so as to resemble fields waving with grain, or shocks rising here and there from the stubble; on one side the vegetation of the torrid zone, high-towering palms and wide-spread banyans, such as are seen in pictures of oriental scenery; on the other, arctic pines stiff frozen, with downcast branches.

Vegetation has been made the type of all growth; but as in crystals the law is more obvious, their material being more simple, and for the most part more transient and fleeting, would it not be as philosophical as convenient to consider all growth, all filling up within the limits of nature, but a crystallization more or less rapid?

On this occasion, in the side of the high bank of the river, wherever the water or other cause had formed a cavity, its throat and outer edge, like the entrance to a citadel, bristled with a glistening ice-armor. In one place you might see minute ostrich-feathers, which seemed the waving plumes of the warriors filing into the fortress; in another, the glancing, fan-shaped banners of the Lilliputian host; and in another, the needle-shaped particles collected into bundles, resembling the plumes of the pine, might pass for a phalanx of spears. From the under side of the ice in the brooks, where there was a thicker ice below, depended a mass of crystallization, four or five inches deep, in the form of prisms, with their lower ends open, which, when the ice was laid on its smooth side, resembled the roofs and steeples of a Gothic city, or the vessels of a crowded haven under a press of canvas. The very mud in the road, where the ice had melted, was crystallized with deep rectilinear fissures, and the crystalline masses in the sides of the ruts resembled exactly asbestos in the disposition of their needles. Around the roots of the stubble and flower-stalks, the frost was gathered into the form of irregular conical shells, or fairy rings. In some places the ice-crystals were lying upon granite rocks, directly over crystals of quartz, the frostwork of a longer night, crystals of a longer period, but, to some eye unprejudiced by the short term of human life, melting as fast as the former.

In the Report on the Invertebrate Animals, this singular fact is recorded, which teaches us to put a new value on time and space: "The distribution of the marine shells is well worthy of notice as a geological fact. Cape Cod, the right arm of the Commonwealth, reaches out into the ocean, some fifty or sixty miles. It is nowhere many miles wide; but this narrow point of land has hitherto proved a barrier to the migrations of many species of Mollusca. Several genera and numerous species, which are separated by the intervention of only a few miles of land, are effectually prevented from mingling by the Cape, and do not pass from one side to the other. . . . Of the one hundred and ninety-seven marine species, eighty-three do not pass to the south shore, and fifty are not found on the north shore of the Cape."

That common mussel, the *Unio complanatus*, or more properly *fluviatilis*, left in the spring by the muskrat upon rocks and stumps, appears to have been an important article of food with the Indians. In one place, where they are said to have feasted, they are found in large quantities, at an elevation of thirty feet above the river, filling the soil to the depth of a foot, and mingled with ashes and Indian remains.

The works we have placed at the head of our chapter, with as much license as the preacher selects his text, are such as imply more labor than enthusiasm. The State wanted complete catalogues of its natural riches, with such additional facts merely as would be directly useful.

The reports on Fishes, Reptiles, Insects, and Invertebrate Animals, however, indicate labor and research, and have a value independent of the object of the legislature.

Those on Herbaceous Plants and Birds cannot be of much value, as long as Bigelow and Nuttall are accessible. They serve but to indicate, with more or less exactness, what species are found in the State. We detect several errors ourselves, and a more practiced eye would no doubt expand the list.

The Quadrupeds deserved a more final and instructive report than they have obtained.

These volumes deal much in measurements and minute descriptions, not interesting to the general reader, with only here and there a colored sentence to allure him, like those plants growing in dark forests, which bear only leaves without blossoms. But the ground was comparatively unbroken, and we will not complain of the pioneer, if he raises no flowers with his first crop. Let us not underrate the value of a fact; it will one day flower in a truth. It is astonishing how few facts of importance are added in a century to the natural history of any animal. The natural history of man himself is still being gradually written. Men are knowing enough after their fashion. Every countryman and dairy-maid knows that the coats of the fourth stomach of the calf will curdle milk, and what particular mushroom is a safe and nutritious diet. You cannot go into any field or wood, but it will seem as if every stone had been turned, and the bark on every tree ripped up. But, after all, it is much easier to discover than to see when the cover is off. It has been well said that "the attitude of inspection is prone." Wisdom does not inspect, but behold. We must look a long time before we can see. Slow are the beginnings of philosophy. He has something demoniacal in him, who can discern a law or couple two facts. We can imagine a time when "Water runs down hill" may have been taught in the schools. The true man of science will know nature better by his finer organization; he will smell, taste, see, hear, feel, better than other men. His will be a deeper and finer experience. We do not learn by inference and deduction and the application of mathematics to philosophy, but by direct intercourse and sympathy. It is with science as with ethics,—we cannot know truth by contrivance and method; the Baconian is as false as any other, and with all the helps of machinery and the arts, the most scientific will still be the healthiest and friendliest man, and possess a more perfect Indian wisdom.

A WINTER WALK

A WINTER WALK.

The wind has gently murmured through the blinds, or puffed with feathery softness against the windows, and occasionally sighed like a summer zephyr lifting the leaves along, the livelong night. The meadow mouse has slept in his snug gallery in the sod, the owl has sat in a hollow tree in the depth of the swamp, the rabbit, the squirrel, and the fox have all been housed. The watch-dog has lain quiet on the hearth, and the cattle have stood silent in their stalls. The earth itself has slept, as it were its first, not its last sleep, save when some street-sign or wood-house door, has faintly creaked upon its hinge, cheering forlorn nature at her midnight work. — The only sound awake twixt Venus and Mars, — advertising us of a remote inward warmth, a divine cheer and fellowship, where gods are met together, but where it is very bleak for men to stand. But while the earth has slumbered, all the air has been alive with feathery flakes, descending, as if some northern Ceres reigned, showering her silvery grain over all the fields.

We sleep and at length awake to the still reality of a winter morning. The snow lies warm as cotton or down upon the window-sill; the broadened sash and frosted panes admit a dim and private light, which enhances the snug cheer within. The stillness of the morning is impressive. The floor creaks under our feet as we move toward the window to look abroad through some clear space over the fields. We see the roofs stand under their snow burden. From the eaves and fences hang stalactites of snow, and in the yard stand stalagmites covering some concealed core. The trees and shrubs rear white arms to the sky on every side, and where were walls and fences, we see fantastic forms stretching in frolic gambols across the dusky landscape, as if nature had strewn her fresh designs over the fields by night as models for man's art.

Silently we unlatch the door, letting the drift fall in, and step abroad to face the cutting air. Already the stars have lost some of their sparkle, and a dull leaden mist skirts the horizon. A lurid brazen light in the east proclaims the approach of day, while the western landscape is

A WINTER WALK

The wind has gently murmured through the blinds, or puffed with feathery softness against the windows, and occasionally sighed like a summer zephyr lifting the leaves along, the livelong night. The meadow mouse has slept in his snug gallery in the sod, the owl has sat in a hollow tree in the depth of the swamp, the rabbit, the squirrel, and the fox have all been housed. The watch-dog has lain quiet on the hearth, and the cattle have stood silent in their stalls. The earth itself has slept, as it were its first, not its last sleep, save when some street-sign or wood-house door has faintly creaked upon its hinge, cheering forlorn nature at her midnight work,—the only sound awake 'twixt Venus and Mars,—advertising us of a remote inward warmth, a divine cheer and fellowship, where gods are met together, but where it is very bleak for men to stand. But while the earth has slumbered, all the air has been alive with feathery flakes descending, as if some northern Ceres reigned, showering her silvery grain over all the fields.

We sleep, and at length awake to the still reality of a winter morning. The snow lies warm as cotton or down upon the window-sill; the broadened sash and frosted panes admit a dim and private light, which enhances the snug cheer within. The stillness of the morning is impressive. The floor creaks under our feet as we move toward the window to look abroad through some clear space over the fields. We see the roofs stand under their snow burden. From the eaves and fences hang stalactites of snow, and in the yard stand stalagmites covering some concealed core.

The trees and shrubs rear white arms to the sky on every side; and where were walls and fences, we see fantastic forms stretching in frolic gambols across the dusky landscape, as if Nature had strewn her fresh designs over the fields by night as models for man's art.

Silently we unlatch the door, letting the drift fall in, and step abroad to face the cutting air. Already the stars have lost some of their sparkle, and a dull, leaden mist skirts the horizon. A lurid brazen light in the east proclaims the approach of day, while the western landscape is dim and spectral still, and clothed in a sombre Tartarean light, like the shadowy realms. They are Infernal sounds only that you hear,—the crowing of cocks, the barking of dogs, the chopping of wood, the lowing of kine, all seem to come from Pluto's barnyard and beyond the Styx,—not for any melancholy they suggest, but their twilight bustle is too solemn and mysterious for earth. The recent tracks of the fox or otter, in the yard, remind us that each hour of the night is crowded with events, and the primeval nature is still working and making tracks in the snow. Opening the gate, we tread briskly along the lone country road, crunching the dry and crisped snow under our feet, or aroused by the sharp, clear creak of the wood-sled, just starting for the distant market, from the early farmer's door, where it has lain the summer long, dreaming amid the chips and stubble; while far through the drifts and powdered windows we see the farmer's early candle, like a paled star, emitting a lonely beam, as if some severe virtue were at its matins there. And one by one the smokes begin to ascend from the chimneys amid the trees and snows.

The sluggish smoke curls up from some deep dell,
The stiffened air exploring in the dawn,
And making slow acquaintance with the day
Delaying now upon its heavenward course,
In wreathèd loiterings dallying with itself,
With as uncertain purpose and slow deed
As its half-wakened master by the hearth,
Whose mind still slumbering and sluggish thoughts
Have not yet swept into the onward current
Of the new day;—and now it streams afar,
The while the chopper goes with step direct,
And mind intent to swing the early axe.
First in the dusky dawn he sends abroad

His early scout, his emissary, smoke,
The earliest, latest pilgrim from the roof,
To feel the frosty air, inform the day;
And while he crouches still beside the hearth,
Nor musters courage to unbar the door,
It has gone down the glen with the light wind,
And o'er the plain unfurled its venturous wreath,
Draped the tree-tops, loitered upon the hill,
And warmed the pinions of the early bird;
And now, perchance, high in the crispy air,
Has caught sight of the day o'er the earth's edge,
And greets its master's eye at his low door,
As some refulgent cloud in the upper sky.

We hear the sound of wood-chopping at the farmers' doors, far over the frozen earth, the baying of the house-dog, and the distant clarion of the cock,—though the thin and frosty air conveys only the finer particles of sound to our ears, with short and sweet vibrations, as the waves subside soonest on the purest and lightest liquids, in which gross substances sink to the bottom. They come clear and bell-like, and from a greater distance in the horizon, as if there were fewer impediments than in summer to make them faint and ragged. The ground is sonorous, like seasoned wood, and even the ordinary rural sounds are melodious, and the jingling of the ice on the trees is sweet and liquid. There is the least possible moisture in the atmosphere, all being dried up or congealed, and it is of such extreme tenuity and elasticity that it becomes a source of delight. The withdrawn and tense sky seems groined like the aisles of a cathedral, and the polished air sparkles as if there were crystals of ice floating in it. As they who have resided in Greenland tell us that when it freezes "the sea smokes like burning turf-land, and a fog or mist arises, called frost-smoke," which "cutting smoke frequently raises blisters on the face and hands, and is very pernicious to the health." But this pure, stinging cold is an elixir to the lungs, and not so much a frozen mist as a crystallized midsummer haze, refined and purified by cold.

The sun at length rises through the distant woods, as if with the faint clashing, swinging sound of cymbals, melting the air with his beams, and with such rapid steps the morning travels, that already his rays are gilding the distant western mountains. Meanwhile we step hastily along through the powdery snow, warmed by an inward heat, enjoying an Indian summer still, in the increased glow of thought and feeling. Probably if our lives were more conformed to nature, we should not need to defend ourselves against her heats and colds, but find her our constant nurse and friend, as do plants and quadrupeds. If our bodies were fed with pure and simple elements, and not with a stimulating and heating diet, they would afford no more pasture for cold than a leafless twig, but thrive like the trees, which find even winter genial to their expansion.

The wonderful purity of nature at this season is a most pleasing fact. Every decayed stump and moss-grown stone and rail, and the dead leaves of autumn, are concealed by a clean napkin of snow. In the bare fields and tinkling woods, see what virtue survives. In the coldest and bleakest places, the warmest charities still maintain a foothold. A cold and searching wind drives away all contagion, and nothing can withstand it but what has a virtue in it, and accordingly, whatever we meet with in cold and bleak places, as the tops of mountains, we respect for a sort of sturdy innocence, a Puritan toughness. All things beside seem to be called in for shelter, and what stays out must be part of the original frame of the universe, and of such valor as God himself. It is invigorating to breathe the cleansed air. Its greater fineness and purity are visible to the eye, and we would fain stay out long and late, that the gales may sigh through us, too, as through the leafless trees, and fit us for the winter,—as if we hoped so to borrow some pure and steadfast virtue, which will stead us in all seasons.

There is a slumbering subterranean fire in nature which never goes out, and which no cold can chill. It finally melts the great snow, and in January or July is only buried under a thicker or thinner covering. In the coldest day it flows somewhere, and the snow melts around every tree. This field of winter rye, which sprouted late in the fall, and now speedily dissolves the snow, is where the fire is very thinly covered. We feel warmed by it. In the winter, warmth stands for all virtue, and we resort in thought to a trickling rill, with its bare stones shining in the sun, and to warm springs in the woods, with as much eagerness as rabbits and robins. The steam which rises from swamps and pools is as dear and domestic as that of our own kettle. What fire could ever equal the sunshine of a winter's day, when the meadow mice come out by the wall-sides, and the chickadee lisps in the defiles of the wood? The warmth comes directly from the sun, and is not radiated from the earth, as in summer; and when we feel his beams on our backs as we are treading some snowy dell, we are grateful as for a special kindness, and bless the sun which has followed us into that by-place.

This subterranean fire has its altar in each man's breast; for in the coldest day, and on the bleakest hill, the traveler cherishes a warmer fire within the folds of his cloak than is kindled on any hearth. A healthy man, indeed, is the complement of the seasons, and in winter, summer is in his heart. There is the south. Thither have all birds and insects migrated, and around the warm springs in his breast are gathered the robin and the lark.

At length, having reached the edge of the woods, and shut out the gadding town, we enter within their covert as we go under the roof of a cottage, and cross its threshold, all ceiled and banked up with snow. They are glad and warm still, and as genial and cheery in winter as in summer. As we stand in the midst of the pines in the flickering and checkered light which straggles but little way into their maze, we wonder if the towns have ever heard their simple story. It seems to us that no traveler has ever explored them, and notwithstanding the wonders which science is elsewhere revealing every day, who would not like to hear their annals? Our humble villages in the plain are their contribution. We borrow from the forest the boards which shelter and the sticks which warm us. How important is their evergreen to the winter, that portion of the summer which does not fade, the permanent year, the unwithered grass! Thus simply, and with little expense of altitude, is the surface of the earth diversified. What would human life be without forests, those natural cities? From the tops of mountains they appear like smooth-shaven lawns, yet whither shall we walk but in this taller grass?

In this glade covered with bushes of a year's growth, see how the silvery dust lies on every seared leaf and twig, deposited in such infinite and luxurious forms as by their very variety atone for the absence of color. Observe the tiny tracks of mice around every stem, and the triangular tracks of the rabbit. A pure elastic heaven hangs over all, as if the impurities of the summer sky, refined and shrunk by the chaste winter's cold, had been winnowed from the heavens upon the earth.

Nature confounds her summer distinctions at this season. The heavens seem to be nearer the earth. The elements are less reserved and distinct. Water turns to ice, rain to snow. The day is but a Scandinavian night. The winter is an arctic summer.

How much more living is the life that is in nature, the furred life which still survives the stinging nights, and, from amidst fields and woods covered with frost and snow, sees the sun rise!

> "The foodless wilds
> Pour forth their brown inhabitants."

The gray squirrel and rabbit are brisk and playful in the remote glens, even on the morning of the cold Friday. Here is our Lapland and Labrador, and for our Esquimaux and Knistenaux, Dog-ribbed Indians, Novazemblaites, and Spitzbergeners, are there not the ice-cutter and woodchopper, the fox, muskrat, and mink?

Still, in the midst of the arctic day, we may trace the summer to its retreats, and sympathize with some contemporary life. Stretched over the brooks, in the midst of the frost-bound meadows, we may observe the submarine cottages of the caddis-worms, the larvæ of the Plicipennes; their small cylindrical cases built around themselves, composed of flags, sticks, grass, and withered leaves, shells, and pebbles, in form and color like the wrecks which strew the bottom,—now drifting along over the pebbly bottom, now whirling in tiny eddies and dashing down steep falls, or sweeping rapidly along with the current, or else swaying to and fro at the end of some grass-blade or root. Anon they will leave their sunken habitations, and, crawling up the stems of plants, or to the surface, like gnats, as perfect insects henceforth, flutter over the surface of the water, or sacrifice their short lives in the flame of our candles at evening. Down yonder little glen the shrubs are drooping under their burden, and the red alder-berries contrast with the white ground. Here are the marks of a myriad feet which have already been abroad. The sun rises as proudly over such a glen as over the valley of the Seine or the Tiber, and it seems the residence of a pure and self-subsistent valor, such as they never witnessed,—which never knew defeat nor fear. Here reign the simplicity and purity of a primitive age, and a health and hope far remote from towns and cities. Standing quite alone, far in the forest, while the wind is shaking down snow from the trees, and leaving the only human tracks behind us, we find our reflections of a richer variety than the life of cities. The chickadee and nuthatch are more inspiring society than statesmen and philosophers, and we shall return to these last as to more vulgar companions. In this lonely glen, with its brook draining the slopes, its creased ice and crystals of all hues, where the spruces and hemlocks stand up on either side, and the rush and sere wild oats in the rivulet itself, our lives are more serene and worthy to contemplate.

As the day advances, the heat of the sun is reflected by the hillsides, and we hear a faint but sweet music, where flows the rill released from its fetters, and the icicles are melting on the trees; and the nuthatch and partridge are heard and seen. The south wind melts the snow at noon, and the bare ground appears with its withered grass and leaves, and we are invigorated by the perfume which exhales from it, as by the scent of strong meats.

Let us go into this deserted woodman's hut, and see how he has passed the long winter nights and the short and stormy days. For here man has lived under this south hillside, and it seems a civilized and public spot. We have such associations as when the traveler stands by the ruins of Palmyra or Hecatompolis. Singing birds and flowers perchance have begun to appear here, for flowers as well as weeds follow in the footsteps of man. These hemlocks whispered over his head, these hickory logs were his fuel, and these pitch pine roots kindled his fire; yonder fuming rill in the hollow, whose thin and airy vapor still ascends as busily as ever, though he is far off now, was his well. These hemlock boughs, and the straw upon this raised platform, were his bed, and this broken dish held his drink. But he has not been here this season, for the phœbes built their nest upon this shelf last summer. I find some embers left as if he had but just gone out, where he baked his pot of beans; and while at evening he smoked his pipe, whose stemless bowl lies in the ashes, chatted with his only companion, if perchance he had any, about the depth of the snow on the morrow, already falling fast and thick without, or disputed whether the last sound was the screech of an owl, or the creak of a bough, or imagination only; and through his broad chimney-throat, in the late winter evening, ere he stretched himself upon the straw, he looked up to learn the progress of the storm, and, seeing the bright stars of Cassiopeia's Chair shining brightly down upon him, fell contentedly asleep.

See how many traces from which we may learn the chopper's history! From this stump we may guess the sharpness of his axe, and from the slope of the stroke, on which side he stood, and whether he cut down the tree without going round it or changing hands; and, from the flexure of the splinters, we may know which way it fell. This one chip contains inscribed on it the whole history of the woodchopper and of the world. On this scrap of paper, which held his sugar or salt, perchance, or was the wadding of his gun, sitting on a log in the forest, with what interest we read the tattle of cities, of those larger huts, empty and to let, like this, in High Streets and Broadways. The eaves are dripping on the south side of this simple roof, while the titmouse lisps in the pine and the genial warmth of the sun around the door is somewhat kind and human.

After two seasons, this rude dwelling does not deform the scene. Already the birds resort to it, to build their nests, and you may track to its door the feet of many quadrupeds. Thus, for a long time, nature overlooks the encroachment and profanity of man. The wood still cheerfully and unsuspiciously echoes the strokes of the axe that fells it, and while they are few and seldom, they enhance its wildness, and all the elements strive to naturalize the sound.

Now our path begins to ascend gradually to the top of this high hill, from whose precipitous south side we can look over the broad country of forest and field and river, to the distant snowy mountains. See yonder thin column of smoke curling up through the woods from some invisible farmhouse, the standard raised over some rural homestead. There must be a warmer and more genial spot there below, as where we detect the vapor from a spring forming a cloud above the trees. What fine relations are established between the traveler who discovers this airy column from some eminence in the forest and him who sits below! Up goes the smoke as silently and naturally as the vapor exhales from the leaves, and as busy disposing itself in wreaths as the housewife on the hearth below. It is a hieroglyphic of man's life, and suggests more intimate and important things than the boiling of a pot. Where its fine column rises above the forest, like an ensign, some human life has planted itself,—and such is the beginning of Rome, the establishment of the arts, and the foundation of empires, whether on the prairies of America or the steppes of Asia.

And now we descend again, to the brink of this woodland lake, which lies in a hollow of the hills, as if it were their expressed juice, and that of the leaves which are annually steeped in it. Without outlet or inlet to the eye, it has still its history, in the lapse of its waves, in the rounded pebbles on its shore, and in the pines which grow down to its brink. It has not been idle, though sedentary, but, like Abu Musa, teaches that "sitting still at home is the heavenly way; the going out is the way of the world." Yet in its evaporation it travels as far as any. In summer it is the earth's liquid eye, a mirror in the breast of nature. The sins of the wood are washed out in it. See how the woods form an amphitheatre about it, and it is an arena for all the genialness of nature. All trees direct the traveler to its brink, all paths seek it out, birds fly to it, quadrupeds flee to it, and the very ground inclines toward it. It is nature's saloon, where she has sat down to her toilet. Consider her silent economy and tidiness; how the sun comes with his evaporation to sweep the dust from its surface each morning, and a fresh surface is constantly welling up; and annually, after whatever impurities have accumulated herein, its liquid transparency appears again in the spring. In summer a hushed music seems to sweep across its surface. But now a plain sheet of snow conceals it from our eyes, except where the wind has swept the ice bare, and the sere leaves are gliding from side to side, tacking and veering on their tiny voyages. Here is one just keeled up against a pebble on shore, a dry beech leaf, rocking still, as if it would start again. A skillful engineer, methinks, might project its course since it fell from the parent stem. Here are all the elements for such a calculation. Its present position, the direction of the wind, the level of the pond, and how much more is given. In its scarred edges and veins is its log rolled up.

We fancy ourselves in the interior of a larger house. The surface of the pond is our deal table or sanded floor, and the woods rise abruptly from its edge, like the walls of a cottage. The lines set to catch pickerel through the ice look like a larger culinary preparation, and the men stand about on the white ground like pieces of forest furniture. The actions of these men, at the distance of half a mile over the ice and snow, impress us as when we read the exploits of Alexander in history. They seem not unworthy of the scenery, and as momentous as the conquest of kingdoms.

Again we have wandered through the arches of the wood, until from its skirts we hear the distant booming of ice from yonder bay of the river, as if it were moved by some other and subtler tide than oceans know. To me it has a strange sound of home, thrilling as the voice of one's distant and noble kindred. A mild summer sun shines over forest and lake, and though there is but one green leaf for many rods, yet nature enjoys a serene health. Every sound is fraught with the same mysterious assurance of health, as well now the creaking of the boughs in January, as the soft sough of the wind in July.

When Winter fringes every bough
  With his fantastic wreath,
And puts the seal of silence now
  Upon the leaves beneath;

When every stream in its penthouse
  Goes gurgling on its way,
And in his gallery the mouse
  Nibbleth the meadow hay;

Methinks the summer still is nigh,
  And lurketh underneath,
As that same meadow mouse doth lie
  Snug in that last year's heath.

And if perchance the chickadee
  Lisp a faint note anon,
The snow is summer's canopy,
  Which she herself put on.

Fair blossoms deck the cheerful trees,
  And dazzling fruits depend;
The north wind sighs a summer breeze,
  The nipping frosts to fend,

Bringing glad tidings unto me,
  The while I stand all ear,
Of a serene eternity,
  Which need not winter fear.

Out on the silent pond straightway
  The restless ice doth crack,
And pond sprites merry gambols play
  Amid the deafening rack.

Eager I hasten to the vale,
  As if I heard brave news,
How nature held high festival,
  Which it were hard to lose.

I gambol with my neighbor ice,
  And sympathizing quake,
As each new crack darts in a trice
  Across the gladsome lake.

One with the cricket in the ground,
  And fagot on the hearth,
Resounds the rare domestic sound
  Along the forest path.

Before night we will take a journey on skates along the course of this meandering river, as full of novelty to one who sits by the cottage fire all the winter's day, as if it were over the polar ice, with Captain Parry or Franklin; following the winding of the stream, now flowing amid hills, now spreading out into fair meadows, and forming a myriad coves and bays where the pine and hemlock overarch. The river flows in the rear of the towns, and we see all things from a new and wilder side. The fields and gardens come down to it with a frankness, and freedom from pretension, which they do not wear on the highway. It is the outside and edge of the earth. Our eyes are not offended by violent contrasts. The last rail of the farmer's fence is some swaying willow bough, which still preserves its freshness, and here at length all fences stop, and we no longer cross any road. We may go far up within the country now by the most retired and level road, never climbing a hill, but by broad levels ascending to the upland meadows. It is a beautiful illustration of the law of obedience, the flow of a river; the path for a sick man, a highway down which an acorn cup may float secure with its freight. Its slight occasional falls, whose precipices would not diversify the landscape, are celebrated by mist and spray, and attract the traveler from far and near. From the remote interior, its current conducts him by broad and easy steps, or by one gentler inclined plane, to the sea. Thus by an early and constant yielding to the inequalities of the ground it secures itself the easiest passage.

No domain of nature is quite closed to man at all times, and now we draw near to the empire of the fishes. Our feet glide swiftly over unfathomed depths, where in summer our line tempted the pout and perch, and where the stately pickerel lurked in the long corridors formed by the bulrushes. The deep, impenetrable marsh, where the heron waded and bittern squatted, is made pervious to our swift shoes, as if a thousand railroads had been made into it. With one impulse we are carried to the cabin of the muskrat, that earliest settler, and see him dart away under the transparent ice, like a furred fish, to his hole in the bank; and we glide rapidly over meadows where lately "the mower whet his scythe," through beds of frozen cranberries mixed with meadow-grass. We skate near to where the blackbird, the pewee, and the kingbird hung their nests over the water, and the hornets builded from the maple in the swamp. How many gay warblers, following the sun, have radiated from this nest of silver birch and thistle-down! On the swamp's outer edge was hung the supermarine village, where no foot penetrated. In this hollow tree the wood duck reared her brood, and slid away each day to forage in yonder fen.

In winter, nature is a cabinet of curiosities, full of dried specimens, in their natural order and position. The meadows and forests are a *hortus siccus*. The leaves and grasses stand perfectly pressed by the air without screw or gum, and the birds' nests are not hung on an artificial twig, but where they builded them. We go about dry-shod to inspect the summer's work in the rank swamp, and see what a growth have got the alders, the willows, and the maples; testifying to how many warm suns, and fertilizing dews and showers. See what strides their boughs took in the luxuriant summer,—and anon these dormant buds will carry them onward and upward another span into the heavens.

Occasionally we wade through fields of snow, under whose depths the river is lost for many rods, to appear again to the right or left, where we least expected; still holding on its way underneath, with a faint, stertorous, rumbling sound, as if, like the bear and marmot, it too had hibernated, and we had followed its faint summer trail to where it earthed itself in snow and ice. At first we should have thought that rivers would be empty and dry in midwinter, or else frozen solid till the spring thawed them; but their volume is not diminished even, for only a superficial cold bridges their surfaces. The thousand springs which feed the lakes and streams are flowing still. The issues of a few surface springs only are closed, and they go to swell the deep reservoirs. Nature's wells are below the frost. The summer brooks are not filled with snow-water, nor does the mower quench his thirst with that alone. The streams are swollen when the snow melts in the spring, because nature's work has been delayed, the water being turned into ice and snow, whose particles are less smooth and round, and do not find their level so soon.

Far over the ice, between the hemlock woods and snow-clad hills, stands the pickerel-fisher, his lines set in some retired cove, like a Finlander, with his arms thrust into the pouches of his dreadnaught; with dull, snowy, fishy thoughts, himself a finless fish, separated a few inches from his race; dumb, erect, and made to be enveloped in clouds and snows, like the pines on shore. In these wild scenes, men stand about in the scenery, or move deliberately and heavily, having sacrificed the sprightliness and vivacity of towns to the dumb sobriety of nature. He does not make the scenery less wild, more than the jays and musk-rats, but stands there as a part of it, as the natives are represented in the voyages of early navigators, at Nootka Sound, and on the North-west coast, with their furs about them, before they were tempted to loquacity by a scrap of iron. He belongs to the natural family of man, and is planted deeper in nature and has more root than the inhabitants of towns. Go to him, ask what luck, and you will learn that he too is a wor-shiper of the unseen. Hear with what sincere deference and waving ges-ture in his tone he speaks of the lake pickerel, which he has never seen, his primitive and ideal race of pickerel. He is connected with the shore still, as by a fish-line, and yet remembers the season when he took fish through the ice on the pond, while the peas were up in his garden at home.

But now, while we have loitered, the clouds have gathered again, and a few straggling snowflakes are beginning to descend. Faster and faster they fall, shutting out the distant objects from sight. The snow falls on every wood and field, and no crevice is forgotten; by the river and the pond, on the hill and in the valley. Quadrupeds are confined to their coverts and the birds sit upon their perches this peaceful hour. There is not so much sound as in fair weather, but silently and gradually every slope, and the gray walls and fences, and the polished ice, and the sere leaves, which were not buried before, are concealed, and the tracks of men and beasts are lost. With so little effort does nature reassert her rule and blot out the traces of men. Hear how Homer has described the same: "The snowflakes fall thick and fast on a winter's day. The winds are lulled, and the snow falls incessant, covering the tops of the mountains, and the hills, and the plains where the lotus-tree grows, and the culti-vated fields, and they are falling by the inlets and shores of the foaming sea, but are silently dissolved by the waves." The snow levels all things, and infolds them deeper in the bosom of nature, as, in the slow summer, vegetation creeps up to the entablature of the temple, and the turrets of the castle, and helps her to prevail over art.

The surly night-wind rustles through the wood, and warns us to re-trace our steps, while the sun goes down behind the thickening storm, and birds seek their roosts, and cattle their stalls.

"Drooping the lab'rer ox
Stands covered o'er with snow, and *now* demands
The fruit of all his toil."

Though winter is represented in the almanac as an old man, facing the wind and sleet, and drawing his cloak about him, we rather think of him as a merry woodchopper, and warm-blooded youth, as blithe as summer. The unexplored grandeur of the storm keeps up the spirits of the traveler. It does not trifle with us, but has a sweet earnestness. In winter we lead a more inward life. Our hearts are warm and cheery, like cottages under drifts, whose windows and doors are half concealed, but from whose chimneys the smoke cheerfully ascends. The imprisoning drifts increase the sense of comfort which the house affords, and in the coldest days we are content to sit over the hearth and see the sky through the chimney-top, enjoying the quiet and serene life that may be had in a warm corner by the chimney-side, or feeling our pulse by listening to the low of cattle in the street, or the sound of the flail in distant barns all the long afternoon. No doubt a skillful physician could determine our health by observing how these simple and natural sounds affected us. We enjoy now, not an Oriental, but a Boreal leisure, around warm stoves and fire-places, and watch the shadow of motes in the sunbeams.

Sometimes our fate grows too homely and familiarly serious ever to be cruel. Consider how for three months the human destiny is wrapped in furs. The good Hebrew Revelation takes no cognizance of all this cheerful snow. Is there no religion for the temperate and frigid zones? We know of no scripture which records the pure benignity of the gods on a New England winter night. Their praises have never been sung, only their wrath deprecated. The best scripture, after all, records but a meagre faith. Its saints live reserved and austere. Let a brave, devout man spend the year in the woods of Maine or Labrador, and see if the Hebrew Scriptures speak adequately to his condition and experience, from the setting in of winter to the breaking up of the ice.

Now commences the long winter evening around the farmer's hearth, when the thoughts of the indwellers travel far abroad, and men are by nature and necessity charitable and liberal to all creatures. Now is the happy resistance to cold, when the farmer reaps his reward, and thinks of his preparedness for winter, and, through the glittering panes, sees with equanimity "the mansion of the northern bear," for now the storm is over,—

> "The full ethereal round,
> Infinite worlds disclosing to the view,
> Shines out intensely keen; and all one cope
> Of starry glitter glows from pole to pole."

PARADISE (TO BE) REGAINED

THE

UNITED STATES MAGAZINE,

AND

DEMOCRATIC REVIEW.

THE BEST GOVERNMENT IS THAT WHICH GOVERNS LEAST."

NEW SERIES.

VOLUME XIII.

NEW YORK:

J. & H. G. LANGLEY, 57 CHATHAM STREET.

1843.

"Paradise (To Be) Regained" appeared in the November 1843 issue of the *Democratic Review*. Thoreau later used a slightly altered version of the journal's motto ("The best government is that which governs least") in the opening sentence of "Civil Disobedience."

*PARADISE (TO BE) REGAINED**

We learn that Mr. Etzler is a native of Germany, and originally published his book in Pennsylvania, ten or twelve years ago; and now a second English edition, from the original American one, is demanded by his readers across the water, owing, we suppose, to the recent spread of Fourier's doctrines. It is one of the signs of the times. We confess that we have risen from reading this book with enlarged ideas, and grander conceptions of our duties in this world. It did expand us a little. It is worth attending to, if only that it entertains large questions. Consider what Mr. Etzler proposes:—

"Fellow-men! I promise to show the means of creating a paradise within ten years, where everything desirable for human life may be had by every man in superabundance, without labor, and without pay; where the whole face of nature shall be changed into the most beautiful forms, and man may live in the most magnificent palaces, in all imaginable refinements of luxury, and in the most delightful gardens; where he may accomplish, without labor, in one year, more than hitherto could be done in thousands of years; may level mountains, sink valleys, create lakes, drain lakes and swamps, and intersect the land everywhere with beautiful canals, and roads for transporting heavy loads of many thousand tons,

**The Paradise within the Reach of all Men, without Labor, by Powers of Nature and Machinery. An Address to all intelligent Men.* In Two Parts. By J. A. Etzler. Part First. Second English Edition. London. 1842. Pp. 55.

and for traveling one thousand miles in twenty-four hours; may cover the ocean with floating islands movable in any desired direction with immense power and celerity, in perfect security, and with all comforts and luxuries, bearing gardens and palaces, with thousands of families, and provided with rivulets of sweet water; may explore the interior of the globe, and travel from pole to pole in a fortnight; provide himself with means, unheard of yet, for increasing his knowledge of the world, and so his intelligence; lead a life of continual happiness, of enjoyments yet unknown; free himself from almost all the evils that afflict mankind, except death, and even put death far beyond the common period of human life, and finally render it less afflicting. Mankind may thus live in and enjoy a new world, far superior to the present, and raise themselves far higher in the scale of being."

It would seem from this and various indications beside, that there is a transcendentalism in mechanics as well as in ethics. While the whole field of the one reformer lies beyond the boundaries of space, the other is pushing his schemes for the elevation of the race to its utmost limits. While one scours the heavens, the other sweeps the earth. One says he will reform himself, and then nature and circumstances will be right. Let us not obstruct ourselves, for that is the greatest friction. It is of little importance though a cloud obstruct the view of the astronomer compared with his own blindness. The other will reform nature and circumstances, and then man will be right. Talk no more vaguely, says he, of reforming the world,—I will reform the globe itself. What matters it whether I remove this humor out of my flesh, or this pestilent humor from the fleshy part of the globe? Nay, is not the latter the more generous course? At present the globe goes with a shattered constitution in its orbit. Has it not asthma, and ague, and fever, and dropsy, and flatulence, and pleurisy, and is it not afflicted with vermin? Has it not its healthful laws counteracted, and its vital energy which will yet redeem it? No doubt the simple powers of nature, properly directed by man, would make it healthy and a paradise; as the laws of man's own constitution but wait to be obeyed, to restore him to health and happiness. Our panaceas cure but few ails, our general hospitals are private and exclusive. We must set up another Hygeia than is now worshiped. Do not the quacks even direct small doses for children, larger for adults, and larger still for oxen and horses? Let us remember that we are to prescribe for the globe itself.

This fair homestead has fallen to us, and how little have we done to improve it, how little have we cleared and hedged and ditched! We are too inclined to go hence to a "better land," without lifting a finger, as our farmers are moving to the Ohio soil; but would it not be more heroic and faithful to till and redeem this New England soil of the world? The still youthful energies of the globe have only to be directed in their proper channel. Every gazette brings accounts of the untutored freaks of the wind,—shipwrecks and hurricanes which the mariner and planter accept as special or general providences; but they touch our consciences, they remind us of our sins. Another deluge would disgrace mankind. We confess we never had much respect for that antediluvian race. A thoroughbred business man cannot enter heartily upon the business of life without first looking into his accounts. How many things are now at loose ends! Who knows which way the wind will blow to-morrow? Let us not succumb to nature. We will marshall the clouds and restrain tempests; we will bottle up pestilent exhalations; we will probe for earthquakes, grub them up, and give vent to the dangerous gas; we will disembowel the volcano, and extract its poison, take its seed out. We will wash water, and warm fire, and cool ice, and underprop the earth. We will teach birds to fly, and fishes to swim, and ruminants to chew the cud. It is time we had looked into these things.

And it becomes the moralist, too, to inquire what man might do to improve and beautify the system; what to make the stars shine more brightly, the sun more cheery and joyous, the moon more placid and content. Could he not heighten the tints of flowers and the melody of birds? Does he perform his duty to the inferior races? Should he not be a god to them? What is the part of magnanimity to the whale and the beaver? Should we not fear to exchange places with them for a day, lest by their behavior they should shame us? Might we not treat with magnanimity the shark and the tiger, not descend to meet them on their own level, with spears of shark's teeth and bucklers of tiger's skin? We slander the hyena; man is the fiercest and cruelest animal. Ah! he is of little faith; even the erring comets and meteors would thank him, and return his kindness in their kind.

How meanly and grossly do we deal with nature! Could we not have a less gross labor? What else do these fine inventions suggest,—magnetism, the daguerreotype, electricity? Can we not do more than cut and trim the forest?—can we not assist in its interior economy, in the circulation of the sap? Now we work superficially and violently. We do not suspect how much might be done to improve our relation to animated nature even; what kindness and refined courtesy there might be.

There are certain pursuits which, if not wholly poetic and true, do at least suggest a nobler and finer relation to nature than we know. The keeping of bees, for instance, is a very slight interference. It is like directing the sunbeams. All nations, from the remotest antiquity, have thus fingered nature. There are Hymettus and Hybla, and how many bee-renowned spots beside! There is nothing gross in the idea of these little herds,—their hum like the faintest low of kine in the meads. A pleasant reviewer has lately reminded us that in some places they are led out to pasture where the flowers are most abundant. "Columella tells us," says he, "that the inhabitants of Arabia sent their hives into Attica to benefit by the later-blowing flowers." Annually are the hives, in immense pyramids, carried up the Nile in boats, and suffered to float slowly down the stream by night, resting by day, as the flowers put forth along the banks; and they determine the richness of any locality, and so the profitableness of delay, by the sinking of the boat in the water. We are told, by the same reviewer, of a man in Germany, whose bees yielded more honey than those of his neighbors, with no apparent advantage; but at length he informed them, that he had turned his hives one degree more to the east, and so his bees, having two hours the start in the morning, got the first sip of honey. True, there is treachery and selfishness behind all this, but these things suggest to the poetic mind what might be done.

Many examples there are of a grosser interference, yet not without their apology. We saw last summer, on the side of a mountain, a dog employed to churn for a farmer's family, traveling upon a horizontal wheel, and though he had sore eyes, an alarming cough, and withal a demure aspect, yet their bread did get buttered for all that. Undoubtedly, in the most brilliant successes, the first rank is always sacrificed. Much useless traveling of horses, *in extenso*, has of late years been improved for man's behoof, only two forces being taken advantage of,—the gravity of the horse, which is the centripetal, and his centrifugal inclination to go ahead. Only these two elements in the calculation. And is not the creature's whole economy better economized thus? Are not all finite beings better pleased with motions relative than absolute? And what is the great globe itself but such a wheel,—a larger tread-mill,—so that our horse's freest steps over prairies are oftentimes balked and rendered of no avail by the earth's motion on its axis? But here he is the central agent and motive-power; and, for variety of scenery, being provided with a window in front, do not the ever-varying activity and fluctuating energy of the creature himself work the effect of the most varied scenery on a country road? It must be confessed that horses at present work too exclusively for men, rarely men for horses; and the brute degenerates in man's society.

It will be seen that we contemplate a time when man's will shall be law to the physical world, and he shall no longer be deterred by such abstractions as time and space, height and depth, weight and hardness, but shall indeed be the lord of creation. "Well," says the faithless reader, " 'life is short, but art is long;' where is the power that will effect all these changes?" This it is the very object of Mr. Etzler's volume to show. At present, he would merely remind us that there are innumerable and immeasurable powers already existing in nature, unimproved on a large scale, or for generous and universal ends, amply sufficient for these purposes. He would only indicate their existence, as a surveyor makes known the existence of a water-power on any stream; but for their application he refers us to a sequel to this book, called the "Mechanical System." A few of the most obvious and familiar of these powers are the Wind, the Tide, the Waves, the Sunshine. Let us consider their value.

First, there is the power of the Wind, constantly exerted over the globe. It appears from observation of a sailing-vessel, and from scientific tables, that the average power of the wind is equal to that of one horse for every one hundred square feet. We do not attach much value to this statement of the comparative power of the wind and horse, for no common ground is mentioned on which they can be compared. Undoubtedly, each is incomparably excellent in its way, and every general comparison made for such practical purposes as are contemplated, which gives a preference to the one, must be made with some unfairness to the other. The scientific tables are, for the most part, true only in a tabular sense. We suspect that a loaded wagon, with a light sail, ten feet square, would not have been blown so far by the end of the year, under equal circumstances, as a common racer or dray horse would have drawn it. And how many crazy structures on our globe's surface, of the same dimensions, would wait for dry-rot if the traces of one horse were hitched to them, even to their windward side? Plainly this is not the principle of comparison. But even the steady and constant force of the horse may be rated as equal to his weight at least. Yet we should prefer to let the zephyrs and gales bear, with all their weight, upon our fences, than that Dobbin, with feet braced, should lean ominously against them for a season.

Nevertheless, here is an almost incalculable power at our disposal, yet how trifling the use we make of it! It only serves to turn a few mills, blow a few vessels across the ocean, and a few trivial ends besides. What a poor compliment do we pay to our indefatigable and energetic servant!

Men having discovered the power of falling water, which, after all, is comparatively slight, how eagerly do they seek out and improve these *privileges*! Let a difference of but a few feet in level be discovered on some stream near a populous town, some slight occasion for gravity to act, and the whole economy of the neighborhood is changed at once. Men do indeed speculate about and with this power as if it were the only privilege. But meanwhile this aerial stream is falling from far greater heights with more constant flow, never shrunk by drought, offering mill-sites wherever the wind blows; a Niagara in the air, with no Canada side;—only the application is hard.

There are the powers, too, of the Tide and Waves, constantly ebbing and flowing, lapsing and relapsing, but they serve man in but few ways. They turn a few tide-mills, and perform a few other insignificant and accidental services only. We all perceive the effect of the tide; how imperceptibly it creeps up into our harbors and rivers, and raises the heaviest navies as easily as the lightest chip. Everything that floats must yield to it. But man, slow to take nature's constant hint of assistance, makes slight and irregular use of this power, in careening ships and getting them afloat when aground.

This power may be applied in various ways. A large body, of the heaviest materials that will float, may first be raised by it, and being attached to the end of a balance reaching from the land, or from a stationary support fastened to the bottom, when the tide falls the whole weight will be brought to bear upon the end of the balance. Also, when the tide rises, it may be made to exert a nearly equal force in the opposite direction. It can be employed wherever a *point d'appui* can be obtained.

Verily, the land would wear a busy aspect at the spring and neap tide, and these island ships, these *terrae infirmae*, which realize the fables of antiquity, affect our imagination. We have often thought that the fittest locality for a human dwelling was on the edge of the land, that there the constant lesson and impression of the sea might sink deep into the life and character of the landsman, and perhaps impart a marine tint to his imagination. It is a noble word, that *mariner*,—one who is conversant with the sea. There should be more of what it signifies in each of us. It is a worthy country to belong to,—we look to see him not disgrace it. Perhaps we should be equally mariners and terreners, and even our Green Mountains need some of that sea-green to be mixed with them.

The computation of the power of the Waves is less satisfactory. While only the average power of the wind and the average height of the tide were taken before, now the extreme height of the waves is used, for they are made to rise ten feet above the level of the sea, to which, adding ten more for depression, we have twenty feet, or the extreme height of a wave. Indeed, the power of the waves, which is produced by the wind blowing obliquely and at disadvantage upon the water, is made to be, not only three thousand times greater than that of the tide, but one hundred times greater than that of the wind itself, meeting its object at right angles. Moreover, this power is measured by the area of the vessel, and not by its length mainly, and it seems to be forgotten that the motion of the waves is chiefly undulatory, and exerts a power only within the limits of a vibration, else the very continents, with their extensive coasts, would soon be set adrift.

Finally, there is the power to be derived from Sunshine, by the principle on which Archimedes contrived his burning-mirrors, a multiplication of mirrors reflecting the rays of the sun upon the same spot, till the requisite degree of heat is obtained. The principal application of this power will be to the boiling of water and production of steam. So much for these few and more obvious powers, already used to a trifling extent. But there are innumerable others in nature, not described nor discovered. These, however, will do for the present. This would be to make the sun and the moon equally our satellites. For, as the moon is the cause of the tides, and the sun the cause of the wind, which, in turn, is the cause of the waves, all the work of this planet would be performed by these far influences.

"We may store up water in some eminent pond, and take out of this store, at any time, as much water through the outlet as we want to employ, by which means the original power may react for many days after it has ceased. . . . Such reservoirs of moderate elevation or size need not be made artificially, but will be found made by nature very frequently, requiring but little aid for their completion. They require no regularity of form. Any valley, with lower grounds in its vicinity, would answer the purpose. Small crevices may be filled up. Such places may be eligible for the beginning of enterprises of this kind."

The greater the height, of course, the less water required. But suppose a level and dry country; then hill and valley, and "eminent pond," are to be constructed by main force; or, if the springs are unusually low, then dirt and stones may be used, and the disadvantage arising from friction will be counterbalanced by their greater gravity. Nor shall a single rood of dry land be sunk in such artificial ponds as may be wanted, but their surfaces "may be covered with rafts decked with fertile earth, and all kinds of vegetables which may grow there as well as anywhere else."

And, finally, by the use of thick envelopes retaining the heat, and other contrivances, "the power of steam caused by sunshine may react at will, and thus be rendered perpetual, no matter how often or how long the sunshine may be interrupted."

Here is power enough, one would think, to accomplish somewhat. These are the Powers below. O ye millwrights, ye engineers, ye operatives and speculators of every class, never again complain of a want of power: it is the grossest form of infidelity. The question is, not how we shall execute, but what. Let us not use in a niggardly manner what is thus generously offered.

Consider what revolutions are to be effected in agriculture. First, in the new country a machine is to move along, taking out trees and stones to any required depth, and piling them up in convenient heaps; then the same machine, "with a little alteration," is to plane the ground perfectly, till there shall be no hills nor valleys, making the requisite canals, ditches, and roads as it goes along. The same machine, "with some other little alterations," is then to sift the ground thoroughly, supply fertile soil from other places if wanted, and plant it; and finally the same machine, "with a little addition," is to reap and gather in the crop, thresh and grind it, or press it to oil, or prepare it any way for final use. For the description of these machines we are referred to "Etzler's Mechanical System," pages 11 to 27. We should be pleased to see that "Mechanical System." We have great faith in it. But we cannot stop for applications now.

Who knows but by accumulating the power until the end of the present century, using meanwhile only the smallest allowance, reserving all that blows, all that shines, all that ebbs and flows, all that dashes, we may have got such a reserved accumulated power as to run the earth off its track into a new orbit, some summer, and so change the tedious vicissitude of the seasons? Or, perchance, coming generations will not abide the dissolution of the globe, but, availing themselves of future inventions in aerial locomotion, and the navigation of space, the entire race may migrate from the earth, to settle some vacant and more western planet, it may be still healthy, perchance unearthy, not composed of dirt and stones, whose primary strata only are strewn, and where no weeds are sown. It took but little art, a simple application of natural laws, a canoe, a paddle, and a sail of matting, to people the isles of the Pacific, and a little more will people the shining isles of space. Do we not see in the firmament the lights carried along the shore by night, as Columbus did? Let us not despair nor mutiny.

"The dwellings also ought to be very different from what is known, if the full benefit of our means is to be enjoyed. They are to be of a structure for which we have no name yet. They are to be neither palaces, nor temples, nor cities, but a combination of all, superior to whatever is known.

"Earth may be baked into bricks, or even vitrified stone by heat,—we may bake large masses of any size and form, into stone and vitrified substance of the greatest durability, lasting even thousands of years, out of clayey earth, or of stones ground to dust, by the application of burning-mirrors. This is to be done in the open air without other preparation than gathering the substance, grinding and mixing it with water and cement, moulding or casting it, and bringing the focus of the burning-mirrors of proper size upon the same."

The character of the architecture is to be quite different from what it ever has been hitherto; large solid masses are to be baked or cast in one piece, ready shaped in any form that may be desired. The building may, therefore, consist of columns two hundred feet high and upwards, of proportionate thickness, and of one entire piece of vitrified substance; huge pieces are to be moulded so as to join and hook on to each other firmly, by proper joints and folds, and not to yield in any way without breaking.

"Foundries, of any description, are to be heated by burning-mirrors, and will require no labor, except the making of the first moulds and the superintendence for gathering the metal and taking the finished articles away."

Alas! in the present state of science, we must take the finished articles away; but think not that man will always be the victim of circumstances.

The countryman who visited the city, and found the streets cluttered with bricks and lumber, reported that it was not yet finished; and one who considers the endless repairs and reforming of our houses might well wonder when they will be done. But why may not the dwellings of men on this earth be built, once for all, of some durable material, some Roman or Etruscan masonry, which will stand, so that time shall only adorn and beautify them? Why may we not finish the outward world for posterity, and leave them leisure to attend to the inner? Surely, all the gross necessities and economies might be cared for in a few years. All might be built and baked and stored up, during this, the term-time of the world, against the vacant eternity, and the globe go provisioned and furnished, like our public vessels, for its voyage through space, as through some Pacific Ocean, while we would "tie up the rudder and sleep before the wind," as those who sail from Lima to Manilla.

But, to go back a few years in imagination, think not that life in these crystal palaces is to bear any analogy to life in our present humble cottages. Far from it. Clothed, once for all, in some "flexible stuff," more durable than George Fox's suit of leather, composed of "fibres of vegetables," "glutinated" together by some "cohesive substances," and made into sheets, like paper, of any size or form, man will put far from him corroding care and the whole host of ills.

"The twenty-five halls in the inside of the square are to be each two hundred feet square and high; the forty corridors, each one hundred feet long and twenty wide; the eighty galleries, each from 1,000 to 1,250 feet long; about 7,000 private rooms, the whole surrounded and intersected by the grandest and most splendid colonnades imaginable; floors, ceilings, columns, with their various beautiful and fanciful intervals, all shining, and reflecting to infinity all objects and persons, with splendid lustre of all beautiful colors, and fanciful shapes and pictures.

"All galleries, outside and within the halls, are to be provided with many thousand commodious and most elegant vehicles, in which persons may move up and down like birds, in perfect security, and without exertion. . . . Any member may procure himself all the common articles of his daily wants, by a short turn of some crank, without leaving his apartment.

"One or two persons are sufficient to direct the kitchen business. They have nothing else to do but to superintend the cookery, and to watch the time of the victuals being done, and then to remove them, with the table and vessels, into the dining-hall, or to the respective private apartments, by a slight motion of the hand at some crank. . . . *Any very ex-*

traordinary desire of any person may be satisfied by going to the place where the thing is to be had; and anything that requires a particular preparation in cooking or baking may be done by the person who desires it."

This is one of those instances in which the individual genius is found to consent, as indeed it always does, at last, with the universal. This last sentence has a certain sad and sober truth, which reminds us of the scripture of all nations. All expression of truth does at length take this deep ethical form. Here is hint of a place the most eligible of any in space, and of a servitor, in comparison with whom all other helps dwindle into insignificance. We hope to hear more of him anon, for even a Crystal Palace would be deficient without his invaluable services.

And as for the environs of the establishment:—

"There will be afforded the most enrapturing views to be fancied, out of the private apartments, from the galleries, from the roof, from its turrets and cupolas,—gardens, as far as the eye can see, full of fruits and flowers, arranged in the most beautiful order, with walks, colonnades, aqueducts, canals, ponds, plains, amphitheatres, terraces, fountains, sculptural works, pavilions, gondolas, places for public amusement, etc., to delight the eye and fancy, the taste and smell. . . . The walks and roads are to be paved with hard vitrified large plates, so as to be always clean from all dirt in any weather or season. . . .

"The walks may be covered with porticoes adorned with magnificent columns, statues, and sculptural works; all of vitrified substance, and lasting forever. At night the roof and the inside and outside of the whole square are illuminated by gas-light, which, in the mazes of many-colored crystal-like colonnades and vaultings, is reflected with a brilliancy that gives to the whole a lustre of precious stones, as far as the eye can see. Such are the future abodes of men. . . . Such is the life reserved to true intelligence, but withheld from ignorance, prejudice, and stupid adherence to custom."

Thus is Paradise to be Regained, and that old and stern decree at length reversed. Man shall no more earn his living by the sweat of his brow. All labor shall be reduced to "a short turn of some crank," and "taking the finished articles away." But there is a crank,—oh, how hard to be turned! Could there not be a crank upon a crank,—an infinitely small crank?—we would fain inquire. No,—alas! not. But there is a certain divine energy in every man, but sparingly employed as yet, which may be called the crank within,—the crank after all,—the prime mover in all machinery,—quite indispensable to all work. Would that we might get our hands on its handle! In fact, no work can be shirked. It may be postponed indefinitely, but not infinitely. Nor can any really important work be made easier by coöperation or machinery. Not one particle of labor now threatening any man can be routed without being performed. It cannot be hunted out of the vicinity like jackals and hyenas. It will not run. You may begin by sawing the little sticks, or you may saw the great sticks first, but sooner or later you must saw them both.

We will not be imposed upon by this vast application of forces. We believe that most things will have to be accomplished still by the application called Industry. We are rather pleased, after all, to consider the small private, but both constant and accumulated, force which stands behind every spade in the field. This it is that makes the valleys shine, and the deserts really bloom. Sometimes, we confess, we are so degenerate as to reflect with pleasure on the days when men were yoked like cattle, and drew a crooked stick for a plow. After all, the great interests and methods were the same.

It is a rather serious objection to Mr. Etzler's schemes, that they require time, men, and money, three very superfluous and inconvenient things for an honest and well-disposed man to deal with. "The whole world," he tells us, "might therefore be really changed into a paradise, within less than ten years, commencing from the first year of an association for the purpose of constructing and applying the machinery." We are sensible of a startling incongruity when time and money are mentioned in this connection. The ten years which are proposed would be a tedious while to wait, if every man were at his post and did his duty, but quite too short a period, if we are to take time for it. But this fault is by no means peculiar to Mr. Etzler's schemes. There is far too much hurry and bustle, and too little patience and privacy, in all our methods, as if something were to be accomplished in centuries. The true reformer does not want time, nor money, nor coöperation, nor advice. What is time but the stuff delay is made of? And depend upon it, our virtue will not live on the interest of our money. He expects no income, but outgoes; so soon as we begin to count the cost, the cost begins. And as for advice, the information floating in the atmosphere of society is as evanescent and unserviceable to him as gossamer for clubs of Hercules. There is absolutely no common sense; it is common nonsense. If we are to risk a cent or a drop of our blood, who then shall advise us? For ourselves, we are too young for experience. Who is old enough? We are older by faith than by experience. In the unbending of the arm to do the deed there is experience worth all the maxims in the world.

"It will now be plainly seen that the execution of the proposals is not proper for individuals. Whether it be proper for government at this time, before the subject has become popular, is a question to be decided; all that is to be done is to step forth, after mature reflection, to confess loudly one's conviction, and to constitute societies. Man is powerful but in union with many. Nothing great, for the improvement of his own condition, or that of his fellow-men, can ever be effected by individual enterprise."

Alas! this is the crying sin of the age, this want of faith in the prevalence of a man. Nothing can be effected but by one man. He who wants help wants everything. True, this is the condition of our weakness, but it can never be the means of our recovery. We must first succeed alone, that we may enjoy our success together. We trust that the social movements which we witness indicate an aspiration not to be thus cheaply satisfied. In this matter of reforming the world, we have little faith in corporations; not thus was it first formed.

But our author is wise enough to say that the raw materials for the accomplishment of his purposes are "iron, copper, wood, earth chiefly, and a union of men whose eyes and understanding are not shut up by preconceptions." Ay, this last may be what we want mainly,—a company of "odd fellows" indeed.

"Small shares of twenty dollars will be sufficient"—in all, from "200,000 to 300,000"—"to create the first establishment for a whole community of from 3,000 to 4,000 individuals;" at the end of five years we shall have a principal of 200 millions of dollars, and so paradise will be wholly regained at the end of the tenth year. But, alas! the ten years have already elapsed, and there are no signs of Eden yet, for want of the requisite funds to begin the enterprise in a hopeful manner. Yet it seems a safe investment. Perchance they could be hired at a low rate, the property being mortgaged for security, and, if necessary, it could be given up in any stage of the enterprise, without loss, with the fixtures.

But we see two main difficulties in the way: first, the successful application of the powers by machinery (we have not yet seen the "Mechanical System"), and, secondly, which is infinitely harder, the application of man to the work by faith. This it is, we fear, which will prolong the ten years to ten thousand at least. It will take a power more than "80,000 times greater than all the men on earth could effect with their nerves" to persuade men to use that which is already offered them. Even a greater than this physical power must be brought to bear upon that moral power. Faith, indeed, is all the reform that is needed; it is itself a reform. Doubtless, we are as slow to conceive of Paradise as of Heaven, of a perfect natural as of a perfect spiritual world. We see how past ages have loitered and erred. "Is perhaps our generation free from irrationality and error? Have we perhaps reached now the summit of human wisdom, and need no more to look out for mental or physical improvement?" Undoubtedly, we are never so visionary as to be prepared for what the next hour may bring forth.

Μέλλει τὸ θεῖον δ' ἐστι τοιοῦτον φύσει.

The Divine is about to be, and such is its nature. In our wisest moments we are secreting a matter, which, like the lime of the shell-fish, incrusts us quite over, and well for us if, like it, we cast our shells from time to time, though they be pearl and of fairest tint. Let us consider under what disadvantages Science has hitherto labored before we pronounce thus confidently on her progress.

Mr. Etzler is not one of the enlightened practical men, the pioneers of the actual, who move with the slow, deliberate tread of science, conserving the world; who execute the dreams of the last century, though they have no dreams of their own; yet he deals in the very raw but still solid material of all inventions. He has more of the practical than usually belongs to so bold a schemer, so resolute a dreamer. Yet his success is in theory, and not in practice, and he feeds our faith rather than contents our understanding. His book wants order, serenity, dignity, everything,—but it does not fail to impart what only man can impart to man of much importance, his own faith. It is true his dreams are not thrilling nor bright enough, and he leaves off to dream where he who dreams just before the dawn begins. His castles in the air fall to the ground, because they are not built lofty enough; they should be secured to heaven's roof. After all, the theories and speculations of men concern us more than their puny accomplishment. It is with a certain coldness and languor that we loiter about the actual and so-called practical. How little do the most wonderful inventions of modern times detain us. They insult nature. Every machine, or particular application, seems a slight outrage against universal laws. How many fine inventions are there which do not clutter the ground? We think that those only succeed which minister to our sensible and animal wants, which bake or brew, wash or warm, or the like. But are those of no account which are patented by fancy and imagination, and succeed so admirably in our dreams that they give the tone still to our waking thoughts? Already nature is serving all those uses which science slowly derives on a much higher and grander scale to him that will be served by her. When the sunshine falls on the path of the poet, he enjoys all those pure benefits and pleasures which the arts slowly and partially realize from age to age. The winds which fan his cheek waft him the sum of that profit and happiness which their lagging inventions supply.

The chief fault of this book is, that it aims to secure the greatest degree of gross comfort and pleasure merely. It paints a Mahometan's heaven, and stops short with singular abruptness when we think it is drawing near to the precincts of the Christian's,—and we trust we have not made here a distinction without a difference. Undoubtedly if we were to reform this outward life truly and thoroughly, we should find no duty of the inner omitted. It would be employment for our whole nature; and what we should do thereafter would be as vain a question as to ask the bird what it will do when its nest is built and its brood reared. But a moral reform must take place first, and then the necessity of the other will be superseded, and we shall sail and plow by its force alone. There is a speedier way than the "Mechanical System" can show to fill up marshes, to drown the roar of the waves, to tame hyenas, secure agreeable environs, diversify the land, and refresh it with "rivulets of sweet water," and that is by the power of rectitude and true behavior. It is only for a little while, only occasionally, methinks, that we want a garden. Surely a good man need not be at the labor to level a hill for the sake of a prospect, or raise fruits and flowers, and construct floating islands, for the sake of a paradise. He enjoys better prospects than lie behind any hill. Where an angel travels it will be paradise all the way, but where Satan travels it will be burning marl and cinders. What says Veeshnoo Sarma? "He whose mind is at ease is possessed of all riches. Is it not the same to one whose foot is inclosed in a shoe, as if the whole surface of the earth were covered with leather?"

He who is conversant with the supernal powers will not worship these inferior deities of the wind, waves, tide, and sunshine. But we would not disparage the importance of such calculations as we have described. They are truths in physics, because they are true in ethics. The moral powers no one would presume to calculate. Suppose we could compare the moral with the physical, and say how many horse-power the force of love, for instance, blowing on every square foot of a man's soul, would equal. No doubt we are well aware of this force; figures would not increase our respect for it; the sunshine is equal to but one ray of its heat. The light of the sun is but the shadow of love. "The souls of men loving and fearing God," says Raleigh, "receive influence from that divine light itself, whereof the sun's clarity, and that of the stars, is by Plato called but a shadow. *Lumen est umbra Dei, Deus est Lumen Luminis.* Light is the shadow of God's brightness, who is the light of light," and, we may add, the heat of heat. Love is the wind, the tide, the waves, the sunshine. Its power is incalculable; it is many horse-power. It never ceases, it never slacks; it can move the globe without a resting-place; it can warm without fire; it can feed without meat; it can clothe without garments; it can shelter without roof; it can make a paradise within which will dispense with a paradise without. But though the wisest men in all ages have labored to publish this force, and every human heart is, sooner or later, more or less, made to feel it, yet how little is actually applied to social ends! True, it is the motive-power of all successful social machinery; but as in physics we have made the elements do only a little drudgery for us,—steam to take the place of a few horses, wind of a few oars, water of a few cranks and hand-mills,—as the mechanical forces have not yet been generously and largely applied to make the physical world answer to the ideal, so the power of love has been but meanly and sparingly applied, as yet. It has patented only such machines as the almshouse, the hospital, and the Bible Society, while its infinite wind is still blowing, and blowing down these very structures too, from time to time. Still less are we accumulating its power, and preparing to act with greater energy at a future time. Shall we not contribute our shares to this enterprise, then?

KTAADN

KTAADN, AND THE MAINE WOODS.

BY HENRY D. THOREAU.

No. V.

THE RETURN JOURNEY.

Perhaps I most fully realized that this was primeval, untamed, and forever untameable *Nature*, or whatever else men call it, while coming down this part of the mountain. We were passing over "Burnt Lands," burnt by lightning, perchance, though they showed no recent marks of fire, hardly so much as a charred stump, but looked rather like a natural pasture for the moose and deer, exceedingly wild and desolate, with occasional strips of timber crossing them, and low poplars springing up, and patches of blueberries here and there. I found myself traversing them familiarly, like some pasture run to waste, or partially reclaimed by man; but when I reflected what man, what brother or sister or kinsman of our race made it and claimed it, I expected the proprietor to rise up and dispute my passage. It is difficult to conceive of a region uninhabited by man. We habitually presume his presence and influence everywhere. And yet we have not seen pure Nature, unless we have seen her thus vast, and drear, and inhuman, though in the midst of cities. Nature was here something savage and awful, though beautiful. I looked with awe at the ground I trod on, to see what the Powers had made there, the form and fashion and material of their work. This was that Earth of which we have heard, made out of Chaos and Old Night. Here was no man's garden, but the unhandselled globe. It was not lawn, nor pasture, nor mead,

The Union Magazine, November 1848

KTAADN

On the 31st of August, 1846, I left Concord in Massachusetts for Bangor and the backwoods of Maine, by way of the railroad and steamboat, intending to accompany a relative of mine engaged in the lumber trade in Bangor, as far as a dam on the west branch of the Penobscot, in which property he was interested. From this place, which is about one hundred miles by the river above Bangor, thirty miles from the Houlton military road, and five miles beyond the last log hut, I proposed to make excursions to mount Ktaadn, the second highest mountain in New England, about thirty miles distant, and to some of the lakes of the Penobscot, either alone or with such company as I might pick up there. It is unusual to find a camp so far in the woods at that season, when lumbering operations have ceased, and I was glad to avail myself of the circumstance of a gang of men being employed there at that time in repairing the injuries caused by the great freshet in the spring. The mountain may be approached more easily and directly on horseback and on foot from the north-east side, by the Aroostook road, and the Wassataquoik river; but in that case you see much less of the wilderness, none of the glorious river and lake scenery, and have no experience of the batteau and the boatman's life. I was fortunate also in the season of the year, for in the summer myriads of black flies, mosquitoes, and midges, or, as the Indians call them, "no-see-ems," make travelling in the woods almost impossible; but now their reign was nearly over.

Ktaadn, whose name is an Indian word signifying highest land, was first ascended by white men in 1804. It was visited by Professor J. W. Bailey of West Point in 1836, by Dr. Charles T. Jackson, the State Geologist, in 1837, and by two young men from Boston in 1845. All these have given accounts of their expeditions. Since I was there, two or three other parties have made the excursion and told their stories. Besides these, very few, even among backwoodsmen and hunters, have ever climbed it, and it will be a long time before the tide of fashionable travel sets that way. The mountainous region of the State of Maine stretches from near the White Mountains, northeasterly one hundred and sixty miles, to the head of the Aroostook river, and is about sixty miles wide. The wild or unsettled portion is far more extensive. So that some hours only of travel in this direction will carry the curious to the verge of a primitive forest, more interesting, perhaps, on all accounts, than they would reach by going a thousand miles westward.

The next forenoon, Tuesday, Sept. 1st, I started with my companion in a buggy from Bangor for "up river," expecting to be overtaken the next day night, at Mattawamkeag Point, some sixty miles off, by two more Bangoreans, who had decided to join us in a trip to the mountain. We had each a knapsack or bag filled with such clothing and other articles as were indispensable, and my companion carried his gun.

Within a dozen miles of Bangor we passed through the villages of Stillwater and Oldtown, built at the falls of the Penobscot, which furnish the principal power by which the Maine woods are converted into lumber. The mills are built directly over and across the river. Here is a close jam, a hard rub, at all seasons; and then the once green tree, long since white, I need not say as the driven snow, but as a driven log, becomes lumber merely. Here your inch, your two and your three inch stuff begin to be, and Mr. Sawyer marks off those spaces which decide the destiny of so many prostrate forests. Through this steel riddle, more or less coarse, is the arrowy Maine forest, from Ktaadn and Chesuncook, and the head waters of the St. John, relentlessly sifted, till it comes out boards, clapboards, laths, and shingles such as the wind can take, still perchance to be slit and slit again, till men get a size that will suit. Think how stood the white-pine tree on the shore of Chesuncook, its branches soughing with the four winds, and every individual needle trembling in the sunlight—think how it stands with it now—sold, perchance to the New England Friction Match Company! There were in 1837, as I read, two hundred and fifty saw mills on the Penobscot and its tributaries above Bangor, the

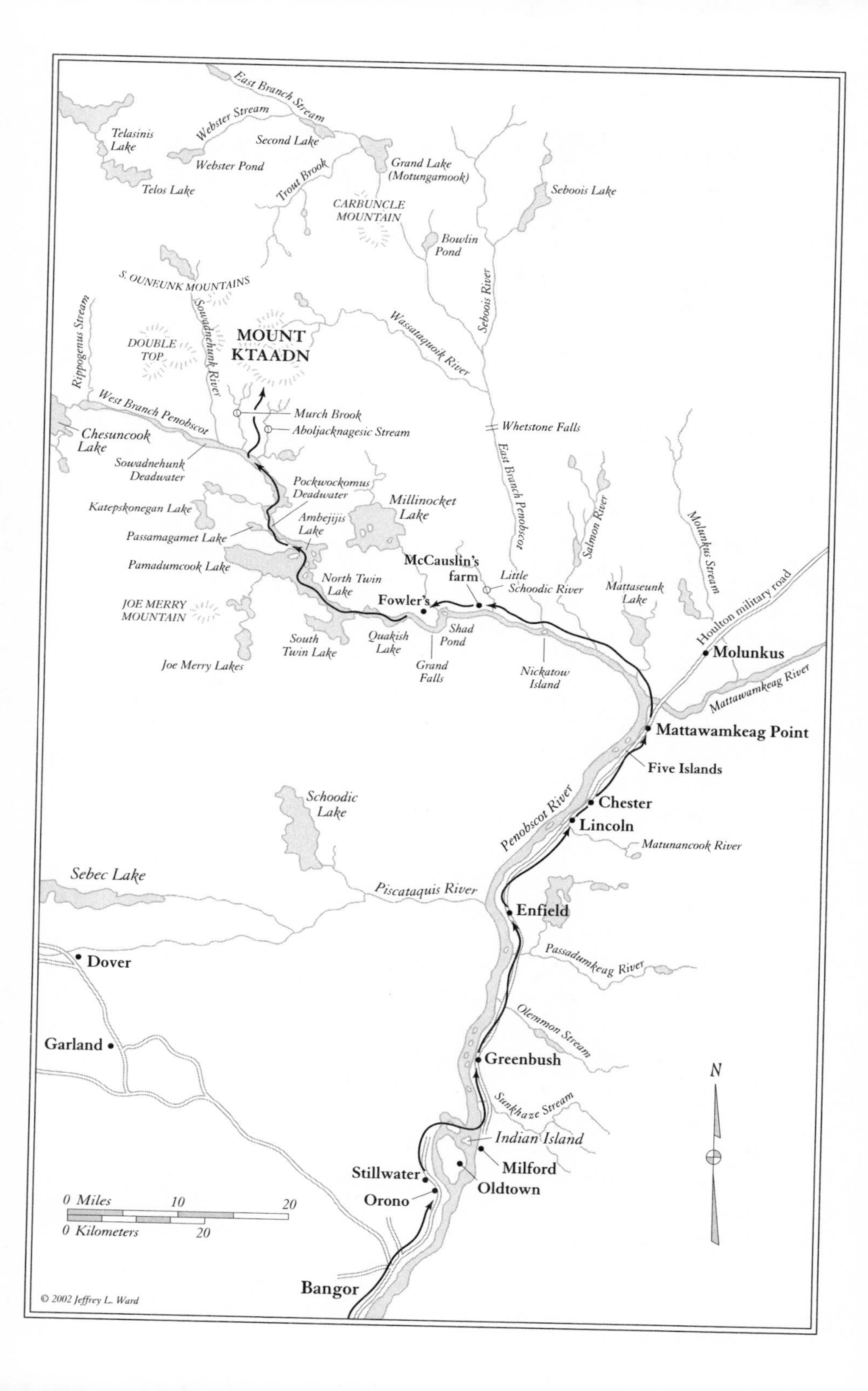
East Branch Stream
Webster Stream
Telasinis Lake
Second Lake
Webster Pond
Telos Lake
Trout Brook
Grand Lake (Motungamook)
Seboois Lake
CARBUNCLE MOUNTAIN
Bowlin Pond
S. OUNEUNK MOUNTAINS
Seboois River
Rippogenus Stream
Sowadnehunk River
Wassataquoik River
DOUBLE TOP
MOUNT KTAADN
West Branch Penobscot
Murch Brook
Aboljacknagesic Stream
Whetstone Falls
Chesuncook Lake
Sowadnehunk Deadwater
East Branch Penobscot
Pockwockomus Deadwater
Millinocket Lake
Katepskonegan Lake
Ambejijis Lake
Salmon River
Molunkus Stream
Passamagamet Lake
Pamadumcook Lake
McCauslin's farm
Little Schoodic River
North Twin Lake
Mattaseunk Lake
Houlton military road
JOE MERRY MOUNTAIN
Fowler's
Shad Pond
Quakish Lake
South Twin Lake
Molunkus
Joe Merry Lakes
Grand Falls
Nickatow Island
Mattawamkeag River
Mattawamkeag Point
Five Islands
Schoodic Lake
Penobscot River
Chester
Lincoln
Matunancook River
Sebec Lake
Piscataquis River
Enfield
Dover
Passadumkeag River
Olemmon Stream
Garland
Greenbush
N
Sunkhaze Stream
Indian Island
Milford
Stillwater
Oldtown
0 Miles
10
20
Orono
0 Kilometers
20
Bangor
© 2002 Jeffrey L. Ward

greater part of them in this immediate neighborhood, and they sawed two hundred millions of feet of boards annually. To this is to be added, the lumber of the Kennebeck, Androscoggin, Saco, Passamaquoddy, and other streams. No wonder that we hear so often of vessels which are becalmed off our coast, being surrounded a week at a time by floating lumber from the Maine woods. The mission of men there seems to be, like so many busy demons, to drive the forest all out of the country, from every solitary beaver swamp, and mountain side, as soon as possible.

At Oldtown we walked into a batteau manufactory. The making of batteaux is quite a business here for the supply of the Penobscot river. We examined some on the stocks. They are light and shapely vessels, calculated for rapid and rocky streams, and to be carried over long portages on men's shoulders, from twenty to thirty feet long, and only four or four and a half wide, sharp at both ends like a canoe, though broadest forward on the bottom, and reaching seven or eight feet over the water, in order that they may slip over rocks as gently as possible. They are made very slight, only two boards to a side, commonly secured to a few light maple or other hard-wood knees, but inward are of the clearest and widest white-pine stuff, of which there is a great waste on account of their form, for the bottom is left perfectly flat, not only from side to side, but from end to end. Sometimes they become "hogging" even, after long use, and the boatmen then turn them over and straighten them by a weight at each end. They told us that one wore out in two years, or often in a single trip, on the rocks, and sold for from fourteen to sixteen dollars. There was something refreshing and wildly musical to my ears in the very name of the white man's canoe, reminding me of Charlevoix and Canadian Voyageurs. The batteau is a sort of mongrel between the canoe and the boat, a fur-trader's boat.

The ferry here took us past the Indian island. As we left the shore, I observed a short shabby washerwoman-looking Indian; they commonly have the woebegone look of the girl that cried for spilt milk—just from "up river,"—land on the Oldtown side near a grocery, and drawing up his canoe, take out a bundle of skins in one hand, and an empty keg or half-barrel in the other, and scramble up the bank with them. This picture will do to put before the Indian's history, that is, the history of his extinction. In 1837, there were three hundred and sixty-two souls left of this tribe. The island seemed deserted to-day, yet I observed some new houses among the weather-stained ones, as if the tribe had still a design upon life; but generally they have a very shabby, forlorn, and cheerless look, being all back side and woodshed, not homesteads, even Indian homesteads, but instead of home or abroad-steads, for their life is *domi aut militiæ*, at home or at war, or now rather *venatus*, that is, a hunting, and most of the latter. The church is the only trim-looking building, but that is not Abenaki, that was Rome's doings. Good Canadian it may be, but it is poor Indian. These were once a powerful tribe. Politics are all the rage with them now. I even thought that a row of wigwams, with a dance of pow-wows, and a prisoner tortured at the stake, would be more respectable than this.

We landed in Milford, and rode along on the east side of the Penobscot, having a more or less constant view of the river, and the Indian islands in it, for they retain all the islands as far up as Nickatow, at the mouth of the East Branch. They are generally well-timbered, and are said to be better soil than the neighboring shores. The river seemed shallow and rocky, and interrupted by rapids, rippling and gleaming in the sun. We paused a moment to see a fish-hawk dive for a fish down straight as an arrow, from a great height, but he missed his prey this time. It was the Houlton Road on which we were now travelling, over which some troops were marched once towards Mars' Hill, though not to Mars' *field*, as it proved. It is the main, almost the only, road in these parts, as straight and well made, and kept in as good repair, as almost any you will find anywhere. Everywhere we saw signs of the great freshet—this house standing awry, and that where it was not founded, but where it was found, at any rate, the next day; and that other with a water-logged look, as if it were still airing and drying its basement, and logs with everybody's marks upon them, and sometimes the marks of their having served as bridges, strewn along the road. We crossed the Sunkhaze, a summery Indian name, the Olemmon, Passadumkeag, and other streams, which make a greater show on the map than they now did on the road. At Passadumkeag, we found anything but what the name implies, earnest politicians, to wit—white ones, I mean—on the alert, to know how the election was likely to go; men who talked rapidly, with subdued voice, and a sort of factitious earnestness, you could not help believing, hardly waiting for an introduction, one on each side of your buggy, endeavoring to say much in little, for they see you hold the whip impatiently, but always saying little in much. Caucuses they have had, it seems, and caucuses they are to have again—victory and defeat: somebody may be elected, somebody may not. One man, a total stranger, who stood by our carriage, in the dusk, actually frightened the horse with his asseverations, growing more solemnly positive as there was less in him to be positive about. So Passadumkeag did not look on the map. At sundown, leaving the river-road awhile for shortness, we went by way of Enfield, where we stopped for the night. This, like most of the localities bearing names on this road, was a place to name, which, in the midst of the unnamed and unincorporated wilderness, was to make a distinction without a difference, it seemed to me. Here, however, I noticed quite an orchard of healthy and well-grown apple trees, in a bearing state, it being the oldest settler's house in this region, but all natural fruit, and comparatively worthless for want of a grafter. And so it is generally lower down the river. It would be a good speculation, as well as a favor conferred on the settlers, for a Massachusetts boy to go down there with a trunk full of choice scions, and his grafting apparatus, in the spring.

The next morning we drove along through a high and hilly country, in view of Cold-Stream Pond, a beautiful lake, four or five miles long, and came into the Houlton road again, here called the Military road, at Lincoln, forty-five miles from Bangor, where there is quite a village, for this country—the principal one above Oldtown. Learning that there were several wigwams here, on one of the Indian islands, we left our horse and wagon, and walked through the forest half a mile, to the river, to procure a guide to the mountain. It was not till after considerable search that we discovered their habitations—small huts, in a retired place, where the scenery was unusually soft and beautiful, and the shore skirted with pleasant meadows and graceful elms. We paddled ourselves across to the island-side in a canoe, which we found on the shore. Near where we landed, sat an Indian girl, ten or twelve years old, on a rock in the water, in the sun, washing, and humming or moaning a song meanwhile. It was an aboriginal strain. A salmon-spear, made wholly of wood, lay on the shore, such as they might have used before white men came. It had an elastic piece of wood fastened to one side of its point, which slipped over and closed upon the fish, somewhat like the contrivance for holding a bucket at the end of a well-pole. As we walked up to the nearest house, we were met by a sally of a dozen wolfish-looking dogs, which may have been lineal descendants from the ancient Indian dogs, which the first voyageurs describe as "their wolves." I suppose they were. The occupant soon appeared, with a long pole in his hand, with which he beat off the dogs, while he parleyed with us. A stalwart, but dull and greasy-looking fellow, who told us, in his sluggish way, in answer to our questions, as if it were the first serious business he had to do that day, that there *were* Indians going "up river,"—he and one other—to-day, before noon. And who was the other? Louis Neptune, who lives in the next house. Well, let us go over and see Louis together. The same doggish reception, and Louis Neptune makes his appearance—a small, wiry man, with puckered and wrinkled face, yet he seemed the chief man of the two; the same, as I remembered, who had accompanied Jackson to the mountain in '37. The same questions were put to Louis, and the same information obtained, while the other Indian stood by. It appeared, that they were going to start by noon, with two canoes, to go up to Chesuncook, to hunt moose—to be gone a month. "Well, Louis, suppose you get to the Point, [to the Five Islands, just below Mattawamkeag,] to camp, we walk on up the West Branch to-morrow—four of us—and wait for you at the dam, or this side. You overtake us to-morrow or next day, and take us into your canoes. We stop for you, you stop for us. We pay you for your trouble." "Ye!" replied Louis, "may be you carry some provision for all—some pork—some bread—and so pay." He said, "Me sure get some moose;" and when I asked, if he thought Pomola would let us go up, he answered that we must plant one bottle of rum on the top, he had planted good many; and when he looked again, the rum was all gone. He had been up two or three times: he had planted letter—English, German, French, &c. These men were slightly clad in shirt and pantaloons, like laborers with us in warm weather. They did not invite us into their houses, but met us outside. So we left the Indians, thinking ourselves lucky to have secured such guides and companions.

There were very few houses along the road, yet they did not altogether fail, as if the law by which men are dispersed over the globe were a very stringent one, and not to be resisted with impunity or for slight reasons. There were even the germs of one or two villages just beginning to expand. The beauty of the road itself was remarkable. The various evergreens, many of which are rare with us—delicate and beautiful specimens of the larch, arbor-vitæ, ball spruce, and fir-balsam, from a few inches to many feet in height, lined its sides, in some places like a long front yard, springing up from the smooth grass-plots which uninterruptedly border it, and are made fertile by its wash; while it was but a step on either hand to the grim untrodden wilderness, whose tangled labyrinth of living, fallen, and decaying trees,—only the deer and moose, the bear and wolf, can easily penetrate. More perfect specimens than any front yard plot can show, grew there to grace the passage of the Houlton teams.

About noon we reached the Mattawamkeag, fifty-six miles from Bangor by the way we had come, and put up at a frequented house, still on the Houlton road, where the Houlton stage stops. Here was a substantial covered bridge over the Mattawamkeag, built, I think they said, some seventeen years before. We had dinner—where, by the way, and even at breakfast, as well as supper—at the public-houses on this road, the front rank is composed of various kinds of "sweet cakes," in a continuous line from one end of the table to the other. I think I may safely say that there was a row of ten or a dozen plates of this kind set before us two here. To account for which, they say, that when the lumberers come out of the woods, they have a craving for cakes and pies, and such sweet things, which there are almost unknown, and this is the *supply* to satisfy that *demand*—the supply is always equal to the demand,—and these hungry men think a good deal of getting their money's worth. No doubt, the balance of victuals is restored by the time they reach Bangor: Mattawamkeag takes off the raw edge. Well, over this front rank, I say, you coming from the "sweet cake" side, with a cheap philosophic indifference though it may be, have to assault what there is behind, which I do not by any means mean to insinuate is insufficient in quantity or quality to supply that other demand of men not from the woods, but from the towns, for venison and strong country fare. After dinner, we strolled down to the "Point," formed by the junction of the two rivers, which is said to be the scene of an ancient battle between the Eastern Indians and the Mohawks, and searched there carefully for relics, though the men at the barroom had never heard of such things; but we found only some flakes of arrow-head stone, some points of arrow-heads, one small leaden-bullet, and some colored beads, the last to be referred, perhaps, to early furtrader days. The Mattawamkeag, though wide, was a mere river's bed, full of rocks and shallows at this time, so that you could cross it almost dry-shod in boots; and I could hardly believe my companion, when he told me that he had been fifty or sixty miles up it in a batteau, through distant and still uncut forests. A batteau could hardly find a harbor now at its mouth. Deer, and caribou, or reindeer, are taken here in the winter, in sight of the house.

Before our companions arrived, we rode on up the Houlton road seven miles, to Molunkus, where the Aroostook road comes into it, and where there is a spacious public house in the woods, called the "Molunkus House," kept by one Libbey, which looked as if it had its hall for dancing and for military drills. There was no other evidence of man but this huge shingle palace in this part of the world; but sometimes even this is filled with travellers. I looked off the piazza round the corner of the house up the Aroostook road, on which there was no clearing in sight. There was a man just adventuring upon it this evening, in a rude, original, what you may call Aroostook, wagon—a mere seat, with a wagon swung under it, a few bags on it, and a dog asleep to watch them. He offered to carry a message for us to anybody in that country, cheerfully. I suspect, that if you should go to the end of the world, you would find somebody there going further, as if just starting for home at sundown, and having a last word before he drove off. Here, too, *was* a small trader, whom I did not see at first, who kept a store—but no great store, certainly—in a small box over the way, behind the Molunkus sign-post. It looked like the balance-box of a patent hay-scales. As for his house, we could only conjecture where that was; he may have been a boarder in the Molunkus House. I saw him standing in his shop-door—his shop was so small, that, if a traveller should make demonstrations of entering in, *he* would have to go out by the back way, and confer with his customer through a window, about his goods in the cellar, or, more probably, bespoken, and yet on the way. I should have gone in, for I felt a real impulse to trade, if I had not stopped to consider what would become of him. The day before, we had walked into a shop, over against an inn where we stopped, the puny beginning of trade, which would grow at last into a firm copartnership, in the future town or city—indeed, it was already "Somebody & Co.," I forget who. The woman came forward from the penetralia of the attached house, for "Somebody & Co." was in the burning, and she sold us percussion-caps, canalés and smooth; and knew their prices and qualities, and which the hunters preferred. Here was a little of everything in a small compass to satisfy the wants and the ambition of the woods, a stock selected with what pains and care, and brought home in the wagon box, or a corner of the Houlton team; but there seemed to me, as usual, a preponderance of children's toys, dogs to bark, and cats to mew, and trumpets to blow, where natives there hardly are yet. As if a child, born into the Maine woods, among the pine cones and cedar berries, could not do without such a sugar-man, or skipping-jack, as the young Rothschild has.

I think that there was not more than one house on the road to Molunkus, or for seven miles. At that place we got over the fence into a new field, planted with potatoes, where the logs were still burning between the hills; and, pulling up the vines, found good-sized potatoes, nearly ripe, growing like weeds, and turnips mixed with them. The mode of clearing and planting, is, to fell the trees, and burn once what will burn, then cut them up into suitable lengths, roll into heaps, and burn again; then, with a hoe, plant potatoes where you can come at the ground between the stumps and charred logs, for a first crop, the ashes sufficing for manure, and no hoeing being necessary the first year. In the fall, cut, roll, and burn again, and so on, till the land is cleared; and soon it is ready for grain, and to be laid down. Let those talk of poverty and hard times who will, in the towns and cities; cannot the emigrant, who can pay his fare to New-York or Boston, pay five dollars more to get here,—I paid three, all told, for my passage from Boston to Bangor, 250 miles,—and be as rich as he pleases, where land virtually costs nothing, and houses only the labor of building, and he may begin life as Adam did? If he will still remember the distinction of poor and rich, let him bespeak him a narrower house forthwith.

When we returned to the Mattawamkeag, the Houlton stage had already put up there; and a Province man was betraying his greenness to the Yankees by his questions.—Why Province money won't pass here at par, when States' money is good at Fredericton—though this, perhaps, was sensible enough. From what I saw then, it appeared that the Province man was now the only real Jonathan, or raw country bumpkin, left so far behind by his enterprising neighbors, that he didn't know enough to put a question to them. No people can long continue provincial in character, who have the propensity for politics and whittling, and rapid travelling, which the Yankees have, and who are leaving the mother country behind in the variety of their notions and inventions. The possession and exercise of practical talent merely, are a sure and rapid means of intellectual culture and independence.

The last edition of Greenleaf's Map of Maine hung on the wall here, and, as we had no pocket map, we resolved to trace a map of the lake country: so dipping a wad of tow into the lamp, we oiled a sheet of paper on the oiled table-cloth, and, in good faith, traced what we afterwards ascertained to be a labyrinth of errors, carefully following the outlines of the imaginary lakes which that map contains. The Map of the Public

Lands of Maine and Massachusetts is the only one I have seen that at all deserves the name. It was while we were engaged in this operation that our companions arrived. They had seen the Indians' fire on the Five Islands, and so we concluded that all was right.

Early the next morning we had mounted our packs, and prepared for a tramp up the West Branch, my companion having turned his horse out to pasture for a week or ten days, thinking that a bite of fresh grass, and a taste of running water, would do him as much good as backwoods fare, and new country influences his master. Leaping over a fence, we began to follow an obscure trail up the northern bank of the Penobscot. There was now no road further, the river being the only highway, and but half a dozen log huts confined to its banks, to be met with for thirty miles; on either hand, and beyond, was a wholly uninhabitated wilderness, stretching to Canada. Neither horse, nor cow, nor vehicle of any kind, had ever passed over this ground. The cattle, and the few bulky articles which the loggers use, being got up in the winter on the ice, and down again before it breaks up. The evergreen woods had a decidedly sweet and bracing fragrance; the air was a sort of diet-drink, and we walked on buoyantly in Indian file, stretching our legs. Occasionally there was a small opening on the bank, made for the purpose of log-rolling, where we got a sight of the river—always a rocky and rippling stream. The roar of the rapids, the note of a whistler-duck on the river, of the jay and chicadee around us, and of the pigeon-woodpecker in the openings, were the sounds that we heard. This was what you might call a bran new country; the only roads were of Nature's making, and the few houses were camps. Here, then, one could no longer accuse institutions and society, but must front the true source of evil.

There are three classes of inhabitants, who either frequent or inhabit the country which we had now entered; first, the loggers, who, for a part of the year, the winter and spring, are far the most numerous, but in the summer, except a few explorers for timber, completely desert it; second, the few settlers I have named, the only permanent inhabitants, who live on the verge of it, and help raise supplies for the former; third, the hunters, mostly Indians, who range over it in their season.

At the end of three miles we came to the Mattaseunk stream and mill, where there was even a rude wooden railroad running down to the Penobscot, the last railroad we were to see. We crossed one tract, on the bank of the river, of more than a hundred acres of heavy timber, which

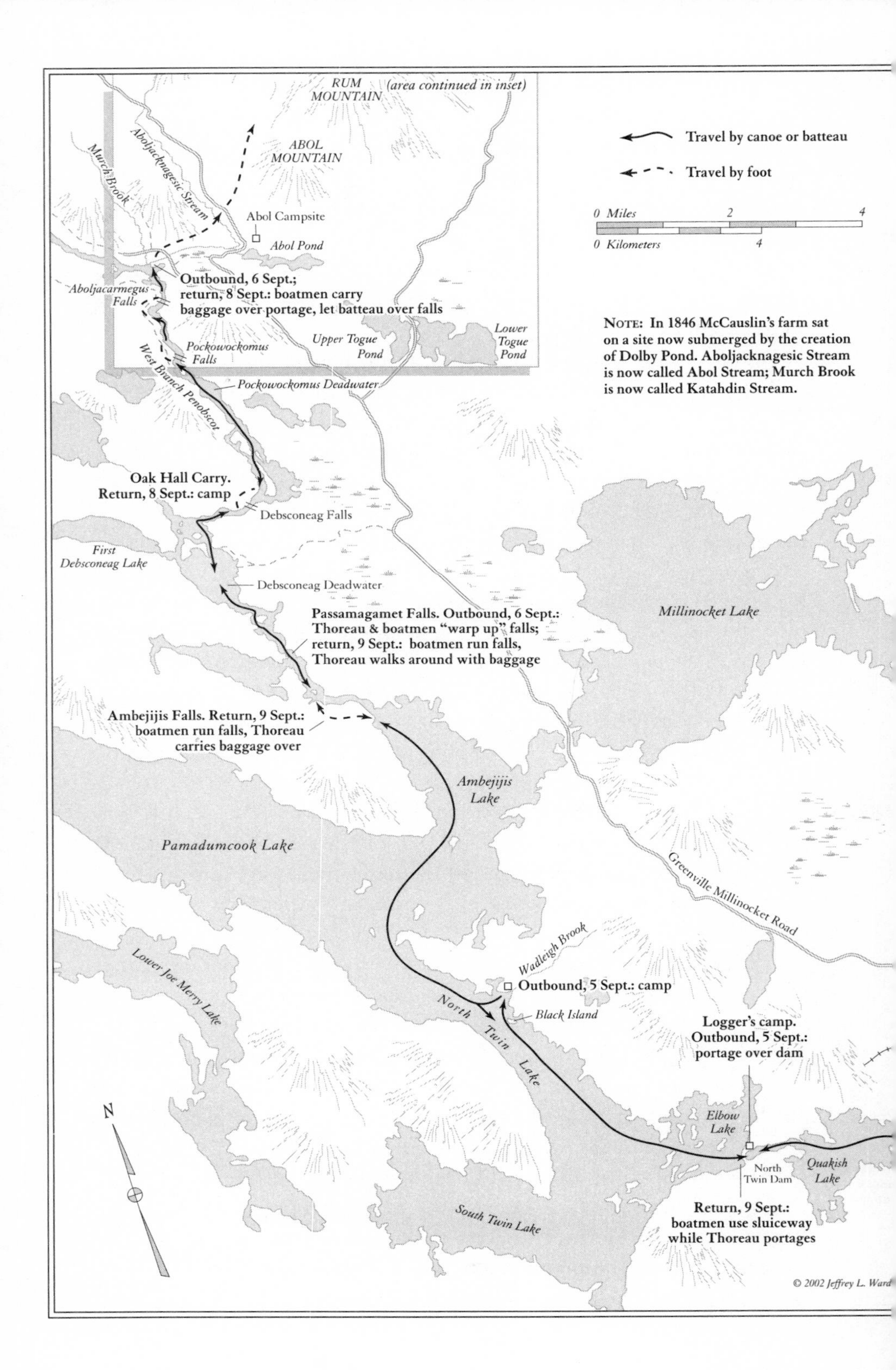

RUM MOUNTAIN
(area continued in inset)
ABOL MOUNTAIN
Travel by canoe or batteau
Travel by foot
0 Miles 2 4
0 Kilometers 4
Murch Brook
Aboljacknagesic Stream
Abol Campsite
Abol Pond
Outbound, 6 Sept.; return, 8 Sept.: boatmen carry baggage over portage, let batteau over falls
Aboljacarmegus Falls
Pockowockomus Falls
Upper Togue Pond
Lower Togue Pond
NOTE: In 1846 McCauslin's farm sat on a site now submerged by the creation of Dolby Pond. Aboljacknagesic Stream is now called Abol Stream; Murch Brook is now called Katahdin Stream.
West Branch Penobscot
Pockowockomus Deadwater
Oak Hall Carry. Return, 8 Sept.: camp
Debsconeag Falls
First Debsconeag Lake
Debsconeag Deadwater
Millinocket Lake
Passamagamet Falls. Outbound, 6 Sept.: Thoreau & boatmen "warp up" falls; return, 9 Sept.: boatmen run falls, Thoreau walks around with baggage
Ambejijis Falls. Return, 9 Sept.: boatmen run falls, Thoreau carries baggage over
Ambejijis Lake
Pamadumcook Lake
Greenville Millinocket Road
Wadleigh Brook
Outbound, 5 Sept.: camp
Black Island
North Twin Lake
Lower Joe Merry Lake
Logger's camp. Outbound, 5 Sept.: portage over dam
Elbow Lake
North Twin Dam
Quakish Lake
N
South Twin Lake
Return, 9 Sept.: boatmen use sluiceway while Thoreau portages
© 2002 Jeffrey L. Ward

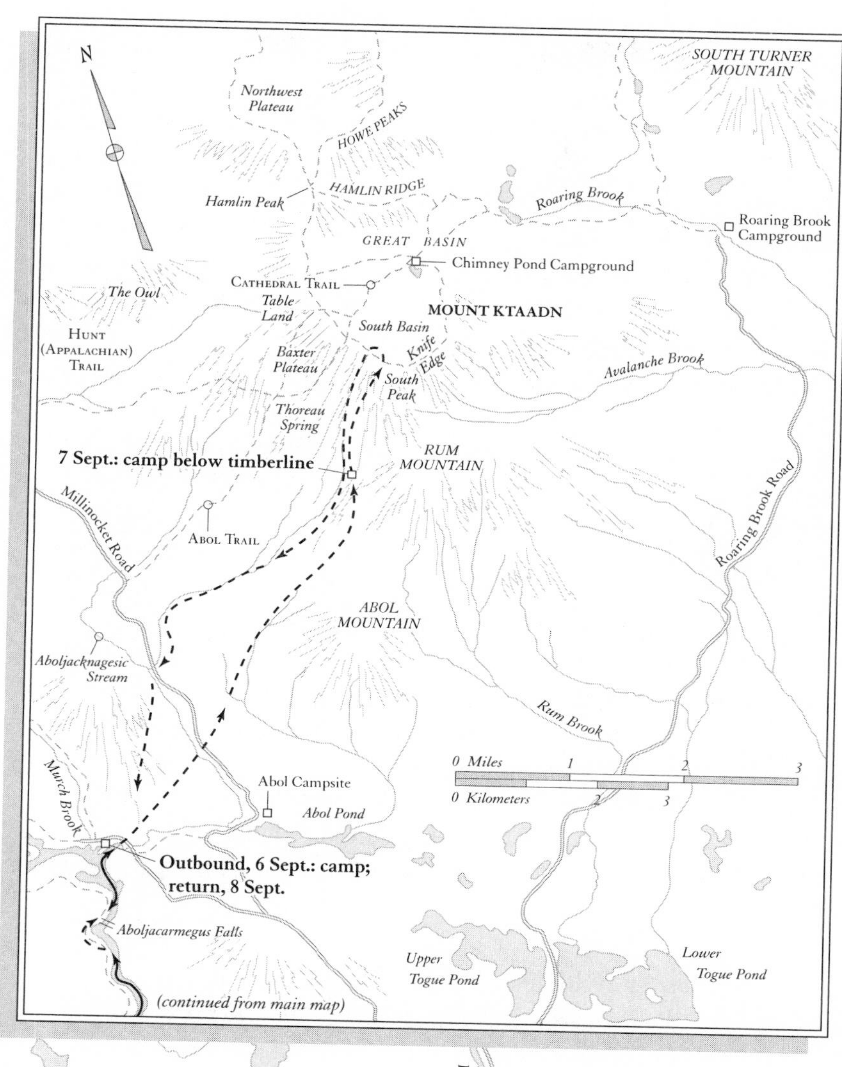
N
Northwest
Plateau
HOWE PEAKS
SOUTH TURNER
MOUNTAIN
Hamlin Peak
HAMLIN RIDGE
Roaring Brook
Roaring Brook
Campground
GREAT BASIN
Chimney Pond Campground
Cathedral Trail
The Owl
Table
Land
MOUNT KTAADN
Hunt
(Appalachian)
Trail
South Basin
Knife
Edge
Baxter
Plateau
South
Peak
Avalanche Brook
Thoreau
Spring
7 Sept.: camp below timberline
RUM
MOUNTAIN
Millinocket Road
Abol Trail
Roaring Brook Road
ABOL
MOUNTAIN
Aboljacknagesic
Stream
Rum Brook
0 Miles
1
2
3
0 Kilometers
2
3
Murch Brook
Abol Campsite
Abol Pond
Outbound, 6 Sept.: camp;
return, 8 Sept.
Aboljacarmegus Falls
Upper
Togue Pond
Lower
Togue Pond
(continued from main map)

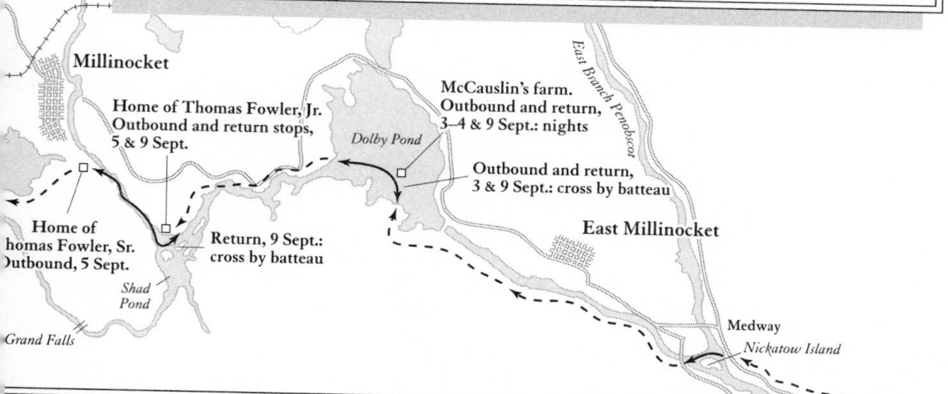
Millinocket
East Branch Penobscot
Home of Thomas Fowler, Jr.
Outbound and return stops,
5 & 9 Sept.
McCauslin's farm.
Outbound and return,
3–4 & 9 Sept.: nights
Dolby Pond
Outbound and return,
3 & 9 Sept.: cross by batteau
Home of
homas Fowler, Sr.
utbound, 5 Sept.
Return, 9 Sept.:
cross by batteau
East Millinocket
Shad
Pond
Medway
Nickatow Island
Grand Falls

had just been felled and burnt over, and was still smoking. Our trail lay through the midst of it, and was well nigh blotted out. The trees lay at full length, four or five feet deep, and crossing each other in all directions, all black as charcoal, but perfectly sound within, still good for fuel or for timber; soon they would be cut into lengths and burnt again. Here were thousands of cords, enough to keep the poor of Boston and New-York amply warm for a winter, which only cumbered the ground, and were in the settler's way. And the whole of that solid and interminable forest is doomed to be gradually devoured thus by fire, like shavings, and no man be warmed by it. At Crocker's log hut, at the mouth of Salmon River, seven miles from the Point, one of the party commenced distributing a store of small cent picture-books among the children, to teach them to read; and also newspapers, more or less recent, among the parents, than which nothing can be more acceptable to a backwoods people. It was really an important item in our outfit, and, at times, the only currency that would circulate. I walked through Salmon River with my shoes on, it being low water, but not without wetting my feet. A few miles further we came to "Marm Howard's," at the end of an extensive clearing, where there were two or three log huts in sight at once, one on the opposite side of the river, and a few graves, even surrounded by a wooden paling, where already the rude forefathers of *a* hamlet lie; and a thousand years hence, perchance, some poet will write his "Elegy in a Country Churchyard." The "Village Hampdens," the "mute, inglorious Miltons," and Cromwells, "guiltless of" their "country's blood," were yet unborn.

> "Perchance in this *wild* spot *there will be* laid
> Some heart once pregnant with celestial fire;
> Hands that the rod of empire might have swayed,
> Or waked to ecstasy the living lyre."

The next house was Fisk's, ten miles from the Point, at the mouth of the East Branch, opposite to the island Nickatow, or the Forks, the last of the Indian islands. I am particular to give the names of the settlers and the distances, since every log hut in these woods is a public house, and such information is of no little consequence to those who may have occasion to travel this way. Our course here crossed the Penobscot, and followed the the southern bank. One of the party, who entered the house in search of some one to set us over, reported a very neat dwelling, with plenty of books, and a new wife, just imported from Boston, wholly new to the woods. We found the East Branch a large and rapid stream at its mouth, and much deeper than it appeared. Having with some difficulty discovered the trail again, we kept up the south side of the West Branch, or main river, passing by some rapids called Rock-Ebeeme, the roar of which we heard through the woods, and, shortly after, in the thickest of the wood, some empty loggers' camps, still new, which were occupied the previous winter. Though we saw a few more afterwards, I will make one account serve for all. These were such houses as the lumberers of Maine spend the winter in, in the wilderness. There were the camps and the hovel for the cattle, hardly distinguishable, except that the latter had no chimney. These camps were about twenty feet long by fifteen wide, built of logs—hemlock, cedar, spruce, or yellow birch—one kind alone, or all together, with the bark on; two or three large ones first, one directly above another, and notched together at the ends, to the height of three or four feet, then of smaller logs resting upon transverse ones at the ends, each of the last successively shorter than the other, to form the roof. The chimney was an oblong square hole in the middle, three or four feet in diameter, with a fence of logs as high as the ridge. The interstices were filled with moss, and the roof was shingled with long and handsome splints of cedar, or spruce, or pine, rifted with a sledge and cleaver. The fire-place, the most important place of all, was in shape and size like the chimney, and directly under it, defined by a log fence or fender on the ground, and a heap of ashes a foot or two deep within, with solid benches of split logs running round it. Here the fire usually melts the snow, and dries the rain before it can descend to quench it. The faded beds of arbor-vitæ leaves extended under the eaves on either hand. There was the place for the water-pail, pork-barrel, and wash-basin, and generally a dingy pack of cards left on a log. Usually a good deal of whittling was expended on the latch, which was made of wood, in the form of an iron one. These houses are made comfortable by the huge fires that can be afforded night and day. Usually the scenery about them is drear and savage enough; and the logger's camp is as completely in the woods as a fungus at the foot of a pine in a swamp; no outlook but to the sky overhead; no more clearing than is made by cutting down the trees of which it is built, and those which are necessary for fuel. If only it be well sheltered and convenient to his work, and near a spring, he wastes no thought on the prospect. They are very proper forest houses, the stems of the trees collected together and piled up around a man to keep out wind and rain: made of living green logs, hanging with moss and lichen, and with the curls and fringes of the yellow-birch bark, and dripping with resin, fresh and moist, and redolent of swampy odors, with that sort of vigor and perennialness even about them that toad-stools suggest.* The logger's fare consists of tea, molasses, flour, pork,—sometimes beef,—and beans. A great proportion of the beans raised in Massachusetts find their market here. On expeditions it is only hard bread and pork, often raw, slice upon slice, with tea or water, as the case may be.

The primitive wood is always and everywhere damp and mossy, so that I travelled constantly with the impression that I was in a swamp; and only when it was remarked that this or that tract, judging from the quality of the timber on it, would make a profitable clearing, was I reminded, that if the sun were let in it would make a dry field, like the few I had seen, at once. The best shod for the most part travel with wet feet. If the ground was so wet and spongy at this, the driest part of a dry season, what must it be in the spring? The woods hereabouts abounded in beech and yellow-birch, of which last there were some very large specimens; also spruce, cedar, fir, and hemlock; but we saw only the stumps of the white pine here, some of them of great size, these having been already culled out, being the only tree much sought after, even as low down as this. Only a little spruce and hemlock beside had been logged here. The eastern wood, which is sold for fuel in Massachusetts, all comes from below Bangor. It was the pine alone, chiefly the white pine, that had tempted any but the hunter to precede us on this route.

Waite's farm, thirteen miles from the Point, is an extensive and elevated clearing, from which we got a fine view of the river, rippling and gleaming far beneath us. My companions had formerly had a good view of Ktaadn and the other mountains here, but to-day it was so smoky that

*Springer, in his "Forest Life" (1851), says that they first remove the leaves and turf from the spot where they intend to build a camp, for fear of fire; also, that "the spruce-tree is generally selected for camp-building, it being light, straight, and quite free from sap;" that "the roof is finally covered with the boughs of the fir, spruce, and hemlock, so that when the snow falls upon the whole, the warmth of the camp is preserved in the coldest weather;" and that they make the log seat before the fire, called the "Deacon's Seat," of a spruce or fir split in halves, with three or four stout limbs left on one side for legs, which are not likely to get loose.

we could see nothing of them. We could overlook an immense country of uninterrupted forest, stretching away up the East Branch toward Canada, on the north and northwest, and toward the Aroostook valley on the northeast: and imagine what wild life was stirring in its midst. Here was quite a field of corn for this region, whose peculiar dry scent we perceived a third of a mile off before we saw it.

Eighteen miles from the Point brought us in sight of McCauslin's, or "Uncle George's," as he was familiarly called by my companions, to whom he was well known, where we intended to break our long fast. His house was in the midst of an extensive clearing of intervale, at the mouth of the Little Schoodic River, on the opposite or north bank of the Penobscot. So we collected on a point of the shore, that we might be seen, and fired our gun as a signal, which brought out his dogs forthwith, and thereafter their master, who in due time took us across in his batteau. This clearing was bounded abruptly on all sides but the river, by the naked stems of the forest, as if you were to cut only a few feet square in the midst of a thousand acres of mowing, and set down a thimble therein. He had a whole heaven and horizon to himself, and the sun seemed to be journeying over his clearing only, the live-long day. Here we concluded to spend the night, and wait for the Indians, as there was no stopping place so convenient above. He had seen no Indians pass, and this did not often happen without his knowledge. He thought that his dogs sometimes gave notice of the approach of Indians, half an hour before they arrived.

McCauslin was a Kennebec man, of Scotch descent, who had been a waterman twenty-two years, and had driven on the lakes and head waters of the Penobscot five or six springs in succession, but was now settled here to raise supplies for the lumberers and for himself. He entertained us a day or two with true Scotch hospitality, and would accept no recompense for it. A man of a dry wit and shrewdness, and a general intelligence which I had not looked for in the backwoods. In fact, the deeper you penetrate into the woods, the more intelligent, and, in one sense, less countrified do you find the inhabitants; for always the pioneer has been a traveller, and, to some extent, a man of the world; and, as the distances with which he is familiar are greater, so is his information more general and far reaching than the villager's. If I were to look for a narrow, uninformed, and countrified mind, as opposed to the intelligence and refinement which are thought to emanate from cities, it would be among the rusty inhabitants of an old-settled country, on farms all run out and gone to seed with life-ever-lasting, in the towns about Boston, even on the high road in Concord, and not in the backwoods of Maine.

Supper was got before our eyes, in the ample kitchen, by a fire which would have roasted an ox; many whole logs, four feet long, were consumed to boil our tea-kettle—birch, or beech, or maple, the same summer and winter; and the dishes were soon smoking on the table, late the arm-chair, against the wall, from which one of the party was expelled. The arms of the chair formed the frame on which the table rested; and, when the round top was turned up against the wall, it formed the back of the chair, and was no more in the way than the wall itself. This, we noticed, was the prevailing fashion in these log houses, in order to economize in room. There were piping hot wheaten-cakes, the flour having been brought up the river in batteaux,—no Indian bread, for the upper part of Maine, it will be remembered, is a wheat country,—and ham, eggs, and potatoes, and milk and cheese, the produce of the farm; and, also, shad and salmon, tea sweetened with molasses, and sweet cakes in contradistinction to the hot cakes not sweetened, the one white, the other yellow, to wind up with. Such, we found, was the prevailing fare, ordinary and extraordinary, along this river. Mountain cranberries (*Vaccinium Vitis-Idæa*), stewed and sweetened, were the common dessert. Everything here was in profusion, and the best of its kind. Butter was in such plenty, that it was commonly used, before it was salted, to grease boots with.

In the night we were entertained by the sound of rain-drops on the cedar splints which covered the roof, and awaked the next morning with a drop or two in our eyes. It had set in for a storm, and we made up our minds not to forsake such comfortable quarters with this prospect, but wait for Indians and fair weather. It rained and drizzled, and gleamed by turns, the live-long day. What we did there, how we killed the time, would, perhaps, be idler to tell; how many times we buttered our boots, and how often a drowsy one was seen to sidle off to the bedroom. When it held up, I strolled up and down the bank and gathered the harebell and cedar berries, which grew there; or else we tried by turns the long-handled axe on the logs before the door. The axe-helves here were made to chop standing on the log—a primitive log of course—and were, therefore, nearly a foot longer than with us. One while we walked over the farm, and visited his well-filled barns with McCauslin. There were one other man and two women only here. He kept horses, cows, oxen, and sheep. I think he said that he was the first to bring a plough and a cow so far; and, he might have added, the last, with only two exceptions. The potato rot had found him out here, too, the previous year, and got half or two-thirds of his crop, though the seed was of his own raising. Oats, grass, and potatoes, were his staples; but he raised, also, a few carrots and turnips, and "a little corn for the hens," for this was all that he dared risk, for fear that it would not ripen. Melons, squashes, sweet-corn, beans, tomatoes, and many other vegetables, could not be ripened there.

The very few settlers along this stream were obviously tempted by the cheapness of the land mainly. When I asked McCauslin why more settlers did not come in, he answered, that one reason was, they could not buy the land, it belonged to individuals or companies who were afraid that their wild lands would be settled, and so incorporated into towns, and they be taxed for them; but to settling on the States' land there was no such hinderance. For his own part, he wanted no neighbors—he didn't wish to see any road by his house. Neighbors, even the best, were a trouble and expense, especially on the score of cattle and fences. They might live across the river, perhaps, but not on the same side.

The chickens here were protected by the dogs. As McCauslin said, "The old one took it up first, and she taught the pup, and now they had got it into their heads that it wouldn't do to have anything of the bird kind on the premises." A hawk hovering over was not allowed to alight, but barked off by the dogs circling underneath; and a pigeon, or a "yellow hammer," as they called the pigeon-woodpecker, on a dead limb or stump, was instantly expelled. It was the main business of their day, and kept them constantly coming and going. One would rush out of the house on the least alarm given by the other.

When it rained hardest, we returned to the house, and took down a tract from the shelf. There was the Wandering Jew, cheap edition, and fine print, the Criminal Calendar, and Parish's Geography, and flash novels two or three. Under the pressure of circumstances, we read a little in these. With such aid, the press is not so feeble an engine after all. This house, which was a fair specimen of those on this river, was built of huge logs, which peeped out everywhere, and were chinked with clay and moss. It contained four or five rooms. There were no sawed boards, or shingles, or clapboards, about it; and scarcely any tool but the axe had been used in its construction. The partitions were made of long clapboard-like splints, of spruce or cedar, turned to a delicate salmon color by the smoke. The roof and sides were covered with the same, instead of shingles and clapboards, and some of a much thicker and larger size were used for the floor. These were all so straight and smooth, that they answered the purpose admirably; and a careless observer would not have suspected that they were not sawed and planed. The chimney and hearth were of vast size, and made of stone. The broom was a few twigs of arbor-vitæ tied to a stick; and a pole was suspended over the hearth, close to the ceiling, to dry stockings and clothes on. I noticed that the floor was full of small, dingy holes, as if made with a gimlet, but which were, in fact, made by the spikes, nearly an inch long, which the lumberers wear in their boots to prevent their slipping on wet logs. Just above McCauslin's, there is a rocky rapid, where logs jam in the spring; and many "drivers" are there collected, who frequent his house for supplies: these were their tracks which I saw.

At sundown, McCauslin pointed away over the forest, across the river, to signs of fair weather amid the clouds—some evening redness there. For even there the points of compass held and there was a quarter of the heavens appropriated to sunrise and another to sunset.

The next morning, the weather proving fair enough for our purpose, we prepared to start; and, the Indians having failed us, persuaded McCauslin, who was not unwilling to re-visit the scenes of his driving, to accompany us in their stead, intending to engage one other boatman on the way. A strip of cotton-cloth for a tent, a couple of blankets, which would suffice for the whole party, fifteen pounds of hard bread, ten pounds of "clear" pork, and a little tea, made up "Uncle George's" pack. The last three articles were calculated to be provision enough for six men for a week, with what we might pick up. A tea-kettle, a frying-pan and an axe, to be obtained at the last house, would complete our outfit.

We were soon out of McCauslin's clearing, and in the ever-green woods again. The obscure trail made by the two settlers above, which even the woodman is sometimes puzzled to discern, ere long crossed a narrow open strip in the woods overrun with weeds, called the Burnt Land, where a fire had raged formerly, stretching northward nine or ten miles, to Millinocket Lake. At the end of three miles we reached Shad Pond, or Noliseemack, an expansion of the river. Hodge, the Assistant State Geologist, who passed through this on the twenty-fifth of June, 1837, says, "We pushed our boat through an acre or more of buck-beans, which had taken root at the bottom, and bloomed above the surface in the greatest profusion and beauty." Thomas Fowler's house is four miles from McCauslin's, on the shore of the Pond, at the mouth of the Millinocket River, and eight miles from the lake of the same name, on the latter stream. This lake affords a more direct course to Ktaadn, but we preferred to follow the Penobscot and the Pamadumcook Lakes. Fowler was just completing a new log hut, and was sawing out a window through the logs nearly two feet thick when we arrived. He had begun to paper his house with spruce bark, turned inside out, which had a good effect, and was in keeping with the circumstances. Instead of water we got here a draught of beer, which, it was allowed, would be better; clear and thin, but strong and stringent as the cedar sap. It was as if we sucked at the very teats of Nature's pine-clad bosom in these parts—the sap of all Millinocket botany commingled—the topmost most fantastic and spiciest sprays of the primitive wood, and whatever invigorating and stringent gum or essence it afforded, steeped and dissolved in it—a lumberer's drink, which would acclimate and naturalize a man at once—which would make him see green, and, if he slept, dream that he heard the wind sough among the pines. Here was a fife, praying to be played on, through which we breathed a few tuneful strains,—brought hither to tame wild beasts. As we stood upon the pile of chips by the door, fish-hawks were sailing over head; and here, over Shad Pond, might daily be witnessed, the tyranny of the bald-eagle over that bird. Tom pointed away over the Lake to a bald-eagle's nest, which was plainly visible more than a mile off, on a pine, high above the surrounding forest, and was frequented from year to year by the same pair, and held sacred by him. There were these two houses only there, his low hut, and the eagles' airy cart-load of fagots. Thomas Fowler, too, was persuaded to join us, for two men were necessary to manage the batteau, which was soon to be our carriage, and these men needed to be cool and skilful for the navigation of the Penobscot. Tom's pack was soon made, for he had not far to look for his waterman's boots, and a red flannel shirt. This is the favorite color with lumbermen; and red flannel is reputed to possess some mysterious virtues, to be most healthful and convenient in respect to perspiration. In every gang there will be a large proportion of red birds. We took here a poor and leaky batteau, and began to pole up the Millinocket two miles, to the elder Fowler's, in order to avoid the Grand Falls of the Penobscot, intending to exchange our batteau there for a better. The Millinocket is a small, shallow and sandy stream, full of what I took to be lamprey-eels' or suckers' nests, and lined with musquash cabins, but free from rapids, according to Fowler, excepting at its outlet from the Lake. He was at this time engaged in cutting the native grass—rush grass and meadow-clover, as he called it—on the meadows and small, low islands, of this stream. We noticed flattened places in the grass on either side, where, he said, a moose had lain down the night before, adding, that there were thousands in these meadows.

Old Fowler's, on the Millinocket, six miles from McCauslin's, and twenty-four from the Point, is the last house. Gibson's, on the Sowadnehunk, is the only clearing above, but that had proved a failure, and was long since deserted. Fowler is the oldest inhabitant of these woods. He formerly lived a few miles from here, on the south side of the West Branch, where he built his house sixteen years ago, the first house built above the Five Islands. Here our new batteau was to be carried over the first portage of two miles, round the Grand Falls of the Penobscot, on a horse-sled made of saplings, to jump the numerous rocks in the way, but we had to wait a couple of hours for them to catch the horses, which were pastured at a distance, amid the stumps, and had wandered still further off. The last of the salmon for this season had just been caught, and were still fresh in pickle, from which enough was extracted to fill our empty kettle, and so graduate our introduction to simpler forest fare. The week before, they had lost nine sheep here out of their first flock, by the wolves. The surviving sheep came round the house, and seemed frightened, which induced them to go and look for the rest, when they found seven dead and lacerated, and two still alive. These last they carried to the house, and, as Mrs. Fowler said, they were merely scratched in the throat, and had no more visible wound than would be produced by the prick of a pin. She sheared off the wool from their throats, and washed them and put on some salve, and turned them out, but in a few moments they were missing, and had not been found since. In fact, they were all poisoned, and those that were found swelled up at once, so that they saved neither skin nor wool. This realized the old fables of the wolves and the sheep, and convinced me that that ancient hostility still existed. Verily, the shepherd boy did not need to sound a false alarm this time. There were steel traps by the door of various sizes, for wolves, otter, and bears, with large claws instead of teeth, to catch in their sinews. Wolves are frequently killed with poisoned bait.

At length, after we had dined here on the usual backwoods fare, the horses arrived, and we hauled our batteau out of the water, and lashed it to its wicker carriage, and, throwing in our packs, walked on before, leaving the boatmen and driver, who was Tom's brother, to manage the concern. The route, which led through the wild pasture where the sheep were killed, was in some places the roughest ever travelled by horses, over rocky hills, where the sled bounced and slid along, like a vessel pitching in a storm; and one man was as necessary to stand at the stern, to prevent the boat from being wrecked, as a helmsman in the roughest sea. The philosophy of our progress was something like this: when the runners struck a rock three or four feet high, the sled bounced back and upwards at the same time; but, as the horses never ceased pulling, it came down on the top of the rock, and so we got over. This portage probably followed the trail of an ancient Indian carry round these falls. By 2 o'clock we, who had walked on before, reached the river above the falls, not far from the outlet of Quakish Lake, and waited for the batteau to come up. We had been here but a short time, when a thunder-shower was seen coming up from the west, over the still invisible lakes, and that pleasant wilderness which we were so eager to become acquainted with; and soon the heavy drops began to patter on the leaves around us. I had just selected the prostrate trunk of a huge pine, five or six feet in diameter, and was crawling under it, when, luckily, the boat arrived. It would have amused a sheltered man to witness the manner in which it was unlashed, and whirled over, while the first water-spout burst upon us. It was no sooner in the hands of the eager company than it was abandoned to the first revolutionary impulse, and to gravity, to adjust it; and they might have been seen all stooping to its shelter, and wriggling under like so many eels, before it was fairly deposited on the ground. When all were under, we propped up the lee side, and busied ourselves there, whittling thole pins for rowing, when we should reach the lakes; and made the woods ring, between the claps of thunder, with such boat-songs as we could remember. The horses stood sleek and shining with the rain, all drooping and crestfallen, while deluge after deluge washed over us; but the bottom of a boat may be relied on for a tight roof. At length, after two hours' delay at this place, a streak of fair weather appeared in the northwest, whither our course now lay, promising a serene evening for our voyage; and the driver returned with his horses, while we made haste to launch our boat, and commence our voyage in good earnest.

There were six of us, including the two boatmen. With our packs heaped up near the bows, and ourselves disposed as baggage to trim the boat, with instructions not to move in case we should strike a rock, more than so many barrels of pork, we pushed out into the first rapid, a slight specimen of the stream we had to navigate. With Uncle George in the stern, and Tom in the bows, each using a spruce pole about twelve feet long, pointed with iron,* and poling on the same side, we shot up the rapids like a salmon, the water rushing and roaring around, so that only a practised eye could distinguish a safe course, or tell what was deep water and what rocks, frequently grazing the latter on one or both sides, with a hundred as narrow escapes as ever the Argo had in passing through the Symplegades. I, who had had some experience in boating, had never experienced any half so exhilarating before. We were lucky to have exchanged our Indians, whom we did not know, for these men, who, together with Tom's brother, were reputed the best boatmen on the river, and were at once indispensable pilots and pleasant companions. The canoe is smaller, more easily upset, and sooner worn out; and the Indian is said not to be so skilful in the management of the batteau. He is, for the most part, less to be relied on, and more disposed to sulks and whims. The utmost familiarity with dead streams, or with the ocean, would not prepare a man for this peculiar navigation; and the most skilful boatman anywhere else would here be obliged to take out his boat and carry round a hundred times, still with great risk, as well as delay, where the practised batteau man poles up with comparative ease and safety. The hardy "voyageur" pushes with incredible perseverance and success quite up to the foot of the falls, and then only carries round some perpendicular ledge, and launches again in "the torrent's smoothness, ere it dash below," to struggle with the boiling rapids above. The Indians say, that the river once ran both ways, one half up and the other down, but, that since the white man came, it all runs down, and now they must laboriously pole their canoes against the stream, and carry them over numerous portages. In the summer, all stores, the grindstone and the plough of the pioneer, flour, pork, and utensils for the explorer, must be conveyed up the river in batteaux; and many a cargo and many a boatman is lost in these waters. In the winter, however, which is very equable and long, the ice is the great highway, and the loggers' team penetrates to Chesuncook

*The Canadians call it *picquer de fond.*

Lake, and still higher up, even two hundred miles above Bangor. Imagine the solitary sled-track running far up into the snowy and evergreen wilderness, hemmed in closely for a hundred miles by the forest, and again stretching straight across the broad surfaces of concealed lakes!

We were soon in the smooth water of the Quakish Lake, and took our turns at rowing and paddling across it. It is a small, irregular, but handsome lake, shut in on all sides by the forest, and showing no traces of man but some low boom in a distant cove, reserved for spring use. The spruce and cedar on its shores, hung with gray lichens, looked at a distance like the ghosts of trees. Ducks were sailing here and there on its surface, and a solitary loon, like a more living wave—a vital spot on the lake's surface—laughed and frolicked, and showed its straight leg, for our amusement. Joe Merry Mountain appeared in the northwest, as if it were looking down on this lake especially; and we had our first, but a partial view of Ktaadn, its summit veiled in clouds, like a dark isthmus in that quarter, connecting the heavens with the earth. After two miles of smooth rowing across this lake, we found ourselves in the river again, which was a continuous rapid for one mile, to the dam, requiring all the strength and skill of our boatmen to pole up it.

This dam is a quite important and expensive work for this country, whither cattle and horses cannot penetrate in the summer, raising the whole river ten feet, and flooding, as they said, some sixty square miles by means of the innumerable lakes with which the river connects. It is a lofty and solid structure, with sloping piers some distance above, made of frames of logs filled with stones, to break the ice.* Here every log pays toll as it passes through the sluices.

We filed into the rude loggers' camp at this place, such as I have described, without ceremony, and the cook, at that moment the sole occupant, at once set about preparing tea for his visitors. His fire-place, which the rain had converted into a mud-puddle, was soon blazing again, and we sat down on the log benches around it to dry us. On the well-flattened, and somewhat faded beds of arbor-vitæ leaves, which stretched on either hand under the eaves behind us, lay an odd leaf of the Bible, some genealogical chapter out of the Old Testament; and, half buried by

*Even the Jesuit missionaries, accustomed to the St. Lawrence and other rivers of Canada, in their first expeditions to the Abnaquiois, speak of rivers *ferrées de rochers*, shod with rocks. See also No. 10 Relations, for 1647, p. 185.

the leaves, we found Emerson's Address on West India Emancipation, which had been left here formerly by one of our company; and *had made two converts to the Liberty party here*, as I was told; also, an odd number of the Westminster Review, for 1834, and a pamphlet entitled History of the Erection of the Monument on the Grave of Myron Holley. This was the readable, or reading matter, in a lumberer's camp in the Maine woods, thirty miles from a road, which would be given up to the bears in a fortnight. These things were well thumbed and soiled. This gang was headed by one John Morrison, a good specimen of a Yankee; and was necessarily composed of men not bred to the business of dam-building, but who were Jacks-at-all-trades, handy with the axe, and other simple implements, and well skilled in wood and water craft. We had hot cakes for our supper even here, white as snow-balls, but without butter, and the never-failing sweet cakes, with which we filled our pockets, foreseeing that we should not soon meet with the like again. Such delicate puffballs seemed a singular diet for backwoodsmen. There was also tea without milk, sweetened with molasses. And so, exchanging a word with John Morrison and his gang when we had returned to the shore, and also exchanging our batteau for a better still, we made haste to improve the little daylight that remained. This camp, exactly twenty-nine miles from Mattawamkeag Point, by the way we had come, and about one hundred from Bangor by the river, was the last human habitation of any kind in this direction. Beyond, there was no trail; and the river and lakes, by batteaux and canoes, was considered the only practicable route. We were about thirty miles by the river from the summit of Ktaadn, which was in sight, though not more than twenty, perhaps, in a straight line.

It being about the full of the moon, and a warm and pleasant evening, we decided to row five miles by moonlight to the head of the North Twin Lake, lest the wind should rise on the morrow. After one mile of river, or what the boatmen call "thoroughfare,"—for the river becomes at length only the connecting link between the lakes,—and some slight rapids which had been mostly made smooth water by the dam, we entered the North Twin Lake just after sundown, and steered across for the river "thoroughfare," four miles distant. This is a noble sheet of water, where one may get the impression which a new country and a "lake of the woods" are fitted to create. There was the smoke of no log-hut nor camp of any kind to greet us, still less was any lover of nature or musing traveller watching our batteau from the distant hills; not even the Indian hunter was there, for he rarely climbs them, but hugs the river like ourselves. No face welcomed us but the fine fantastic sprays of free and happy evergreen trees, waving one above another in their ancient home. At first the red clouds hung over the western shore as gorgeously as if over a city, and the lake lay open to the light with even a civilized aspect, as if expecting trade and commerce, and towns and villas. We could distinguish the inlet to the South Twin, which is said to be the larger, where the shore was misty and blue, and it was worth the while to look thus through a narrow opening across the entire expanse of a concealed lake to its own yet more dim and distant shore. The shores rose gently to ranges of low hills covered with forests; and though in fact the most valuable white pine timber, even about this lake, had been culled out, this would never have been suspected by the voyager. The impression, which indeed corresponded with the fact, was as if we were upon a high table land between the States and Canada, the northern side of which is drained by the St. John and Chaudiere, the southern by the Penobscot and Kennebec. There was no bold mountainous shore, as we might have expected, but only isolated hills and mountains rising here and there from the plateau. The country is an archipelago of lakes,—the lake-country of New England. Their levels vary but a few feet, and the boatmen, by short portages, or by none at all, pass easily from one to another. They say that at very high water the Penobscot and the Kennebec flow into each other, or at any rate, that you may lie with your face in the one and your toes in the other. Even the Penobscot and St. John have been connected by a canal, so that the lumber of the Allagash, instead of going down the St. John, comes down the Penobscot; and the Indian's tradition that the Penobscot once ran both ways for his convenience, is, in one sense, partially realized to-day.

None of our party but McCauslin had been above this lake, so we trusted to him to pilot us, and we could not but confess the importance of a pilot on these waters. While it is river, you will not easily forget which way is up stream; but when you enter a lake, the river is completely lost, and you scan the distant shores in vain to find where it comes in. A stranger is, for the time at least, lost, and must set about a voyage of discovery first of all to find the river. To follow the windings of the shore when the lake is ten miles or even more in length, and of an irregularity which will not soon be mapped, is a wearisome voyage, and will spend his time and his provisions. They tell a story of a gang of experienced woodmen sent to a location on this stream, who were thus lost in the wilderness of lakes. They cut their way through thickets, and carried their baggage and their boats over from lake to lake, sometimes several miles. They carried into Millinocket lake, which is on another stream, and is ten miles square, and contains a hundred islands. They explored its shores thoroughly, and then carried into another and another, and it was a week of toil and anxiety before they found the Penobscot river again, and then their provisions were exhausted, and they were obliged to return.

While Uncle George steered for a small island near the head of the lake, now just visible like a speck on the water, we rowed by turns swiftly over its surface, singing such boat-songs as we could remember. The shores seemed at an indefinite distance in the moonlight. Occasionally we paused in our singing and rested on our oars, while we listened to hear if the wolves howled, for this is a common serenade, and my companions affirmed that it was the most dismal and unearthly of sounds; but we heard none this time.—If we did not *hear*, however, we did *listen*, not without a reasonable expectation; that at least I have to tell,—only some utterly uncivilized, big-throated owl hooted loud and dismally in the drear and boughy wilderness, plainly not nervous about his solitary life, nor afraid to hear the echoes of his voice there. We remembered also that possibly moose were silently watching us from the distant coves, or some surly bear, or timid caribou had been startled by our singing. It was with new emphasis that we sang there the Canadian boat-song—

> "Row, brothers, row, the stream runs fast,
> The Rapids are near and the daylight's past!"—

which described precisely our own adventure, and was inspired by the experience of a similar kind of life,—for the rapids were ever near, and the daylight long past; the woods on shore looked dim, and many an Utawas' tide here emptied into the lake.

> "Why should we yet our sail unfurl?
> There is not a breath the blue wave to curl!
> But, when the wind blows off the shore,
> O sweetly we'll rest our weary oar."

"Utawas' tide! this trembling moon,
Shall see us float o'er thy surges soon."

At last we glided past the "green isle" which had been our landmark, all joining in the chorus; as if by the watery links of rivers and of lakes we were about to float over unmeasured zones of earth, bound on unimaginable adventures.

"Saint of this green isle! hear our prayers,
O grant us cool heavens and favoring airs!"

About nine o'clock we reached the river, and ran our boat into a natural haven between some rocks, and drew her out on the sand. This camping ground McCauslin had been familiar with in his lumbering days, and he now struck it unerringly in the moonlight, and we heard the sound of the rill which would supply us with cool water emptying into the lake. The first business was to make a fire, an operation which was a little delayed by the wetness of the fuel and the ground, owing to the heavy showers of the afternoon. The fire is the main comfort of a camp, whether in summer or winter, and is about as ample at one season as at another. It is as well for cheerfulness, as for warmth and dryness. It forms one side of the camp; one bright side at any rate. Some were dispersed to fetch in dead trees and boughs, while Uncle George felled the birches and beeches which stood convenient, and soon we had a fire some ten feet long by three or four high, which rapidly dried the sand before it. This was calculated to burn all night. We next proceeded to pitch our tent; which operation was performed by sticking our two spike poles into the ground in a slanting direction, about ten feet apart, for rafters, and then drawing our cotton cloth over them, and tying it down at the ends, leaving it open in front, shed-fashion. But this evening the wind carried the sparks on to the tent and burned it. So we hastily drew up the batteau just within the edge of the woods before the fire, and propping up one side three or four feet high, spread the tent on the ground to lie on; and with the corner of a blanket, or what more or less we could get to put over us, lay down with our heads and bodies under the boat, and our feet and legs on the sand toward the fire. At first we lay awake, talking of our course, and finding ourselves in so convenient a posture for studying the heavens, with the moon and stars shining in our faces, our conversation naturally turned upon astronomy, and we recounted by turns the most interesting discoveries in that science. But at length we composed ourselves seriously to sleep. It was interesting, when awakened at midnight, to watch the grotesque and fiendlike forms and motions of some one of the party, who, not being able to sleep, had got up silently to arouse the fire, and add fresh fuel, for a change; now stealthily lugging a dead tree from out the dark, and heaving it on, now stirring up the embers with his fork, or tiptoeing about to observe the stars, watched, perchance, by half the prostrate party in breathless silence; so much the more intense because they were awake, while each supposed his neighbor sound asleep. Thus aroused, I too brought fresh fuel to the fire, and then rambled along the sandy shore in the moonlight, hoping to meet a moose come down to drink, or else a wolf. The little rill tinkled the louder, and peopled all the wilderness for me; and the glassy smoothness of the sleeping lake, laving the shores of a new world, with the dark, fantastic rocks rising here and there from its surface, made a scene not easily described. It has left such an impression of stern yet gentle wildness on my memory as will not soon be effaced. Not far from midnight, we were one after another awakened by rain falling on our extremities; and as each was made aware of the fact by cold or wet, he drew a long sigh and then drew up his legs, until gradually we had all sidled round from lying at right angles with the boat, till our bodies formed an acute angle with it, and were wholly protected. When next we awoke, the moon and stars were shining again, and there were signs of dawn in the east. I have been thus particular in order to convey some idea of a night in the woods.

We had soon launched and loaded our boat, and, leaving our fire blazing, were off again before breakfast. The lumberers rarely trouble themselves to put out their fires, such is the dampness of the primitive forest; and this is one cause, no doubt, of the frequent fires in Maine, of which we hear so much on smoky days in Massachusetts. The forests are held cheap after the white pine has been culled out; and the explorers and hunters pray for rain only to clear the atmosphere of smoke. The woods were so wet to-day, however, that there was no danger of our fire spreading. After poling up half a mile of river, or thoroughfare, we rowed a mile across the foot of Pamadumcook Lake, which is the name given on the map to this whole chain of lakes, as if there was but one, though they are, in each instance, distinctly separated by a reach of the river, with its narrow and rocky channel and its rapids. This lake, which is one of the largest, stretched north-west ten miles, to hills and mountains in the distance. McCauslin pointed to some distant and, as yet, inaccessible forests of white pine, on the sides of a mountain in that direction. The Joe Merry Lakes, which lay between us and Moosehead, on the west, were recently, if they are not still, "surrounded by some of the best timbered land in the state." By another thoroughfare we passed into Deep Cove, a part of the same lake, which makes up two miles, toward the north-east, and rowing two miles across this, by another short thoroughfare, entered Ambejijis Lake.

At the entrance to a lake we sometimes observed what is technically called "fencing stuff," or the unhewn timbers of which booms are formed, either secured together in the water, or laid up on the rocks and lashed to trees, for spring use. But it was always startling to discover so plain a trail of civilized man there. I remember that I was strangely affected when we were returning, by the sight of a ring-bolt well drilled into a rock, and fastened with lead, at the head of this solitary Ambejijis Lake.

It was easy to see, that driving logs must be an exciting as well as arduous and dangerous business. All winter long the logger goes on piling up the trees which he has trimmed and hauled in some dry ravine at the head of a stream, and then in the spring he stands on the bank, and whistles for Rain and Thaw, ready to wring the perspiration out of his shirt to swell the tide, till suddenly, with a whoop and halloo from him, shutting his eyes, as if to bid farewell to the existing state of things, a fair proportion of his winter's work goes scrambling down the country, followed by his faithful dogs, Thaw, and Rain, and Freshet, and Wind, the whole pack in full cry, toward the Orono Mills. Every log is marked with the owner's name, cut in the sapwood with an axe, or bored with an auger, so deep as not to be worn off in the driving, and yet not so as to injure the timber; and it requires considerable ingenuity to invent new and simple marks where there are so many owners. They have quite an alphabet of their own, which only the practised can read. One of my companions read off from his memorandum book some marks of his own logs, among which there were crosses, belts, crow's feet, girdles, &c., as Y—girdle—crow-foot, and various other devices. When the logs have run the gauntlet of innumerable rapids and falls, each on its own account, with more or less jamming and bruising, those bearing various owners' marks being mixed up together, since all must take advantage of the same freshet, they are collected together at the heads of the lakes, and surrounded by a boom fence of floating logs, to prevent their being dispersed by the wind, and are thus towed all together, like a flock of sheep, across the lake, where there is no current, by a windlass, or boom-head, such as we sometimes saw standing on an island or head-land, and, if circumstances permit, with the aid of sails and oars. Sometimes, notwithstanding, the logs are dispersed over many miles of lake surface in a few hours by winds and freshets, and thrown up on distant shores, where the driver can pick up only one or two at a time, and return with them to the thoroughfare; and, before he gets his flock well through Ambejijis or Pamadumcook, he makes many a wet and uncomfortable camp on the shore. He must be able to navigate a log as if it were a canoe, and be as indifferent to cold and wet as a muskrat. He uses a few efficient tools,—a lever commonly of rock-maple, six or seven feet long, with a stout spike in it, strongly ferruled on, and a long spike-pole, with a screw at the end of the spike to make it hold. The boys along shore learn to walk on floating logs as city boys on sidewalks. Sometimes the logs are thrown up on rocks in such positions as to be irrecoverable but by another freshet as high, or they jam together at rapids and falls, and accumulate in vast piles, which the driver must start at the risk of his life. Such is the lumber business, which depends on many accidents, as the early freezing of the rivers, that the teams may get up in season, a sufficient freshet in the spring, to fetch the logs down, and many others.* I quote Michaux on Lumbering on the Kennebec, then the source of the best white-pine lumber carried to England. "The persons engaged in this branch of industry are generally emigrants from New Hampshire. . . . In the summer they unite in small companies, and traverse these vast solitudes in every direction, to ascertain the places in which the pines abound. After cutting the grass and converting it into hay for the nourishment of the cattle to be employed in their labor, they return home. In the beginning of the winter they enter the forests again, establish themselves in huts covered with the bark of the canoe-birch, or the arbor-vitæ; and, though the cold is so intense that the mercury sometimes remains for several weeks from 40° to

*"A steady current or pitch of water is preferable to one either rising or diminishing; as, when rising rapidly, the water at the middle of the river is considerably higher than at the shores,—so much so as to be distinctly perceived by the eye of a spectator on the banks, presenting an appearance like a turnpike road. The lumber, therefore, is always sure to incline from the centre of the channel toward either shore."—Springer.

50° [Fahr.] below the point of congelation, they persevere, with unabated courage, in their work." According to Springer, the company consists of choppers, swampers,—who make roads,—barker and loader, teamster, and cook. "When the trees are felled, they cut them into logs from fourteen to eighteen feet long, and, by means of their cattle, which they employ with great dexterity, drag them to the river, and after stamping on them a mark of property, roll them on its frozen bosom. At the breaking of the ice, in the spring, they float down with the current. . . . The logs that are not sawn the first year," adds Michaux, "are attacked by large worms, which form holes about two lines in diameter, in every direction; but, if stripped of their bark, they will remain uninjured for thirty years."

Ambejijis, this quiet Sunday morning, struck me as the most beautiful lake we had seen. It is said to be one of the deepest. We had the fairest view of Joe Merry, Double Top, and Ktaadn, from its surface. The summit of the latter had a singularly flat table-land appearance, like a short highway, where a demigod might be let down to take a turn or two in an afternoon, to settle his dinner. We rowed a mile and a half to near the head of the lake, and, pushing through a field of lily pads, landed, to cook our breakfast by the side of a large rock, known to McCauslin. Our breakfast consisted of tea, with hard bread and pork, and fried salmon, which we ate with forks neatly whittled from alder-twigs, which grew there, off strips of birch-bark for plates. The tea was black tea, without milk to color or sugar to sweeten it, and two tin dippers were our tea cups. This beverage is as indispensable to the loggers as to any gossiping old women in the land, and they, no doubt, derive great comfort from it. Here was the site of an old loggers' camp, remembered by McCauslin, now overgrown with weeds and bushes. In the midst of a dense underwood, we noticed a whole brick, on a rock, in a small run, clean, and red, and square, as in a brick-yard, which had been brought thus far formerly for tamping. Some of us afterward regretted that we had not carried this on with us to the top of the mountain, to be left there for our mark. It would certainly have been a simple evidence of civilized man. McCauslin said, that large wooden crosses made of oak, still sound, were sometimes found standing in this wilderness, which were set up by the first Catholic missionaries who came through to the Kennebec.

In the next nine miles, which were the extent of our voyage, and which it took us the rest of the day to get over, we rowed across several small lakes, poled up numerous rapids and thoroughfares, and carried over four portages. I will give the names and distances, for the benefit of future tourists. First, after leaving Ambejijis Lake, we had a quarter of a mile of rapids to the portage, or carry of ninety rods around Ambejijis Falls; then a mile and a half through Passamagamet Lake, which is narrow and river-like, to the falls of the same name—Ambejijis stream coming in on the right; then two miles through Katepskonegan Lake to the portage of ninety rods around Katepskonegan Falls, which name signifies "carrying place"—Passamagamet stream coming in on the left; then three miles through Pockwockomus Lake, a slight expansion of the river, to the portage of forty rods around the falls of the same name—Katepskonegan stream coming in on the left; then three quarters of a mile through Aboljacarmegus Lake, similar to the last, to the portage of forty rods around the falls of the same name; then half a mile of rapid water to the Sowadnehunk dead-water, and the Aboljacknagesic stream.

This is generally the order of names as you ascend the river:—First, the lake, or, if there is no expansion, the dead-water; then the falls; then the stream emptying into the lake or river above, all of the same name. First we came to Passamagamet Lake, then to Passamagamet Falls, then to Passamagamet stream, emptying in. This order and identity of names, it will be perceived, is quite philosophical, since the dead-water or lake is always at least partially produced by the stream emptying in above; and the first fall below, which is the inlet of that lake, and where that tributary water makes its first plunge, also naturally bears the same name.

At the portage around Ambejijis Falls, I observed a pork-barrel on the shore, with a hole eight or nine inches square cut in one side, which was set against an upright rock; but the bears, without turning or upsetting the barrel, had gnawed a hole in the opposite side, which looked exactly like an enormous rat hole, big enough to put their heads in; and at the bottom of the barrel were still left a few mangled and slabbered slices of pork. It is usual for the lumberers to leave such supplies as they cannot conveniently carry along with them at carries or camps, to which the next comers do not scruple to help themselves, they being the property commonly not of an individual, but a company, who can afford to deal liberally.

I will describe particularly how we got over some of these portages and rapids, in order that the reader may get an idea of the boatman's life. At Ambejijis Falls, for instance, there was the roughest path imaginable cut through the woods; at first up hill at an angle of nearly forty-five degrees, over rocks and logs without end. This was the manner of the portage:—We first carried over our baggage, and deposited it on the shore at the other end; then returning to the batteau, we dragged it up the hill by the painter, and onward, with frequent pauses, over half the portage. But this was a bungling way, and would soon have worn out the boat. Commonly, three men walk over with a batteau weighing from three to five or six hundred pounds on their heads and shoulders, the tallest standing under the middle of the boat, which is turned over, and one at each end, or else there are two at the bows. More cannot well take hold at once. But this requires some practice, as well as strength, and is in any case extremely laborious, and wearing to the constitution, to follow. We were, on the whole, rather an invalid party, and could render our boatmen but little assistance. Our two men at length took the batteau upon their shoulders, and, while two of us steadied it, to prevent it from rocking and wearing into their shoulders, on which they placed their hats folded, walked bravely over the remaining distance, with two or three pauses. In the same manner they accomplished the other portages. With this crushing weight they must climb and stumble along over fallen trees and slippery rocks of all sizes, where those who walked by the sides were continually brushed off, such was the narrowness of the path. But we were fortunate not to have to cut our path in the first place. Before we launched our boat, we scraped the bottom smooth again with our knives, where it had rubbed on the rocks, to save friction.

To avoid the difficulties of the portage, our men determined to "warp up" the Passamagamet Falls: so while the rest walked over the portage with the baggage, I remained in the batteau, to assist in warping up. We were soon in the midst of the rapids, which were more swift and tumultuous than any we had poled up, and had turned to the side of the stream for the purpose of warping, when the boatmen, who felt some pride in their skill, and were ambitious to do something more than usual, for my benefit, as I surmised, took one more view of the rapids, or rather the falls; and in answer to one's question, whether we couldn't get up there, the other answered that he guessed he'd try it: so we pushed again into the midst of the stream, and began to struggle with the current. I sat in the middle of the boat, to trim it, moving slightly to the right or left as it grazed a rock. With an uncertain and wavering motion we wound and bolted our way up, until the bow was actually raised two feet above the stern at the steepest pitch; and then, when everything depended upon his exertions, the bowman's pole snapped in two; but before he had time to take the spare one, which I reached him, he had saved himself with the fragment upon a rock; and so we got up by a hair's breadth; and Uncle George exclaimed, that that was never done before; and he had not tried it, if he had not known whom he had got in the bow—nor he in the bow, if he had not known him in the stern. At this place there was a regular portage cut through the woods; and our boatmen had never known a batteau to ascend the falls. As near as I can remember, there was a perpendicular fall here, at the worst place, of the whole Penobscot River, two or three feet at least. I could not sufficiently admire the skill and coolness with which they performed this feat, never speaking to each other. The bowman, not looking behind, but knowing exactly what the other is about, works as if he worked alone; now sounding in vain for a bottom in fifteen feet of water, while the boat falls back several rods, held straight only with the greatest skill and exertion; or, while the sternman obstinately holds his ground, like a turtle, the bowman springs from side to side with wonderful suppleness and dexterity, scanning the rapids and the rocks with a thousand eyes; and now, having got a bite at last, with a lusty shove which makes his pole bend and quiver, and the whole boat tremble, he gains a few feet upon the river. To add to the danger, the poles are liable at any time to be caught between the rocks, and wrenched out of their hands, leaving them at the mercy of the rapids—the rocks, as it were, lying in wait, like so many alligators, to catch them in their teeth, and jerk them from your hands, before you have stolen an effectual shove against their palates. The pole is set close to the boat, and the prow is made to overshoot, and just turn the corners of the rocks, in the very teeth of the rapids. Nothing but the length and lightness, and the slight draught of the batteau, enables them to make any headway. The bowman must quickly choose his course; there is no time to deliberate. Frequently the boat is shoved between rocks where both sides touch, and the waters on either hand are a perfect maelstrom.

Half a mile above this, two of us tried our hands at poling up a slight rapid; and we were just surmounting the last difficulty, when an unlucky rock confounded our calculations; and while the batteau was sweeping round irrecoverably amid the whirlpool, we were obliged to resign the poles to more skilful hands.

Katepskonegan is one of the shallowest and weediest of the lakes, and looked as if it might abound in pickerel. The falls of the same name, where we stopped to dine, are considerable and quite picturesque. Here Uncle George had seen trout caught by the barrel-full; but they would not rise to our bait at this hour. Half way over this carry, thus far in the Maine wilderness on its way to the Provinces, we noticed a large flaming Oak Hall hand-bill, about two feet long, wrapped round the trunk of a pine, from which the bark had been stript, and to which it was fast glued by the pitch. This should be recorded among the advantages of this mode of advertising, that so, possibly, even the bears and wolves, moose, deer, otter, and beaver, not to mention the Indian, may learn where they can fit themselves according to the latest fashion, or, at least, recover some of their own lost garments. We christened this the Oak Hall carry.

The forenoon was as serene and placid on this wild stream in the woods as we are wont to imagine that Sunday in summer usually is in Massachusetts. We were occasionally startled by the scream of a bald-eagle, sailing over the stream in front of our batteau; or of the fish-hawks, on whom he levies his contributions. There were, at intervals, small meadows of a few acres on the sides of the stream, waving with uncut grass, which attracted the attention of our boatmen, who regretted that they were not nearer to their clearings, and calculated how many stacks they might cut. Two or three men sometimes spend the summer by themselves, cutting the grass in these meadows, to sell to the loggers in the winter, since it will fetch a higher price on the spot than in any market in the state. On a small isle, covered with this kind of rush, or cut grass, on which we landed, to consult about our further course, we noticed the recent track of a moose, a large, roundish hole, in the soft wet ground, evincing the great size and weight of the animal that made it. They are fond of the water; and visit all these island-meadows, swimming as easily from island to island as they make their way through the thickets on land. Now and then we passed what McCauslin called a pokelogan, an Indian term for what the drivers might have reason to call a poke-logs-in, an inlet that leads nowhere: if you get in you have got to get out again the same way. These, and the frequent "run-rounds," which come into the river again, would embarrass an inexperienced voyager not a little.

The carry around Pockwockomus Falls was exceedingly rough and rocky, the batteau having to be lifted directly from the water up four or five feet on to a rock, and launched again down a similar bank. The rocks on this portage were covered with the dents made by the spikes in the lumberers' boots while staggering over under the weight of their batteaux; and you could see where the surface of some large rocks on which they had rested their batteaux was worn quite smooth with use. As it was, we had carried over but half the usual portage at this place for this stage of the water, and launched our boat in the smooth wave just curving to the fall, prepared to struggle with the most violent rapid we had to encounter. The rest of the party walked over the remainder of the portage, while I remained with the boatmen to assist in warping up. One had to hold the boat while the others got in to prevent it from going over the falls. When we had pushed up the rapids as far as possible, keeping close to the shore, Tom seized the painter and leaped out upon a rock just visible in the water, but he lost his footing notwithstanding his spiked boots, and was instantly amid the rapids; but recovering himself by good luck, and reaching another rock, he passed the painter to me, who had followed him, and took his place again in the bows. Leaping from rock to rock in the shoal water close to the shore, and now and then getting a bite with the rope round an upright one, I held the boat while one reset his pole, and then all three forced it upward against any rapid. This was "warping up." When a part of us walked round at such a place, we generally took the precaution to take out the most valuable part of the baggage, for fear of being swamped.

As we poled up a swift rapid for half a mile above Aboljacarmegus Falls, some of the party read their own marks on the huge logs which lay piled up high and dry on the rocks on either hand, the relics probably of a jam which had taken place here in the Great Freshet in the spring. Many of these would have to wait for another great freshet, perchance, if they lasted so long, before they could be got off. It was singular enough to meet with property of theirs which they had never seen, and where they had never been before, thus detained by freshets and rocks when on its way to them. Methinks that must be where all my property lies, cast up on the rocks on some distant and unexplored stream, and waiting for an unheard-of freshet to fetch it down. O make haste, ye gods, with your winds and rains, and start the jam before it rots!

The last half mile carried us to the Sowadnehunk dead-water, so called from the stream of the same name, signifying "running between mountains," an important tributary which comes in a mile above. Here we decided to camp, about twenty miles from the Dam, at the mouth of Murch Brook and the Aboljacknagesic, mountain streams, broad off from Ktaadn, and about a dozen miles from its summit; having made fifteen miles this day.

We had been told by McCauslin that we should here find trout enough: so while some prepared the camp, the rest fell to fishing. Seizing the birch poles which some party of Indians or white hunters had left on the shore, and baiting our hooks with pork, and with trout, as soon as they were caught, we cast our lines into the mouth of the Aboljacknagesic, a clear, swift, shallow stream, which came in from Ktaadn. Instantly a shoal of white chivin, (leucisci pulchelli,) silvery roaches, cousin-trout, or what not, large and small, prowling thereabouts, fell upon our bait, and one after another were landed amidst the bushes. Anon their cousins, the true trout, took their turn, and alternately the speckled trout, and the silvery roaches, swallowed the bait as fast as we could throw in; and the finest specimens of both that I have ever seen, the largest one weighing three pounds, were heaved upon the shore, though at first in vain, to wriggle down into the water again, for we stood in the boat; but soon we learned to remedy this evil: for one, who had lost his hook, stood on shore to catch them as they fell in a perfect shower around him—sometimes, wet and slippery, full in his face and bosom, as his arms were outstretched to receive them. While yet alive, before their tints had faded, they glistened like the fairest flowers, the product of primitive rivers; and he could hardly trust his senses, as he stood over them, that these jewels should have swum away in that Aboljacknagesic water for so long, so many dark ages;—these bright fluviatile flowers, seen of Indians only, made beautiful, the Lord only knows why, to swim there! I could understand better, for this, the truth of mythology, the fables of Proteus, and all those beautiful sea-monsters,—how all history, indeed, put to a terrestrial use, is mere history; but put to a celestial, is mythology always.

But there is the rough voice of Uncle George, who commands at the frying-pan, to send over what you've got, and then you may stay till morning. The pork sizzles, and cries for fish. Luckily for the foolish race, and this particularly foolish generation of trout, the night shut down at last, not a little deepened by the dark side of Ktaadn, which, like a permanent shadow, reared itself from the eastern bank. Lescarbot, writing in 1609, tells us that the Sieur Champdoré, who, with one of the people of the Sieur de Monts, ascended some fifty leagues up the St. John in 1608, found the fish so plenty, "qu'en mettant la chaudière sur le feu ils en avoient pris suffisamment pour eux dîsner avant que l'eau fust chaude."

Their descendants here are no less numerous. So we accompanied Tom into the woods, to cut cedar-twigs for our bed. While he went ahead with the axe, and lopped off the smallest twigs of the flat-leaved cedar, the arbor-vitæ of the gardens, we gathered them up, and returned with them to the boat, until it was loaded. Our bed was made with as much care and skill as a roof is shingled; beginning at the foot, and laying the twig end of the cedar upward, we advanced to the head, a course at a time, thus successively covering the stub-ends, and producing a soft and level bed. For us six it was about ten feet long by six in breadth. This time we lay under our tent, having pitched it more prudently with reference to the wind and the flame, and the usual huge fire blazed in front. Supper was eaten off a large log, which some freshet had thrown up. This night we had a dish of arbor-vitæ, or cedar tea, which the lumberer sometimes uses when other herbs fail,—

> "A quart of *arbor*-vitæ,
> To make him strong and mighty,"—

but I had no wish to repeat the experiment. It had too medicinal a taste for my palate. There was the skeleton of a moose here, whose bones some Indian hunters had picked on this very spot.

In the night I dreamed of trout-fishing; and, when at length I awoke, it seemed a fable, that this painted fish swam there so near my couch, and rose to our hooks the last evening—and I doubted if I had not dreamed it all. So I arose before dawn to test its truth, while my companions were still sleeping. There stood Ktaadn with distinct and cloudless outline in the moonlight; and the rippling of the rapids was the only sound to break the stillness. Standing on the shore, I once more cast my line into the stream, and found the dream to be real, and the fable true. The speckled trout and silvery roach, like flying fish, sped swiftly through the moonlight air, describing bright arcs on the dark side of Ktaadn, until moonlight, now fading into daylight, brought satiety to my mind, and the minds of my companions, who had joined me.

By six o'clock, having mounted our packs and a good blanket full of trout, ready dressed, and swung up such baggage and provision as we wished to leave behind upon the tops of saplings, to be out of the reach of bears, we started for the summit of the mountain, distant, as Uncle George said the boatmen called it, about four miles, but as I judged, and as it proved, nearer fourteen. He had never been any nearer the mountain than this, and there was not the slightest trace of man to guide us further in this direction. At first, pushing a few rods up the Aboljacknagesic, or "open-land stream," we fastened our batteau to a tree, and travelled up the north side, through burnt lands, now partially overgrown with young aspens, and other shrubbery; but soon, recrossing this stream, where it was about fifty or sixty feet wide, upon a jam of logs and rocks, and you could cross it by this means almost anywhere, we struck at once for the highest peak, over a mile or more of comparatively open land still, very gradually ascending the while. Here it fell to my lot, as the oldest mountain-climber, to take the lead: so scanning the woody side of the mountain, which lay still at an indefinite distance, stretched out some seven or eight miles in length before us, we determined to steer directly for the base of the highest peak, leaving a large slide, by which, as I have since learned, some of our predecessors ascended, on our left. This course would lead us parallel to a dark seam in the forest, which marked the bed of a torrent, and over a slight spur, which extended southward from the main mountain, from whose bare summit we could get an outlook over the country, and climb directly up the peak, which would then be close at hand. Seen from this point, a bare ridge at the extremity of the open land, Ktaadn presented a different aspect from any mountain I have seen, there being a greater proportion of naked rock, rising abruptly from the forest; and we looked up at this blue barrier as if it were some fragment of a wall which anciently bounded the earth in that direction. Setting the compass for a north-east course, which was the bearing of the southern base of the highest peak, we were soon buried in the woods.

We soon began to meet with traces of bears and moose, and those of rabbits were everywhere visible. The tracks of moose, more or less recent, to speak literally covered every square rod on the sides of the mountain; and these animals are probably more numerous there now than ever before, being driven into this wilderness from all sides by the settlements. The track of a full-grown moose is like that of a cow, or larger, and of the young, like that of a calf. Sometimes we found ourselves travelling in faint paths, which they had made, like cow-paths in the woods, only far more indistinct, being rather openings, affording imperfect vistas through the dense underwood, than trodden paths; and everywhere the twigs had been browsed by them, clipt as smoothly as if by a knife. The bark of trees was stript up by them to the height of eight or nine feet, in long narrow strips, an inch wide, still showing the distinct marks of their teeth. We expected nothing less than to meet a herd of them every moment, and our Nimrod held his shooting-iron in readiness; but we did not go out of our way to look for them, and, though numerous, they are so wary, that the unskilful hunter might range the forest a long time before he could get sight of one. They are sometimes dangerous to encounter, and will not turn out for the hunter, but furiously rush upon him, and trample him to death, unless he is lucky enough to avoid them by dodging round a tree. The largest are nearly as large as a horse, and weigh sometimes one thousand pounds; and it is said that they can step over a five-foot gate in their ordinary walk. They are described as exceedingly awkward-looking animals, with their long legs and short bodies, making a ludicrous figure when in full run, but making great headway nevertheless. It seemed a mystery to us how they could thread these woods, which it required all our suppleness to accomplish, climbing, stooping, and winding, alternately. They are said to drop their long and branching horns, which usually spread five or six feet, on their backs, and make their way easily by the weight of their bodies. Our boatmen said, but I know not with how much truth, that their horns are apt to be gnawed away by vermin while they sleep. Their flesh, which is more like beef than venison, is common in Bangor market.

We had proceeded on thus seven or eight miles, till about noon, with frequent pauses to refresh the weary ones, crossing a considerable mountain stream, which we conjectured to be Murch Brook, at whose mouth we had camped, all the time in woods, without having once seen the summit, and rising very gradually, when the boatmen, beginning to despair a little, and fearing that we were leaving the mountain on one side of us, for they had not entire faith in the compass, McCauslin climbed a tree, from the top of which he could see the peak, when it appeared that we had not swerved from a right line, the compass down below still ranging with his arm, which pointed to the summit. By the side of a cool mountain rill, amid the woods, where the water began to partake of the purity and transparency of the air, we stopped to cook some of our fishes, which we had brought thus far in order to save our hard bread and pork, in the use of which we had put ourselves on short allowance. We soon had a fire blazing, and stood around it, under the damp and sombre forest of firs and birches, each with a sharpened stick, three or four feet in length, upon which he had spitted his trout, or roach, previously well gashed and salted, our sticks radiating like the spokes of a wheel from one centre, and each crowding his particular fish into the most desirable exposure, not with the truest regard always to his neighbor's rights. Thus we regaled ourselves, drinking meanwhile at the spring, till one man's pack, at least, was considerably lightened, when we again took up our line of march.

At length we reached an elevation sufficiently bare to afford a view of the summit, still distant and blue, almost as if retreating from us. A torrent, which proved to be the same we had crossed, was seen tumbling down in front, literally from out of the clouds. But this glimpse at our whereabouts was soon lost, and we were buried in the woods again. The wood was chiefly yellow birch, spruce, fir, mountain-ash, or round-wood, as the Maine people call it, and moose-wood. It was the worst kind of travelling; sometimes like the densest scrub-oak patches with us. The cornel, or bunch-berries, were very abundant, as well as Solomon's seal and moose-berries. Blue-berries were distributed along our whole route; and in one place the bushes were drooping with the weight of the fruit, still as fresh as ever. It was the seventh of September. Such patches afforded a grateful repast, and served to bait the tired party forward. When any lagged behind, the cry of "blue-berries" was most effectual to bring them up. Even at this elevation we passed through a moose-yard, formed by a large flat rock, four or five rods square, where they tread down the snow in winter. At length, fearing that if we held the direct course to the summit, we should not find any water near our camping-ground, we gradually swerved to the west, till, at four o'clock, we struck again the torrent which I have mentioned, and here, in view of the summit, the weary party decided to camp that night.

While my companions were seeking a suitable spot for this purpose, I improved the little daylight that was left in climbing the mountain alone. We were in a deep and narrow ravine, sloping up to the clouds, at an angle of nearly forty-five degrees, and hemmed in by walls of rock, which were at first covered with low trees, then with impenetrable thickets of scraggy birches and spruce-trees, and with moss, but at last bare of all vegetation but lichens, and almost continually draped in clouds. Following up the course of the torrent which occupied this—and I mean to lay some emphasis on this word *up*—pulling myself up by the side of perpendicular falls of twenty or thirty feet, by the roots of firs and birches, and then, perhaps, walking a level rod or two in the thin stream, for it took up the whole road, ascending by huge steps, as it were, a giant's stairway, down which a river flowed, I had soon cleared the trees, and paused on the successive shelves, to look back over the country. The torrent was from fifteen to thirty feet wide, without a tributary, and seemingly not diminishing in breadth as I advanced; but still it came rushing and roaring down, with a copious tide, over and amidst masses of bare rock, from the very clouds, as though a water-spout had just burst over the mountain. Leaving this at last, I began to work my way, scarcely less arduous than Satan's anciently through Chaos, up the nearest, though not the highest peak. At first scrambling on all fours over the tops of ancient black spruce-trees, (*Abies nigra*,) old as the flood, from two to ten or twelve feet in height, their tops flat and spreading, and their foliage blue and nipt with cold, as if for centuries they had ceased growing upward against the bleak sky, the solid cold. I walked some good rods erect upon the tops of these trees, which were overgrown with moss and mountain-cranberries. It seemed that in the course of time they had filled up the intervals between the huge rocks, and the cold wind had uniformly levelled all over. Here the principle of vegetation was hard put to it. There was apparently a belt of this kind running quite round the mountain, though, perhaps, nowhere so remarkable as here. Once, slumping through, I looked down ten feet, into a dark and cavernous region, and saw the stem of a spruce, on whose top I stood, as on a mass of coarse basket-work, fully nine inches in diameter at the ground. These holes were bears' dens, and the bears were even then at home. This was the sort of garden I made my way *over*, for an eighth of a mile, at the risk, it is true, of treading on some of the plants, not seeing any path *through* it—certainly the most treacherous and porous country I ever travelled.

> "——nigh founder'd, on he fares,
> Treading the crude consistence, half on foot,
> Half flying."

But nothing could exceed the toughness of the twigs,—not one snapped under my weight, for they had slowly grown. Having slumped, scrambled, rolled, bounced, and walked, by turns, over this scraggy country, I arrived upon a side-hill, or rather side-mountain, where rocks, gray, silent rocks, were the flocks and herds that pastured, chewing a rocky cud at sunset. They looked at me with hard gray eyes, without a bleat or a low. This brought me to the skirt of a cloud, and bounded my walk that night. But I had already seen that Maine country when I turned about, waving, flowing, rippling, down below.

When I returned to my companions, they had selected a camping-ground on the torrent's edge, and were resting on the ground; one was on the sick list, rolled in a blanket, on a damp shelf of rock. It was a savage and dreary scenery enough; so wildly rough, that they looked long to find a level and open space for the tent. We could not well camp higher, for want of fuel; and the trees here seemed so evergreen and sappy, that we almost doubted if they would acknowledge the influence of fire; but fire prevailed at last, and blazed here, too, like a good citizen of the world. Even at this height we met with frequent traces of moose, as well as of bears. As here was no cedar, we made our bed of coarser feathered spruce; but at any rate the feathers were plucked from the live tree. It was, perhaps, even a more grand and desolate place for a night's lodging than the summit would have been, being in the neighborhood of those wild trees, and of the torrent. Some more aerial and finer-spirited winds rushed and roared through the ravine all night, from time to time arousing our fire, and dispersing the embers about. It was as if we lay in the very nest of a young whirlwind. At midnight, one of my bedfellows, being startled in his dreams by the sudden blazing up to its top of a fir-tree, whose green boughs were dried by the heat, sprang up, with a cry, from his bed, thinking the world on fire, and drew the whole camp after him.

In the morning, after whetting our appetite on some raw pork, a wafer of hard bread, and a dipper of condensed cloud or water-spout, we all together began to make our way up the falls, which I have described; this time choosing the right hand, or highest peak, which was not the one I had approached before. But soon my companions were lost to my sight behind the mountain ridge in my rear, which still seemed ever retreating before me, and I climbed alone over huge rocks, loosely poised, a mile or more, still edging toward the clouds—for though the day was clear elsewhere, the summit was concealed by mist. The mountain seemed a vast aggregation of loose rocks, as if sometime it had rained rocks, and they lay as they fell on the mountain sides, nowhere fairly at rest, but leaning on each other, all rocking-stones, with cavities between, but scarcely any soil or smoother shelf. They were the raw materials of a planet dropped from an unseen quarry, which the vast chemistry of nature would anon work up, or work down, into the smiling and verdant plains and valleys of earth. This was an undone extremity of the globe; as in lignite we see coal in the process of formation.

At length I entered within the skirts of the cloud which seemed forever drifting over the summit, and yet would never be gone, but was generated out of that pure air as fast as it flowed away; and when, a quarter of a mile further, I reached the summit of the ridge, which those who have seen in clearer weather say is about five miles long, and contains a thousand acres of table-land, I was deep within the hostile ranks of clouds, and all objects were obscured by them. Now the wind would blow me out a yard of clear sunlight, wherein I stood; then a gray, dawning light was all it could accomplish, the cloud-line ever rising and falling with the wind's intensity. Sometimes it seemed as if the summit would be cleared in a few moments and smile in sunshine: but what was gained on one side was lost on another. It was like sitting in a chimney and waiting for the smoke to blow away. It was, in fact, a cloud-factory,—these were the cloud-works, and the wind turned them off done from the cool, bare rocks. Occasionally, when the windy columns broke in to me, I caught sight of a dark, damp crag to the right or left; the mist driving ceaselessly between it and me. It reminded me of the creations of the old epic and dramatic poets, of Atlas, Vulcan, the Cyclops, and Prometheus. Such was Caucasus and the rock where Prometheus was bound. Æschylus had no doubt visited such scenery as this. It was vast, Titanic, and such as man never inhabits. Some part of the beholder, even some vital part, seems to escape through the loose grating of his ribs as he ascends. He is more lone than you can imagine. There is less of substantial thought and fair understanding in him, than in the plains where men inhabit. His reason is dispersed and shadowy, more thin and subtile like the air. Vast, Titanic, inhuman Nature has got him at disadvantage, caught him alone, and pilfers him of some of his divine faculty. She does not smile on him as in the plains. She seems to say sternly, why came ye here before your time? This ground is not prepared for you. Is it not enough that I smile in the valleys? I have never made this soil for thy feet, this air for thy breathing, these rocks for thy neighbors. I cannot pity nor fondle thee here, but forever relentlessly drive thee hence to where I *am* kind. Why seek me where I have not called thee, and then complain because you find me but a stepmother? Shouldst thou freeze or starve, or shudder thy life away, here is no shrine, nor altar, nor any access to my ear.

"Chaos and ancient Night, I come no spy
With purpose to explore or to disturb
The secrets of your realm, but * * *
* * * * * * * as my way
Lies through your spacious empire up to light."

The tops of mountains are among the unfinished parts of the globe, whither it is a slight insult to the gods to climb and pry into their secrets, and try their effect on our humanity. Only daring and insolent men, perchance, go there. Simple races, as savages, do not climb mountains—their tops are sacred and mysterious tracts never visited by them. Pomola is always angry with those who climb to the summit of Ktaadn.

According to Jackson, who in his capacity of geological surveyor of the state, has accurately measured it—the altitude of Ktaadn is 5,300 feet, or a little more than one mile above the level of the sea—and he adds: "It is then evidently the highest point in the State of Maine, and is the most abrupt granite mountain in New England." The peculiarities of that spacious table-land on which I was standing, as well as the remarkable semicircular precipice or basin on the eastern side, were all concealed by the mist. I had brought my whole pack to the top, not knowing but I should have to make my descent to the river, and possibly to the settled portion of the state alone and by some other route, and wishing to have a complete outfit with me. But at length, fearing that my companions would be anxious to reach the river before night, and knowing that the clouds might rest on the mountain for days, I was compelled to descend. Occasionally, as I came down, the wind would blow me a vista open through which I could see the country eastward, boundless forests, and lakes, and streams, gleaming in the sun, some of them emptying into the East Branch. There were also new mountains in sight in that direction. Now and then some small bird of the sparrow family would flit away before me, unable to command its course, like a fragment of the gray rock blown off by the wind.

I found my companions where I had left them, on the side of the peak, gathering the mountain cranberries, which filled every crevice between the rocks, together with blue berries, which had a spicier flavor the higher up they grew, but were not the less agreeable to our palates. When the country is settled and roads are made, these cranberries will perhaps become an article of commerce. From this elevation, just on the skirts of the clouds, we could overlook the country west and south for a hundred miles. There it was, the State of Maine, which we had seen on the map, but not much like that. Immeasurable forest for the sun to shine on, that eastern *stuff* we hear of in Massachusetts. No clearing, no house. It did not look as if a solitary traveller had cut so much as a walking-stick there. Countless lakes,—Moosehead in the southwest, forty miles long by ten wide, like a gleaming silver platter at the end of the table; Chesuncook, eighteen long by three wide, without an island; Millinocket, on the south, with its hundred islands; and a hundred others without a name; and mountains also, whose names, for the most part, are known only to the Indians. The forest looked like a firm grass sward, and the effect of these lakes in its midst has been well compared by one who has since visited this same spot, to that of a "mirror broken into a thousand fragments, and wildly scattered over the grass, reflecting the full blaze of the sun." It was a large farm for somebody, when cleared. According to the Gazetteer, which was printed before the boundary question was settled, this single Penobscot county in which we were, was larger than the whole State of Vermont, with its fourteen counties; and this was only a part of the wild lands of Maine. We are concerned now, however, about natural, not political limits. We were about eighty miles as the bird flies from Bangor, or one hundred and fifteen as we had ridden, and walked, and paddled. We had to console ourselves with the reflection that this view was probably as good as that from the peak, as far as it went, and what were a mountain without its attendant clouds and mists? Like ourselves, neither Bailey nor Jackson had obtained a clear view from the summit.

Setting out on our return to the river, still at an early hour in the day, we decided to follow the course of the torrent, which we supposed to be Murch Brook, as long as it would not lead us too far out of our way. We thus travelled about four miles in the very torrent itself, continually crossing and recrossing it, leaping from rock to rock, and jumping with the stream down falls of seven or eight feet, or sometimes sliding down on our backs in a thin sheet of water. This ravine had been the scene of an extraordinary freshet in the spring, apparently accompanied by a slide from the mountain. It must have been filled with a stream of stones and water, at least twenty feet above the present level of the torrent. For a rod or two on either side of its channel, the trees were barked and splintered up to their tops, the birches bent over, twisted, and sometimes finely split like a stable-broom; some a foot in diameter snapped off, and whole clumps of trees bent over with the weight of rocks piled on them. In one place we noticed a rock two or three feet in diameter, lodged nearly twenty feet high in the crotch of a tree. For the whole four miles, we saw but one rill emptying in, and the volume of water did not seem to be increased from the first. We travelled thus very rapidly with a downward impetus, and grew remarkably expert at leaping from rock to rock, for leap we must, and leap we did, whether there was any rock at the right distance or not. It was a pleasant picture when the foremost turned about and looked up the winding ravine, walled in with rocks and the green forest, to see at intervals of a rod or two, a red-shirted or green-jacketed mountaineer against the white torrent, leaping down the channel with his pack on his back, or pausing upon a convenient rock in the midst of the torrent to mend a rent in his clothes, or unstrap the dipper at his belt to take a draught of the water. At one place we were startled by seeing, on a little sandy shelf by the side of the stream, the fresh print of a man's foot, and for a moment realized how Robinson Crusoe felt in a similar case; but at last we remembered that we had struck this stream on our way up, though we could not have told where, and one had descended into the ravine for a drink. The cool air above, and the continual bathing of our bodies in mountain water, alternate foot, sitz, douche, and plunge baths, made this walk exceedingly refreshing, and we had travelled only a mile or two after leaving the torrent, before every thread of our clothes was as dry as usual, owing perhaps to a peculiar quality in the atmosphere.

After leaving the torrent, being in doubt about our course, Tom threw down his pack at the foot of the loftiest spruce tree at hand, and shinned up the bare trunk some twenty feet, and then climbed through the green tower, lost to our sight, until he held the topmost spray in his hand.* McCauslin, in his younger days, had marched through the wilderness with a body of troops, under General Somebody, and with one

*"The spruce-tree," says Springer in '51, "is generally selected, principally for the superior facilities which its numerous limbs afford the climber. To gain the first limbs of this tree, which are from twenty to forty feet from the ground, a smaller tree is undercut and lodged against it, clambering up which the top of the spruce is reached. In some cases, when a very elevated position is desired, the spruce-tree is lodged against the trunk of some lofty pine, up which we ascend to a height twice that of the surrounding forest."

To indicate the direction of pines, he throws down a branch, and a man at the ground takes the bearing.

other man did all the scouting and spying service. The General's word was: "Throw down the top of that tree," and there was no tree in the Maine woods so high that it did not lose its top in such a case. I have heard a story of two men being lost once in these woods, nearer to the settlements than this, who climbed the loftiest pine they could find, some six feet in diameter at the ground, from whose top they discovered a solitary clearing and its smoke. When at this height, some two hundred feet from the ground, one of them became dizzy, and fainted in his companion's arms, and the latter had to accomplish the descent with him, alternately fainting and reviving, as best he could. To Tom we cried, where away does the summit bear? where the burnt lands? The last he could only conjecture; he descried, however, a little meadow and pond, lying probably in our course, which we concluded to steer for. On reaching this secluded meadow, we found fresh tracks of moose on the shore of the pond, and the water was still unsettled as if they had fled before us. A little further, in a dense thicket, we seemed to be still on their trail. It was a small meadow, of a few acres, on the mountain side, concealed by the forest, and perhaps never seen by a white man before, where one would think that the moose might browse and bathe, and rest in peace. Pursuing this course, we soon reached the open land, which went sloping down some miles toward the Penobscot.

Perhaps I most fully realized that this was primeval, untamed, and forever untameable *Nature*, or whatever else men call it, while coming down this part of the mountain. We were passing over "Burnt Lands," burnt by lightning, perchance, though they showed no recent marks of fire, hardly so much as a charred stump, but looked rather like a natural pasture for the moose and deer, exceedingly wild and desolate, with occasional strips of timber crossing them, and low poplars springing up, and patches of blueberries here and there. I found myself traversing them familiarly, like some pasture run to waste, or partially reclaimed by man; but when I reflected what man, what brother or sister or kinsman of our race made it and claimed it, I expected the proprietor to rise up and dispute my passage. It is difficult to conceive of a region uninhabited by man. We habitually presume his presence and influence everywhere. And yet we have not seen pure Nature, unless we have seen her thus vast, and drear, and inhuman, though in the midst of cities. Nature was here something savage and awful, though beautiful. I looked with awe at the ground I trod on, to see what the Powers had made there, the form and fashion and material of their work. This was that Earth of which we have heard, made out of Chaos and Old Night. Here was no man's garden, but the unhandselled globe. It was not lawn, nor pasture, nor mead, nor woodland, nor lea, nor arable, nor waste-land. It was the fresh and natural surface of the planet Earth, as it was made forever and ever,—to be the dwelling of man, we say,—so Nature made it, and man may use it if he can. Man was not to be associated with it. It was Matter, vast, terrific,—not his Mother Earth that we have heard of, not for him to tread on, or be buried in,—no, it were being too familiar even to let his bones lie there—the home this of Necessity and Fate. There was there felt the presence of a force not bound to be kind to man. It was a place for heathenism and superstitious rites,—to be inhabited by men nearer of kin to the rocks and to wild animals than we. We walked over it with a certain awe, stopping from time to time to pick the blueberries which grew there, and had a smart and spicy taste. Perchance where *our* wild pines stand, and leaves lie on their forest floor in Concord, there were once reapers, and husbandmen planted grain; but here not even the surface had been scarred by man, but it was a specimen of what God saw fit to make this world. What is it to be admitted to a museum, to see a myriad of particular things, compared with being shown some star's surface, some hard matter in its home! I stand in awe of my body, this matter to which I am bound has become so strange to me. I fear not spirits, ghosts, of which I am one,—*that* my body might,—but I fear bodies, I tremble to meet them. What is this Titan that has possession of me? Talk of mysteries!—Think of our life in nature,—daily to be shown matter, to come in contact with it,—rocks, trees, wind on our cheeks! the *solid* earth! the *actual* world! the *common sense! Contact! Contact! Who* are we? *where* are we?

Ere long we recognized some rocks and other features in the landscape which we had purposely impressed on our memories, and quickening our pace, by two o'clock we reached the batteau.* Here we had expected to dine on trout, but in this glaring sunlight they were slow to take the bait, so we were compelled to make the most of the crumbs of our hard bread and our pork, which were both nearly exhausted. Meanwhile we deliberated whether we should go up the river a mile farther to

*The bears had not touched things on our possessions. They sometimes tear a batteau to pieces for the sake of the tar with which it is besmeared.

Gibson's clearing on the Sowadnehunk, where there was a deserted log hut, in order to get a half-inch auger, to mend one of our spike-poles with. There were young spruce trees enough around us, and we had a spare spike, but nothing to make a hole with. But as it was uncertain whether we should find any tools left there, we patched up the broken pole as well as we could for the downward voyage, in which there would be but little use for it. Moreover, we were unwilling to lose any time in this expedition, lest the wind should rise before we reached the larger lakes, and detain us, for a moderate wind produces quite a sea on these waters, in which a batteau will not live for a moment; and on one occasion McCauslin had been delayed a week at the head of the North Twin, which is only four miles across. We were nearly out of provisions, and ill prepared in this respect for what might possibly prove a week's journey round by the shore, fording innumerable streams, and threading a trackless forest, should any accident happen to our boat.

It was with regret that we turned our backs on Chesuncook, which McCauslin had formerly logged on, and the Allagash lakes. There were still longer rapids and portages above; among the last the Rippogenus Portage, which he described as the most difficult on the river, and three miles long. The whole length of the Penobscot is two hundred and seventy-five miles, and we are still nearly one hundred miles from its source. Hodge, the assistant State Geologist, passed up this river in 1837, and by a portage of only one mile and three-quarters, crossed over into the Allagash, and so went down that into the St. John, and up the Madawaska to the Grand Portage across to the St. Lawrence. His is the only account that I know, of an expedition through to Canada in this direction. He thus describes his first sight of the latter river, which, to compare small things with great, is like Balboa's first sight of the Pacific from the mountains of the Isthmus of Darien. "When we first came in sight of the St. Lawrence," he says, "from the top of a high hill, the view was most striking, and much more interesting to me from having been shut up in the woods for the two previous months. Directly before us lay the broad river, extending across nine or ten miles, its surface broken by a few islands and reefs; and two ships riding at anchor near the shore. Beyond, extended ranges of uncultivated hills, parallel with the river. The sun was just going down behind them, and gilding the whole scene with its parting rays."

About four o'clock the same afternoon, we commenced our return voyage, which would require but little if any poling. In shooting rapids, the boatmen use large and broad paddles, instead of poles, to guide the boat with. Though we glided so swiftly and often smoothly down, where it had cost us no slight effort to get up, our present voyage was attended with far more danger: for if we once fairly struck one of the thousand rocks by which we were surrounded, the boat would be swamped in an instant. When a boat is swamped under these circumstances, the boatmen commonly find no difficulty in keeping afloat at first, for the current keeps both them and their cargo up for a long way down the stream; and if they can swim, they have only to work their way gradually to the shore. The greatest danger is of being caught in an eddy behind some larger rock, where the water rushes up stream faster than elsewhere it does down, and being carried round and round under the surface till they are drowned. McCauslin pointed out some rocks which had been the scene of a fatal accident of this kind. Sometimes the body is not thrown out for several hours. He himself had performed such a circuit once, only his legs being visible to his companions; but he was fortunately thrown out in season to recover his breath.* In shooting the rapids, the boatman has this problem to solve: to choose a circuitous and safe course amid a thousand sunken rocks, scattered over a quarter or half a mile, at the same time that he is moving steadily on at the rate of fifteen miles an hour. Stop he cannot; the only question is, where will he go? The bow-man chooses the course with all his eyes about him, striking broad off with his paddle, and drawing the boat by main force into her course. The stern-man faithfully follows the bow.

We were soon at the Aboljacarmegus Falls. Anxious to avoid the delay as well as the labor of the portage here, our boatmen went forward first to reconnoitre, and concluded to let the batteau down the falls, carrying the baggage only over the portage. Jumping from rock to rock until nearly in the middle of the stream, we were ready to receive the boat and let her down over the first fall, some six or seven feet perpendicular. The boatmen stand upon the edge of a shelf of rock where the fall is perhaps nine or ten feet perpendicular, in from one to two feet of rapid wa-

*I cut this from a newspaper. "On the 11th (instant?) [May, '49], on Rappogenes Falls, Mr. John Delantee, of Orono, Me., was drowned while running logs. He was a citizen of Orono, and was twenty-six years of age. His companions found his body, enclosed it in bark, and buried it in the solemn woods."

ter, one on each side of the boat, and let it slide gently over, till the bow is run out ten or twelve feet in the air; then letting it drop squarely, while one holds the painter, the other leaps in, and his companion following, they are whirled down the rapids to a new fall, or to smooth water. In a very few minutes they had accomplished a passage in safety, which would be as fool-hardy for the unskilful to attempt as the descent of Niagara itself. It seemed as if it needed only a little familiarity, and a little more skill, to navigate down such falls as Niagara itself with safety. At any rate, I should not despair of such men in the rapids above Table-Rock, until I saw them actually go over the falls, so cool, so collected, so fertile in resources are they. One might have thought that these were falls, and that falls were not to be waded through with impunity like a mud-puddle. There was really danger of their losing their sublimity in losing their power to harm us. Familiarity breeds contempt. The boatman pauses, perchance, on some shelf beneath a table-rock under the fall, standing in some cove of back-water two feet deep, and you hear his rough voice come up through the spray, coolly giving directions how to launch the boat this time.

Having carried round Pockwockomus Falls, our oars soon brought us to the Katepskonegan, or Oak Hall carry, where we decided to camp half way over, leaving our batteau to be carried over in the morning on fresh shoulders. One shoulder of each of the boatmen showed a red spot as large as one's hand, worn by the batteau on this expedition; and this shoulder, as it did all the work, was perceptibly lower than its fellow, from long service. Such toil soon wears out the strongest constitution. The drivers are accustomed to work in the cold water in the spring, rarely ever dry; and if one falls in all over, he rarely changes his clothes till night, if then, even. One who takes this precaution is called by a particular nickname, or is turned off. None can lead this life who are not almost amphibious. McCauslin said soberly, what is at any rate a good story to tell, that he had seen where six men were wholly under water at once, at a jam, with their shoulders to handspikes. If the log did not start, then they had to put out their heads to breathe. The driver works as long as he can see, from dark to dark, and at night has not time to eat his supper and dry his clothes fairly, before he is asleep on his cedar bed. We lay that night on the very bed made by such a party, stretching our tent over the poles which were still standing, but reshingling the damp and faded bed with fresh leaves.

In the morning, we carried our boat over and launched it, making haste lest the wind should rise. The boatmen ran down Passamagamet, and, soon after, Ambejijis Falls, while we walked round with the baggage. We made a hasty breakfast at the head of Ambejijis lake, on the remainder of our pork, and were soon rowing across its smooth surface again, under a pleasant sky, the mountain being now clear of clouds in the northeast. Taking turns at the oars, we shot rapidly across Deep Cove, the Foot of Pamadumcook, and the North Twin, at the rate of six miles an hour, the wind not being high enough to disturb us, and reached the Dam at noon. The boatmen went through one of the log sluices in the batteau, where the fall was ten feet at the bottom, and took us in below. Here was the longest rapid in our voyage, and perhaps the running this was as dangerous and arduous a task as any. Shooting down sometimes at the rate, as we judged, of fifteen miles an hour, if we struck a rock, we were split from end to end in an instant. Now like a bait bobbing for some river monster amid the eddies, now darting to this side of the stream, now to that, gliding swift and smooth near to our destruction, or striking broad off with the paddle and drawing the boat to right or left with all our might, in order to avoid a rock. I suppose that it was like running the rapids of the Sault de Ste. Marie, at the outlet of Lake Superior, and our boatmen probably displayed no less dexterity than the Indians there do. We soon ran through this mile, and floated in Quakish lake.

After such a voyage, the troubled and angry waters, which once had seemed terrible and not to be trifled with, appeared tamed and subdued; they had been bearded and worried in their channels, pricked and whipped into submission with the spike-pole and paddle, gone through and through with impunity, and all their spirit and their danger taken out of them, and the most swollen and impetuous rivers seemed but playthings henceforth. I began, at length, to understand the boatman's familiarity with and contempt for the rapids. "Those Fowler boys," said Mrs. McCauslin, "are perfect ducks for the water." They had run down to Lincoln, according to her, thirty or forty miles, in a batteau, in the night, for a doctor, when it was so dark that they could not see a rod before them, and the river was swollen so as to be almost a continuous rapid, so that the doctor *cried*, when they brought him up by daylight, "Why, Tom, how did you see to steer?" "We didn't steer much,—only kept her straight." And yet they met with no accident. It is true, the more difficult rapids are higher up than this.

When we reached the Millinocket opposite to Tom's house, and were waiting for his folks to set us over, for we had left our batteau above the Grand Falls, we discovered two canoes with two men in each, turning up this stream from Shad Pond, one keeping the opposite side of a small island before us, while the other approached the side where we were standing, examining the banks carefully for muskrats as they came along. The last proved to be Louis Neptune and his companion, now at last on their way up to Chesuncook after moose; but they were so disguised that we hardly knew them. At a little distance, they might have been taken for Quakers, with their broad-brimmed hats, and overcoats with broad capes, the spoils of Bangor, seeking a settlement in this Sylvania,—or, nearer at hand, for fashionable gentlemen, the morning after a spree. Met face to face, these Indians in their native woods looked like the sinister and slouching fellows whom you meet picking up strings and paper in the streets of a city. There is, in fact, a remarkable and unexpected resemblance between the degraded savage and the lowest classes in a great city. The one is no more a child of nature than the other. In the progress of degradation, the distinction of races is soon lost. Neptune at first was only anxious to know what we "kill," seeing some partridges in the hands of one of the party, but we had assumed too much anger to permit of a reply. We thought Indians had some honor before. But—"Me been sick. O, me unwell now. You make bargain, then me go." They had in fact been delayed so long by a drunken frolic at the Five Islands, and they had not yet recovered from its effects. They had some young musquash in their canoes, which they dug out of the banks with a hoe for food, not for their skins, for musquash are their principal food on these expeditions. So they went on up the Millinocket, and we kept down the bank of the Penobscot, after recruiting ourselves with a draught of Tom's beer, leaving Tom at his home.

Thus a man shall lead his life away here on the edge of the wilderness, on Indian Millinocket stream, in a new world, far in the dark of a continent, and have a flute to play at evening here, while his strains echo to the stars, amid the howling of wolves; shall live, as it were, in the primitive age of the world, a primitive man. Yet he shall spend a sunny day, and in this century be my contemporary; perchance shall read some scattered leaves of literature, and sometimes talk with me. Why read history then if the ages and the generations are now? He lives three thousand years deep into time, an age not yet described by poets. Can you well go further back in history than this? Ay! ay!—for there turns up but now into the mouth of Millinocket stream a still more ancient and primitive man, whose history is not brought down even to the former. In a bark vessel sewn with the roots of the spruce, with horn-beam paddles he dips his way along. He is but dim and misty to me, obscured by the æons that lie between the bark canoe and the batteau. He builds no house of logs, but a wigwam of skins. He eats no hot-bread and sweet-cake, but musquash and moose-meat and the fat of bears. He glides up the Millinocket and is lost to my sight, as a more distant and misty cloud is seen flitting by behind a nearer, and is lost in space. So he goes about his destiny, the red face of man.

After having passed the night and buttered our boots for the last time at Uncle George's, whose dogs almost devoured him for joy at his return, we kept on down the river the next day about eight miles on foot, and then took a batteau with a man to pole it to Mattawamkeag, ten more. At the middle of that very night, to make a swift conclusion to a long story, we dropped our buggy over the half-finished bridge at Oldtown, where we heard the confused din and clink of a hundred saws which never rest, and at six o'clock the next morning one of the party was steaming his way to Massachusetts.

What is most striking in the Maine wilderness is, the continuousness of the forest, with fewer open intervals or glades than you had imagined. Except the few burnt lands, the narrow intervals on the rivers, the bare tops of the high mountains, and the lakes and streams, the forest is uninterrupted. It is even more grim and wild than you had anticipated, a damp and intricate wilderness, in the spring everywhere wet and miry. The aspect of the country indeed is universally stern and savage, excepting the distant views of the forest from hills, and the lake prospects, which are mild and civilizing in a degree. The lakes are something which you are unprepared for: they lie up so high exposed to the light, and the forest is diminished to a fine fringe on their edges, with here and there a blue mountain, like amethyst jewels set around some jewel of the first water,—so anterior, so superior to all the changes that are to take place on their shores, even now civil and refined, and fair, as they can ever be. These are not the artificial forests of an English king—a royal preserve merely. Here prevail no forest laws, but those of nature. The aborigines have never been dispossessed, nor nature disforested.

It is a country full of evergreen trees, of mossy silver birches and watery maples, the ground dotted with insipid, small red berries, and strewn with damp and moss-grown rocks—a country diversified with innumerable lakes and rapid streams, peopled with trout and various species of *leucisci*, with salmon, shad and pickerel, and other fishes; the forest resounding at rare intervals with the note of the chicadee, the blue-jay, and the woodpecker, the scream of the fish-hawk and the eagle, the laugh of the loon, and the whistle of ducks along the solitary streams; and at night, with the hooting of owls and howling of wolves; in summer, swarming with myriads of black flies and mosquitoes, more formidable than wolves to the white man. Such is the home of the moose, the bear, the caribou, the wolf, the beaver, and the Indian. Who shall describe the inexpressible tenderness and immortal life of the grim forest, where Nature, though it be mid-winter, is ever in her spring, where the moss-grown and decaying trees are not old, but seem to enjoy a perpetual youth; and blissful, innocent Nature, like a serene infant, is too happy to make a noise, except by a few tinkling, lisping birds and trickling rills?

What a place to live, what a place to die and be buried in! There certainly men would live forever, and laugh at death and the grave. There they could have no such thoughts as are associated with the village graveyard,—that make a grave out of one of those moist evergreen hummocks!

Die and be buried who will,
  I mean to live here still;
My nature grows ever more young
  The primitive pines among.

I am reminded by my journey how exceedingly new this country still is. You have only to travel for a few days into the interior and back parts even of many of the old states, to come to that very America which the Northmen, and Cabot, and Gosnold, and Smith and Raleigh visited. If Columbus was the first to discover the islands, Americus Vespucius, and Cabot, and the Puritans, and we their descendants, have discovered only the shores of America. While the republic has already acquired a history world-wide, America is still unsettled and unexplored. Like the English in New Holland, we live only on the shores of a continent even yet, and hardly know where the rivers come from which float our navy. The very timber and boards, and shingles, of which our houses are made, grew but yesterday in a wilderness where the Indian still hunts and the moose runs wild. New-York has her wilderness within her own borders; and though the sailors of Europe are familiar with the soundings of her Hudson, and Fulton long since invented the steamboat on its waters, an Indian is still necessary to guide her scientific men to its head-waters in the Adirondac country.

Have we even so much as discovered and settled the shores? Let a man travel on foot along the coast, from the Passamaquoddy to the Sabine, or to the Rio Bravo, or to wherever the end is now, if he is swift enough to overtake it, faithfully following the windings of every inlet and of every cape, and stepping to the music of the surf—with a desolate fishing-town once a week, and a city's port once a month to cheer him, and putting up at the light-houses, when there are any, and tell me if it looks like a discovered and settled country, and not rather, for the most part, like a desolate island, and No-man's Land.

We have advanced by leaps to the Pacific, and left many a lesser Oregon and California unexplored behind us. Though the railroad and the telegraph have been established on the shores of Maine, the Indian still looks out from her interior mountains over all these to the sea. There stands the city of Bangor, fifty miles up the Penobscot, at the head of navigation for vessels of the largest class, the principal lumber depot on this continent, with a population of twelve thousand, like a star on the edge of night, still hewing at the forests of which it is built, already overflowing with the luxuries and refinement of Europe, and sending its vessels to Spain, to England, and to the West Indies for its groceries,—and yet only a few axe-men have gone "up river" into the howling wilderness which feeds it. The bear and deer are still found within its limits; and the moose, as he swims the Penobscot, is entangled amid its shipping and taken by foreign sailors in its harbor. Twelve miles in the rear, twelve miles of railroad, are Orono and the Indian Island, the home of the Penobscot tribe, and then commence the batteau and the canoe, and the military road; and, sixty miles above, the country is virtually unmapped and unexplored, and there still waves the virgin forest of the New World.

CIVIL DISOBEDIENCE

TABLE OF CONTENTS.

POETRY.

Aesthetic Papers, 1849. Thoreau's lecture was delivered in January 1848.

CIVIL DISOBEDIENCE

I heartily accept the motto, "That government is best which governs least;" and I should like to see it acted up to more rapidly and systematically. Carried out, it finally amounts to this, which also I believe,—"That government is best which governs not at all;" and when men are prepared for it, that will be the kind of government which they will have. Government is at best but an expedient; but most governments are usually, and all governments are sometimes, inexpedient. The objections which have been brought against a standing army, and they are many and weighty, and deserve to prevail, may also at last be brought against a standing government. The standing army is only an arm of the standing government. The government itself, which is only the mode which the people have chosen to execute their will, is equally liable to be abused and perverted before the people can act through it. Witness the present Mexican war, the work of comparatively a few individuals using the standing government as their tool; for, in the outset, the people would not have consented to this measure.

This American government,—what is it but a tradition, though a recent one, endeavoring to transmit itself unimpaired to posterity, but each instant losing some of its integrity? It has not the vitality and force of a single living man; for a single man can bend it to his will. It is a sort of wooden gun to the people themselves. But it is not the less necessary for this; for the people must have some complicated machinery or other, and hear its din, to satisfy that idea of government which they have. Governments show thus how successfully men can be imposed on, even impose on themselves, for their own advantage. It is excellent, we must all allow. Yet this government never of itself furthered any enterprise, but by the alacrity with which it got out of its way. *It* does not keep the country free. *It* does not settle the West. *It* does not educate. The character inherent in the American people has done all that has been accomplished; and it would have done somewhat more, if the government had not sometimes got in its way. For government is an expedient by which men would fain succeed in letting one another alone; and, as has been said, when it is most expedient, the governed are most let alone by it. Trade and commerce, if they were not made of india-rubber, would never manage to bounce over the obstacles which legislators are continually putting in their way; and, if one were to judge these men wholly by the effects of their actions and not partly by their intentions, they would deserve to be classed and punished with those mischievous persons who put obstructions on the railroads.

But, to speak practically and as a citizen, unlike those who call themselves no-government men, I ask for, not at once no government, but *at once* a better government. Let every man make known what kind of government would command his respect, and that will be one step toward obtaining it.

After all, the practical reason why, when the power is once in the hands of the people, a majority are permitted, and for a long period continue, to rule is not because they are most likely to be in the right, nor because this seems fairest to the minority, but because they are physically the strongest. But a government in which the majority rule in all cases cannot be based on justice, even as far as men understand it. Can there not be a government in which majorities do not virtually decide right and wrong, but conscience?—in which majorities decide only those questions to which the rule of expediency is applicable? Must the citizen ever for a moment, or in the least degree, resign his conscience to the legislator? Why has every man a conscience, then? I think that we should be men first, and subjects afterward. It is not desirable to cultivate a respect for the law, so much as for the right. The only obligation which I have a right to assume is to do at any time what I think right. It is truly enough said that a corporation has no conscience; but a corporation of conscientious men is a corporation *with* a conscience. Law never made men a whit more just; and, by means of their respect for it, even the well-disposed are daily made the agents of injustice. A common and natural result of an undue respect for law is, that you may see a file of soldiers, colonel, captain, corporal, privates, powder-monkeys, and all, marching in admirable order over hill and dale to the wars, against their wills, ay, against their common sense and consciences, which makes it very steep marching indeed, and produces a palpitation of the heart. They have no doubt that it is a damnable business in which they are concerned; they are all peaceably inclined. Now, what are they? Men at all? or small movable forts and magazines, at the service of some unscrupulous man in power? Visit the Navy-Yard, and behold a marine, such a man as an American government can make, or such as it can make a man with its black arts,—a mere shadow and reminiscence of humanity, a man laid out alive and standing, and already, as one may say, buried under arms with funeral accompaniments, though it may be,—

> "Not a drum was heard, not a funeral note,
> As his corse to the rampart we hurried;
> Not a soldier discharged his farewell shot
> O'er the grave where our hero we buried."

The mass of men serve the state thus, not as men mainly, but as machines, with their bodies. They are the standing army, and the militia, jailers, constables, *posse comitatus*, etc. In most cases there is no free exercise whatever of the judgment or of the moral sense; but they put themselves on a level with wood and earth and stones; and wooden men can perhaps be manufactured that will serve the purpose as well. Such command no more respect than men of straw or a lump of dirt. They have the same sort of worth only as horses and dogs. Yet such as these even are commonly esteemed good citizens. Others—as most legislators, politicians, lawyers, ministers, and office-holders—serve the state chiefly with their heads; and, as they rarely make any moral distinctions, they are as likely to serve the devil, without *intending* it, as God. A very few—as heroes, patriots, martyrs, reformers in the great sense, and *men*—serve the state with their consciences also, and so necessarily resist it for the most part; and they are commonly treated as enemies by it. A wise man will only be useful as a man, and will not submit to be "clay," and "stop a hole to keep the wind away," but leave that office to his dust at least:—

"I am too high-born to be propertied,
To be a secondary at control,
Or useful serving-man and instrument
To any sovereign state throughout the world."

He who gives himself entirely to his fellow-men appears to them useless and selfish; but he who gives himself partially to them is pronounced a benefactor and philanthropist.

How does it become a man to behave toward this American government to-day? I answer, that he cannot without disgrace be associated with it. I cannot for an instant recognize that political organization as *my* government which is the *slave's* government also.

All men recognize the right of revolution; that is, the right to refuse allegiance to, and to resist, the government, when its tyranny or its inefficiency are great and unendurable. But almost all say that such is not the case now. But such was the case, they think, in the Revolution of '75. If one were to tell me that this was a bad government because it taxed certain foreign commodities brought to its ports, it is most probable that I should not make an ado about it, for I can do without them. All machines have their friction; and possibly this does enough good to counterbalance the evil. At any rate, it is a great evil to make a stir about it. But when the friction comes to have its machine, and oppression and robbery are organized, I say, let us not have such a machine any longer. In other words, when a sixth of the population of a nation which has undertaken to be the refuge of liberty are slaves, and a whole country is unjustly overrun and conquered by a foreign army, and subjected to military law, I think that it is not too soon for honest men to rebel and revolutionize. What makes this duty the more urgent is the fact that the country so overrun is not our own, but ours is the invading army.

Paley, a common authority with many on moral questions, in his chapter on the "Duty of Submission to Civil Government," resolves all civil obligation into expediency; and he proceeds to say that "so long as the interest of the whole society requires it, that is, so long as the established government cannot be resisted or changed without public inconveniency, it is the will of God . . . that the established government be obeyed,—and no longer. This principle being admitted, the justice of every particular case of resistance is reduced to a computation of the quantity of the danger and grievance on the one side, and of the probability and expense of redressing it on the other." Of this, he says, every man shall judge for himself. But Paley appears never to have contemplated those cases to which the rule of expediency does not apply, in which a people, as well as an individual, must do justice, cost what it may. If I have unjustly wrested a plank from a drowning man, I must restore it to him though I drown myself. This, according to Paley, would be inconvenient. But he that would save his life, in such a case, shall lose it. This people must cease to hold slaves, and to make war on Mexico, though it cost them their existence as a people.

In their practice, nations agree with Paley; but does any one think that Massachusetts does exactly what is right at the present crisis?

> "A drab of state, a cloth-o'-silver slut,
> To have her train borne up, and her soul trail in the dirt."

Practically speaking, the opponents to a reform in Massachusetts are not a hundred thousand politicians at the South, but a hundred thousand merchants and farmers here, who are more interested in commerce and agriculture than they are in humanity, and are not prepared to do justice to the slave and to Mexico, *cost what it may.* I quarrel not with far-off foes, but with those who, near at home, coöperate with, and do the bidding of, those far away, and without whom the latter would be harmless. We are accustomed to say, that the mass of men are unprepared; but improvement is slow, because the few are not materially wiser or better than the many. It is not so important that many should be as good as you, as that there be some absolute goodness somewhere; for that will leaven the whole lump. There are thousands who are *in opinion* opposed to slavery and to the war, who yet in effect do nothing to put an end to them; who, esteeming themselves children of Washington and Franklin, sit down with their hands in their pockets, and say that they know not what to do, and do nothing; who even postpone the question of freedom to the question of free trade, and quietly read the prices-current along with the latest advices from Mexico, after dinner, and, it may be, fall asleep over them both. What is the price-current of an honest man and patriot today? They hesitate, and they regret, and sometimes they petition; but they do nothing in earnest and with effect. They will wait, well disposed, for others to remedy the evil, that they may no longer have it to regret. At most, they give only a cheap vote, and a feeble countenance and Godspeed, to the right, as it goes by them. There are nine hundred and ninety-nine patrons of virtue to one virtuous man. But it is easier to deal with the real possessor of a thing than with the temporary guardian of it.

All voting is a sort of gaming, like checkers or backgammon, with a slight moral tinge to it, a playing with right and wrong, with moral questions; and betting naturally accompanies it. The character of the voters is not staked. I cast my vote, perchance, as I think right; but I am not vitally concerned that that right should prevail. I am willing to leave it to the majority. Its obligation, therefore, never exceeds that of expediency. Even voting *for the right* is *doing* nothing for it. It is only expressing to men feebly your desire that it should prevail. A wise man will not leave the right to the mercy of chance, nor wish it to prevail through the power of the majority. There is but little virtue in the action of masses of men. When the majority shall at length vote for the abolition of slavery, it will be because they are indifferent to slavery, or because there is but little slavery left to be abolished by their vote. *They* will then be the only slaves. Only *his* vote can hasten the abolition of slavery who asserts his own freedom by his vote.

I hear of a convention to be held at Baltimore, or elsewhere, for the selection of a candidate for the Presidency, made up chiefly of editors, and men who are politicians by profession; but I think, what is it to any independent, intelligent, and respectable man what decision they may come to? Shall we not have the advantage of his wisdom and honesty, nevertheless? Can we not count upon some independent votes? Are there not many individuals in the country who do not attend conventions? But no: I find that the respectable man, so called, has immediately drifted from his position, and despairs of his country, when his country has more reason to despair of him. He forthwith adopts one of the candidates thus selected as the only *available* one, thus proving that he is himself *available* for any purposes of the demagogue. His vote is of no more worth than that of any unprincipled foreigner or hireling native, who may have been bought. O for a man who is a *man*, and, as my neighbor says, has a bone in his back which you cannot pass your hand through! Our statistics are at fault: the population has been returned too large. How many *men* are there to a square thousand miles in this country? Hardly one. Does not America offer any inducement for men to settle here? The American has dwindled into an Odd Fellow,—one who may be known by the development of his organ of gregariousness, and a manifest lack of intellect and cheerful self-reliance; whose first and chief concern, on coming into the world, is to see that the almshouses are in good repair; and, before yet he has lawfully donned the virile garb, to collect a fund for the support of the widows and orphans that may be; who, in short, ventures to live only by the aid of the Mutual Insurance company, which has promised to bury him decently.

It is not a man's duty, as a matter of course, to devote himself to the eradication of any, even the most enormous, wrong; he may still properly have other concerns to engage him; but it is his duty, at least, to wash his hands of it, and, if he gives it no thought longer, not to give it practically his support. If I devote myself to other pursuits and contemplations, I must first see, at least, that I do not pursue them sitting upon another man's shoulders. I must get off him first, that he may pursue his contemplations too. See what gross inconsistency is tolerated. I have heard some of my townsmen say, "I should like to have them order me out to help put down an insurrection of the slaves, or to march to Mexico;—see if I would go;" and yet these very men have each, directly by their allegiance, and so indirectly, at least, by their money, furnished a substitute. The soldier is applauded who refuses to serve in an unjust war by those who do not refuse to sustain the unjust government which makes the war; is applauded by those whose own act and authority he disregards and sets at naught; as if the state were penitent to that degree that it hired one to scourge it while it sinned, but not to that degree that it left off sinning for a moment. Thus, under the name of Order and Civil Government, we are all made at last to pay homage to and support our own meanness. After the first blush of sin comes its indifference; and from immoral it becomes, as it were, *un*moral, and not quite unnecessary to that life which we have made.

The broadest and most prevalent error requires the most disinterested virtue to sustain it. The slight reproach to which the virtue of patriotism is commonly liable, the noble are most likely to incur. Those who, while they disapprove of the character and measures of a government, yield to it their allegiance and support are undoubtedly its most conscientious supporters, and so frequently the most serious obstacles to reform. Some are petitioning the State to dissolve the Union, to disregard the requisitions of the President. Why do they not dissolve it themselves,—the union between themselves and the State,—and refuse to pay their quota into its treasury? Do not they stand in the same relation to the State that the State does to the Union? And have not the same reasons prevented the State from resisting the Union which have prevented them from resisting the State?

How can a man be satisfied to entertain an opinion merely, and enjoy *it*? Is there any enjoyment in it, if his opinion is that he is aggrieved? If you are cheated out of a single dollar by your neighbor, you do not rest satisfied with knowing that you are cheated, or with saying that you are cheated, or even with petitioning him to pay you your due; but you take effectual steps at once to obtain the full amount, and see that you are never cheated again. Action from principle, the perception and the performance of right, changes things and relations; it is essentially revolutionary, and does not consist wholly with anything which was. It not only divides States and churches, it divides families; ay, it divides the *individual*, separating the diabolical in him from the divine.

Unjust laws exist: shall we be content to obey them, or shall we endeavor to amend them, and obey them until we have succeeded, or shall we transgress them at once? Men generally, under such a government as this, think that they ought to wait until they have persuaded the majority to alter them. They think that, if they should resist, the remedy would be worse than the evil. But it is the fault of the government itself that the remedy *is* worse than the evil. *It* makes it worse. Why is it not more apt to anticipate and provide for reform? Why does it not cherish its wise minority? Why does it cry and resist before it is hurt? Why does it not encourage its citizens to be on the alert to point out its faults, and *do* better than it would have them? Why does it always crucify Christ, and excommunicate Copernicus and Luther, and pronounce Washington and Franklin rebels?

One would think, that a deliberate and practical denial of its authority was the only offence never contemplated by government; else, why has it not assigned its definite, its suitable and proportionate, penalty? If a man who has no property refuses but once to earn nine shillings for the State, he is put in prison for a period unlimited by any law that I know, and determined only by the discretion of those who placed him there; but if he should steal ninety times nine shillings from the State, he is soon permitted to go at large again.

If the injustice is part of the necessary friction of the machine of government, let it go, let it go: perchance it will wear smooth,—certainly the machine will wear out. If the injustice has a spring, or a pulley, or a rope, or a crank, exclusively for itself, then perhaps you may consider whether the remedy will not be worse than the evil; but if it is of such a nature that it requires you to be the agent of injustice to another, then, I say, break the law. Let your life be a counter-friction to stop the machine. What I have to do is to see, at any rate, that I do not lend myself to the wrong which I condemn.

As for adopting the ways which the State has provided for remedying the evil, I know not of such ways. They take too much time, and a man's life will be gone. I have other affairs to attend to. I came into this world, not chiefly to make this a good place to live in, but to live in it, be it good or bad. A man has not everything to do, but something; and because he cannot do *everything*, it is not necessary that he should do *something* wrong. It is not my business to be petitioning the Governor or the Legislature any more than it is theirs to petition me; and if they should not hear my petition, what should I do then? But in this case the State has provided no way: its very Constitution is the evil. This may seem to be harsh and stubborn and unconciliatory; but it is to treat with the utmost kindness and consideration the only spirit that can appreciate or deserves it. So is all change for the better, like birth and death, which convulse the body.

I do not hesitate to say, that those who call themselves Abolitionists should at once effectually withdraw their support, both in person and property, from the government of Massachusetts, and not wait till they constitute a majority of one, before they suffer the right to prevail through them. I think that it is enough if they have God on their side, without waiting for that other one. Moreover, any man more right than his neighbors constitutes a majority of one already.

I meet this American government, or its representative, the State government, directly, and face to face, once a year—no more—in the person of its tax-gatherer; this is the only mode in which a man situated as I am necessarily meets it; and it then says distinctly, Recognize me; and the simplest, the most effectual, and, in the present posture of affairs, the indispensablest mode of treating with it on this head, of expressing your little satisfaction with and love for it, is to deny it then. My civil neighbor, the tax-gatherer, is the very man I have to deal with,—for it is, after all, with men and not with parchment that I quarrel,—and he has voluntarily chosen to be an agent of the government. How shall he ever know well what he is and does as an officer of the government, or as a man, until he is obliged to consider whether he shall treat me, his neighbor, for whom he has respect, as a neighbor and well-disposed man, or as a maniac and disturber of the peace, and see if he can get over this obstruction to his neighborliness without a ruder and more impetuous thought or speech corresponding with his action. I know this well, that if one thousand, if one hundred, if ten men whom I could name,—if ten *honest* men only,—ay, if *one* HONEST man, in this State of Massachusetts, *ceasing to hold slaves*, were actually to withdraw from this copartnership, and be locked up in the county jail therefor, it would be the abolition of slavery in America. For it matters not how small the beginning may seem to be: what is once well done is done forever. But we love better to talk about it: that we say is our mission. Reform keeps many scores of newspapers in its service, but not one man. If my esteemed neighbor, the State's ambassador, who will devote his days to the settlement of the question of human rights in the Council Chamber, instead of being threatened with the prisons of Carolina, were to sit down the prisoner of Massachusetts, that State which is so anxious to foist the sin of slavery upon her sister,—though at present she can discover only an act of inhospitality to be the ground of a quarrel with her,—the Legislature would not wholly waive the subject the following winter.

Under a government which imprisons any unjustly, the true place for a just man is also a prison. The proper place to-day, the only place which Massachusetts has provided for her freer and less desponding spirits, is in her prisons, to be put out and locked out of the State by her own act, as they have already put themselves out by their principles. It is there that the fugitive slave, and the Mexican prisoner on parole, and the Indian come to plead the wrongs of his race should find them; on that separate, but more free and honorable, ground, where the State places those who are not *with* her, but *against* her,—the only house in a slave State in which a free man can abide with honor. If any think that their influence would be lost there, and their voices no longer afflict the ear of the State, that they would not be as an enemy within its walls, they do not know by how much truth is stronger than error, nor how much more eloquently and effectively he can combat injustice who has experienced a little in his own person. Cast your whole vote, not a strip of paper merely, but your whole influence. A minority is powerless while it conforms to the majority; it is not even a minority then; but it is irresistible when it clogs by its whole weight. If the alternative is to keep all just men in prison, or give up war and slavery, the State will not hesitate which to choose. If a thousand men were not to pay their tax-bills this year, that would not be a violent and bloody measure, as it would be to pay them, and enable the State to commit violence and shed innocent blood. This is, in fact, the definition of a peaceable revolution, if any such is possible. If the tax-gatherer, or any other public officer, asks me, as one has done, "But what shall I do?" my answer is, "If you really wish to do anything, resign your office." When the subject has refused allegiance, and the officer has resigned his office, then the revolution is accomplished. But even suppose blood should flow. Is there not a sort of blood shed when the conscience is wounded? Through this wound a man's real manhood and immortality flow out, and he bleeds to an everlasting death. I see this blood flowing now.

I have contemplated the imprisonment of the offender, rather than the seizure of his goods,—though both will serve the same purpose,—because they who assert the purest right, and consequently are most dangerous to a corrupt State, commonly have not spent much time in accumulating property. To such the State renders comparatively small service, and a slight tax is wont to appear exorbitant, particularly if they are obliged to earn it by special labor with their hands. If there were one who lived wholly without the use of money, the State itself would hesitate to demand it of him. But the rich man—not to make any invidious comparison—is always sold to the institution which makes him rich. Absolutely speaking, the more money, the less virtue; for money comes between a man and his objects, and obtains them for him; and it was certainly no great virtue to obtain it. It puts to rest many questions which he would otherwise be taxed to answer; while the only new question which it puts is the hard but superfluous one, how to spend it. Thus his moral ground is taken from under his feet. The opportunities of living are diminished in proportion as what are called the "means" are increased. The best thing a man can do for his culture when he is rich is to endeavor to carry out those schemes which he entertained when he was poor. Christ answered the Herodians according to their condition. "Show me the tribute-money," said he;—and one took a penny out of his pocket;—if you use money which has the image of Cæsar on it, and which he has made current and valuable, that is, *if you are men of the State*, and gladly enjoy the advantages of Cæsar's government, then pay him back some of his own when he demands it. "Render therefore to Cæsar that which is Cæsar's, and to God those things which are

God's,"—leaving them no wiser than before as to which was which; for they did not wish to know.

When I converse with the freest of my neighbors, I perceive that, whatever they may say about the magnitude and seriousness of the question, and their regard for the public tranquillity, the long and the short of the matter is, that they cannot spare the protection of the existing government, and they dread the consequences to their property and families of disobedience to it. For my own part, I should not like to think that I ever rely on the protection of the State. But, if I deny the authority of the State when it presents its tax-bill, it will soon take and waste all my property, and so harass me and my children without end. This is hard. This makes it impossible for a man to live honestly, and at the same time comfortably, in outward respects. It will not be worth the while to accumulate property; that would be sure to go again. You must hire or squat somewhere, and raise but a small crop, and eat that soon. You must live within yourself, and depend upon yourself always tucked up and ready for a start, and not have many affairs. A man may grow rich in Turkey even, if he will be in all respects a good subject of the Turkish government. Confucius said: "If a state is governed by the principles of reason, poverty and misery are subjects of shame; if a state is not governed by the principles of reason, riches and honors are the subjects of shame." No: until I want the protection of Massachusetts to be extended to me in some distant Southern port, where my liberty is endangered, or until I am bent solely on building up an estate at home by peaceful enterprise, I can afford to refuse allegiance to Massachusetts, and her right to my property and life. It costs me less in every sense to incur the penalty of disobedience to the State than it would to obey. I should feel as if I were worth less in that case.

Some years ago, the State met me in behalf of the Church, and commanded me to pay a certain sum toward the support of a clergyman whose preaching my father attended, but never I myself. "Pay," it said, "or be locked up in the jail." I declined to pay. But, unfortunately, another man saw fit to pay it. I did not see why the schoolmaster should be taxed to support the priest, and not the priest the schoolmaster; for I was not the State's schoolmaster, but I supported myself by voluntary subscription. I did not see why the lyceum should not present its tax-bill, and have the State to back its demand, as well as the Church. However, at the request of the selectmen, I condescended to make some such statement as this in writing:—"Know all men by these presents, that I, Henry Thoreau, do not wish to be regarded as a member of any incorporated society which I have not joined." This I gave to the town clerk; and he has it. The State, having thus learned that I did not wish to be regarded as a member of that church, has never made a like demand on me since; though it said that it must adhere to its original presumption that time. If I had known how to name them, I should then have signed off in detail from all the societies which I never signed on to; but I did not know where to find a complete list.

I have paid no poll-tax for six years. I was put into a jail once on this account, for one night; and, as I stood considering the walls of solid stone, two or three feet thick, the door of wood and iron, a foot thick, and the iron grating which strained the light, I could not help being struck with the foolishness of that institution which treated me as if I were mere flesh and blood and bones, to be locked up. I wondered that it should have concluded at length that this was the best use it could put me to, and had never thought to avail itself of my services in some way. I saw that, if there was a wall of stone between me and my townsmen, there was a still more difficult one to climb or break through before they could get to be as free as I was. I did not for a moment feel confined, and the walls seemed a great waste of stone and mortar. I felt as if I alone of all my townsmen had paid my tax. They plainly did not know how to treat me, but behaved like persons who are underbred. In every threat and in every compliment there was a blunder; for they thought that my chief desire was to stand the other side of that stone wall. I could not but smile to see how industriously they locked the door on my meditations, which followed them out again without let or hindrance, and *they* were really all that was dangerous. As they could not reach me, they had resolved to punish my body; just as boys, if they cannot come at some person against whom they have a spite, will abuse his dog. I saw that the State was half-witted, that it was timid as a lone woman with her silver spoons, and that it did not know its friends from its foes, and I lost all my remaining respect for it, and pitied it.

Thus the State never intentionally confronts a man's sense, intellectual or moral, but only his body, his senses. It is not armed with superior wit or honesty, but with superior physical strength. I was not born to be forced. I will breathe after my own fashion. Let us see who is the strongest. What force has a multitude? They only can force me who obey a higher law than I. They force me to become like themselves. I do not hear of *men* being *forced* to live this way or that by masses of men. What sort of life were that to live? When I meet a government which says to me, "Your money or your life," why should I be in haste to give it my money? It may be in a great strait, and not know what to do: I cannot help that. It must help itself; do as I do. It is not worth the while to snivel about it. I am not responsible for the successful working of the machinery of society. I am not the son of the engineer. I perceive that, when an acorn and a chestnut fall side by side, the one does not remain inert to make way for the other, but both obey their own laws, and spring and grow and flourish as best they can, till one, perchance, overshadows and destroys the other. If a plant cannot live according to its nature, it dies; and so a man.

The night in prison was novel and interesting enough. The prisoners in their shirt-sleeves were enjoying a chat and the evening air in the doorway, when I entered. But the jailer said, "Come, boys, it is time to lock up;" and so they dispersed, and I heard the sound of their steps returning into the hollow apartments. My roommate was introduced to me by the jailer as "a first-rate fellow and a clever man." When the door was locked, he showed me where to hang my hat, and how he managed matters there. The rooms were whitewashed once a month; and this one, at least, was the whitest, most simply furnished, and probably the neatest apartment in the town. He naturally wanted to know where I came from, and what brought me there; and, when I had told him, I asked him in my turn how he came there, presuming him to be an honest man, of course; and, as the world goes, I believe he was. "Why," said he, "they accuse me of burning a barn; but I never did it." As near as I could discover, he had probably gone to bed in a barn when drunk, and smoked his pipe there; and so a barn was burnt. He had the reputation of being a clever man, had been there some three months waiting for his trial to come on, and would have to wait as much longer; but he was quite domesticated and contented, since he got his board for nothing, and thought that he was well treated.

He occupied one window, and I the other; and I saw that if one stayed there long, his principal business would be to look out the window. I had soon read all the tracts that were left there, and examined where former prisoners had broken out, and where a grate had been sawed off, and heard the history of the various occupants of that room; for I found that even here there was a history and a gossip which never circulated beyond the walls of the jail. Probably this is the only house in the town where verses are composed, which are afterward printed in a circular form, but not published. I was shown quite a long list of verses which were composed by some young men who had been detected in an attempt to escape, who avenged themselves by singing them.

I pumped my fellow-prisoner as dry as I could, for fear I should never see him again; but at length he showed me which was my bed, and left me to blow out the lamp.

It was like traveling into a far country, such as I had never expected to behold, to lie there for one night. It seemed to me that I never had heard the town clock strike before, nor the evening sounds of the village; for we slept with the windows open, which were inside the grating. It was to see my native village in the light of the Middle Ages, and our Concord was turned into a Rhine stream, and visions of knights and castles passed before me. They were the voices of old burghers that I heard in the streets. I was an involuntary spectator and auditor of whatever was done and said in the kitchen of the adjacent village inn,—a wholly new and rare experience to me. It was a closer view of my native town. I was fairly inside of it. I never had seen its institutions before. This is one of its peculiar institutions; for it is a shire town. I began to comprehend what its inhabitants were about.

In the morning, our breakfasts were put through the hole in the door, in small oblong-square tin pans, made to fit, and holding a pint of chocolate, with brown bread, and an iron spoon. When they called for the vessels again, I was green enough to return what bread I had left; but my comrade seized it, and said that I should lay that up for lunch or dinner. Soon after he was let out to work at haying in a neighboring field, whither he went every day, and would not be back till noon; so he bade me good-day, saying that he doubted if he should see me again.

When I came out of prison,—for some one interfered, and paid that tax,—I did not perceive that great changes had taken place on the common, such as he observed who went in a youth and emerged a tottering and gray-headed man; and yet a change had to my eyes come over the scene,—the town, and State, and country,—greater than any that mere time could effect. I saw yet more distinctly the State in which I lived. I saw to what extent the people among whom I lived could be trusted as good neighbors and friends; that their friendship was for summer weather only; that they did not greatly propose to do right; that they were a distinct race from me by their prejudices and superstitions, as the Chinamen and Malays are; that in their sacrifices to humanity they ran no risks, not even to their property; that after all they were not so noble but they treated the thief as he had treated them, and hoped, by a certain outward observance and a few prayers, and by walking in a particular straight though useless path from time to time, to save their souls. This may be to judge my neighbors harshly; for I believe that many of them are not aware that they have such an institution as the jail in their village.

It was formerly the custom in our village, when a poor debtor came out of jail, for his acquaintances to salute him, looking through their fingers, which were crossed to represent the grating of a jail window, "How do ye do?" My neighbors did not thus salute me, but first looked at me, and then at one another, as if I had returned from a long journey. I was put into jail as I was going to the shoemaker's to get a shoe which was mended. When I was let out the next morning, I proceeded to finish my errand, and, having put on my mended shoe, joined a huckleberry party, who were impatient to put themselves under my conduct; and in half an hour,—for the horse was soon tackled,—was in the midst of a huckleberry field, on one of our highest hills, two miles off, and then the State was nowhere to be seen.

This is the whole history of "My Prisons."

I have never declined paying the highway tax, because I am as desirous of being a good neighbor as I am of being a bad subject; and as for supporting schools, I am doing my part to educate my fellow-countrymen now. It is for no particular item in the tax-bill that I refuse to pay it. I simply wish to refuse allegiance to the State, to withdraw and stand aloof from it effectually. I do not care to trace the course of my dollar, if I could, till it buys a man or a musket to shoot one with,—the dollar is innocent,—but I am concerned to trace the effects of my allegiance. In fact, I quietly declare war with the State, after my fashion, though I will still make what use and get what advantage of her I can, as is usual in such cases.

If others pay the tax which is demanded of me, from a sympathy with the State, they do but what they have already done in their own case, or rather they abet injustice to a greater extent than the State requires. If they pay the tax from a mistaken interest in the individual taxed, to save his property, or prevent his going to jail, it is because they have not considered wisely how far they let their private feelings interfere with the public good.

This, then, is my position at present. But one cannot be too much on his guard in such a case, lest his action be biased by obstinacy or an undue regard for the opinions of men. Let him see that he does only what belongs to himself and to the hour.

I think sometimes, Why, this people mean well, they are only ignorant; they would do better if they knew how: why give your neighbors this pain to treat you as they are not inclined to? But I think again, This is no reason why I should do as they do, or permit others to suffer much greater pain of a different kind. Again, I sometimes say to myself, When many millions of men, without heat, without ill will, without personal feeling of any kind, demand of you a few shillings only, without the possibility, such is their constitution, of retracting or altering their present demand, and without the possibility, on your side, of appeal to any other millions, why expose yourself to this overwhelming brute force? You do not resist cold and hunger, the winds and the waves, thus obstinately; you quietly submit to a thousand similar necessities. You do not put your head into the fire. But just in proportion as I regard this as not wholly a brute force, but partly a human force, and consider that I have relations to those millions as to so many millions of men, and not of mere brute or inanimate things, I see that appeal is possible, first and instantaneously, from them to the Maker of them, and, secondly, from them to themselves. But if I put my head deliberately into the fire, there is no appeal to fire or to the Maker of fire, and I have only myself to blame. If I could convince myself that I have any right to be satisfied with men as they are, and to treat them accordingly, and not according, in some respects, to my requisitions and expectations of what they and I ought to be, then, like a good Mussulman and fatalist, I should endeavor to be satisfied with things as they are, and say it is the will of God. And, above all, there is this difference between resisting this and a purely brute or natural force, that I can resist this with some effect; but I cannot expect, like Orpheus, to change the nature of the rocks and trees and beasts.

I do not wish to quarrel with any man or nation. I do not wish to split hairs, to make fine distinctions, or set myself up as better than my neighbors. I seek rather, I may say, even an excuse for conforming to the laws of the land. I am but too ready to conform to them. Indeed, I have reason to suspect myself on this head; and each year, as the tax-gatherer comes round, I find myself disposed to review the acts and position of the general and State governments, and the spirit of the people, to discover a pretext for conformity.

> "We must affect our country as our parents,
> And if at any time we alienate
> Our love or industry from doing it honor,
> We must respect effects and teach the soul
> Matter of conscience and religion,
> And not desire of rule or benefit."

I believe that the State will soon be able to take all my work of this sort out of my hands, and then I shall be no better a patriot than my fellow-countrymen. Seen from a lower point of view, the Constitution, with all its faults, is very good; the law and the courts are very respectable; even this State and this American government are, in many respects, very admirable, and rare things, to be thankful for, such as a great many have described them; but seen from a point of view a little higher, they are what I have described them; seen from a higher still, and the highest, who shall say what they are, or that they are worth looking at or thinking of at all?

However, the government does not concern me much, and I shall bestow the fewest possible thoughts on it. It is not many moments that I live under a government, even in this world. If a man is thought-free, fancy-free, imagination-free, that which *is not* never for a long time appearing *to be* to him, unwise rulers or reformers cannot fatally interrupt him.

I know that most men think differently from myself; but those whose lives are by profession devoted to the study of these or kindred subjects content me as little as any. Statesmen and legislators, standing so completely within the institution, never distinctly and nakedly behold it. They speak of moving society, but have no resting-place without it. They may be men of a certain experience and discrimination, and have no doubt invented ingenious and even useful systems, for which we sincerely thank them; but all their wit and usefulness lie within certain not very wide limits. They are wont to forget that the world is not governed by policy and expediency. Webster never goes behind government, and so cannot speak with authority about it. His words are wisdom to those legislators who contemplate no essential reform in the existing government; but for thinkers, and those who legislate for all time, he never once glances at the subject. I know of those whose serene and wise speculations on this theme would soon reveal the limits of his mind's range and hospitality. Yet, compared with the cheap professions of most reformers, and the still cheaper wisdom and eloquence of politicians in general, his are almost the only sensible and valuable words, and we thank Heaven for him. Comparatively, he is always strong, original, and, above all, practical. Still, his quality is not wisdom, but prudence. The lawyer's truth is not Truth, but consistency or a consistent expediency. Truth is always in harmony with herself, and is not concerned chiefly to reveal the justice that may consist with wrong-doing. He well deserves to be called, as he has been called, the Defender of the Constitution. There are really no blows to be given by him but defensive ones. He is not a leader, but a follower. His leaders are the men of '87. "I have never made an effort," he says, "and never propose to make an effort; I have never countenanced an effort, and never mean to countenance an effort, to disturb the arrangement as originally made, by which the various States came into the Union." Still thinking of the sanction which the Constitution gives to slavery, he says, "Because it was a part of the original compact,—let it stand." Notwithstanding his special acuteness and ability, he is unable to take a fact out of its merely political relations, and behold it as it lies absolutely to be disposed of by the intellect,—what, for instance, it behooves a man to do here in America to-day with regard to slavery,—but ventures, or is driven, to make some such desperate answer as the following, while professing to speak absolutely, and as a private man,—from which what new and singular code of social duties might be inferred? "The manner," says he, "in which the governments of those States where slavery exists are to regulate it is for their own consideration, under their responsibility to their constituents, to the general laws of propriety, humanity, and justice, and to God. Associations formed elsewhere, springing from a feeling of humanity, or any other cause, have nothing whatever to do with it. They have never received any encouragement from me, and they never will."*

They who know of no purer sources of truth, who have traced up its stream no higher, stand, and wisely stand, by the Bible and the Constitution, and drink at it there with reverence and humility; but they who behold where it comes trickling into this lake or that pool, gird up their loins once more, and continue their pilgrimage toward its fountain-head.

No man with a genius for legislation has appeared in America. They are rare in the history of the world. There are orators, politicians, and eloquent men, by the thousand; but the speaker has not yet opened his mouth to speak who is capable of settling the much-vexed questions of the day. We love eloquence for its own sake, and not for any truth which it may utter, or any heroism it may inspire. Our legislators have not yet learned the comparative value of free trade and of freedom, of union, and of rectitude, to a nation. They have no genius or talent for comparatively humble questions of taxation and finance, commerce and manufactures and agriculture. If we were left solely to the wordy wit of legislators in Congress for our guidance, uncorrected by the seasonable experience and the effectual complaints of the people, America would not long retain her rank among the nations. For eighteen hundred years, though perchance I have no right to say it, the New Testament has been written; yet where is the legislator who has wisdom and practical talent enough to avail himself of the light which it sheds on the science of legislation?

The authority of government, even such as I am willing to submit to,—for I will cheerfully obey those who know and can do better than I, and in many things even those who neither know nor can do so well,—is still an impure one: to be strictly just, it must have the sanction and consent of the governed. It can have no pure right over my person and property but what I concede to it. The progress from an absolute to a limited monarchy, from a limited monarchy to a democracy, is a progress toward a true respect for the individual. Even the Chinese philosopher was wise enough to regard the individual as the basis of the empire. Is a democ-

*These extracts have been inserted since the lecture was read.

racy, such as we know it, the last improvement possible in government? Is it not possible to take a step further towards recognizing and organizing the rights of man? There will never be a really free and enlightened State until the State comes to recognize the individual as a higher and independent power, from which all its own power and authority are derived, and treats him accordingly. I please myself with imagining a State at last which can afford to be just to all men, and to treat the individual with respect as a neighbor; which even would not think it inconsistent with its own repose if a few were to live aloof from it, not meddling with it, nor embraced by it, who fulfilled all the duties of neighbors and fellow-men. A State which bore this kind of fruit, and suffered it to drop off as fast as it ripened, would prepare the way for a still more perfect and glorious State, which also I have imagined, but not yet anywhere seen.

WALKING

I feel that I owe my au-
dience an apology for speaking
to them to night on any other
subject than the Fugitive Slave
Law on which every man is bound
to express ~~his opinion~~ a distinct
opinion, — but I had prepared
myself to speak a word now
for Nature — for absolute
freedom & wildness, as contrasted with a freedom and
culture simply civil — to regard
man as an inhabitant or a
part and parcel of nature —
rather than a member of
society. I wish to make an
extreme statement, if so I may
make an emphatic one — for
there are enough champions
of civilization — the minister
and the school committee —
and every one of you will take
care of that

Manuscript page of an 1851 draft of Thoreau's lecture "Walking, or the Wild." The first sentence refers to the case of Thomas Sims, an escaped slave who had been captured in Boston and remanded to Georgia in April of that year: "I feel that I owe my audience an apology for speaking to them tonight on any other subject than the Fugitive Slave Law, on which every man is bound to express a distinct opinion,—but I had prepared myself to speak a word now for *nature*—for absolute freedom & wildness . . ."

WALKING

I wish to speak a word for Nature, for absolute freedom and wildness, as contrasted with a freedom and culture merely civil,—to regard man as an inhabitant, or a part and parcel of Nature, rather than a member of society. I wish to make an extreme statement, if so I may make an emphatic one, for there are enough champions of civilization: the minister and the school committee and every one of you will take care of that.

I have met with but one or two persons in the course of my life who understood the art of Walking, that is, of taking walks,—who had a genius, so to speak, for *sauntering*, which word is beautifully derived "from idle people who roved about the country, in the Middle Ages, and asked charity, under pretense of going *à la Sainte Terre*," to the Holy Land, till the children exclaimed, "There goes a *Sainte-Terrer*," a Saunterer, a Holy-Lander. They who never go to the Holy Land in their walks, as they pretend, are indeed mere idlers and vagabonds; but they who do go there are saunterers in the good sense, such as I mean. Some, however, would derive the word from *sans terre*, without land or a home, which, therefore, in the good sense, will mean, having no particular home, but equally at home everywhere. For this is the secret of successful sauntering. He who sits still in a house all the time may be the greatest vagrant of all; but the saunterer, in the good sense, is no more vagrant than the meandering river, which is all the while sedulously seeking the shortest course to the sea. But I prefer the first, which, indeed, is the most probable derivation. For every walk is a sort of crusade, preached by some Peter the Hermit in us, to go forth and reconquer this Holy Land from the hands of the Infidels.

It is true, we are but faint-hearted crusaders, even the walkers, nowadays, who undertake no persevering, never-ending enterprises. Our expeditions are but tours, and come round again at evening to the old hearth-side from which we set out. Half the walk is but retracing our steps. We should go forth on the shortest walk, perchance, in the spirit of undying adventure, never to return,—prepared to send back our embalmed hearts only as relics to our desolate kingdoms. If you are ready to leave father and mother, and brother and sister, and wife and child and friends, and never see them again,—if you have paid your debts, and made your will, and settled all your affairs, and are a free man, then you are ready for a walk.

To come down to my own experience, my companion and I, for I sometimes have a companion, take pleasure in fancying ourselves knights of a new, or rather an old, order,—not Equestrians or Chevaliers, not Ritters or Riders, but Walkers, a still more ancient and honorable class, I trust. The chivalric and heroic spirit which once belonged to the Rider seems now to reside in, or perchance to have subsided into, the Walker,—not the Knight, but Walker, Errant. He is a sort of fourth estate, outside of Church and State and People.

We have felt that we almost alone hereabouts practiced this noble art; though, to tell the truth, at least if their own assertions are to be received, most of my townsmen would fain walk sometimes, as I do, but they cannot. No wealth can buy the requisite leisure, freedom, and independence which are the capital in this profession. It comes only by the grace of God. It requires a direct dispensation from Heaven to become a walker. You must be born into the family of the Walkers. *Ambulator nascitur, non fit.* Some of my townsmen, it is true, can remember and have described to me some walks which they took ten years ago, in which they were so blessed as to lose themselves for half an hour in the woods; but I know very well that they have confined themselves to the highway ever since, whatever pretensions they may make to belong to this select class. No doubt they were elevated for a moment as by the reminiscence of a previous state of existence, when even they were foresters and outlaws.

"When he came to grene wode,
In a mery mornynge,
There he herde the notes small
Of byrdes mery syngynge.

"It is ferre gone, sayd Robyn,
That I was last here;
Me lyste a lytell for to shote
At the donne dere."

I think that I cannot preserve my health and spirits, unless I spend four hours a day at least—and it is commonly more than that—sauntering through the woods and over the hills and fields, absolutely free from all worldly engagements. You may safely say, A penny for your thoughts, or a thousand pounds. When sometimes I am reminded that the mechanics and shopkeepers stay in their shops not only all the forenoon, but all the afternoon too, sitting with crossed legs, so many of them,—as if the legs were made to sit upon, and not to stand or walk upon,—I think that they deserve some credit for not having all committed suicide long ago.

I, who cannot stay in my chamber for a single day without acquiring some rust, and when sometimes I have stolen forth for a walk at the eleventh hour, or four o'clock in the afternoon, too late to redeem the day, when the shades of night were already beginning to be mingled with the daylight, have felt as if I had committed some sin to be atoned for,—I confess that I am astonished at the power of endurance, to say nothing of the moral insensibility, of my neighbors who confine themselves to shops and offices the whole day for weeks and months, aye, and years almost together. I know not what manner of stuff they are of,—sitting there now at three o'clock in the afternoon, as if it were three o'clock in the morning. Bonaparte may talk of the three-o'clock-in-the-morning courage, but it is nothing to the courage which can sit down cheerfully at this hour in the afternoon over against one's self whom you have known all the morning, to starve out a garrison to whom you are bound by such strong ties of sympathy. I wonder that about this time, or say between four and five o'clock in the afternoon, too late for the morning papers and too early for the evening ones, there is not a general explosion heard up and down the street, scattering a legion of antiquated and house-bred notions and whims to the four winds for an airing,—and so the evil cure itself.

How womankind, who are confined to the house still more than men, stand it I do not know; but I have ground to suspect that most of them do not *stand* it at all. When, early in a summer afternoon, we have been shaking the dust of the village from the skirts of our garments, making haste past those houses with purely Doric or Gothic fronts, which have such an air of repose about them, my companion whispers that probably about these times their occupants are all gone to bed. Then it is that I appreciate the beauty and the glory of architecture, which itself never turns in, but forever stands out and erect, keeping watch over the slumberers.

No doubt temperament, and, above all, age, have a good deal to do with it. As a man grows older, his ability to sit still and follow indoor occupations increases. He grows vespertinal in his habits as the evening of life approaches, till at last he comes forth only just before sundown, and gets all the walk that he requires in half an hour.

But the walking of which I speak has nothing in it akin to taking exercise, as it is called, as the sick take medicine at stated hours,—as the swinging of dumbbells or chairs; but is itself the enterprise and adventure of the day. If you would get exercise, go in search of the springs of life. Think of a man's swinging dumbbells for his health, when those springs are bubbling up in far-off pastures unsought by him!

Moreover, you must walk like a camel, which is said to be the only beast which ruminates when walking. When a traveler asked Wordsworth's servant to show him her master's study, she answered, "Here is his library, but his study is out of doors."

Living much out of doors, in the sun and wind, will no doubt produce a certain roughness of character,—will cause a thicker cuticle to grow over some of the finer qualities of our nature, as on the face and hands, or as severe manual labor robs the hands of some of their delicacy of touch. So staying in the house, on the other hand, may produce a softness and smoothness, not to say thinness of skin, accompanied by an increased sensibility to certain impressions. Perhaps we should be more susceptible to some influences important to our intellectual and moral growth, if the sun had shone and the wind blown on us a little less; and no doubt it is a nice matter to proportion rightly the thick and thin skin. But methinks that is a scurf that will fall off fast enough,—that the natural remedy is to be found in the proportion which the night bears to the day, the winter to the summer, thought to experience. There will be so much the more air and sunshine in our thoughts. The callous palms of the laborer are conversant with finer tissues of self-respect and heroism, whose touch thrills the heart, than the languid fingers of idleness. That is mere sentimentality that lies abed by day and thinks itself white, far from the tan and callus of experience.

When we walk, we naturally go to the fields and woods: what would become of us, if we walked only in a garden or a mall? Even some sects of philosophers have felt the necessity of importing the woods to themselves, since they did not go to the woods. "They planted groves and walks of Platanes," where they took *subdiales ambulationes* in porticos open to the air. Of course it is of no use to direct our steps to the woods, if they do not carry us thither. I am alarmed when it happens that I have walked a mile into the woods bodily, without getting there in spirit. In my afternoon walk I would fain forget all my morning occupations and my obligations to society. But it sometimes happens that I cannot easily shake off the village. The thought of some work will run in my head and I am not where my body is,—I am out of my senses. In my walks I would fain return to my senses. What business have I in the woods, if I am thinking of something out of the woods? I suspect myself, and cannot help a shudder, when I find myself so implicated even in what are called good works,—for this may sometimes happen.

My vicinity affords many good walks; and though for so many years I have walked almost every day, and sometimes for several days together, I have not yet exhausted them. An absolutely new prospect is a great happiness, and I can still get this any afternoon. Two or three hours' walking will carry me to as strange a country as I expect ever to see. A single farmhouse which I had not seen before is sometimes as good as the dominions of the King of Dahomey. There is in fact a sort of harmony discoverable between the capabilities of the landscape within a circle of ten miles' radius, or the limits of an afternoon walk, and the threescore years and ten of human life. It will never become quite familiar to you.

Nowadays almost all man's improvements, so called, as the building of houses and the cutting down of the forest and of all large trees, simply deform the landscape, and make it more and more tame and cheap. A people who would begin by burning the fences and let the forest stand! I saw the fences half consumed, their ends lost in the middle of the prairie, and some worldly miser with a surveyor looking after his bounds, while heaven had taken place around him, and he did not see the angels going to and fro, but was looking for an old post-hole in the midst of paradise.

I looked again, and saw him standing in the middle of a boggy Stygian fen, surrounded by devils, and he had found his bounds without a doubt, three little stones, where a stake had been driven, and looking nearer, I saw that the Prince of Darkness was his surveyor.

I can easily walk ten, fifteen, twenty, any number of miles, commencing at my own door, without going by any house, without crossing a road except where the fox and the mink do: first along by the river, and then the brook, and then the meadow and the woodside. There are square miles in my vicinity which have no inhabitant. From many a hill I can see civilization and the abodes of man afar. The farmers and their works are scarcely more obvious than woodchucks and their burrows. Man and his affairs, church and state and school, trade and commerce, and manufactures and agriculture, even politics, the most alarming of them all,—I am pleased to see how little space they occupy in the landscape. Politics is but a narrow field, and that still narrower highway yonder leads to it. I sometimes direct the traveler thither. If you would go to the political world, follow the great road,—follow that market-man, keep his dust in your eyes, and it will lead you straight to it; for it, too, has its place merely, and does not occupy all space. I pass from it as from a bean-field into the forest, and it is forgotten. In one half-hour I can walk off to some portion of the earth's surface where a man does not stand from one year's end to another, and there, consequently, politics are not, for they are but as the cigar-smoke of a man.

The village is the place to which the roads tend, a sort of expansion of the highway, as a lake of a river. It is the body of which roads are the arms and legs,—a trivial or quadrivial place, the thoroughfare and ordinary of travelers. The word is from the Latin *villa*, which together with *via*, a way, or more anciently *ved* and *vella*, Varro derives from *veho*, to carry, because the villa is the place to and from which things are carried. They who got their living by teaming were said *vellaturam facere*. Hence, too, the Latin word *vilis* and our vile, also *villain*. This suggests what kind of degeneracy villagers are liable to. They are wayworn by the travel that goes by and over them, without traveling themselves.

Some do not walk at all; others walk in the highways; a few walk across lots. Roads are made for horses and men of business. I do not travel in them much, comparatively, because I am not in a hurry to get to any tavern or grocery or livery-stable or depot to which they lead. I am a good horse to travel, but not from choice a roadster. The landscape-painter uses the figures of men to mark a road. He would not make that use of my figure. I walk out into a nature such as the old prophets and poets, Menu, Moses, Homer, Chaucer, walked in. You may name it America, but it is not America; neither Americus Vespucius, nor Columbus, nor the rest were the discoverers of it. There is a truer account of it in mythology than in any history of America, so called, that I have seen.

However, there are a few old roads that may be trodden with profit, as if they led somewhere now that they are nearly discontinued. There is the Old Marlborough Road, which does not go to Marlborough now, methinks, unless that is Marlborough where it carries me. I am the bolder to speak of it here, because I presume that there are one or two such roads in every town.

THE OLD MARLBOROUGH ROAD

Where they once dug for money,
But never found any;
Where sometimes Martial Miles
Singly files,
And Elijah Wood,
I fear for no good:
No other man,
Save Elisha Dugan,—
O man of wild habits,
Partridges and rabbits,
Who hast no cares
Only to set snares,
Who liv'st all alone,
Close to the bone,
And where life is sweetest
Constantly eatest.
When the spring stirs my blood
With the instinct to travel,
I can get enough gravel
On the Old Marlborough Road.
Nobody repairs it,
For nobody wears it;
It is a living way,

As the Christians say.
Not many there be
Who enter therein,
Only the guests of the
Irishman Quin.
What is it, what is it,
But a direction out there,
And the bare possibility
Of going somewhere?
Great guide-boards of stone,
But travelers none;
Cenotaphs of the towns
Named on their crowns.
It is worth going to see
Where you *might* be.
What king
Did the thing,
I am still wondering;
Set up how or when,
By what selectmen,
Gourgas or Lee,
Clark or Darby?
They 're a great endeavor
To be something forever;
Blank tablets of stone,
Where a traveler might groan,
And in one sentence
Grave all that is known;
Which another might read,
In his extreme need.
I know one or two
Lines that would do,
Literature that might stand
All over the land,
Which a man could remember
Till next December,
And read again in the spring,
After the thawing.

If with fancy unfurled
You leave your abode,
You may go round the world
By the Old Marlborough Road.

At present, in this vicinity, the best part of the land is not private property; the landscape is not owned, and the walker enjoys comparative freedom. But possibly the day will come when it will be partitioned off into so-called pleasure-grounds, in which a few will take a narrow and exclusive pleasure only,—when fences shall be multiplied, and man-traps and other engines invented to confine men to the *public* road, and walking over the surface of God's earth shall be construed to mean trespassing on some gentleman's grounds. To enjoy a thing exclusively is commonly to exclude yourself from the true enjoyment of it. Let us improve our opportunities, then, before the evil days come.

What is it that makes it so hard sometimes to determine whither we will walk? I believe that there is a subtle magnetism in Nature, which, if we unconsciously yield to it, will direct us aright. It is not indifferent to us which way we walk. There is a right way; but we are very liable from heedlessness and stupidity to take the wrong one. We would fain take that walk, never yet taken by us through this actual world, which is perfectly symbolical of the path which we love to travel in the interior and ideal world; and sometimes, no doubt, we find it difficult to choose our direction, because it does not yet exist distinctly in our idea.

When I go out of the house for a walk, uncertain as yet whither I will bend my steps, and submit myself to my instinct to decide for me, I find, strange and whimsical as it may seem, that I finally and inevitably settle southwest, toward some particular wood or meadow or deserted pasture or hill in that direction. My needle is slow to settle,—varies a few degrees, and does not always point due southwest, it is true, and it has good authority for this variation, but it always settles between west and south-southwest. The future lies that way to me, and the earth seems more unexhausted and richer on that side. The outline which would bound my walks would be, not a circle, but a parabola, or rather like one of those cometary orbits which have been thought to be non-returning curves, in this case opening westward, in which my house occupies the place of the sun. I turn round and round irresolute sometimes for a quarter of an hour, until I decide, for a thousandth time, that I will walk into the southwest or west. Eastward I go only by force; but westward I go free. Thither no business leads me. It is hard for me to believe that I shall find fair landscapes or sufficient wildness and freedom behind the eastern horizon. I am not excited by the prospect of a walk thither; but I believe that the forest which I see in the western horizon stretches uninterruptedly toward the setting sun, and there are no towns nor cities in it of enough consequence to disturb me. Let me live where I will, on this side is the city, on that the wilderness, and ever I am leaving the city more and more, and withdrawing into the wilderness. I should not lay so much stress on this fact, if I did not believe that something like this is the prevailing tendency of my countrymen. I must walk toward Oregon, and not toward Europe. And that way the nation is moving, and I may say that mankind progress from east to west. Within a few years we have witnessed the phenomenon of a southeastward migration, in the settlement of Australia; but this affects us as a retrograde movement, and, judging from the moral and physical character of the first generation of Australians, has not yet proved a successful experiment. The eastern Tartars think that there is nothing west beyond Thibet. "The world ends there," say they; "beyond there is nothing but a shoreless sea." It is unmitigated East where they live.

We go eastward to realize history and study the works of art and literature, retracing the steps of the race; we go westward as into the future, with a spirit of enterprise and adventure. The Atlantic is a Lethean stream, in our passage over which we have had an opportunity to forget the Old World and its institutions. If we do not succeed this time, there is perhaps one more chance for the race left before it arrives on the banks of the Styx; and that is in the Lethe of the Pacific, which is three times as wide.

I know not how significant it is, or how far it is an evidence of singularity, that an individual should thus consent in his pettiest walk with the general movement of the race; but I know that something akin to the migratory instinct in birds and quadrupeds,—which, in some instances, is known to have affected the squirrel tribe, impelling them to a general and mysterious movement, in which they were seen, say some, crossing the broadest rivers, each on its particular chip, with its tail raised for a sail, and bridging narrower streams with their dead,—that something like the *furor* which affects the domestic cattle in the spring, and which is referred to a worm in their tails, affects both nations and individuals, either perennially or from time to time. Not a flock of wild geese cackles over our town, but it to some extent unsettles the value of real estate here, and, if I were a broker, I should probably take that disturbance into account.

> "Than longen folk to gon on pilgrimages,
> And palmeres for to seken strange strondes."

Every sunset which I witness inspires me with the desire to go to a West as distant and as fair as that into which the sun goes down. He appears to migrate westward daily, and tempt us to follow him. He is the Great Western Pioneer whom the nations follow. We dream all night of those mountain-ridges in the horizon, though they may be of vapor only, which were last gilded by his rays. The island of Atlantis, and the islands and gardens of the Hesperides, a sort of terrestrial paradise, appear to have been the Great West of the ancients, enveloped in mystery and poetry. Who has not seen in imagination, when looking into the sunset sky, the gardens of the Hesperides, and the foundation of all those fables?

Columbus felt the westward tendency more strongly than any before. He obeyed it, and found a New World for Castile and Leon. The herd of men in those days scented fresh pastures from afar.

> "And now the sun had stretched out all the hills,
> And now was dropped into the western bay;
> At last *he* rose, and twitched his mantle blue;
> To-morrow to fresh woods and pastures new."

Where on the globe can there be found an area of equal extent with that occupied by the bulk of our States, so fertile and so rich and varied in its productions, and at the same time so habitable by the European, as this is? Michaux, who knew but part of them, says that "the species of large trees are much more numerous in North America than in Europe; in the United States there are more than one hundred and forty species that exceed thirty feet in height; in France there are but thirty that attain this size." Later botanists more than confirm his observations. Humboldt came to America to realize his youthful dreams of a tropical vegetation, and he beheld it in its greatest perfection in the primitive forests of the Amazon, the most gigantic wilderness on the earth, which he has so eloquently described. The geographer Guyot, himself a European, goes farther,—farther than I am ready to follow him; yet not when he says: "As the plant is made for the animal, as the vegetable world is made for the animal world, America is made for the man of the Old World. . . . The man of the Old World sets out upon his way. Leaving the highlands of Asia, he descends from station to station towards Europe. Each of his steps is marked by a new civilization superior to the preceding, by a greater power of development. Arrived at the Atlantic, he pauses on the shore of this unknown ocean, the bounds of which he knows not, and turns upon his footprints for an instant." When he has exhausted the rich soil of Europe, and reinvigorated himself, "then recommences his adventurous career westward as in the earliest ages." So far Guyot.

From this western impulse coming in contact with the barrier of the Atlantic sprang the commerce and enterprise of modern times. The younger Michaux, in his "Travels West of the Alleghanies in 1802," says that the common inquiry in the newly settled West was, " 'From what part of the world have you come?' As if these vast and fertile regions would naturally be the place of meeting and common country of all the inhabitants of the globe."

To use an obsolete Latin word, I might say, *Ex Oriente lux; ex Occidente* FRUX. From the East light; from the West fruit.

Sir Francis Head, an English traveler and a Governor-General of Canada, tells us that "in both the northern and southern hemispheres of the New World, Nature has not only outlined her works on a larger scale, but has painted the whole picture with brighter and more costly colors than she used in delineating and in beautifying the Old World. . . . The heavens of America appear infinitely higher, the sky is bluer, the air is fresher, the cold is intenser, the moon looks larger, the stars are brighter, the thunder is louder, the lightning is vivider, the wind is stronger, the rain is heavier, the mountains are higher, the rivers longer, the forests bigger, the plains broader." This statement will do at least to set against Buffon's account of this part of the world and its productions.

Linnæus said long ago, "Nescio quae facies *laeta, glabra* plantis Americanis" (I know not what there is of joyous and smooth in the aspect of American plants); and I think that in this country there are no, or at most very few, *Africanae bestiae*, African beasts, as the Romans called them, and that in this respect also it is peculiarly fitted for the habitation of man. We are told that within three miles of the centre of the East-Indian city of Singapore, some of the inhabitants are annually carried off by tigers; but the traveler can lie down in the woods at night almost anywhere in North America without fear of wild beasts.

These are encouraging testimonies. If the moon looks larger here than in Europe, probably the sun looks larger also. If the heavens of America appear infinitely higher, and the stars brighter, I trust that these facts are symbolical of the height to which the philosophy and poetry and religion of her inhabitants may one day soar. At length, perchance, the immaterial heaven will appear as much higher to the American mind, and the intimations that star it as much brighter. For I believe that climate does thus react on man,—as there is something in the mountain air that feeds the spirit and inspires. Will not man grow to greater perfection intellectually as well as physically under these influences? Or is it unimportant how many foggy days there are in his life? I trust that we shall be more imaginative, that our thoughts will be clearer, fresher, and more ethereal, as our sky,—our understanding more comprehensive and broader, like our plains,—our intellect generally on a grander scale, like our thunder and lightning, our rivers and mountains and forests,—and our hearts shall even correspond in breadth and depth and grandeur to our inland seas. Perchance there will appear to the traveler something, he knows not what, of *laeta* and *glabra*, of joyous and serene, in our very faces. Else to what end does the world go on, and why was America discovered?

To Americans I hardly need to say,—

"Westward the star of empire takes its way."

As a true patriot, I should be ashamed to think that Adam in paradise was more favorably situated on the whole than the backwoodsman in this country.

Our sympathies in Massachusetts are not confined to New England; though we may be estranged from the South, we sympathize with the West. There is the home of the younger sons, as among the Scandinavians they took to the sea for their inheritance. It is too late to be studying Hebrew; it is more important to understand even the slang of to-day.

Some months ago I went to see a panorama of the Rhine. It was like a dream of the Middle Ages. I floated down its historic stream in something more than imagination, under bridges built by the Romans, and repaired by later heroes, past cities and castles whose very names were music to my ears, and each of which was the subject of a legend. There were Ehrenbreitstein and Rolandseck and Coblentz, which I knew only in history. They were ruins that interested me chiefly. There seemed to come up from its waters and its vine-clad hills and valleys a hushed music as of Crusaders departing for the Holy Land. I floated along under the spell of enchantment, as if I had been transported to an heroic age, and breathed an atmosphere of chivalry.

Soon after, I went to see a panorama of the Mississippi, and as I worked my way up the river in the light of to-day, and saw the steamboats wooding up, counted the rising cities, gazed on the fresh ruins of Nauvoo, beheld the Indians moving west across the stream, and, as before I had looked up the Moselle, now looked up the Ohio and the Missouri and heard the legends of Dubuque and of Wenona's Cliff,—still thinking more of the future than of the past or present,—I saw that this was a Rhine stream of a different kind; that the foundations of castles were yet to be laid, and the famous bridges were yet to be thrown over the river; and I felt that *this was the heroic age itself*, though we know it not, for the hero is commonly the simplest and obscurest of men.

The West of which I speak is but another name for the Wild; and what I have been preparing to say is, that in Wildness is the preservation of the World. Every tree sends its fibres forth in search of the Wild. The cities import it at any price. Men plow and sail for it. From the forest and wilderness come the tonics and barks which brace mankind. Our ancestors were savages. The story of Romulus and Remus being suckled by a wolf is not a meaningless fable. The founders of every state which has risen to eminence have drawn their nourishment and vigor from a similar wild source. It was because the children of the Empire were not suckled by the wolf that they were conquered and displaced by the children of the northern forests who were.

I believe in the forest, and in the meadow, and in the night in which the corn grows. We require an infusion of hemlock spruce or arbor-vitæ in our tea. There is a difference between eating and drinking for strength and from mere gluttony. The Hottentots eagerly devour the marrow of the koodoo and other antelopes raw, as a matter of course. Some of our northern Indians eat raw the marrow of the Arctic reindeer, as well as various other parts, including the summits of the antlers as long as they are soft. And herein, perchance, they have stolen a march on the cooks of Paris. They get what usually goes to feed the fire. This is probably better than stall-fed beef and slaughter-house pork to make a man of. Give me a wildness whose glance no civilization can endure,—as if we lived on the marrow of koodoos devoured raw.

There are some intervals which border the strain of the wood thrush, to which I would migrate,—wild lands where no settler has squatted; to which, methinks, I am already acclimated.

The African hunter Cumming tells us that the skin of the eland, as well as that of most other antelopes just killed, emits the most delicious perfume of trees and grass. I would have every man so much like a wild antelope, so much a part and parcel of nature, that his very person should thus sweetly advertise our senses of his presence, and remind us of those parts of nature which he most haunts. I feel no disposition to be satirical, when the trapper's coat emits the odor of musquash even; it is a sweeter scent to me than that which commonly exhales from the merchant's or the scholar's garments. When I go into their wardrobes and handle their vestments, I am reminded of no grassy plains and flowery meads which they have frequented, but of dusty merchants' exchanges and libraries rather.

A tanned skin is something more than respectable, and perhaps olive is a fitter color than white for a man,—a denizen of the woods. "The pale white man!" I do not wonder that the African pitied him. Darwin the naturalist says, "A white man bathing by the side of a Tahitian was like a plant bleached by the gardener's art, compared with a fine, dark green one, growing vigorously in the open fields."

Ben Jonson exclaims,—

"How near to good is what is fair!"

So I would say,—

How near to good is what is *wild*!

Life consists with wildness. The most alive is the wildest. Not yet subdued to man, its presence refreshes him. One who pressed forward incessantly and never rested from his labors, who grew fast and made infinite demands on life, would always find himself in a new country or wilderness, and surrounded by the raw material of life. He would be climbing over the prostrate stems of primitive forest-trees.

Hope and the future for me are not in lawns and cultivated fields, not in towns and cities, but in the impervious and quaking swamps. When, formerly, I have analyzed my partiality for some farm which I had contemplated purchasing, I have frequently found that I was attracted solely by a few square rods of impermeable and unfathomable bog,—a natural sink in one corner of it. That was the jewel which dazzled me. I derive more of my subsistence from the swamps which surround my native town than from the cultivated gardens in the village. There are no richer parterres to my eyes than the dense beds of dwarf andromeda (*Cassandra calyculata*) which cover these tender places on the earth's surface. Botany cannot go farther than tell me the names of the shrubs which grow there,—the high blueberry, panicled andromeda, lambkill, azalea, and rhodora,—all standing in the quaking sphagnum. I often think that I should like to have my house front on this mass of dull red bushes, omitting other flower plots and borders, transplanted spruce and trim box, even graveled walks,—to have this fertile spot under my windows, not a few imported barrowfuls of soil only to cover the sand which was thrown out in digging the cellar. Why not put my house, my parlor, behind this plot, instead of behind that meagre assemblage of curiosities, that poor apology for a Nature and Art, which I call my front yard? It is an effort to clear up and make a decent appearance when the carpenter and mason have departed, though done as much for the passer-by as the dweller within. The most tasteful front-yard fence was never an agreeable object of study to me; the most elaborate ornaments, acorn tops, or what not, soon wearied and disgusted me. Bring your sills up to the very edge of the swamp, then (though it may not be the best place for a dry cellar), so that there be no access on that side to citizens. Front yards are not made to walk in, but, at most, through, and you could go in the back way.

Yes, though you may think me perverse, if it were proposed to me to dwell in the neighborhood of the most beautiful garden that ever human art contrived, or else of a Dismal Swamp, I should certainly decide for the swamp. How vain, then, have been all your labors, citizens, for me!

My spirits infallibly rise in proportion to the outward dreariness. Give me the ocean, the desert, or the wilderness! In the desert, pure air and solitude compensate for want of moisture and fertility. The traveler Burton says of it: "Your *morale* improves; you become frank and cordial, hospitable and single-minded. . . . In the desert, spirituous liquors excite only disgust. There is a keen enjoyment in a mere animal existence." They who have been traveling long on the steppes of Tartary say, "On reëntering cultivated lands, the agitation, perplexity, and turmoil of civilization oppressed and suffocated us; the air seemed to fail us, and we felt every moment as if about to die of asphyxia." When I would recreate myself, I seek the darkest wood, the thickest and most interminable and, to the citizen, most dismal, swamp. I enter a swamp as a sacred place, a *sanctum sanctorum*. There is the strength, the marrow, of Nature. The wildwood covers the virgin mould, and the same soil is good for men and for trees. A man's health requires as many acres of meadow to his prospect as his farm does loads of muck. There are the strong meats on which he feeds. A town is saved, not more by the righteous men in it than by the woods and swamps that surround it. A township where one primitive forest waves above while another primitive forest rots below,—such a town is fitted to raise not only corn and potatoes, but poets and philosophers for the coming ages. In such a soil grew Homer and Confucius and the rest, and out of such a wilderness comes the Reformer eating locusts and wild honey.

To preserve wild animals implies generally the creation of a forest for them to dwell in or resort to. So it is with man. A hundred years ago they sold bark in our streets peeled from our own woods. In the very aspect of those primitive and rugged trees there was, methinks, a tanning principle which hardened and consolidated the fibres of men's thoughts. Ah! already I shudder for these comparatively degenerate days of my native village, when you cannot collect a load of bark of good thickness, and we no longer produce tar and turpentine.

The civilized nations—Greece, Rome, England—have been sustained by the primitive forests which anciently rotted where they stand. They survive as long as the soil is not exhausted. Alas for human culture! little is to be expected of a nation, when the vegetable mould is exhausted, and it is compelled to make manure of the bones of its fathers. There the poet sustains himself merely by his own superfluous fat, and the philosopher comes down on his marrow-bones.

It is said to be the task of the American "to work the virgin soil," and that "agriculture here already assumes proportions unknown everywhere else." I think that the farmer displaces the Indian even because he redeems the meadow, and so makes himself stronger and in some respects more natural. I was surveying for a man the other day a single straight line one hundred and thirty-two rods long, through a swamp at whose entrance might have been written the words which Dante read over the entrance to the infernal regions, "Leave all hope, ye that enter,"—that is, of ever getting out again; where at one time I saw my employer actually up to his neck and swimming for his life in his property, though it was still winter. He had another similar swamp which I could not survey at all, because it was completely under water, and nevertheless, with regard to a third swamp, which I did *survey* from a distance, he remarked to me, true to his instincts, that he would not part with it for any consideration, on account of the mud which it contained. And that man intends to put a girdling ditch round the whole in the course of forty months, and so redeem it by the magic of his spade. I refer to him only as the type of a class.

The weapons with which we have gained our most important victories, which should be handed down as heirlooms from father to son, are not the sword and the lance, but the bushwhack, the turf-cutter, the spade, and the bog hoe, rusted with the blood of many a meadow, and begrimed with the dust of many a hard-fought field. The very winds blew the Indian's cornfield into the meadow, and pointed out the way which he had not the skill to follow. He had no better implement with which to intrench himself in the land than a clamshell. But the farmer is armed with plow and spade.

In literature it is only the wild that attracts us. Dullness is but another name for tameness. It is the uncivilized free and wild thinking in Hamlet and the Iliad, in all the scriptures and mythologies, not learned in the schools, that delights us. As the wild duck is more swift and beautiful than the tame, so is the wild—the mallard—thought, which 'mid falling dews wings its way above the fens. A truly good book is something as natural, and as unexpectedly and unaccountably fair and perfect, as a wild-flower discovered on the prairies of the West or in the jungles of the East. Genius is a light which makes the darkness visible, like the lightning's flash, which perchance shatters the temple of knowledge itself,—and not a taper lighted at the hearth-stone of the race, which pales before the light of common day.

English literature, from the days of the minstrels to the Lake Poets,—Chaucer and Spenser and Milton, and even Shakespeare, included,—breathes no quite fresh and, in this sense, wild strain. It is an essentially tame and civilized literature, reflecting Greece and Rome. Her wilderness is a greenwood, her wild man a Robin Hood. There is plenty of genial love of Nature, but not so much of Nature herself. Her chronicles inform us when her wild animals, but not when the wild man in her, became extinct.

The science of Humboldt is one thing, poetry is another thing. The poet to-day, notwithstanding all the discoveries of science, and the accumulated learning of mankind, enjoys no advantage over Homer.

Where is the literature which gives expression to Nature? He would be a poet who could impress the winds and streams into his service, to speak for him; who nailed words to their primitive senses, as farmers drive down stakes in the spring, which the frost has heaved; who derived his words as often as he used them,—transplanted them to his page with earth adhering to their roots; whose words were so true and fresh and natural that they would appear to expand like the buds at the approach of spring, though they lay half smothered between two musty leaves in a library,—aye, to bloom and bear fruit there, after their kind, annually, for the faithful reader, in sympathy with surrounding Nature.

I do not know of any poetry to quote which adequately expresses this yearning for the Wild. Approached from this side, the best poetry is tame. I do not know where to find in any literature, ancient or modern, any account which contents me of that Nature with which even I am acquainted. You will perceive that I demand something which no Augustan nor Elizabethan age, which no *culture*, in short, can give. Mythology comes nearer to it than anything. How much more fertile a Nature, at least, has Grecian mythology its root in than English literature! Mythology is the crop which the Old World bore before its soil was exhausted, before the fancy and imagination were affected with blight; and which it still bears, wherever its pristine vigor is unabated. All other literatures endure only as the elms which overshadow our houses; but this is like the great dragon-tree of the Western Isles, as old as mankind, and, whether that does or not, will endure as long; for the decay of other literatures makes the soil in which it thrives.

The West is preparing to add its fables to those of the East. The valleys of the Ganges, the Nile, and the Rhine having yielded their crop, it remains to be seen what the valleys of the Amazon, the Plate, the Orinoco, the St. Lawrence, and the Mississippi will produce. Perchance, when, in the course of ages, American liberty has become a fiction of the past,—as it is to some extent a fiction of the present,—the poets of the world will be inspired by American mythology.

The wildest dreams of wild men, even, are not the less true, though they may not recommend themselves to the sense which is most common among Englishmen and Americans to-day. It is not every truth that recommends itself to the common sense. Nature has a place for the wild clematis as well as for the cabbage. Some expressions of truth are reminiscent,—others merely *sensible*, as the phrase is,—others prophetic. Some forms of disease, even, may prophesy forms of health. The geologist has discovered that the figures of serpents, griffins, flying dragons, and other fanciful embellishments of heraldry, have their prototypes in the forms of fossil species which were extinct before man was created, and hence "indicate a faint and shadowy knowledge of a previous state of organic existence." The Hindoos dreamed that the earth rested on an elephant, and the elephant on a tortoise, and the tortoise on a serpent; and though it may be an unimportant coincidence, it will not be out of place here to state, that a fossil tortoise has lately been discovered in Asia large enough to support an elephant. I confess that I am partial to these wild fancies, which transcend the order of time and development. They are the sublimest recreation of the intellect. The partridge loves peas, but not those that go with her into the pot.

In short, all good things are wild and free. There is something in a strain of music, whether produced by an instrument or by the human voice,—take the sound of a bugle in a summer night, for instance,—which by its wildness, to speak without satire; reminds me of the cries emitted by wild beasts in their native forests. It is so much of their wildness as I can understand. Give me for my friends and neighbors wild men, not tame ones. The wildness of the savage is but a faint symbol of the awful ferity with which good men and lovers meet.

I love even to see the domestic animals reassert their native rights,—any evidence that they have not wholly lost their original wild habits and vigor; as when my neighbor's cow breaks out of her pasture early in the spring and boldly swims the river, a cold, gray tide, twenty-five or thirty rods wide, swollen by the melted snow. It is the buffalo crossing the Mississippi. This exploit confers some dignity on the herd in my eyes,—already dignified. The seeds of instinct are preserved under the thick hides of cattle and horses, like seeds in the bowels of the earth, an indefinite period.

Any sportiveness in cattle is unexpected. I saw one day a herd of a dozen bullocks and cows running about and frisking in unwieldy sport, like huge rats, even like kittens. They shook their heads, raised their tails, and rushed up and down a hill, and I perceived by their horns, as well as by their activity, their relation to the deer tribe. But, alas! a sudden loud *Whoa!* would have damped their ardor at once, reduced them from venison to beef, and stiffened their sides and sinews like the locomotive. Who but the Evil One has cried "Whoa!" to mankind? Indeed, the life of cattle, like that of many men, is but a sort of locomotiveness; they move a side at a time, and man, by his machinery, is meeting the horse and the ox half-way. Whatever part the whip has touched is thenceforth palsied. Who would ever think of a *side* of any of the supple cat tribe, as we speak of a *side* of beef?

I rejoice that horses and steers have to be broken before they can be made the slaves of men, and that men themselves have some wild oats still left to sow before they become submissive members of society. Undoubtedly, all men are not equally fit subjects for civilization; and because the majority, like dogs and sheep, are tame by inherited disposition, this is no reason why the others should have their natures broken that they may be reduced to the same level. Men are in the main alike, but they were made several in order that they might be various. If a low use is to be served, one man will do nearly or quite as well as another; if a high one, individual excellence is to be regarded. Any man can stop a hole to keep the wind away, but no other man could serve so rare a use as the author of this illustration did. Confucius says, "The skins of the tiger and the leopard, when they are tanned, are as the skins of the dog and the sheep tanned." But it is not the part of a true culture to tame tigers, any more than it is to make sheep ferocious; and tanning their skins for shoes is not the best use to which they can be put.

When looking over a list of men's names in a foreign language, as of military officers, or of authors who have written on a particular subject, I am reminded once more that there is nothing in a name. The name Menschikoff, for instance, has nothing in it to my ears more human than a whisker, and it may belong to a rat. As the names of the Poles and Russians are to us, so are ours to them. It is as if they had been named by the child's rigmarole, *Iery wiery ichery van, tittle-tol-tan.* I see in my mind a herd of wild creatures swarming over the earth, and to each the herdsman has affixed some barbarous sound in his own dialect. The names of men are, of course, as cheap and meaningless as *Bose* and *Tray*, the names of dogs.

Methinks it would be some advantage to philosophy if men were named merely in the gross, as they are known. It would be necessary only to know the genus and perhaps the race or variety, to know the individual. We are not prepared to believe that every private soldier in a Roman army had a name of his own,—because we have not supposed that he had a character of his own.

At present our only true names are nicknames. I knew a boy who, from his peculiar energy, was called "Buster" by his playmates, and this rightly supplanted his Christian name. Some travelers tell us that an Indian had no name given him at first, but earned it, and his name was his fame; and among some tribes he acquired a new name with every new exploit. It is pitiful when a man bears a name for convenience merely, who has earned neither name nor fame.

I will not allow mere names to make distinctions for me, but still see men in herds for all them. A familiar name cannot make a man less strange to me. It may be given to a savage who retains in secret his own wild title earned in the woods. We have a wild savage in us, and a savage name is perchance somewhere recorded as ours. I see that my neighbor, who bears the familiar epithet William or Edwin, takes it off with his jacket. It does not adhere to him when asleep or in anger, or aroused by any passion or inspiration. I seem to hear pronounced by some of his kin at such a time his original wild name in some jaw-breaking or else melodious tongue.

Here is this vast, savage, howling mother of ours, Nature, lying all around, with such beauty, and such affection for her children, as the leopard; and yet we are so early weaned from her breast to society, to that culture which is exclusively an interaction of man on man,—a sort of breeding in and in, which produces at most a merely English nobility, a civilization destined to have a speedy limit.

In society, in the best institutions of men, it is easy to detect a certain precocity. When we should still be growing children, we are already little men. Give me a culture which imports much muck from the meadows, and deepens the soil,—not that which trusts to heating manures, and improved implements and modes of culture only!

Many a poor sore-eyed student that I have heard of would grow faster, both intellectually and physically, if, instead of sitting up so very late, he honestly slumbered a fool's allowance.

There may be an excess even of informing light. Niepce, a Frenchman, discovered "actinism," that power in the sun's rays which produces a chemical effect; that granite rocks, and stone structures, and statues of metal "are all alike destructively acted upon during the hours of sunshine, and, but for provisions of Nature no less wonderful, would soon perish under the delicate touch of the most subtile of the agencies of the universe." But he observed that "those bodies which underwent this change during the daylight possessed the power of restoring themselves to their original conditions during the hours of night, when this excitement was no longer influencing them." Hence it has been inferred that "the hours of darkness are as necessary to the inorganic creation as we know night and sleep are to the organic kingdom." Not even does the moon shine every night, but gives place to darkness.

I would not have every man nor every part of a man cultivated, any more than I would have every acre of earth cultivated: part will be tillage, but the greater part will be meadow and forest, not only serving an immediate use, but preparing a mould against a distant future, by the annual decay of the vegetation which it supports.

There are other letters for the child to learn than those which Cadmus invented. The Spaniards have a good term to express this wild and dusky knowledge, *Gramática parda*, tawny grammar, a kind of mother-wit derived from that same leopard to which I have referred.

We have heard of a Society for the Diffusion of Useful Knowledge. It is said that knowledge is power, and the like. Methinks there is equal need of a Society for the Diffusion of Useful Ignorance, what we will call Beautiful Knowledge, a knowledge useful in a higher sense: for what is most of our boasted so-called knowledge but a conceit that we know something, which robs us of the advantage of our actual ignorance? What we call knowledge is often our positive ignorance; ignorance our negative knowledge. By long years of patient industry and reading of the newspapers,—for what are the libraries of science but files of newspapers?—a man accumulates a myriad facts, lays them up in his memory, and then when in some spring of his life he saunters abroad into the

Great Fields of thought, he, as it were, goes to grass like a horse and leaves all his harness behind in the stable. I would say to the Society for the Diffusion of Useful Knowledge, sometimes,—Go to grass. You have eaten hay long enough. The spring has come with its green crop. The very cows are driven to their country pastures before the end of May; though I have heard of one unnatural farmer who kept his cow in the barn and fed her on hay all the year round. So, frequently, the Society for the Diffusion of Useful Knowledge treats its cattle.

A man's ignorance sometimes is not only useful, but beautiful,—while his knowledge, so called, is oftentimes worse than useless, besides being ugly. Which is the best man to deal with,—he who knows nothing about a subject, and, what is extremely rare, knows that he knows nothing, or he who really knows something about it, but thinks that he knows all?

My desire for knowledge is intermittent, but my desire to bathe my head in atmosphere unknown to my feet is perennial and constant. The highest that we can attain to is not Knowledge, but Sympathy with Intelligence. I do not know that this higher knowledge amounts to anything more definite than a novel and grand surprise on a sudden revelation of the insufficiency of all that we called Knowledge before,—a discovery that there are more things in heaven and earth than are dreamed of in our philosophy. It is the lighting up of the mist by the sun. Man cannot *know* in any higher sense than this, any more than he can look serenely and with impunity in the face of the sun: *'Ως τὶ νοων, οὐ κεῖνον νοήσεις*, "You will not perceive that, as perceiving a particular thing," say the Chaldean Oracles.

There is something servile in the habit of seeking after a law which we may obey. We may study the laws of matter at and for our convenience, but a successful life knows no law. It is an unfortunate discovery certainly, that of a law which binds us where we did not know before that we were bound. Live free, child of the mist,—and with respect to knowledge we are all children of the mist. The man who takes the liberty to live is superior to all the laws, by virtue of his relation to the lawmaker. "That is active duty," says the Vishnu Purana, "which is not for our bondage; that is knowledge which is for our liberation: all other duty is good only unto weariness; all other knowledge is only the cleverness of an artist."

It is remarkable how few events or crises there are in our histories, how little exercised we have been in our minds, how few experiences we have had. I would fain be assured that I am growing apace and rankly, though my very growth disturb this dull equanimity,—though it be with struggle through long, dark, muggy nights or seasons of gloom. It would be well if all our lives were a divine tragedy even, instead of this trivial comedy or farce. Dante, Bunyan, and others appear to have been exercised in their minds more than we: they were subjected to a kind of culture such as our district schools and colleges do not contemplate. Even Mahomet, though many may scream at his name, had a good deal more to live for, aye, and to die for, than they have commonly.

When, at rare intervals, some thought visits one, as perchance he is walking on a railroad, then, indeed, the cars go by without his hearing them. But soon, by some inexorable law, our life goes by and the cars return.

> "Gentle breeze, that wanderest unseen,
> And bendest the thistles round Loira of storms,
> Traveler of the windy glens,
> Why hast thou left my ear so soon?"

While almost all men feel an attraction drawing them to society, few are attracted strongly to Nature. In their reaction to Nature men appear to me for the most part, notwithstanding their arts, lower than the animals. It is not often a beautiful relation, as in the case of the animals. How little appreciation of the beauty of the landscape there is among us! We have to be told that the Greeks called the world Κόσμος, Beauty, or Order, but we do not see clearly why they did so, and we esteem it at best only a curious philological fact.

For my part, I feel that with regard to Nature I live a sort of border life, on the confines of a world into which I make occasional and transient forays only, and my patriotism and allegiance to the state into whose territories I seem to retreat are those of a moss-trooper. Unto a life which I call natural I would gladly follow even a will-o'-the-wisp through bogs and sloughs unimaginable, but no moon nor firefly has shown me the causeway to it. Nature is a personality so vast and universal that we have never seen one of her features. The walker in the familiar fields which stretch around my native town sometimes finds himself in another land than is described in their owners' deeds, as it were in some faraway field on the confines of the actual Concord, where her jurisdiction ceases, and the idea which the word Concord suggests ceases to be suggested. These farms which I have myself surveyed, these bounds which I have set up, appear dimly still as through a mist; but they have no chemistry to fix them; they fade from the surface of the glass, and the picture which the painter painted stands out dimly from beneath. The world with which we are commonly acquainted leaves no trace, and it will have no anniversary.

I took a walk on Spaulding's Farm the other afternoon. I saw the setting sun lighting up the opposite side of a stately pine wood. Its golden rays straggled into the aisles of the wood as into some noble hall. I was impressed as if some ancient and altogether admirable and shining family had settled there in that part of the land called Concord, unknown to me,—to whom the sun was servant,—who had not gone into society in the village,—who had not been called on. I saw their park, their pleasure-ground, beyond through the wood, in Spaulding's cranberry-meadow. The pines furnished them with gables as they grew. Their house was not obvious to vision; the trees grew through it. I do not know whether I heard the sounds of a suppressed hilarity or not. They seemed to recline on the sunbeams. They have sons and daughters. They are quite well. The farmer's cart-path, which leads directly through their hall, does not in the least put them out, as the muddy bottom of a pool is sometimes seen through the reflected skies. They never heard of Spaulding, and do not know that he is their neighbor,—notwithstanding I heard him whistle as he drove his team through the house. Nothing can equal the serenity of their lives. Their coat-of-arms is simply a lichen. I saw it painted on the pines and oaks. Their attics were in the tops of the trees. They are of no politics. There was no noise of labor. I did not perceive that they were weaving or spinning. Yet I did detect, when the wind lulled and hearing was done away, the finest imaginable sweet musical hum,—as of a distant hive in May,—which perchance was the sound of their thinking. They had no idle thoughts, and no one without could see their work, for their industry was not as in knots and excrescences embayed.

But I find it difficult to remember them. They fade irrevocably out of my mind even now while I speak, and endeavor to recall them and recollect myself. It is only after a long and serious effort to recollect my best thoughts that I become again aware of their cohabitancy. If it were not for such families as this, I think I should move out of Concord.

We are accustomed to say in New England that few and fewer pigeons visit us every year. Our forests furnish no mast for them. So, it would seem, few and fewer thoughts visit each growing man from year to year, for the grove in our minds is laid waste,—sold to feed unnecessary fires of ambition, or sent to mill,—and there is scarcely a twig left for them to perch on. They no longer build nor breed with us. In some more genial season, perchance, a faint shadow flits across the landscape of the mind, cast by the *wings* of some thought in its vernal or autumnal migration, but, looking up, we are unable to detect the substance of the thought itself. Our winged thoughts are turned to poultry. They no longer soar, and they attain only to a Shanghai and Cochin-China grandeur. Those *gra-a-ate thoughts*, those *gra-a-ate men* you hear of!

We hug the earth,—how rarely we mount! Methinks we might elevate ourselves a little more. We might climb a tree, at least. I found my account in climbing a tree once. It was a tall white pine, on the top of a hill; and though I got well pitched, I was well paid for it, for I discovered new mountains in the horizon which I had never seen before,—so much more of the earth and the heavens. I might have walked about the foot of the tree for threescore years and ten, and yet I certainly should never have seen them. But, above all, I discovered around me,—it was near the end of June,—on the ends of the topmost branches only, a few minute and delicate red cone-like blossoms, the fertile flower of the white pine looking heavenward. I carried straightway to the village the topmost spire, and showed it to stranger jurymen who walked the streets,—for it was court week,—and to farmers and lumber-dealers and woodchoppers and hunters, and not one had ever seen the like before, but they wondered as at a star dropped down. Tell of ancient architects finishing their works on the tops of columns as perfectly as on the lower and more visible parts! Nature has from the first expanded the minute blossoms of the forest only toward the heavens, above men's heads and unobserved by them. We see only the flowers that are under our feet in the meadows. The pines have developed their delicate blossoms on the highest twigs of the wood every summer for ages, as well over the heads of Nature's red children as of her white ones; yet scarcely a farmer or hunter in the land has ever seen them.

Above all, we cannot afford not to live in the present. He is blessed over all mortals who loses no moment of the passing life in remembering the past. Unless our philosophy hears the cock crow in every barn-yard within our horizon, it is belated. That sound commonly reminds us that we are growing rusty and antique in our employments and habits of thought. His philosophy comes down to a more recent time than ours. There is something suggested by it that is a newer testament,—the gospel according to this moment. He has not fallen astern; he has got up early and kept up early, and to be where he is is to be in season, in the foremost rank of time. It is an expression of the health and soundness of Nature, a brag for all the world,—healthiness as of a spring burst forth, a new fountain of the Muses, to celebrate this last instant of time. Where he lives no fugitive slave laws are passed. Who has not betrayed his master many times since last he heard that note?

The merit of this bird's strain is in its freedom from all plaintiveness. The singer can easily move us to tears or to laughter, but where is he who can excite in us a pure morning joy? When, in doleful dumps, breaking the awful stillness of our wooden sidewalk on a Sunday, or, perchance, a watcher in the house of mourning, I hear a cockerel crow far or near, I think to myself, "There is one of us well, at any rate,"—and with a sudden gush return to my senses.

We had a remarkable sunset one day last November. I was walking in a meadow, the source of a small brook, when the sun at last, just before setting, after a cold, gray day, reached a clear stratum in the horizon, and the softest, brightest morning sunlight fell on the dry grass and on the stems of the trees in the opposite horizon and on the leaves of the shrub oaks on the hillside, while our shadows stretched long over the meadow eastward, as if we were the only motes in its beams. It was such a light as we could not have imagined a moment before, and the air also was so warm and serene that nothing was wanting to make a paradise of that meadow. When we reflected that this was not a solitary phenomenon, never to happen again, but that it would happen forever and ever, an infinite number of evenings, and cheer and reassure the latest child that walked there, it was more glorious still.

The sun sets on some retired meadow, where no house is visible, with all the glory and splendor that it lavishes on cities, and perchance as it has never set before,—where there is but a solitary marsh hawk to have his wings gilded by it, or only a musquash looks out from his cabin, and there is some little black-veined brook in the midst of the marsh, just beginning to meander, winding slowly round a decaying stump. We walked in so pure and bright a light, gilding the withered grass and leaves, so softly and serenely bright, I thought I had never bathed in such a golden flood, without a ripple or a murmur to it. The west side of every wood and rising ground gleamed like the boundary of Elysium, and the sun on our backs seemed like a gentle herdsman driving us home at evening.

So we saunter toward the Holy Land, till one day the sun shall shine more brightly than ever he has done, shall perchance shine into our minds and hearts, and light up our whole lives with a great awakening light, as warm and serene and golden as on a bankside in autumn.

SLAVERY IN MASSACHUSETTS

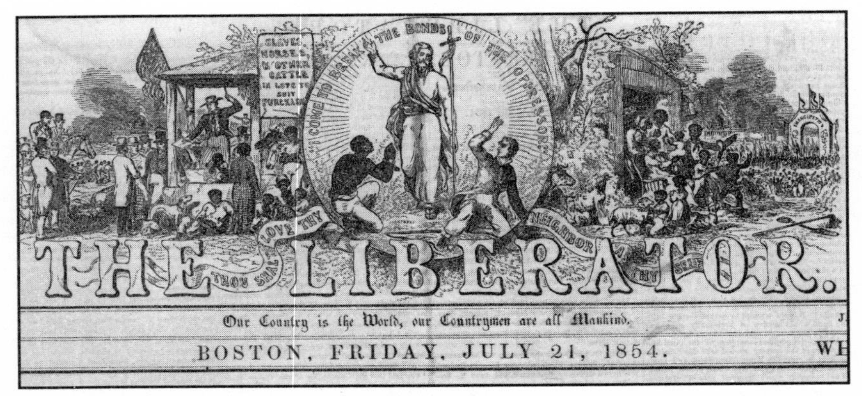

Colophon of *The Liberator*, July 21, 1854, the issue in which "Slavery in Massachusetts" first appeared.

SLAVERY IN MASSACHUSETTS

I lately attended a meeting of the citizens of Concord, expecting, as one among many, to speak on the subject of slavery in Massachusetts; but I was surprised and disappointed to find that what had called my townsmen together was the destiny of Nebraska, and not of Massachusetts, and that what I had to say would be entirely out of order. I had thought that the house was on fire, and not the prairie; but though several of the citizens of Massachusetts are now in prison for attempting to rescue a slave from her own clutches, not one of the speakers at that meeting expressed regret for it, not one even referred to it. It was only the disposition of some wild lands a thousand miles off, which appeared to concern them. The inhabitants of Concord are not prepared to stand by one of their own bridges, but talk only of taking up a position on the highlands beyond the Yellowstone river. Our Buttricks, and Davises, and Hosmers are retreating thither, and I fear that they will have no Lexington Common between them and the enemy. There is not one slave in Nebraska; there are perhaps a million slaves in Massachusetts.

They who have been bred in the school of politics fail now and always to face the facts. Their measures are half measures and make-shifts, merely. They put off the day of settlement indefinitely, and meanwhile, the debt accumulates. Though the Fugitive Slave Law had not been the subject of discussion on that occasion, it was at length faintly resolved by my townsmen, at an adjourned meeting, as I learn, that the compromise compact of 1820 having been repudiated by one of the parties,

"Therefore, . . . the Fugitive Slave Law must be repealed." But this is not the reason why an iniquitous law should be repealed. The fact which the politician faces is merely, that there is less honor among thieves than was supposed, and not the fact that they are thieves.

As I had no opportunity to express my thoughts at that meeting, will you allow me to do so here?

Again it happens that the Boston Court House is full of armed men, holding prisoner and trying a MAN, to find out if he is not really a SLAVE. Does any one think that Justice or God awaits Mr. Loring's decision? For him to sit there deciding still, when this question is already decided from eternity to eternity, and the unlettered slave himself, and the multitude around, have long since heard and assented to the decision, is simply to make himself ridiculous. We may be tempted to ask from whom he received his commission, and who he is that received it; what novel statutes he obeys, and what precedents are to him of authority. Such an arbiter's very existence is an impertinence. We do not ask him to make up his mind, but to make up his pack.

I listen to hear the voice of a Governor, Commander-in-Chief of the forces of Massachusetts. I hear only the creaking of crickets and the hum of insects which now fill the summer air. The Governor's exploit is to review the troops on muster days. I have seen him on horseback, with his hat off, listening to a chaplain's prayer. It chances that is all I have ever seen of a Governor. I think that I could manage to get along without one. If *he* is not of the least use to prevent my being kidnapped, pray of what important use is he likely to be to me? When freedom is most endangered, he dwells in the deepest obscurity. A distinguished clergyman told me that he chose the profession of a clergyman, because it afforded the most leisure for literary pursuits. I would recommend to him the profession of a Governor.

Three years ago, also, when the Simm's tragedy was acted, I said to myself, there is such an officer, if not such a man, as the Governor of Massachusetts,—what has he been about the last fortnight? Has he had as much as he could do to keep on the fence during this moral earthquake? It seemed to me that no keener satire could have been aimed at, no more cutting insult have been offered to that man, than just what happened—the absence of all inquiry after him in that crisis. The worst and the most I chance to know of him is, that he did not improve that opportunity to make himself known, and worthily known. He could at least have *resigned* himself into fame. It appeared to be forgotten that there was such a man, or such an office. Yet no doubt he was endeavoring to fill the gubernatorial chair all the while. He was no Governor of mine. He did not govern me.

But at last, in the present case, the Governor was heard from. After he and the United States Government had perfectly succeeded in robbing a poor innocent black man of his liberty for life, and, as far as they could, of his Creator's likeness in his breast, he made a speech to his accomplices, at a congratulatory supper!

I have read a recent law of this State, making it penal for "any officer of the Commonwealth" to "detain, or aid in the . . . detention," any where within its limits, "of any person, for the reason that he is claimed as a fugitive slave." Also, it was a matter of notoriety that a writ of replevin to take the fugitive out of the custody of the United States Marshal could not be served, for want of sufficient force to aid the officer.

I had thought that the Governor was in some sense the executive officer of the State; that it was his business, as a Governor, to see that the laws of the State were executed; while, as a man, he took care that he did not, by so doing, break the laws of humanity; but when there is any special important use for him, he is useless, or worse than useless, and permits the laws of the State to go unexecuted. Perhaps I do not know what are the duties of a Governor; but if to be a Governor requires to subject one's self to so much ignominy without remedy, if it is to put a restraint upon my manhood, I shall take care never to be Governor of Massachusetts. I have not read far in the statutes of this Commonwealth. It is not profitable reading. They do not always say what is true; and they do not always mean what they say. What I am concerned to know is, that that man's influence and authority were on the side of the slaveholder, and not of the slave—of the guilty, and not of the innocent—of injustice, and not of justice. I never saw him of whom I speak; indeed, I did not know that he was Governor until this event occurred. I heard of him and Anthony Burns at the same time, and thus, undoubtedly, most will hear of him. So far am I from being governed by him. I do not mean that it was any thing to his discredit that I had not heard of him, only that I heard what I did. The worst I shall say of him is, that he proved no better than the majority of his constituents would be likely to prove. In my opinion, he was not equal to the occasion.

The whole military force of the State is at the service of a Mr. Suttle, a slaveholder from Virginia, to enable him to catch a man whom he calls his property; but not a soldier is offered to save a citizen of Massachusetts from being kidnapped! Is this what all these soldiers, all this *training* has been for these seventy-nine years past? Have they been trained merely to rob Mexico, and carry back fugitive slaves to their masters?

These very nights, I heard the sound of a drum in our streets. There were men *training* still; and for what? I could with an effort pardon the cockerels of Concord for crowing still, for they, perchance, had not been beaten that morning; but I could not excuse this rub-a-dub of the "trainers." The slave was carried back by exactly such as these, i.e., by the soldier, of whom the best you can say in this connection is, that he is a fool made conspicuous by a painted coat.

Three years ago, also, just a week after the authorities of Boston assembled to carry back a perfectly innocent man, and one whom they knew to be innocent, into slavery, the inhabitants of Concord caused the bells to be rung and the cannons to be fired, to celebrate their liberty—and the courage and love of liberty of their ancestors who fought at the bridge. As if *those* three millions had fought for the right to be free themselves, but to hold in slavery three million others. Now-a-days, men wear a fool's cap, and call it a liberty cap. I do not know but there are some, who, if they were tied to a whipping-post, and could but get one hand free, would use it to ring the bells and fire the cannons, to celebrate *their* liberty. So some of my townsmen took the liberty to ring and fire; that was the extent of their freedom; and when the sound of the bells died away, their liberty died away also; when the powder was all expended, their liberty went off with the smoke.

The joke could be no broader, if the inmates of the prisons were to subscribe for all the powder to be used in such salutes, and hire the jailers to do the firing and ringing for them, while they enjoyed it through the grating.

This is what I thought about my neighbors.

Every humane and intelligent inhabitant of Concord, when he or she heard those bells and those cannons, thought not with pride of the events of the 19th of April, 1775, but with shame of the events of the 12th of April, 1851. But now we have half buried that old shame under a new one.

Massachusetts sat waiting Mr. Loring's decision, as if it could in any way affect her own criminality. Her crime, the most conspicuous and fatal crime of all, was permitting him to be the umpire in such a case. It was really the trial of Massachusetts. Every moment that she hesitated to set this man free—every moment that she now hesitates to atone for her crime, she is convicted. The Commissioner on her case is God; not Edward G. God, but simple God.

I wish my countrymen to consider, that whatever the human law may be, neither an individual nor a nation can ever commit the least act of injustice against the obscurest individual, without having to pay the penalty for it. A government which deliberately enacts injustice, and persists in it, will at length ever become the laughing-stock of the world.

Much has been said about American slavery, but I think that we do not even yet realize what slavery is. If I were seriously to propose to Congress to make mankind into sausages, I have no doubt that most of the members would smile at my proposition, and if any believed me to be in earnest, they would think that I proposed something much worse than Congress had ever done. But if any of them will tell me that to make a man into a sausage would be much worse,—would be any worse, than to make him into a slave,—than it was to enact the Fugitive Slave Law, I will accuse him of foolishness, of intellectual incapacity, of making a distinction without a difference. The one is just as sensible a proposition as the other.

I hear a good deal said about trampling this law under foot. Why, one need not go out of his way to do that. This law rises not to the level of the head or the reason; its natural habitat is in the dirt. It was born and bred, and has its life only in the dust and mire, on a level with the feet, and he who walks with freedom, and does not with Hindoo mercy avoid treading on every venomous reptile, will inevitably tread on it, and so trample it under foot,—and Webster, its maker, with it, like the dirt-bug and its ball.

Recent events will be valuable as a criticism on the administration of justice in our midst, or, rather, as showing what are the true resources of justice in any community. It has come to this, that the friends of liberty, the friends of the slave, have shuddered when they have understood that his fate was left to the legal tribunals of the country to be decided. Free men have no faith that justice will be awarded in such a case; the judge may decide this way or that; it is a kind of accident, at best. It is evident that he is not a competent authority in so important a case. It is no time, then, to be judging according to his precedents, but to establish a precedent for the future. I would much rather trust to the sentiment of the people. In their vote, you would get something of some value, at least, however small; but, in the other case, only the trammelled judgment of an individual, of no significance, be it which way it might.

It is to some extent fatal to the courts, when the people are compelled to go behind them. I do not wish to believe that the courts were made for fair weather, and for very civil cases merely,—but think of leaving it to any court in the land to decide whether more than three millions of people, in this case, a sixth part of a nation, have a right to be freemen or not! But it has been left to the courts of *justice*, so-called—to the Supreme Court of the land—and, as you all know, recognizing no authority but the Constitution, it has decided that the three millions are, and shall continue to be, slaves. Such judges as these are merely the inspectors of a pick-lock and murderer's tools, to tell him whether they are in working order or not, and there they think that their responsibility ends. There was a prior case on the docket, which they, as judges appointed by God, had no right to skip; which having been justly settled, they would have been saved from this humiliation. It was the case of the murderer himself.

The law will never make men free; it is men who have got to make the law free. They are the lovers of law and order, who observe the law when the government breaks it.

Among human beings, the judge whose words seal the fate of a man furthest into eternity, is not he who merely pronounces the verdict of the law, but he, whoever he may be, who, from a love of truth, and unprejudiced by any custom or enactment of men, utters a true opinion or *sentence* concerning him. He it is that *sentences* him. Whoever has discerned truth, has received his commission from a higher source than the chiefest justice in the world, who can discern only law. He finds himself constituted judge of the judge.—Strange that it should be necessary to state such simple truths.

I am more and more convinced that, with reference to any public question, it is more important to know what the country thinks of it, than what the city thinks. The city does not *think* much. On any moral question, I would rather have the opinion of Boxboro than of Boston and New York put together. When the former speaks, I feel as if somebody *had* spoken, as if *humanity* was yet, and a reasonable being had asserted its rights,—as if some unprejudiced men among the country's hills had at length turned their attention to the subject, and by a few sensible words redeemed the reputation of the race. When, in some obscure country town, the farmers come together to a special town meeting, to express their opinion on some subject which is vexing the land, that, I think, is the true Congress, and the most respectable one that is ever assembled in the United States.

It is evident that there are, in this Commonwealth, at least, two parties, becoming more and more distinct—the party of the city, and the party of the country. I know that the country is mean enough, but I am glad to believe that there is a slight difference in her favor. But as yet, she has few, if any organs, through which to express herself. The editorials which she reads, like the news, come from the sea-board. Let us, the inhabitants of the country, cultivate self-respect. Let us not send to the city for aught more essential than our broadcloths and groceries, or, if we read the opinions of the city, let us entertain opinions of our own.

Among measures to be adopted, I would suggest to make as earnest and vigorous an assault on the Press as has already been made, and with effect, on the Church. The Church has much improved within a few years; but the Press is almost, without exception, corrupt. I believe that, in this country, the press exerts a greater and a more pernicious influence than the Church did in its worst period. We are not a religious people, but we are a nation of politicians. We do not care for the Bible, but we do care for the newspaper. At any meeting of politicians,—like that at Concord the other evening, for instance,—how impertinent it would be to quote from the Bible! how pertinent to quote from a newspaper or from the Constitution! The newspaper is a Bible which we read every morning and every afternoon, standing and sitting, riding and walking. It is a Bible which every man carries in his pocket, which lies on every table and counter, and which the mail, and thousands of missionaries, are continually dispensing. It is, in short, the only book which America has printed, and which America reads. So wide is its influence. The editor is a preacher whom you voluntarily support. Your tax is commonly one cent daily, and it costs nothing for pew hire. But how many of these preachers preach the truth? I repeat the testimony of many an intelligent foreigner, as well as my own convictions, when I say, that probably no country was ever ruled by so mean a class of tyrants as, with a few noble exceptions, are the editors of the periodical press in *this* country. And as they live and rule only by their servility, and appealing to the worst, and not the better nature of man, the people who read them are in the condition of the dog that returns to his vomit.

The *Liberator* and the *Commonwealth* were the only papers in Boston, as far as I know, which made themselves heard in condemnation of the cowardice and meanness of the authorities of that city, as exhibited in '51. The other journals, almost without exception, by their manner of referring to and speaking of the Fugitive Slave Law, and the carrying back of the slave Simms, insulted the common sense of the country, at least. And, for the most part, they did this, one would say, because they thought so to secure the approbation of their patrons, not being aware that a sounder sentiment prevailed to any extent in the heart of the Commonwealth. I am told that some of them have improved of late; but they are still eminently time-serving. Such is the character they have won.

But, thank fortune, this preacher can be even more easily reached by the weapons of the reformer than could the recreant priest. The free men of New England have only to refrain from purchasing and reading these sheets, have only to withhold their cents, to kill a score of them at once. One whom I respect told me that he purchased Mitchell's *Citizen* in the cars, and then threw it out the window. But would not his contempt have been more fatally expressed, if he had not bought it?

Are they Americans? are they New Englanders? are they inhabitants of Lexington, and Concord, and Framingham, who read and support the Boston *Post*, *Mail*, *Journal*, *Advertiser*, *Courier*, and *Times*? Are these the Flags of our Union? I am not a newspaper reader, and may omit to name the worst.

Could slavery suggest a more complete servility than some of these journals exhibit? Is there any dust which their conduct does not lick, and make fouler still with its slime? I do not know whether the Boston *Herald* is still in existence, but I remember to have seen it about the streets when Simms was carried off. Did it not act its part well—serve its master faithfully? How could it have gone lower on its belly? How can a man stoop lower than he is low? do more than put his extremities in the place of the head he has? than make his head his lower extremity? When I have taken up this paper with my cuffs turned up, I have heard the gurgling of the sewer through every column. I have felt that I was handling a paper picked out of the public gutters, a leaf from the gospel of the gambling-house, the groggery and the brothel, harmonizing with the gospel of the Merchants' Exchange.

The majority of the men of the North, and of the South, and East, and West, are not men of principle. If they vote, they do not send men to Congress on errands of humanity, but while their brothers and sisters are being scourged and hung for loving liberty, while——I might here insert all that slavery implies and is,——it is the mismanagement of wood and iron and stone and gold which concerns them. Do what you will, O Government! with my wife and children, my mother and brother, my father and sister, I will obey your commands to the letter. It will indeed grieve me if you hurt them, if you deliver them to overseers to be hunted by hounds or to be whipped to death; but nevertheless, I will peaceably pursue my chosen calling on this fair earth, until perchance, one day, when I have put on mourning for them dead, I shall have persuaded you to relent. Such is the attitude, such are the words of Massachusetts.

Rather than do thus, I need not say what match I would touch, what system endeavor to blow up,—but as I love my life, I would side with the light, and let the dark earth roll from under me, calling my mother and my brother to follow.

I would remind my countrymen, that they are to be men first, and Americans only at a late and convenient hour. No matter how valuable law may be to protect your property, even to keep soul and body together, if it do not keep you and humanity together.

I am sorry to say, that I doubt if there is a judge in Massachusetts who is prepared to resign his office, and get his living innocently, whenever it is required of him to pass sentence under a law which is merely contrary to the law of God. I am compelled to see that they put themselves, or rather, are by character, in this respect, exactly on a level with the marine who discharges his musket in any direction he is ordered to. They are just as much tools and as little men. Certainly, they are not the more to be respected, because their master enslaves their understandings and consciences, instead of their bodies.

The judges and lawyers,—simply as such, I mean,—and all men of expediency, try this case by a very low and incompetent standard. They consider, not whether the Fugitive Slave Law is right, but whether it is what they call *constitutional*. Is virtue constitutional, or vice? Is equity constitutional, or iniquity? In important moral and vital questions like this, it is just as impertinent to ask whether a law is constitutional or not, as to ask whether it is profitable or not. They persist in being the servants of the worst of men, and not the servants of humanity. The question is not whether you or your grandfather, seventy years ago, did not enter into an agreement to serve the devil, and that service is not accordingly now due; but whether you will not now, for once and at last, serve God,—in spite of your own past recreancy, or that of your ancestor,—by obeying that eternal and only just CONSTITUTION, which He, and not any Jefferson or Adams, has written in your being.

The amount of it is, if the majority vote the devil to be God, the minority will live and behave accordingly, and obey the successful candidate, trusting that some time or other, by some Speaker's casting vote, perhaps, they may reinstate God. This is the highest principle I can get out of or invent for my neighbors. These men act as if they believed that they could safely slide down hill a little way—or a good way—and would surely come to a place, by and by, where they could begin to slide up again. This is expediency, or choosing that course which offers the slightest obstacles to the feet, that is, a down-hill one. But there is no such thing as accomplishing a righteous reform by the use of "expediency." There is no such thing as sliding up hill. In morals, the only sliders are backsliders.

Thus we steadily worship Mammon, both School, and State, and Church, and the Seventh Day curse God with a tintamar from one end of the Union to the other.

Will mankind never learn that policy is not morality—that it never secures any moral right, but considers merely what is expedient? chooses the available candidate, who is invariably the devil,—and what right have his constituents to be surprised, because the devil does not behave like an angel of light? What is wanted is men, not of policy, but of probity—who recognize a higher law than the Constitution, or the decision of the majority. The fate of the country does not depend on how you vote at the polls—the worst man is as strong as the best at that game; it does not depend on what kind of paper you drop into the ballot-box once a year, but on what kind of man you drop from your chamber into the street every morning.

What should concern Massachusetts is not the Nebraska Bill, nor the Fugitive Slave Bill, but her own slaveholding and servility. Let the State dissolve her union with the slaveholder. She may wriggle and hesitate, and ask leave to read the Constitution once more; but she can find no respectable law or precedent which sanctions the continuance of such a Union for an instant.

Let each inhabitant of the State dissolve his union with her, as long as she delays to do her duty.

The events of the past month teach me to distrust Fame. I see that she does not finely discriminate, but coarsely hurrahs. She considers not the simple heroism of an action, but only as it is connected with its apparent consequences. She praises till she is hoarse the easy exploit of the Boston tea party, but will be comparatively silent about the braver and more disinterestedly heroic attack on the Boston Court-House, simply because it was unsuccessful!

Covered with disgrace, the State has sat down coolly to try for their lives and liberties the men who attempted to do its duty for it. And this is called *justice*! They who have shown that they can behave particularly well may perchance be put under bonds for *their good behavior*. They whom truth requires at present to plead guilty, are of all the inhabitants of the State, pre-eminently innocent. While the Governor, and the Mayor, and countless officers of the Commonwealth, are at large, the champions of liberty are imprisoned.

Only they are guiltless, who commit the crime of contempt of such a Court. It behoves every man to see that his influence is on the side of justice, and let the courts make their own characters. My sympathies in this case are wholly with the accused, and wholly against the accusers and their judges. Justice is sweet and musical; but injustice is harsh and discordant. The judge still sits grinding at his organ, but it yields no music, and we hear only the sound of the handle. He believes that all the music resides in the handle, and the crowd toss him their coppers the same as before.

Do you suppose that that Massachusetts which is now doing these things,—which hesitates to crown these men, some of whose lawyers, and even judges, perchance, may be driven to take refuge in some poor quibble, that they may not wholly outrage their instinctive sense of justice,—do you suppose that she is any thing but base and servile? that she is the champion of liberty?

Show me a free State, and a court truly of justice, and I will fight for them, if need be; but show me Massachusetts, and I refuse her my allegiance, and express contempt for her courts.

The effect of a good government is to make life more valuable,—of a bad one, to make it less valuable. We can afford that railroad, and all merely material stock, should lose some of its value, for that only compels us to live more simply and economically; but suppose that the value of life itself should be diminished! How can we make a less demand on man and nature, how live more economically in respect to virtue and all noble qualities, than we do? I have lived for the last month,—and I think that every man in Massachusetts capable of the sentiment of patriotism must have had a similar experience,—with the sense of having suffered a vast and indefinite loss. I did not know at first what ailed me. At last it occurred to me that what I had lost was a country. I had never respected the Government near to which I had lived, but I had foolishly thought that I might manage to live here, minding my private affairs, and forget it. For my part, my old and worthiest pursuits have lost I cannot say how much of their attraction, and I feel that my investment in life here is worth many per cent. less since Massachusetts last deliberately sent back an innocent man, Anthony Burns, to slavery. I dwelt before, perhaps, in the illusion that my life passed somewhere only *between* heaven and hell, but now I cannot persuade myself that I do not dwell *wholly within* hell. The site of that political organization called Massachusetts is to me morally covered with volcanic scoriæ and cinders, such as Milton describes in the infernal regions. If there is any hell more unprincipled than our rulers, and we, the ruled, I feel curious to see it. Life itself being worth less, all things with it, which minister to it, are worth less. Suppose you have a small library, with pictures to adorn the walls—a garden laid out around—and contemplate scientific and literary pursuits, &c., and discover all at once that your villa, with all its contents, is located in hell, and that the justice of the peace has a cloven foot and a forked tail—do not these things suddenly lose their value in your eyes?

I feel that, to some extent, the State has fatally interfered with my lawful business. It has not only interrupted me in my passage through Court street on errands of trade, but it has interrupted me and every man on his onward and upward path, on which he had trusted soon to leave Court street far behind. What right had it to remind me of Court street? I have found that hollow which even I had relied on for solid.

I am surprised to see men going about their business as if nothing had happened. I say to myself—Unfortunates! they have not heard the news. I am surprised that the man whom I just met on horseback should be so earnest to overtake his newly-bought cows running away—since all property is insecure—and if they do not run away again, they may be taken away from him when he gets them. Fool! does he not know that his seed-corn is worth less this year—that all beneficent harvests fail as you approach the empire of hell? No prudent man will build a stone house under these circumstances, or engage in any peaceful enterprise which it requires a long time to accomplish. Art is as long as ever, but life is more interrupted and less available for a man's proper pursuits. It is not an era of repose. We have used up all our inherited freedom. If we would save our lives, we must fight for them.

I walk toward one of our ponds, but what signifies the beauty of nature when men are base? We walk to lakes to see our serenity reflected in them; when we are not serene, we go not to them. Who can be serene in a country where both the rulers and the ruled are without principle? The remembrance of my country spoils my walk. My thoughts are murder to the State, and involuntarily go plotting against her.

But it chanced the other day that I scented a white water-lily, and a season I had waited for had arrived. It is the emblem of purity. It bursts up so pure and fair to the eye, and so sweet to the scent, as if to show us what purity and sweetness reside in, and can be extracted from, the slime and muck of earth. I think I have plucked the first one that has opened for a mile. What confirmation of our hopes is in the fragrance of this flower! I shall not so soon despair of the world for it, notwithstanding slavery, and the cowardice and want of principle of Northern men. It suggests what kind of laws have prevailed longest and widest, and still prevail, and that the time may come when man's deeds will smell as sweet. Such is the odor which the plant emits. If Nature can compound this fragrance still annually, I shall believe her still young and full of vigor, her integrity and genius unimpaired, and that there is virtue even in man, too, who is fitted to perceive and love it. It reminds me that Nature has been partner to no Missouri Compromise. I scent no compromise in the fragrance of the water-lily. It is not a *Nymphæa Douglasii*. In it, the sweet, and pure, and innocent, are wholly sundered from the obscene and baleful. I do not scent in this the time-serving irresolution of a Massachusetts Governor, nor of a Boston Mayor. So behave that the odor of your actions may enhance the general sweetness of the atmosphere, that when we behold or scent a flower, we may not be reminded how inconsistent your deeds are with it; for all odor is but one form of advertisement of a moral quality, and if fair actions had not been performed, the lily would not smell sweet. The foul slime stands for the sloth and vice of man, the decay of humanity; the fragrant flower that springs from it, for the purity and courage which are immortal.

Slavery and servility have produced no sweet-scented flower annually, to charm the senses of men, for they have no real life: they are merely a decaying and a death, offensive to all healthy nostrils. We do not complain that they *live*, but that they do not *get buried*. Let the living bury them; even they are good for manure.

LIFE WITHOUT PRINCIPLE

LECTURES IN PROVIDENCE.

The second course of Independent Lectures commenced in the city of Providence Nov. 1st, by an Introductory from Rev. Theodore Parker, and the 15th and 29th, by Mrs. Emma R. Coe, and Rev. Thomas W. Higginson, of Worcester. The list is filled by the following names, well known to the public :—

HENRY D. THOREAU, Concord, Mass., Dec. 6.
MRS. ERNESTINE L. ROSE, Dec. 13.
CASSIUS M. CLAY, Esq., Dec. 27.
Rev. ANTOINETTE L. BROWN, January 3.
WILLIAM LLOYD GARRISON, January 10.
LUCY STONE.
WENDELL PHILLIPS.

The above may be varied as to time, in two or three instances, of which due notice will be given.

The lecture by Mr. Parker was an able production, and was attentively listened to by a large audience. The two following were also successful, as we trust those to come will be. The people are anticipating the remaining lectures with a great deal of interest, and the names of the lecturers are a sufficient guarantee that their anticipations will not be disappointed.

A. F.

The first notice of the first presentation of "What Shall It Profit?" Years later Thoreau changed the title to "Life without Principle." From *The Liberator*, December 1, 1854.

LIFE WITHOUT PRINCIPLE

At a lyceum, not long since, I felt that the lecturer had chosen a theme too foreign to himself, and so failed to interest me as much as he might have done. He described things not in or near to his heart, but toward his extremities and superficies. There was, in this sense, no truly central or centralizing thought in the lecture. I would have had him deal with his privatest experience, as the poet does. The greatest compliment that was ever paid me was when one asked me what *I thought*, and attended to my answer. I am surprised, as well as delighted, when this happens, it is such a rare use he would make of me, as if he were acquainted with the tool. Commonly, if men want anything of me, it is only to know how many acres I make of their land,—since I am a surveyor,—or, at most, what trivial news I have burdened myself with. They never will go to law for my meat; they prefer the shell. A man once came a considerable distance to ask me to lecture on Slavery; but on conversing with him, I found that he and his clique expected seven-eighths of the lecture to be theirs, and only one-eighth mine; so I declined. I take it for granted, when I am invited to lecture anywhere,—for I have had a little experience in that business,—that there is a desire to hear what I *think* on some subject, though I may be the greatest fool in the country,—and not that I should say pleasant things merely, or such as the audience will assent to; and I resolve, accordingly, that I will give them a strong dose of myself. They have sent for me, and engaged to pay for me, and I am determined that they shall have me, though I bore them beyond all precedent.

So now I would say something similar to you, my readers. Since *you* are my readers, and I have not been much of a traveller, I will not talk about people a thousand miles off, but come as near home as I can. As the time is short, I will leave out all the flattery, and retain all the criticism.

Let us consider the way in which we spend our lives.

This world is a place of business. What an infinite bustle! I am awaked almost every night by the panting of the locomotive. It interrupts my dreams. There is no sabbath. It would be glorious to see mankind at leisure for once. It is nothing but work, work, work. I cannot easily buy a blank-book to write thoughts in; they are commonly ruled for dollars and cents. An Irishman, seeing me making a minute in the fields, took it for granted that I was calculating my wages. If a man was tossed out of a window when an infant, and so made a cripple for life, or scared out of his wits by the Indians, it is regretted chiefly because he was thus incapacitated for—business! I think that there is nothing, not even crime, more opposed to poetry, to philosophy, ay, to life itself, than this incessant business.

There is a coarse and boisterous money-making fellow in the outskirts of our town, who is going to build a bank-wall under the hill along the edge of his meadow. The powers have put this into his head to keep him out of mischief, and he wishes me to spend three weeks digging there with him. The result will be that he will perhaps get some more money to hoard, and leave for his heirs to spend foolishly. If I do this, most will commend me as an industrious and hardworking man; but if I choose to devote myself to certain labors which yield more real profit, though but little money, they may be inclined to look on me as an idler. Nevertheless, as I do not need the police of meaningless labor to regulate me, and do not see anything absolutely praiseworthy in this fellow's undertaking, any more than in many an enterprise of our own or foreign governments, however amusing it may be to him or them, I prefer to finish my education at a different school.

If a man walk in the woods for love of them half of each day, he is in danger of being regarded as a loafer; but if he spends his whole day as a speculator, shearing off those woods and making earth bald before her time, he is esteemed an industrious and enterprising citizen. As if a town had no interest in its forests but to cut them down!

Most men would feel insulted, if it were proposed to employ them in throwing stones over a wall, and then in throwing them back, merely that they might earn their wages. But many are no more worthily employed now. For instance: just after sunrise, one summer morning, I noticed one of my neighbors walking beside his team, which was slowly drawing a heavy hewn stone swung under the axle, surrounded by an atmosphere of industry,—his day's work begun,—his brow commenced to sweat,—a reproach to all sluggards and idlers,—pausing abreast the shoulders of his oxen, and half turning round with a flourish of his merciful whip, while they gained their length on him. And I thought, Such is the labor which the American Congress exists to protect,—honest, manly toil,—honest as the day is long,—that makes his bread taste sweet, and keeps society sweet,—which all men respect and have consecrated: one of the sacred band, doing the needful, but irksome drudgery. Indeed, I felt a slight reproach, because I observed this from the window, and was not abroad and stirring about a similar business. The day went by, and at evening I passed the yard of another neighbor, who keeps many servants, and spends much money foolishly, while he adds nothing to the common stock, and there I saw the stone of the morning lying beside a whimsical structure intended to adorn this Lord Timothy Dexter's premises, and the dignity forthwith departed from the teamster's labor, in my eyes. In my opinion, the sun was made to light worthier toil than this. I may add, that his employer has since run off, in debt to a good part of the town, and, after passing through Chancery, has settled somewhere else, there to become once more a patron of the arts.

The ways by which you may get money almost without exception lead downward. To have done anything by which you earned money *merely* is to have been truly idle or worse. If the laborer gets no more than the wages which his employer pays him, he is cheated, he cheats himself. If you would get money as a writer or lecturer, you must be popular, which is to go down perpendicularly. Those services which the community will most readily pay for it is most disagreeable to render. You are paid for being something less than a man. The State does not commonly reward a genius any more wisely. Even the poet-laureate would rather not have to celebrate the accidents of royalty. He must be bribed with a pipe of wine; and perhaps another poet is called away from his muse to gauge that very pipe. As for my own business, even that kind of surveying which I could do with most satisfaction my employers do not want. They would prefer that I should do my work coarsely and not too well, ay, not well enough. When I observe that there are different ways of surveying, my employer commonly asks which will give him the most land, not which is most correct. I once invented a rule for measuring cord-wood, and tried to introduce it in Boston; but the measurer there told me that the sellers did not wish to have their wood measured correctly,—that he was already too accurate for them, and therefore they commonly got their wood measured in Charlestown before crossing the bridge.

The aim of the laborer should be, not to get his living, to get "a good job," but to perform well a certain work; and, even in a pecuniary sense, it would be economy for a town to pay its laborers so well that they would not feel that they were working for low ends, as for a livelihood merely, but for scientific, or even moral ends. Do not hire a man who does your work for money, but him who does it for love of it.

It is remarkable that there are few men so well employed, so much to their minds, but that a little money or fame would commonly buy them off from their present pursuit. I see advertisements for *active* young men, as if activity were the whole of a young man's capital. Yet I have been surprised when one has with confidence proposed to me, a grown man, to embark in some enterprise of his, as if I had absolutely nothing to do, my life having been a complete failure hitherto. What a doubtful compliment this is to pay me! As if he had met me half-way across the ocean beating up against the wind, but bound nowhere, and proposed to me to go along with him! If I did, what do you think the underwriters would say? No, no! I am not without employment at this stage of the voyage. To tell the truth, I saw an advertisement for able-bodied seamen, when I was a boy, sauntering in my native port, and as soon as I came of age I embarked.

The community has no bribe that will tempt a wise man. You may raise money enough to tunnel a mountain, but you cannot raise money enough to hire a man who is minding *his own* business. An efficient and valuable man does what he can, whether the community pay him for it or not. The inefficient offer their inefficiency to the highest bidder, and are forever expecting to be put into office. One would suppose that they were rarely disappointed.

Perhaps I am more than usually jealous with respect to my freedom. I feel that my connection with and obligation to society are still very slight and transient. Those slight labors which afford me a livelihood, and by which it is allowed that I am to some extent serviceable to my contemporaries, are as yet commonly a pleasure to me, and I am not often reminded that they are a necessity. So far I am successful. But I foresee, that, if my wants should be much increased, the labor required to supply them would become a drudgery. If I should sell both my forenoons and afternoons to society, as most appear to do, I am sure, that, for me, there would be nothing left worth living for. I trust that I shall never thus sell my birthright for a mess of pottage. I wish to suggest that a man may be very industrious, and yet not spend his time well. There is no more fatal blunderer than he who consumes the greater part of his life getting his living. All great enterprises are self-supporting. The poet, for instance, must sustain his body by his poetry, as a steam planing-mill feeds its boilers with the shavings it makes. You must get your living by loving. But as it is said of the merchants that ninety-seven in a hundred fail, so the life of men generally, tried by this standard, is a failure, and bankruptcy may be surely prophesied.

Merely to come into the world the heir of a fortune is not to be born, but to be still-born, rather. To be supported by the charity of friends, or a government-pension,—provided you continue to breathe,—by whatever fine synonymes you describe these relations, is to go into the almshouse. On Sundays the poor debtor goes to church to take an account of stock, and finds, of course, that his outgoes have been greater than his income. In the Catholic Church, especially, they go into Chancery, make a clean confession, give up all, and think to start again. Thus men will lie on their backs, talking about the fall of man, and never make an effort to get up.

As for the comparative demand which men make on life, it is an important difference between two, that the one is satisfied with a level success, that his marks can all be hit by point-blank shots, but the other, however low and unsuccessful his life may be, constantly elevates his aim, though at a very slight angle to the horizon. I should much rather be the last man,—though, as the Orientals say, "Greatness doth not approach him who is forever looking down; and all those who are looking high are growing poor."

It is remarkable that there is little or nothing to be remembered written on the subject of getting a living: how to make getting a living not merely honest and honorable, but altogether inviting and glorious; for if *getting* a living is not so, then living is not. One would think, from looking at literature, that this question had never disturbed a solitary individual's musings. Is it that men are too much disgusted with their experience to speak of it? The lesson of value which money teaches, which the Author of the Universe has taken so much pains to teach us, we are inclined to skip altogether. As for the means of living, it is wonderful how indifferent men of all classes are about it, even reformers, so called,—whether they inherit, or earn, or steal it. I think that society has done nothing for us in this respect, or at least has undone what she has done. Cold and hunger seem more friendly to my nature than those methods which men have adopted and advise to ward them off.

The title *wise* is, for the most part, falsely applied. How can one be a wise man, if he does not know any better how to live than other men?—if he is only more cunning and intellectually subtle? Does Wisdom work in a tread-mill? or does she teach how to succeed *by her example*? Is there any such thing as wisdom not applied to life? Is she merely the miller who grinds the finest logic? It is pertinent to ask if Plato got his *living* in a better way or more successfully than his contemporaries,—or did he succumb to the difficulties of life like other men? Did he seem to prevail over some of them merely by indifference, or by assuming grand airs? or find it easier to live, because his aunt remembered him in her will? The ways in which most men get their living, that is, live, are mere makeshifts, and a shirking of the real business of life,—chiefly because they do not know, but partly because they do not mean, any better.

The rush to California, for instance, and the attitude, not merely of merchants, but of philosophers and prophets, so called, in relation to it, reflect the greatest disgrace on mankind. That so many are ready to live by luck, and so get the means of commanding the labor of others less lucky, without contributing any value to society! And that is called enterprise! I know of no more startling development of the immorality of trade, and all the common modes of getting a living. The philosophy and poetry and religion of such a mankind are not worth the dust of a puffball. The hog that gets his living by rooting, stirring up the soil so, would be ashamed of such company. If I could command the wealth of all the worlds by lifting my finger, I would not pay *such* a price for it. Even Mahomet knew that God did not make this world in jest. It makes God to be a moneyed gentleman who scatters a handful of pennies in order to see mankind scramble for them. The world's raffle! A subsistence in the domains of Nature a thing to be raffled for! What a comment, what a satire on our institutions! The conclusion will be, that mankind will hang itself upon a tree. And have all the precepts in all the Bibles taught men only this? and is the last and most admirable invention of the human race only an improved muck-rake? Is this the ground on which Orientals and Occidentals meet? Did God direct us so to get our living, digging where we never planted,—and He would, perchance, reward us with lumps of gold?

God gave the righteous man a certificate entitling him to food and raiment, but the unrighteous man found a *facsimile* of the same in God's coffers, and appropriated it, and obtained food and raiment like the former. It is one of the most extensive systems of counterfeiting that the world has seen. I did not know that mankind were suffering for want of gold. I have seen a little of it. I know that it is very malleable, but not so malleable as wit. A grain of gold will gild a great surface, but not so much as a grain of wisdom.

The gold-digger in the ravines of the mountains is as much a gambler as his fellow in the saloons of San Francisco. What difference does it make, whether you shake dirt or shake dice? If you win, society is the loser. The gold-digger is the enemy of the honest laborer, whatever checks and compensations there may be. It is not enough to tell me that you worked hard to get your gold. So does the Devil work hard. The way of transgressors may be hard in many respects. The humblest observer who goes to the mines sees and says that gold-digging is of the character of a lottery; the gold thus obtained is not the same thing with the wages of honest toil. But, practically, he forgets what he has seen, for he has seen only the fact, not the principle, and goes into trade there, that is, buys a ticket in what commonly proves another lottery, where the fact is not so obvious.

After reading Howitt's account of the Australian gold-diggings one evening, I had in my mind's eye, all night, the numerous valleys, with their streams, all cut up with foul pits, from ten to one hundred feet deep, and half a dozen feet across, as close as they can be dug, and partly filled with water,—the locality to which men furiously rush to probe for their fortunes,—uncertain where they shall break ground,—not knowing but the gold is under their camp itself,—sometimes digging one hundred and sixty feet before they strike the vein, or then missing it by a foot,—turned into demons, and regardless of each other's rights, in their thirst for riches,—whole valleys, for thirty miles, suddenly honey-combed by the pits of the miners, so that even hundreds are drowned in them,—standing in water, and covered with mud and clay, they work night and day, dying of exposure and disease. Having read this, and partly forgotten it, I was thinking, accidentally, of my own unsatisfactory life, doing as others do; and with that vision of the diggings still before me, I asked myself, why *I* might not be washing some gold daily, though it were only the finest particles,—why *I* might not sink a shaft down to the gold within me, and work that mine. *There* is a Ballarat, a Bendigo for you,—what though it were a Sulky Gully? At any rate, I might pursue some path, however solitary and narrow and crooked, in which I could walk with love and reverence. Wherever a man separates from the multitude, and goes his own way in this mood, there indeed is a fork in the road, though ordinary travellers may see only a gap in the paling. His solitary path across-lots will turn out the *higher way* of the two.

Men rush to California and Australia as if the true gold were to be found in that direction; but that is to go to the very opposite extreme to where it lies. They go prospecting farther and farther away from the true lead, and are most unfortunate when they think themselves most successful. Is not our *native* soil auriferous? Does not a stream from the golden mountains flow through our native valley? and has not this for more than geologic ages been bringing down the shining particles and forming the nuggets for us? Yet, strange to tell, if a digger steal away, prospecting for this true gold, into the unexplored solitudes around us, there is no danger that any will dog his steps, and endeavor to supplant him. He may claim and undermine the whole valley even, both the cultivated and the uncultivated portions, his whole life long in peace, for no one will ever dispute his claim. They will not mind his cradles or his toms. He is not confined to a claim twelve feet square, as at Ballarat, but may mine anywhere, and wash the whole wide world in his tom.

Howitt says of the man who found the great nugget which weighed twenty-eight pounds, at the Bendigo diggings in Australia:—"He soon began to drink; got a horse and rode all about, generally at full gallop, and when he met people, called out to inquire if they knew who he was, and then kindly informed them that he was 'the bloody wretch that had found the nugget.' At last he rode full speed against a tree, and nearly knocked his brains out." I think, however, there was no danger of that, for he had already knocked his brains out against the nugget. Howitt adds, "He is a hopelessly ruined man." But he is a type of the class. They are all fast men. Hear some of the names of the places where they dig:—"Jackass Flat,"—"Sheep's-Head Gully,"—"Murderer's Bar," etc. Is there no satire in these names? Let them carry their ill-gotten wealth where they will, I am thinking it will still be "Jackass Flat," if not "Murderer's Bar," where they live.

The last resource of our energy has been the robbing of graveyards on the Isthmus of Darien, an enterprise which appears to be but in its infancy; for, according to late accounts, an act has passed its second reading in the legislature of New Granada, regulating this kind of mining; and a correspondent of the *Tribune* writes:—"In the dry season, when the weather will permit of the country being properly prospected, no doubt other rich '*guacas*' [that is, graveyards] will be found." To emigrants he says:—"Do not come before December; take the Isthmus route in preference to the Boca del Toro one; bring no useless baggage, and do not cumber yourself with a tent; but a good pair of blankets will be necessary; a pick, shovel, and axe of good material will be almost all that is required": advice which might have been taken from the "Burker's Guide." And he concludes with this line in Italics and small capitals: "*If you are doing well at home*, STAY THERE," which may fairly be interpreted to mean, "If you are getting a good living by robbing graveyards at home, stay there."

But why go to California for a text? She is the child of New England, bred at her own school and church.

It is remarkable that among all the preachers there are so few moral teachers. The prophets are employed in excusing the ways of men. Most reverend seniors, the *illuminati* of the age, tell me, with a gracious, reminiscent smile, betwixt an aspiration and a shudder, not to be too tender about these things,—to lump all that, that is, make a lump of gold of it. The highest advice I have heard on these subjects was grovelling. The burden of it was,—It is not worth your while to undertake to reform the world in this particular. Do not ask how your bread is buttered; it will make you sick, if you do,—and the like. A man had better starve at once than lose his innocence in the process of getting his bread. If within the sophisticated man there is not an unsophisticated one, then he is but one of the Devil's angels. As we grow old, we live more coarsely, we relax a little in our disciplines, and, to some extent, cease to obey our finest instincts. But we should be fastidious to the extreme of sanity, disregarding the gibes of those who are more unfortunate than ourselves.

In our science and philosophy, even, there is commonly no true and absolute account of things. The spirit of sect and bigotry has planted its hoof amid the stars. You have only to discuss the problem, whether the stars are inhabited or not, in order to discover it. Why must we daub the heavens as well as the earth? It was an unfortunate discovery that Dr. Kane was a Mason, and that Sir John Franklin was another. But it was a more cruel suggestion that possibly that was the reason why the former went in search of the latter. There is not a popular magazine in this country that would dare to print a child's thought on important subjects without comment. It must be submitted to the D. D.s. I would it were the chickadee-dees.

You come from attending the funeral of mankind to attend to a natural phenomenon. A little thought is sexton to all the world.

I hardly know an *intellectual* man, even, who is so broad and truly liberal that you can think aloud in his society. Most with whom you endeavor to talk soon come to a stand against some institution in which they appear to hold stock,—that is, some particular, not universal, way of viewing things. They will continually thrust their own low roof, with its narrow skylight, between you and the sky, when it is the unobstructed heavens you would view. Get out of the way with your cobwebs, wash your windows, I say! In some lyceums they tell me that they have voted to exclude the subject of religion. But how do I know what their religion is, and when I am near to or far from it? I have walked into such an arena and done my best to make a clean breast of what religion I have experienced, and the audience never suspected what I was about. The lecture was as harmless as moonshine to them. Whereas, if I had read to them the biography of the greatest scamps in history, they might have thought that I had written the lives of the deacons of their church. Ordinarily, the inquiry is, Where did you come from? or, Where are you going? That was a more pertinent question which I overheard one of my auditors put to another once,—"What does he lecture for?" It made me quake in my shoes.

To speak impartially, the best men that I know are not serene, a world in themselves. For the most part, they dwell in forms, and flatter and study effect only more finely than the rest. We select granite for the underpinning of our houses and barns; we build fences of stone; but we do not ourselves rest on an underpinning of granitic truth, the lowest primitive rock. Our sills are rotten. What stuff is the man made of who is not coexistent in our thought with the purest and subtilest truth? I often accuse my finest acquaintances of an immense frivolity; for, while there are manners and compliments we do not meet, we do not teach one another the lessons of honesty and sincerity that the brutes do, or of steadiness and solidity that the rocks do. The fault is commonly mutual, however; for we do not habitually demand any more of each other.

That excitement about Kossuth, consider how characteristic, but superficial, it was!—only another kind of politics or dancing. Men were making speeches to him all over the country, but each expressed only the thought, or the want of thought, of the multitude. No man stood on truth. They were merely banded together, as usual, one leaning on another, and all together on nothing; as the Hindoos made the world rest on an elephant, the elephant on a tortoise, and the tortoise on a serpent, and had nothing to put under the serpent. For all fruit of that stir we have the Kossuth hat.

Just so hollow and ineffectual, for the most part, is our ordinary conversation. Surface meets surface. When our life ceases to be inward and private, conversation degenerates into mere gossip. We rarely meet a man who can tell us any news which he has not read in a newspaper, or been told by his neighbor; and, for the most part, the only difference between us and our fellow is, that he has seen the newspaper, or been out to tea, and we have not. In proportion as our inward life fails, we go more constantly and desperately to the post-office. You may depend on it, that the poor fellow who walks away with the greatest number of letters, proud of his extensive correspondence, has not heard from himself this long while.

I do not know but it is too much to read one newspaper a week. I have tried it recently, and for so long it seems to me that I have not dwelt in my native region. The sun, the clouds, the snow, the trees say not so much to me. You cannot serve two masters. It requires more than a day's devotion to know and to possess the wealth of a day.

We may well be ashamed to tell what things we have read or heard in our day. I do not know why my news should be so trivial,—considering what one's dreams and expectations are, why the developments should be so paltry. The news we hear, for the most part, is not news to our genius. It is the stalest repetition. You are often tempted to ask, why such stress is laid on a particular experience which you have had,—that, after twenty-five years, you should meet Hobbins, Registrar of Deeds, again on the sidewalk. Have you not budged an inch, then? Such is the daily news. Its facts appear to float in the atmosphere, insignificant as the sporules of fungi, and impinge on some neglected *thallus*, or surface of our minds, which affords a basis for them, and hence a parasitic growth. We should wash ourselves clean of such news. Of what consequence, though our planet explode, if there is no character involved in the explosion? In health we have not the least curiosity about such events. We do not live for idle amusement. I would not run round a corner to see the world blow up.

All summer, and far into the autumn, perchance, you unconsciously went by the newspapers and the news, and now you find it was because the morning and the evening were full of news to you. Your walks were full of incidents. You attended, not to the affairs of Europe, but to your own affairs in Massachusetts fields. If you chance to live and move and have your being in that thin stratum in which the events that make the news transpire,—thinner than the paper on which it is printed,—then these things will fill the world for you; but if you soar above or dive below that plane, you cannot remember nor be reminded of them. Really to see the sun rise or go down every day, so to relate ourselves to a universal fact, would preserve us sane forever. Nations! What are nations? Tartars, and Huns, and Chinamen! Like insects, they swarm. The historian strives in vain to make them memorable. It is for want of a man that there are so many men. It is individuals that populate the world. Any man thinking may say with the Spirit of Lodin,—

> "I look down from my height on nations,
> And they become ashes before me;—
> Calm is my dwelling in the clouds;
> Pleasant are the great fields of my rest."

Pray, let us live without being drawn by dogs, Esquimaux-fashion, tearing over hill and dale, and biting each other's ears.

Not without a slight shudder at the danger, I often perceive how near I had come to admitting into my mind the details of some trivial affair,—the news of the street; and I am astonished to observe how willing men are to lumber their minds with such rubbish,—to permit idle rumors and incidents of the most insignificant kind to intrude on ground which should be sacred to thought. Shall the mind be a public arena, where the affairs of the street and the gossip of the tea-table chiefly are discussed? Or shall it be a quarter of heaven itself,—an hypæthral temple, consecrated to the service of the gods? I find it so difficult to dispose of the few facts which to me are significant, that I hesitate to burden my attention with those which are insignificant, which only a divine mind could illustrate. Such is, for the most part, the news in newspapers and conversation. It is important to preserve the mind's chastity in this respect. Think of admitting the details of a single case of the criminal court into our thoughts, to stalk profanely through their very *sanctum sanctorum* for an hour, ay, for many hours! to make a very bar-room of the mind's inmost apartment, as if for so long the dust of the street had occupied us,—the very street itself, with all its travel, its bustle, and filth had passed through our thoughts' shrine! Would it not be an intellectual and moral suicide? When I have been compelled to sit spectator and auditor in a court-room for some hours, and have seen my neighbors, who were not compelled, stealing in from time to time, and tiptoeing about with washed hands and faces, it has appeared to my mind's eye, that, when they took off their hats, their ears suddenly expanded into vast hoppers for sound, between which even their narrow heads were crowded. Like the vanes of windmills, they caught the broad, but shallow stream of sound, which, after a few titillating gyrations in their coggy brains, passed out the other side. I wondered if, when they got home, they were as careful to wash their ears as before their hands and faces. It has seemed to me, at such a time, that the auditors and the witnesses, the jury and the counsel, the judge and the criminal at the bar,—if I may presume him guilty before he is convicted,—were all equally criminal, and a thunderbolt might be expected to descend and consume them all together.

By all kinds of traps and sign-boards, threatening the extreme penalty of the divine law, exclude such trespassers from the only ground which can be sacred to you. It is so hard to forget what it is worse than useless to remember! If I am to be a thoroughfare, I prefer that it be of the mountain-brooks, the Parnassian streams, and not the town-sewers. There is inspiration, that gossip which comes to the ear of the attentive mind from the courts of heaven. There is the profane and stale revelation of the bar-room and the police court. The same ear is fitted to receive both communications. Only the character of the hearer determines to which it shall be open, and to which closed. I believe that the mind can be permanently profaned by the habit of attending to trivial things, so that all our thoughts shall be tinged with triviality. Our very intellect shall be macadamized, as it were,—its foundation broken into fragments for the wheels of travel to roll over; and if you would know what will make the most durable pavement, surpassing rolled stones, spruce blocks, and asphaltum, you have only to look into some of our minds which have been subjected to this treatment so long.

If we have thus desecrated ourselves,—as who has not?—the remedy will be by wariness and devotion to reconsecrate ourselves, and make once more a fane of the mind. We should treat our minds, that is, ourselves, as innocent and ingenuous children, whose guardians we are, and be careful what objects and what subjects we thrust on their attention. Read not the Times. Read the Eternities. Conventionalities are at length as bad as impurities. Even the facts of science may dust the mind by their dryness, unless they are in a sense effaced each morning, or rather rendered fertile by the dews of fresh and living truth. Knowledge does not come to us by details, but in flashes of light from heaven. Yes, every thought that passes through the mind helps to wear and tear it, and to deepen the ruts, which, as in the streets of Pompeii, evince how much it has been used. How many things there are concerning which we might well deliberate, whether we had better know them,—had better let their peddling-carts be driven, even at the slowest trot or walk, over that bridge of glorious span by which we trust to pass at last from the farthest brink of time to the nearest shore of eternity! Have we no culture, no refinement,—but skill only to live coarsely and serve the Devil?—to acquire a little worldly wealth, or fame, or liberty, and make a false show with it, as if we were all husk and shell, with no tender and living kernel to us? Shall our institutions be like those chestnut-burs which contain abortive nuts, perfect only to prick the fingers?

America is said to be the arena on which the battle of freedom is to be fought; but surely it cannot be freedom in a merely political sense that is meant. Even if we grant that the American has freed himself from a political tyrant, he is still the slave of an economical and moral tyrant. Now that the republic—the *res-publica*—has been settled, it is time to look after the *res-privata*,—the private state,—to see, as the Roman senate charged its consuls, "*ne quid res-*PRIVATA *detrimenti caperet*," that the *private* state receive no detriment.

Do we call this the land of the free? What is it to be free from King George and continue the slaves of King Prejudice? What is it to be born free and not to live free? What is the value of any political freedom, but as a means to moral freedom? Is it a freedom to be slaves, or a freedom to be free, of which we boast? We are a nation of politicians, concerned about the outmost defences only of freedom. It is our children's children who may perchance be really free. We tax ourselves unjustly. There is a part of us which is not represented. It is taxation without representation. We quarter troops, we quarter fools and cattle of all sorts upon ourselves. We quarter our gross bodies on our poor souls, till the former eat up all the latter's substance.

With respect to a true culture and manhood, we are essentially provincial still, not metropolitan,—mere Jonathans. We are provincial, because we do not find at home our standards,—because we do not worship truth, but the reflection of truth,—because we are warped and narrowed by an exclusive devotion to trade and commerce and manufactures and agriculture and the like, which are but means, and not the end.

So is the English Parliament provincial. Mere country-bumpkins, they betray themselves, when any more important question arises for them to settle, the Irish question, for instance,—the English question why did I not say? Their natures are subdued to what they work in. Their "good breeding" respects only secondary objects. The finest manners in the world are awkwardness and fatuity, when contrasted with a finer intelligence. They appear but as the fashions of past days,—mere courtliness, knee-buckles and small-clothes, out of date. It is the vice, but not the excellence of manners, that they are continually being deserted by the character; they are cast-off clothes or shells, claiming the respect which belonged to the living creature. You are presented with the shells instead of the meat, and it is no excuse generally, that, in the case of some fishes, the shells are of more worth than the meat. The man who thrusts his manners upon me does as if he were to insist on introducing me to his cabinet of curiosities, when I wished to see himself. It was not in this sense that the poet Decker called Christ "the first true gentleman that ever breathed." I repeat that in this sense the most splendid court in Christendom is provincial, having authority to consult about Transalpine interests only, and not the affairs of Rome. A praetor or proconsul would suffice to settle the questions which absorb the attention of the English Parliament and the American Congress.

Government and legislation! these I thought were respectable professions. We have heard of heaven-born Numas, Lycurguses, and Solons, in the history of the world, whose *names* at least may stand for ideal legislators; but think of legislating to *regulate* the breeding of slaves, or the exportation of tobacco! What have divine legislators to do with the exportation or the importation of tobacco? what humane ones with the breeding of slaves? Suppose you were to submit the question to any son of God,—and has He no children in the nineteenth century? is it a family which is extinct?—in what condition would you get it again? What shall a State like Virginia say for itself at the last day, in which these have been the principal, the staple productions? What ground is there for patriotism in such a State? I derive my facts from statistical tables which the States themselves have published.

A commerce that whitens every sea in quest of nuts and raisins, and makes slaves of its sailors for this purpose! I saw, the other day, a vessel which had been wrecked, and many lives lost, and her cargo of rags, juniper-berries, and bitter almonds were strewn along the shore. It seemed hardly worth the while to tempt the dangers of the sea between Leghorn and New York for the sake of a cargo of juniper-berries and bitter almonds. America sending to the Old World for her bitters! Is not the sea-brine, is not shipwreck, bitter enough to make the cup of life go down here? Yet such, to a great extent, is our boasted commerce; and there are those who style themselves statesmen and philosophers who are so blind as to think that progress and civilization depend on precisely this kind of interchange and activity,—the activity of flies about a molasses-hogshead. Very well, observes one, if men were oysters. And very well, answer I, if men were mosquitoes.

Lieutenant Herndon, whom our Government sent to explore the Amazon, and, it is said, to extend the area of Slavery, observed that there was wanting there "an industrious and active population, who know what the comforts of life are, and who have artificial wants to draw out the great resources of the country." But what are the "artificial wants" to be encouraged? Not the love of luxuries, like the tobacco and slaves of, I believe, his native Virginia, nor the ice and granite and other material wealth of our native New England; nor are "the great resources of a country" that fertility or barrenness of soil which produces these. The chief want, in every State that I have been into, was a high and earnest purpose in its inhabitants. This alone draws out "the great resources" of Nature, and at last taxes her beyond her resources; for man naturally dies out of her. When we want culture more than potatoes, and illumination more than sugar-plums, then the great resources of a world are taxed and drawn out, and the result, or staple production, is, not slaves, nor operatives, but men,—those rare fruits called heroes, saints, poets, philosophers, and redeemers.

In short, as a snow-drift is formed where there is a lull in the wind, so, one would say, where there is a lull of truth, an institution springs up. But the truth blows right on over it, nevertheless, and at length blows it down.

What is called politics is comparatively something so superficial and inhuman, that, practically, I have never fairly recognized that it concerns me at all. The newspapers, I perceive, devote some of their columns specially to politics or government without charge; and this, one would say, is all that saves it; but, as I love literature, and, to some extent, the truth also, I never read those columns at any rate. I do not wish to blunt my sense of right so much. I have not got to answer for having read a single President's Message. A strange age of the world this, when empires, kingdoms, and republics come a-begging to a private man's door, and utter their complaints at his elbow! I cannot take up a newspaper but I find that some wretched government or other, hard pushed, and on its last legs, is interceding with me, the reader, to vote for it,—more importunate than an Italian beggar; and if I have a mind to look at its certificate, made, perchance, by some benevolent merchant's clerk, or the skipper that brought it over, for it cannot speak a word of English itself, I shall probably read of the eruption of some Vesuvius, or the overflowing of some Po, true or forged, which brought it into this condition. I do not hesitate, in such a case, to suggest work, or the almshouse; or why not keep its castle in silence, as I do commonly? The poor President, what with preserving his popularity and doing his duty, is completely bewildered. The newspapers are the ruling power. Any other government is reduced to a few marines at Fort Independence. If a man neglects to read the Daily Times, Government will go down on its knees to him, for this is the only treason in these days.

Those things which now most engage the attention of men, as politics and the daily routine, are, it is true, vital functions of human society, but should be unconsciously performed, like the corresponding functions of the physical body. They are *infra*-human, a kind of vegetation. I sometimes awake to a half-consciousness of them going on about me, as a man may become conscious of some of the processes of digestion in a morbid state, and so have the dyspepsia, as it is called. It is as if a thinker submitted himself to be rasped by the great gizzard of creation. Politics is, as it were, the gizzard of society, full of grit and gravel, and the two political parties are its two opposite halves,—sometimes split into quarters, it may be, which grind on each other. Not only individuals, but States, have thus a confirmed dyspepsia, which expresses itself, you can imagine by what sort of eloquence. Thus our life is not altogether a forgetting, but also, alas! to a great extent, a remembering of that which we should never have been conscious of, certainly not in our waking hours. Why should we not meet, not always as dyspeptics, to tell our bad dreams, but sometimes as *eu*peptics, to congratulate each other on the ever glorious morning? I do not make an exorbitant demand, surely.

AUTUMNAL TINTS

At Thoreau's request, this engraving of a scarlet oak leaf accompanied the first publication of "Autumnal Tints" in *The Atlantic Monthly*, October 1862. It was drawn from a specimen in his own herbarium. See page 237: "[T]his leaf reminds me of some fair wild island in the ocean."

AUTUMNAL TINTS

Europeans coming to America are surprised by the brilliancy of our autumnal foliage. There is no account of such a phenomenon in English poetry, because the trees acquire but few bright colors there. The most that Thomson says on this subject in his "Autumn" is contained in the lines,—

> "But see the fading many-colored woods
> Shade deepening over shade, the country round
> Imbrown; a crowded umbrage, dusk and dun,
> Of every hue, from wan declining green
> To sooty dark;"

and in the line in which he speaks of

> "Autumn beaming o'er the yellow woods."

The autumnal change of our woods has not made a deep impression on our own literature yet. October has hardly tinged our poetry.

A great many, who have spent their lives in cities, and have never chanced to come into the country at this season, have never seen this, the flower, or rather the ripe fruit, of the year. I remember riding with one such citizen, who, though a fortnight too late for the most brilliant tints, was taken by surprise, and would not believe that there had been any brighter. He had never heard of this phenomenon before. Not only many in our towns have never witnessed it, but it is scarcely remembered by the majority from year to year.

Most appear to confound changed leaves with withered ones, as if they were to confound ripe apples with rotten ones. I think that the change to some higher color in a leaf is an evidence that it has arrived at a late and perfect maturity, answering to the maturity of fruits. It is generally the lowest and oldest leaves which change first. But as the perfect-winged and usually bright-colored insect is short-lived, so the leaves ripen but to fall.

Generally, every fruit, on ripening, and just before it falls, when it commences a more independent and individual existence, requiring less nourishment from any source, and that not so much from the earth through its stem as from the sun and air, acquires a bright tint. So do leaves. The physiologist says it is "due to an increased absorption of oxygen." That is the scientific account of the matter,—only a reassertion of the fact. But I am more interested in the rosy cheek than I am to know what particular diet the maiden fed on. The very forest and herbage, the pellicle of the earth, must acquire a bright color, an evidence of its ripeness,—as if the globe itself were a fruit on its stem, with ever a cheek toward the sun.

Flowers are but colored leaves, fruits but ripe ones. The edible part of most fruits is, as the physiologist says, "the parenchyma or fleshy tissue of the leaf," of which they are formed.

Our appetites have commonly confined our views of ripeness and its phenomena, color, mellowness, and perfectness, to the fruits which we eat, and we are wont to forget that an immense harvest which we do not eat, hardly use at all, is annually ripened by Nature. At our annual cattle-shows and horticultural exhibitions, we make, as we think, a great show of fair fruits, destined, however, to a rather ignoble end, fruits not valued for their beauty chiefly. But round about and within our towns there is annually another show of fruits, on an infinitely grander scale, fruits which address our taste for beauty alone.

October is the month for painted leaves. Their rich glow now flashes round the world. As fruits and leaves and the day itself acquire a bright tint just before they fall, so the year near its setting. October is its sunset sky; November the later twilight.

I formerly thought that it would be worth the while to get a specimen leaf from each changing tree, shrub, and herbaceous plant, when it had acquired its brightest characteristic color, in its transition from the green to the brown state, outline it, and copy its color exactly, with paint, in a book, which should be entitled "October, or Autumnal Tints,"—beginning with the earliest reddening woodbine and the lake of radical leaves, and coming down through the maples, hickories, and sumachs, and many beautifully freckled leaves less generally known, to the latest oaks and aspens. What a memento such a book would be! You would need only to turn over its leaves to take a ramble through the autumn woods whenever you pleased. Or if I could preserve the leaves themselves, unfaded, it would be better still. I have made but little progress toward such a book, but I have endeavored, instead, to describe all these bright tints in the order in which they present themselves. The following are some extracts from my notes.

THE PURPLE GRASSES

By the twentieth of August, everywhere in woods and swamps we are reminded of the fall, both by the richly spotted sarsaparilla leaves and brakes, and the withering and blackened skunk-cabbage and hellebore, and, by the riverside, the already blackening pontederia.

The purple grass (*Eragrostis pectinacea*) is now in the height of its beauty. I remember still when I first noticed this grass particularly. Standing on a hillside near our river, I saw, thirty or forty rods off, a stripe of purple half a dozen rods long, under the edge of a wood, where the ground sloped toward a meadow. It was as high-colored and interesting, though not quite so bright, as the patches of rhexia, being a darker purple, like a berry's stain laid on close and thick. On going to and examining it, I found it to be a kind of grass in bloom, hardly a foot high, with but few green blades, and a fine spreading panicle of purple flowers, a shallow, purplish mist trembling around me. Close at hand it appeared but a dull purple, and made little impression on the eye; it was even difficult to detect; and if you plucked a single plant, you were surprised to find how thin it was, and how little color it had. But viewed at a distance in a favorable light, it was of a fine lively purple, flower-like, enriching the earth. Such puny causes combine to produce these decided effects. I was the more surprised and charmed because grass is commonly of a sober and humble color.

With its beautiful purple blush it reminds me, and supplies the place, of the rhexia, which is now leaving off, and it is one of the most interesting phenomena of August. The finest patches of it grow on waste strips or selvages of land at the base of dry hills, just above the edge of the meadows, where the greedy mower does not deign to swing his scythe; for this is a thin and poor grass, beneath his notice. Or, it may be, because it is so beautiful he does not know that it exists; for the same eye does not see this and timothy. He carefully gets the meadow-hay and the more nutritious grasses which grow next to that, but he leaves this fine purple mist for the walker's harvest,—fodder for his fancy stock. Higher up the hill, perchance, grow also blackberries, John's-wort, and neglected, withered, and wiry June-grass. How fortunate that it grows in such places, and not in the midst of the rank grasses which are annually cut! Nature thus keeps use and beauty distinct. I know many such localities, where it does not fail to present itself annually, and paint the earth with its blush. It grows on the gentle slopes, either in a continuous patch or in scattered and rounded tufts a foot in diameter, and it lasts till it is killed by the first smart frosts.

In most plants the corolla or calyx is the part which attains the highest color, and is the most attractive; in many it is the seed-vessel or fruit; in others, as the red maple, the leaves; and in others still it is the very culm itself which is the principal flower or blooming part.

The last is especially the case with the poke or garget (*Phytolacca decandra*). Some which stand under our cliffs quite dazzle me with their purple stems now and early in September. They are as interesting to me as most flowers, and one of the most important fruits of our autumn. Every part is flower (or fruit), such is its superfluity of color,—stem, branch, peduncle, pedicel, petiole, and even the at length yellowish, purple-veined leaves. Its cylindrical racemes of berries of various hues, from green to dark purple, six or seven inches long, are gracefully drooping on all sides, offering repasts to the birds; and even the sepals from which the birds have picked the berries are a brilliant lake red, with crimson flame-like reflections, equal to anything of the kind,—all on fire with ripeness. Hence the *lacca*, from *lac*, lake. There are at the same time flower-buds, flowers, green berries, dark-purple or ripe ones, and these flower-like sepals, all on the same plant.

We love to see any redness in the vegetation of the temperate zone. It is the color of colors. This plant speaks to our blood. It asks a bright sun on it to make it show to best advantage, and it must be seen at this season of the year. On warm hillsides its stems are ripe by the twenty-third of August. At that date I walked through a beautiful grove of them, six or seven feet high, on the side of one of our cliffs, where they ripen early. Quite to the ground they were a deep, brilliant purple, with a bloom contrasting with the still clear green leaves. It appears a rare triumph of Nature to have produced and perfected such a plant, as if this were enough for a summer. What a perfect maturity it arrives at! It is the emblem of a successful life concluded by a death not premature, which is an ornament to Nature. What if we were to mature as perfectly, root and branch, glowing in the midst of our decay, like the poke! I confess that it excites me to behold them. I cut one for a cane, for I would fain handle and lean on it. I love to press the berries between my fingers, and see their juice staining my hand. To walk amid these upright, branching casks of purple wine, which retain and diffuse a sunset glow, tasting each one with your eye, instead of counting the pipes on a London dock, what a privilege! For Nature's vintage is not confined to the vine. Our poets have sung of wine, the product of a foreign plant which commonly they never saw, as if our own plants had no juice in them more than the singers. Indeed, this has been called by some the American grape, and, though a native of America, its juices are used in some foreign countries to improve the color of the wine; so that the poetaster may be celebrating the virtues of the poke without knowing it. Here are berries enough to paint afresh the western sky, and play the bacchanal with, if you will. And what flutes its ensanguined stems would make, to be used in such a dance! It is truly a royal plant. I could spend the evening of the year musing amid the poke stems. And perchance amid these groves might arise at last a new school of philosophy or poetry. It lasts all through September.

At the same time with this, or near the end of August, a to me very interesting genus of grasses, andropogons, or beard-grasses, is in its prime: *Andropogon furcatus*, forked beard-grass, or call it purple-fingered grass; *Andropogon scoparius*, purple wood-grass; and *Andropogon* (now called *Sorghum*) *nutans*, Indian-grass. The first is a very tall and slender-culmed grass, three to seven feet high, with four or five purple finger-like spikes raying upward from the top. The second is also quite slender, growing in tufts two feet high by one wide, with culms often somewhat curving, which, as the spikes go out of bloom, have a whitish, fuzzy look. These two are prevailing grasses at this season on dry and sandy fields and hillsides. The culms of both, not to mention their pretty flowers, reflect a purple tinge, and help to declare the ripeness of the year. Perhaps I have the more sympathy with them because they are despised by the farmer, and occupy sterile and neglected soil. They are high-colored, like ripe grapes, and express a maturity which the spring did not suggest. Only the August sun could have thus burnished these culms and leaves. The farmer has long since done his upland haying, and he will not condescend to bring his scythe to where these slender wild grasses have at length flowered thinly; you often see spaces of bare sand amid them. But I walk encouraged between the tufts of purple wood-grass over the sandy fields, and along the edge of the shrub oaks, glad to recognize these simple contemporaries. With thoughts cutting a broad swathe I "get" them, with horse-raking thoughts I gather them into windrows. The fine-eared poet may hear the whetting of my scythe. These two were almost the first grasses that I learned to distinguish, for I had not known by how many friends I was surrounded; I had seen them simply as grasses standing. The purple of their culms also excites me like that of the poke-weed stems.

Think what refuge there is for one, before August is over, from college commencements and society that isolates! I can skulk amid the tufts of purple wood-grass on the borders of the "Great Fields." Wherever I walk these afternoons, the purple-fingered grass also stands like a guide-board, and points my thoughts to more poetic paths than they have lately traveled.

A man shall perhaps rush by and trample down plants as high as his head, and cannot be said to know that they exist, though he may have cut many tons of them, littered his stables with them, and fed them to his cattle for years. Yet, if he ever favorably attends to them, he may be overcome by their beauty. Each humblest plant, or weed, as we call it, stands there to express some thought or mood of ours; and yet how long it stands in vain! I had walked over those Great Fields so many Augusts, and never yet distinctly recognized these purple companions that I had there. I had brushed against them and trodden on them, forsooth; and now, at last, they, as it were, rose up and blessed me. Beauty and true wealth are always thus cheap and despised. Heaven might be defined as the place which men avoid. Who can doubt that these grasses, which the farmer says are of no account to him, find some compensation in your appreciation of them? I may say that I never saw them before; though, when I came to look them face to face, there did come down to me a purple gleam from previous years; and now, wherever I go, I see hardly anything else. It is the reign and presidency of the andropogons.

Almost the very sands confess the ripening influence of the August sun, and methinks, together with the slender grasses waving over them, reflect a purple tinge. The impurpled sands! Such is the consequence of all this sunshine absorbed into the pores of plants and of the earth. All sap or blood is now wine-colored. At last we have not only the purple sea, but the purple land.

The chestnut beard-grass, Indian-grass, or wood-grass, growing here and there in waste places, but more rare than the former (from two to four or five feet high), is still handsomer and of more vivid colors than its congeners, and might well have caught the Indian's eye. It has a long, narrow, one-sided, and slightly nodding panicle of bright purple and yellow flowers, like a banner raised above its reedy leaves. These bright standards are now advanced on the distant hillsides, not in large armies, but in scattered troops or single file, like the red men. They stand thus fair and bright, representative of the race which they are named after, but for the most part unobserved as they. The expression of this grass haunted me for a week, after I first passed and noticed it, like the glance of an eye. It stands like an Indian chief taking a last look at his favorite hunting-grounds.

THE RED MAPLE

By the twenty-fifth of September, the red maples generally are beginning to be ripe. Some large ones have been conspicuously changing for a week, and some single trees are now very brilliant. I notice a small one, half a mile off across a meadow, against the green woodside there, a far brighter red than the blossoms of any tree in summer, and more conspicuous. I have observed this tree for several autumns invariably changing earlier than its fellows, just as one tree ripens its fruit earlier than another. It might serve to mark the season, perhaps. I should be sorry if it were cut down. I know of two or three such trees in different parts of our town, which might, perhaps, be propagated from, as early ripeners or September trees, and their seed be advertised in the market, as well as that of radishes, if we cared as much about them.

At present these burning bushes stand chiefly along the edge of the meadows, or I distinguish them afar on the hillsides here and there. Sometimes you will see many small ones in a swamp turned quite crimson when all other trees around are still perfectly green, and the former appear so much the brighter for it. They take you by surprise, as you are going by on one side, across the fields, thus early in the season, as if it were some gay encampment of the red men, or other foresters, of whose arrival you had not heard.

Some single trees, wholly bright scarlet, seen against others of their kind still freshly green, or against evergreens, are more memorable than whole groves will be by and by. How beautiful, when a whole tree is like one great scarlet fruit full of ripe juices, every leaf, from lowest limb to topmost spire, all aglow, especially if you look toward the sun! What more remarkable object can there be in the landscape? Visible for miles, too fair to be believed. If such a phenomenon occurred but once, it would be handed down by tradition to posterity, and get into the mythology at last.

The whole tree thus ripening in advance of its fellows attains a singular preëminence, and sometimes maintains it for a week or two. I am thrilled at the sight of it, bearing aloft its scarlet standard for the regiment of green-clad foresters around, and I go half a mile out of my way to examine it. A single tree becomes thus the crowning beauty of some meadowy vale, and the expression of the whole surrounding forest is at once more spirited for it.

A small red maple has grown, perchance, far away at the head of some retired valley, a mile from any road, unobserved. It has faithfully discharged the duties of a maple there, all winter and summer, neglected none of its economies, but added to its stature in the virtue which belongs to a maple, by a steady growth for so many months, never having gone gadding abroad, and is nearer heaven than it was in the spring. It has faithfully husbanded its sap, and afforded a shelter to the wandering bird, has long since ripened its seeds and committed them to the winds, and has the satisfaction of knowing, perhaps, that a thousand little well-behaved maples are already settled in life somewhere. It deserves well of Mapledom. Its leaves have been asking it from time to time, in a whisper, "When shall we redden?" And now, in this month of September, this month of traveling, when men are hastening to the seaside, or the mountains, or the lakes, this modest maple, still without budging an inch, travels in its reputation,—runs up its scarlet flag on that hillside, which shows that it has finished its summer's work before all other trees, and withdraws from the contest. At the eleventh hour of the year, the tree which no scrutiny could have detected here when it was most industrious is thus, by the tint of its maturity, by its very blushes, revealed at last to the careless and distant traveler, and leads his thoughts away from the dusty road into those brave solitudes which it inhabits. It flashes out conspicuous with all the virtue and beauty of a maple,—*Acer rubrum.* We may now read its title, or *rubric*, clear. Its *virtues*, not its sins, are as scarlet.

Notwithstanding the red maple is the most intense scarlet of any of our trees, the sugar maple has been the most celebrated, and Michaux in his "Sylva" does not speak of the autumnal color of the former. About the second of October, these trees, both large and small, are most brilliant, though many are still green. In "sprout-lands" they seem to vie with one another, and ever some particular one in the midst of the crowd will be of a peculiarly pure scarlet, and by its more intense color attract our eye even at a distance, and carry off the palm. A large red maple swamp, when at the height of its change, is the most obviously brilliant of all tangible things, where I dwell, so abundant is this tree with us. It varies much both in form and color. A great many are merely yellow; more, scarlet; others, scarlet deepening into crimson, more red than common. Look at yonder swamp of maples mixed with pines, at the base of a pine-clad hill, a quarter of a mile off, so that you get the full effect of the bright colors, without detecting the imperfections of the leaves, and see their yellow, scarlet, and crimson fires, of all tints, mingled and contrasted with the green. Some maples are yet green, only yellow or crimson-tipped on the edges of their flakes, like the edges of a hazelnut bur; some are wholly brilliant scarlet, raying out regularly and finely every way, bilaterally, like the veins of a leaf; others, of more irregular form, when I turn my head slightly, emptying out some of its earthiness and concealing the trunk of the tree, seem to rest heavily flake on flake, like yellow and scarlet clouds, wreath upon wreath, or like snow-drifts driving through the air, stratified by the wind. It adds greatly to the beauty of such a swamp at this season, that, even though there may be no other trees interspersed, it is not seen as a simple mass of color, but, different trees being of different colors and hues, the outline of each crescent treetop is distinct, and where one laps on to another. Yet a painter would hardly venture to make them thus distinct a quarter of a mile off.

As I go across a meadow directly toward a low rising ground this bright afternoon, I see, some fifty rods off toward the sun, the top of a maple swamp just appearing over the sheeny russet edge of the hill, a stripe apparently twenty rods long by ten feet deep, of the most intensely brilliant scarlet, orange, and yellow, equal to any flowers or fruits, or any tints ever painted. As I advance, lowering the edge of the hill which makes the firm foreground or lower frame of the picture, the depth of the brilliant grove revealed steadily increases, suggesting that the whole of the inclosed valley is filled with such color. One wonders that the tithing-men and fathers of the town are not out to see what the trees mean by their high colors and exuberance of spirits, fearing that some mischief is brewing. I do not see what the Puritans did at this season, when the maples blaze out in scarlet. They certainly could not have worshiped in groves then. Perhaps that is what they built meetinghouses and fenced them round with horse-sheds for.

THE ELM

Now too, the first of October, or later, the elms are at the height of their autumnal beauty,—great brownish-yellow masses, warm from their September oven, hanging over the highway. Their leaves are perfectly ripe. I wonder if there is any answering ripeness in the lives of the men who live beneath them. As I look down our street, which is lined with them, they remind me both by their form and color of yellowing sheaves of grain, as if the harvest had indeed come to the village itself, and we might expect to find some maturity and *flavor* in the thoughts of the villagers at last. Under those bright rustling yellow piles just ready to fall on the heads of the walkers, how can any crudity or greenness of thought or act prevail? When I stand where half a dozen large elms droop over a house, it is as if I stood within a ripe pumpkin-rind, and I feel as mellow as if I were the pulp, though I may be somewhat stringy and seedy withal. What is the late greenness of the English elm, like a cucumber out of season, which does not know when to have done, compared with the early and golden maturity of the American tree? The street is the scene of a great harvest-home. It would be worth the while to set out these trees, if only for their autumnal value. Think of these great yellow canopies or parasols held over our heads and houses by the mile together, making the village all one and compact,—an *ulmarium*, which is at the same time a nursery of men! And then how gently and unobserved they drop their burden and let in the sun when it is wanted, their leaves not heard when they fall on our roofs and in our streets; and thus the village parasol is shut up and put away! I see the market-man driving into the village, and disappearing under its canopy of elm-tops, with *his* crop, as into a great granary or barn-yard. I am tempted to go thither as to a husking of thoughts, now dry and ripe, and ready to be separated from their integuments; but, alas! I foresee that it will be chiefly husks and little thought, blasted pig-corn, fit only for cob-meal,—for, as you sow, so shall you reap.

FALLEN LEAVES

By the sixth of October the leaves generally begin to fall, in successive showers, after frost or rain; but the principal leaf-harvest, the acme of the *Fall*, is commonly about the sixteenth. Some morning at that date there is perhaps a harder frost than we have seen, and ice formed under the pump, and now, when the morning wind rises, the leaves come down in denser showers than ever. They suddenly form thick beds or carpets on the ground, in this gentle air, or even without wind, just the size and form of the tree above. Some trees, as small hickories, appear to have dropped their leaves instantaneously, as a soldier grounds arms at a signal; and those of the hickory, being bright yellow still, though withered, reflect a blaze of light from the ground where they lie. Down they have come on all sides, at the first earnest touch of autumn's wand, making a sound like rain.

Or else it is after moist and rainy weather that we notice how great a fall of leaves there has been in the night, though it may not yet be the touch that loosens the rock maple leaf. The streets are thickly strewn with the trophies, and fallen elm leaves make a dark brown pavement under our feet. After some remarkably warm Indian-summer day or days, I perceive that it is the unusual heat which, more than anything, causes the leaves to fall, there having been, perhaps, no frost nor rain for some time. The intense heat suddenly ripens and wilts them, just as it softens and ripens peaches and other fruits, and causes them to drop.

The leaves of late red maples, still bright, strew the earth, often crimson-spotted on a yellow ground, like some wild apples,—though they preserve these bright colors on the ground but a day or two, especially if it rains. On causeways I go by trees here and there all bare and smoke-like, having lost their brilliant clothing; but there it lies, nearly as bright as ever, on the ground on one side, and making nearly as regular a figure as lately on the tree. I would rather say that I first observe the trees thus flat on the ground like a permanent colored shadow, and they suggest to look for the boughs that bore them. A queen might be proud to walk where these gallant trees have spread their bright cloaks in the mud. I see wagons roll over them as a shadow or a reflection, and the drivers heed them just as little as they did their shadows before.

Birds' nests, in the huckleberry and other shrubs, and in trees, are already being filled with the withered leaves. So many have fallen in the woods that a squirrel cannot run after a falling nut without being heard. Boys are raking them in the streets, if only for the pleasure of dealing with such clean, crisp substances. Some sweep the paths scrupulously neat, and then stand to see the next breath strew them with new trophies. The swamp floor is thickly covered, and the *Lycopodium lucidulum* looks suddenly greener amid them. In dense woods they half cover pools that are three or four rods long. The other day I could hardly find a well-known spring, and even suspected that it had dried up, for it was completely concealed by freshly fallen leaves; and when I swept them aside and revealed it, it was like striking the earth, with Aaron's rod, for a new spring. Wet grounds about the edges of swamps look dry with them. At one swamp, where I was surveying, thinking to step on a leafy shore from a rail, I got into the water more than a foot deep.

When I go to the river the day after the principal fall of leaves, the sixteenth, I find my boat all covered, bottom and seats, with the leaves of the golden willow under which it is moored, and I set sail with a cargo of them rustling under my feet. If I empty it, it will be full again to-morrow. I do not regard them as litter, to be swept out, but accept them as suitable straw or matting for the bottom of my carriage. When I turn up into the mouth of the Assabet, which is wooded, large fleets of leaves are floating on its surface, as it were getting out to sea, with room to tack; but next the shore, a little farther up, they are thicker than foam, quite concealing the water for a rod in width, under and amid the alders, button-bushes, and maples, still perfectly light and dry, with fibre unrelaxed; and at a rocky bend where they are met and stopped by the morning wind, they sometimes form a broad and dense crescent quite across the river. When I turn my prow that way, and the wave which it makes strikes them, list what a pleasant rustling from these dry substances getting on one another! Often it is their undulation only which reveals the water beneath them. Also every motion of the wood turtle on the shore is betrayed by their rustling there. Or even in mid-channel, when the wind rises, I hear them blown with a rustling sound. Higher up they are slowly moving round and round in some great eddy which the river makes, as that at the "Leaning Hemlocks," where the water is deep, and the current is wearing into the bank.

Perchance, in the afternoon of such a day, when the water is perfectly calm and full of reflections, I paddle gently down the main stream, and, turning up the Assabet, reach a quiet cove, where I unexpectedly find myself surrounded by myriads of leaves, like fellow-voyagers, which seem to have the same purpose, or want of purpose, with myself. See this great fleet of scattered leaf-boats which we paddle amid, in this smooth river-bay, each one curled up on every side by the sun's skill, each nerve a stiff spruce knee,—like boats of hide, and of all patterns,—Charon's boat probably among the rest,—and some with lofty prows and poops, like the stately vessels of the ancients, scarcely moving in the sluggish current,—like the great fleets, the dense Chinese cities of boats, with which you mingle on entering some great mart, some New York or Canton, which we are all steadily approaching together. How gently each has been deposited on the water! No violence has been used towards them yet, though, perchance, palpitating hearts were present at the launching. And painted ducks, too, the splendid wood duck among the rest, often come to sail and float amid the painted leaves,—barks of a nobler model still!

What wholesome herb drinks are to be had in the swamps now! What strong medicinal but rich scents from the decaying leaves! The rain falling on the freshly dried herbs and leaves, and filling the pools and ditches into which they have dropped thus clean and rigid, will soon convert them into tea,—green, black, brown, and yellow teas, of all degrees of strength, enough to set all Nature a-gossiping. Whether we drink them or not, as yet, before their strength is drawn, these leaves, dried on great Nature's coppers, are of such various pure and delicate tints as might make the fame of Oriental teas.

How they are mixed up, of all species, oak and maple and chestnut and birch! But Nature is not cluttered with them; she is a perfect husbandman; she stores them all. Consider what a vast crop is thus annually shed on the earth! This, more than any mere grain or seed, is the great harvest of the year. The trees are now repaying the earth with interest what they have taken from it. They are discounting. They are about to add a leaf's thickness to the depth of the soil. This is the beautiful way in which Nature gets her muck, while I chaffer with this man and that, who talks to me about sulphur and the cost of carting. We are all the richer for their decay. I am more interested in this crop than in the English grass alone or in the corn. It prepares the virgin mould for future corn-fields and forests, on which the earth fattens. It keeps our homestead in good heart.

For beautiful variety no crop can be compared with this. Here is not merely the plain yellow of the grains, but nearly all the colors that we know, the brightest blue not excepted: the early blushing maple, the poison sumach blazing its sins as scarlet, the mulberry ash, the rich chrome yellow of the poplars, the brilliant red huckleberry, with which the hills' backs are painted, like those of sheep. The frost touches them, and, with the slightest breath of returning day or jarring of earth's axle, see in what showers they come floating down! The ground is all parti-colored with them. But they still live in the soil, whose fertility and bulk they increase, and in the forests that spring from it. They stoop to rise, to mount higher in coming years, by subtle chemistry, climbing by the sap in the trees; and the sapling's first fruits thus shed, transmuted at last, may adorn its crown, when, in after years, it has become the monarch of the forest.

It is pleasant to walk over the beds of these fresh, crisp, and rustling leaves. How beautifully they go to their graves! how gently lay themselves down and turn to mould!—painted of a thousand hues, and fit to make the beds of us living. So they troop to their last resting-place, light and frisky. They put on no weeds, but merrily they go scampering over the earth, selecting the spot, choosing a lot, ordering no iron fence, whispering all through the woods about it,—some choosing the spot where the bodies of men are mouldering beneath, and meeting them half-way. How many flutterings before they rest quietly in their graves! They that soared so loftily, how contentedly they return to dust again, and are laid low, resigned to lie and decay at the foot of the tree, and afford nourishment to new generations of their kind, as well as to flutter on high! They teach us how to die. One wonders if the time will ever come when men, with their boasted faith in immortality, will lie down as gracefully and as ripe,—with such an Indian-summer serenity will shed their bodies, as they do their hair and nails.

When the leaves fall, the whole earth is a cemetery pleasant to walk in. I love to wander and muse over them in their graves. Here are no lying nor vain epitaphs. What though you own no lot at Mount Auburn? Your lot is surely cast somewhere in this vast cemetery, which has been consecrated from of old. You need attend no auction to secure a place. There is room enough here. The loosestrife shall bloom and the huckleberry-bird sing over your bones. The woodman and hunter shall be your sextons, and the children shall tread upon the borders as much as they will. Let us walk in the cemetery of the leaves; this is your true Greenwood Cemetery.

THE SUGAR MAPLE

But think not that the splendor of the year is over; for as one leaf does not make a summer, neither does one falling leaf make an autumn. The smallest sugar maples in our streets make a great show as early as the fifth of October, more than any other trees there. As I look up the main street, they appear like painted screens standing before the houses; yet many are green. But now, or generally by the seventeenth of October, when almost all red maples and some white maples are bare, the large sugar maples also are in their glory, glowing with yellow and red, and show unexpectedly bright and delicate tints. They are remarkable for the contrast they often afford of deep blushing red on one half and green on the other. They become at length dense masses of rich yellow with a deep scarlet blush, or more than blush, on the exposed surfaces. They are the brightest trees now in the street.

The large ones on our Common are particularly beautiful. A delicate but warmer than golden yellow is now the prevailing color, with scarlet cheeks. Yet, standing on the east side of the Common just before sundown, when the western light is transmitted through them, I see that their yellow even, compared with the pale lemon yellow of an elm close by, amounts to a scarlet, without noticing the bright scarlet portions. Generally, they are great regular oval masses of yellow and scarlet. All the sunny warmth of the season, the Indian summer, seems to be absorbed in their leaves. The lowest and inmost leaves next the bole are, as usual, of the most delicate yellow and green, like the complexion of young men brought up in the house. There is an auction on the Common to-day, but its red flag is hard to be discerned amid this blaze of color.

Little did the fathers of the town anticipate this brilliant success, when they caused to be imported from farther in the country some straight poles with their tops cut off, which they called sugar maples; and, as I remember, after they were set out, a neighboring merchant's clerk, by way of jest, planted beans about them. Those which were then jestingly called bean-poles are to-day far the most beautiful objects noticeable in our streets. They are worth all and more than they have cost,—though one of the selectmen, while setting them out, took the cold which occasioned his death,—if only because they have filled the open eyes of children with their rich color unstintedly so many Octobers. We will not ask them to yield us sugar in the spring, while they afford us so fair a prospect in the autumn. Wealth indoors may be the inheritance of few, but it is equally distributed on the Common. All children alike can revel in this golden harvest.

Surely trees should be set in our streets with a view to their October splendor, though I doubt whether this is ever considered by the "Tree Society." Do you not think it will make some odds to these children that they were brought up under the maples? Hundreds of eyes are steadily drinking in this color, and by these teachers even the truants are caught and educated the moment they step abroad. Indeed, neither the truant nor the studious is at present taught color in the schools. These are instead of the bright colors in apothecaries' shops and city windows. It is a pity that we have no more *red* maples, and some hickories, in our streets as well. Our paint-box is very imperfectly filled. Instead of, or beside, supplying such paint-boxes as we do, we might supply these natural colors to the young. Where else will they study color under greater advantages? What School of Design can vie with this? Think how much the eyes of painters of all kinds, and of manufacturers of cloth and paper, and paper-stainers, and countless others, are to be educated by these autumnal colors. The stationer's envelopes may be of very various tints, yet not so various as those of the leaves of a single tree. If you want a different shade or tint of a particular color, you have only to look farther within or without the tree or the wood. These leaves are not many dipped in one dye, as at the dye-house, but they are dyed in light of infinitely various degrees of strength and left to set and dry there.

Shall the names of so many of our colors continue to be derived from those of obscure foreign localities, as Naples yellow, Prussian blue, raw Sienna, burnt Umber, Gamboge? (surely the Tyrian purple must have faded by this time), or from comparatively trivial articles of commerce,—chocolate, lemon, coffee, cinnamon, claret? (shall we compare our hickory to a lemon, or a lemon to a hickory?) or from ores and oxides which few ever see? Shall we so often, when describing to our neighbors the color of something we have seen, refer them, not to some natural object in our neighborhood, but perchance to a bit of earth fetched from the other side of the planet, which possibly they may find at the apothecary's, but which probably neither they nor we ever saw? Have we not an *earth* under our feet,—aye, and a sky over our heads? Or is the last *all* ultramarine? What do we know of sapphire, amethyst, emerald, ruby, amber, and the like,—most of us who take these names in vain? Leave these precious words to cabinet-keepers, virtuosos, and maids-of-honor,—to the Nabobs, Begums, and Chobdars of Hindostan, or wherever else. I do not see why, since America and her autumn woods have been discovered, our leaves should not compete with the precious stones in giving names to colors; and, indeed, I believe that in course of time the names of some of our trees and shrubs, as well as flowers, will get into our popular chromatic nomenclature.

But of much more importance than a knowledge of the names and distinctions of color is the joy and exhilaration which these colored leaves excite. Already these brilliant trees throughout the street, without any more variety, are at least equal to an annual festival and holiday, or a week of such. These are cheap and innocent gala-days, celebrated by one and all without the aid of committees or marshals, such a show as may safely be licensed, not attracting gamblers or rum-sellers, not requiring any special police to keep the peace. And poor indeed must be that New England village's October which has not the maple in its streets. This October festival costs no powder, nor ringing of bells, but every tree is a living liberty-pole on which a thousand bright flags are waving.

No wonder that we must have our annual cattle-show, and fall training, and perhaps cornwallis, our September courts, and the like. Nature herself holds her annual fair in October, not only in the streets, but in every hollow and on every hillside. When lately we looked into that red maple swamp all ablaze, where the trees were clothed in their vestures of most dazzling tints, did it not suggest a thousand gypsies beneath,—a race capable of wild delight,—or even the fabled fauns, satyrs, and wood-nymphs come back to earth? Or was it only a congregation of wearied woodchoppers, or of proprietors come to inspect their lots, that we thought of? Or, earlier still, when we paddled on the river through that fine-grained September air, did there not appear to be something new going on under the sparkling surface of the stream, a shaking of props, at least, so that we made haste in order to be up in time? Did not the rows of yellowing willows and button-bushes on each side seem like rows of booths, under which, perhaps, some fluviatile egg-pop equally yellow was effervescing? Did not all these suggest that man's spirits should rise as high as Nature's,—should hang out their flag, and the routine of his life be interrupted by an analogous expression of joy and hilarity?

No annual training or muster of soldiery, no celebration with its scarfs and banners, could import into the town a hundredth part of the annual splendor of our October. We have only to set the trees, or let them stand, and Nature will find the colored drapery,—flags of all her nations, some of whose private signals hardly the botanist can read,—while we walk under the triumphal arches of the elms. Leave it to Nature to appoint the days, whether the same as in neighboring States or not, and let the clergy read her proclamations, if they can understand them. Behold what a brilliant drapery is her woodbine flag! What public-spirited merchant, think you, has contributed this part of the show? There is no handsomer shingling and paint than this vine, at present covering a whole side of some houses. I do not believe that the ivy *never sere* is comparable to it. No wonder it has been extensively introduced into London. Let us have a good many maples and hickories and scarlet oaks, then, I say. Blaze away! Shall that dirty roll of bunting in the gun-house be all the colors a village can display? A village is not complete, unless it have these trees to mark the season in it. They are important, like the town clock. A village that has them not will not be found to work well. It has a screw loose, an essential part is wanting. Let us have willows for spring, elms for summer, maples and walnuts and tupeloes for autumn, evergreens for winter, and oaks for all seasons. What is a gallery in a house to a gallery in the streets, which every market-man rides through, whether he will or not? Of course, there is not a picture-gallery in the country which would be worth so much to us as is the western view at sunset under the elms of our main street. They are the frame to a picture which is daily painted behind them. An avenue of elms as large as our largest and three miles long would seem to lead to some admirable place, though only C—— were at the end of it.

A village needs these innocent stimulants of bright and cheering prospects to keep off melancholy and superstition. Show me two villages, one embowered in trees and blazing with all the glories of October, the other a merely trivial and treeless waste, or with only a single tree or two for suicides, and I shall be sure that in the latter will be found the most starved and bigoted religionists and the most desperate drinkers. Every wash-tub and milk-can and gravestone will be exposed. The inhabitants will disappear abruptly behind their barns and houses, like desert Arabs amid their rocks, and I shall look to see spears in their hands. They will be ready to accept the most barren and forlorn doctrine,—as that the world is speedily coming to an end, or has already got to it, or that they themselves are turned wrong side outward. They will perchance crack their dry joints at one another and call it a spiritual communication.

But to confine ourselves to the maples. What if we were to take half as much pains in protecting them as we do in setting them out,—not stupidly tie our horses to our dahlia stems?

What meant the fathers by establishing this *perfectly living* institution before the church,—this institution which needs no repairing nor repainting, which is continually enlarged and repaired by its growth? Surely they

> "Wrought in a sad sincerity;
> Themselves from God they could not free;
> They *planted* better than they knew;—
> The conscious *trees* to beauty grew."

Verily these maples are cheap preachers, permanently settled, which preach their half-century, and century, aye, and century-and-a-half sermons, with constantly increasing unction and influence, ministering to many generations of men; and the least we can do is to supply them with suitable colleagues as they grow infirm.

THE SCARLET OAK

Belonging to a genus which is remarkable for the beautiful form of its leaves, I suspect that some scarlet oak leaves surpass those of all other oaks in the rich and wild beauty of their outlines. I judge from an acquaintance with twelve species, and from drawings which I have seen of many others.

Stand under this tree and see how finely its leaves are cut against the sky,—as it were, only a few sharp points extending from a midrib. They look like double, treble, or quadruple crosses. They are far more ethereal than the less deeply scalloped oak leaves. They have so little leafy *terra firma* that they appear melting away in the light, and scarcely obstruct our view. The leaves of very young plants are, like those of full-grown oaks of other species, more entire, simple, and lumpish in their outlines, but these, raised high on old trees, have solved the leafy problem. Lifted higher and higher, and sublimated more and more, putting off some earthiness and cultivating more intimacy with the light each year, they have at length the least possible amount of earthy matter, and the greatest spread and grasp of skyey influences. There they dance, arm in arm with the light,—tripping it on fantastic points, fit partners in those aerial halls. So intimately mingled are they with it, that, what with their slenderness and their glossy surfaces, you can hardly tell at last what in the dance is leaf and what is light. And when no zephyr stirs, they are at most but a rich tracery to the forest windows.

I am again struck with their beauty, when, a month later, they thickly strew the ground in the woods, piled one upon another under my feet. They are then brown above, but purple beneath. With their narrow lobes and their bold, deep scallops reaching almost to the middle, they suggest that the material must be cheap, or else there has been a lavish expense in their creation, as if so much had been cut out. Or else they seem to us the remnants of the stuff out of which leaves have been cut with a die. Indeed, when they lie thus one upon another, they remind me of a pile of scrap-tin.

Or bring one home, and study it closely at your leisure, by the fireside. It is a type, not from any Oxford font, not in the Basque nor the arrow-headed character, not found on the Rosetta Stone, but destined to be copied in sculpture one day, if they ever get to whittling stone here. What a wild and pleasing outline, a combination of graceful curves and angles! The eye rests with equal delight on what is not leaf and on what is leaf,—on the broad, free, open sinuses, and on the long, sharp, bristle-pointed lobes. A simple oval outline would include it all, if you connected the points of the leaf; but how much richer is it than that, with its half-dozen deep scallops, in which the eye and thought of the beholder are embayed! If I were a drawing-master, I would set my pupils to copying these leaves, that they might learn to draw firmly and gracefully.

Regarded as water, it is like a pond with half a dozen broad rounded promontories extending nearly to its middle, half from each side, while its watery bays extend far inland, like sharp friths, at each of whose heads several fine streams empty in,—almost a leafy archipelago.

But it oftener suggests land, and, as Dionysius and Pliny compared the form of the Morea to that of the leaf of the Oriental plane tree, so this leaf reminds me of some fair wild island in the ocean, whose extensive coast, alternate rounded bays with smooth strands, and sharp-pointed rocky capes, mark it as fitted for the habitation of man, and destined to become a centre of civilization at last. To the sailor's eye, it is a much indented shore. Is it not, in fact, a shore to the aerial ocean, on which the windy surf beats? At sight of this leaf we are all mariners,—if not vikings, buccaneers, and filibusters. Both our love of repose and our spirit of adventure are addressed. In our most casual glance, perchance, we think that if we succeed in doubling those sharp capes we shall find deep, smooth, and secure havens in the ample bays. How different from the white oak leaf, with its rounded headlands, on which no lighthouse need be placed! That is an England, with its long civil history, that may be read. This is some still unsettled New-found Island or Celebes. Shall we go and be rajahs there?

By the twenty-sixth of October the large scarlet oaks are in their prime, when other oaks are usually withered. They have been kindling their fires for a week past, and now generally burst into a blaze. This alone of *our* indigenous deciduous trees (excepting the dogwood, of which I do not know half a dozen, and they are but large bushes) is now in its glory. The two aspens and the sugar maple come nearest to it in date, but they have lost the greater part of their leaves. Of evergreens, only the pitch pine is still commonly bright.

But it requires a particular alertness, if not devotion to these phenomena, to appreciate the wide-spread, but late and unexpected glory of the scarlet oaks. I do not speak here of the small trees and shrubs, which are commonly observed, and which are now withered, but of the large trees. Most go in and shut their doors, thinking that bleak and colorless November has already come, when some of the most brilliant and memorable colors are not yet lit.

This very perfect and vigorous one, about forty feet high, standing in an open pasture, which was quite glossy green on the twelfth, is now, the twenty-sixth, completely changed to bright dark-scarlet,—every leaf, between you and the sun, as if it had been dipped into a scarlet dye. The whole tree is much like a heart in form, as well as color. Was not this worth waiting for? Little did you think, ten days ago, that that cold green tree would assume such color as this. Its leaves are still firmly attached, while those of other trees are falling around it. It seems to say: "I am the last to blush, but I blush deeper than any of ye. I bring up the rear in my red coat. We scarlet ones, alone of oaks, have not given up the fight."

The sap is now, and even far into November, frequently flowing fast in these trees, as in maples in the spring; and apparently their bright tints, now that most other oaks are withered, are connected with this phenomenon. They are full of life. It has a pleasantly astringent, acorn-like taste, this strong oak wine, as I find on tapping them with my knife.

Looking across this woodland valley, a quarter of a mile wide, how rich those scarlet oaks embosomed in pines, their bright red branches intimately intermingled with them! They have their full effect there. The pine boughs are the green calyx to their red petals. Or, as we go along a road in the woods, the sun striking endwise through it, and lighting up the red tents of the oaks, which on each side are mingled with the liquid green of the pines, makes a very gorgeous scene. Indeed, without the evergreens for contrast, the autumnal tints would lose much of their effect.

The scarlet oak asks a clear sky and the brightness of late October days. These bring out its colors. If the sun goes into a cloud they become comparatively indistinct. As I sit on a cliff in the southwest part of our town, the sun is now getting low, and the woods in Lincoln, south and east of me, are lit up by its more level rays; and in the scarlet oaks, scattered so equally over the forest, there is brought out a more brilliant redness than I had believed was in them. Every tree of this species which is visible in those directions, even to the horizon, now stands out distinctly red. Some great ones lift their red backs high above the woods, in the next town, like huge roses with a myriad of fine petals; and some more slender ones, in a small grove of white pines on Pine Hill in the east, on the very verge of the horizon, alternating with the pines on the edge of the grove, and shouldering them with their red coats, look like soldiers in red amid hunters in green. This time it is Lincoln green, too. Till the sun got low, I did not believe that there were so many redcoats in the forest army. Theirs is an intense, burning red, which would lose some of its strength, methinks, with every step you might take toward them; for the shade that lurks amid their foliage does not report itself at this distance, and they are unanimously red. The focus of their reflected color is in the atmosphere far on this side. Every such tree becomes a nucleus of red, as it were, where, with the declining sun, that color grows and glows. It is partly borrowed fire, gathering strength from the sun on its way to your eye. It has only some comparatively dull red leaves for a rallying-point, or kindling-stuff, to start it, and it becomes an intense scarlet or red mist, or fire, which finds fuel for itself in the very atmosphere. So vivacious is redness. The very rails reflect a rosy light at this hour and season. You see a redder tree than exists.

If you wish to count the scarlet oaks, do it now. In a clear day stand thus on a hilltop in the woods, when the sun is an hour high, and every one within range of your vision, excepting in the west, will be revealed. You might live to the age of Methuselah and never find a tithe of them, otherwise. Yet sometimes even in a dark day I have thought them as bright as I ever saw them. Looking westward, their colors are lost in a blaze of light; but in other directions the whole forest is a flower-garden, in which these late roses burn, alternating with green, while the so-called "gardeners," walking here and there, perchance, beneath, with spade and water-pot, see only a few little asters amid withered leaves.

These are *my* China-asters, *my* late garden-flowers. It costs me nothing for a gardener. The falling leaves, all over the forest, are protecting the roots of my plants. Only look at what is to be seen, and you will have garden enough, without deepening the soil in your yard. We have only to elevate our view a little, to see the whole forest as a garden. The blossoming of the scarlet oak,—the forest-flower, surpassing all in splendor (at least since the maple)! I do not know but they interest me more than the maples, they are so widely and equally dispersed throughout the forest; they are so hardy, a nobler tree on the whole; our chief November flower, abiding the approach of winter with us, imparting warmth to early November prospects. It is remarkable that the latest bright color that is general should be this deep, dark scarlet and red, the intensest of colors. The ripest fruit of the year; like the cheek of a hard, glossy red apple, from the cold Isle of Orleans, which will not be mellow for eating till next spring! When I rise to a hilltop, a thousand of these great oak roses, distributed on every side, as far as the horizon! I admire them four or five miles off! This my unfailing prospect for a fortnight past! This late forest-flower surpasses all that spring or summer could do. Their colors were but rare and dainty specks comparatively (created for the near-sighted, who walk amid the humblest herbs and underwoods), and made no impression on a distant eye. Now it is an extended forest or a mountain-side, through or along which we journey from day to day, that bursts into bloom. Comparatively, our gardening is on a petty scale,—the gardener still nursing a few asters amid dead weeds, ignorant of the gigantic asters and roses which, as it were, overshadow him, and ask for none of his care. It is like a little red paint ground on a saucer, and held up against the sunset sky. Why not take more elevated and broader views, walk in the great garden; not skulk in a little "debauched" nook of it? consider the beauty of the forest, and not merely of a few impounded herbs?

Let your walks now be a little more adventurous; ascend the hills. If, about the last of October, you ascend any hill in the outskirts of our town, and probably of yours, and look over the forest, you may see—well, what I have endeavored to describe. All this you surely *will* see, and much more, if you are prepared to see it,—if you *look* for it. Otherwise, regular and universal as this phenomenon is, whether you stand on the hilltop or in the hollow, you will think for threescore years and ten that all the wood is, at this season, sere and brown. Objects are concealed from our view, not so much because they are out of the course of our visual ray as because we do not bring our minds and eyes to bear on them; for there is no power to see in the eye itself, any more than in any other jelly. We do not realize how far and widely, or how near and narrowly, we are to look. The greater part of the phenomena of Nature are for this reason concealed from us all our lives. The gardener sees only the gardener's garden. Here, too, as in political economy, the supply answers to the demand. Nature does not cast pearls before swine. There is just as much beauty visible to us in the landscape as we are prepared to appreciate,—not a grain more. The actual objects which one man will see from a particular hilltop are just as different from those which another will see as the beholders are different. The scarlet oak must, in a sense, be in your eye when you go forth. We cannot see anything until we are possessed with the idea of it, take it into our heads,—and then we can hardly see anything else. In my botanical rambles I find that, first, the idea, or image, of a plant occupies my thoughts, though it may seem very foreign to this locality,—no nearer than Hudson's Bay,—and for some weeks or months I go thinking of it, and expecting it, unconsciously, and at length I surely see it. This is the history of my finding a score or more of rare plants which I could name. A man sees only what concerns him. A botanist absorbed in the study of grasses does not distinguish the grandest pasture oaks. He, as it were, tramples down oaks unwittingly in his walk, or at most sees only their shadows. I have found that it required a different intention of the eye, in the same locality, to see different plants, even when they were closely allied, as *Juncaceae* and *Gramineae*: when I was looking for the former, I did not see the latter in the midst of them. How much more, then, it requires different intentions of the eye and of the mind to attend to different departments of knowledge! How differently the poet and the naturalist look at objects!

Take a New England selectman, and set him on the highest of our hills, and tell him to look,—sharpening his sight to the utmost, and putting on the glasses that suit him best (aye, using a spy-glass, if he likes),—and make a full report. What, probably, will he *spy*?—what will he *select* to look at? Of course, he will see a Brocken spectre of himself. He will see several meetinghouses, at least, and, perhaps, that somebody ought to be assessed higher than he is, since he has so handsome a wood-lot. Now take Julius Cæsar, or Emanuel Swedenborg, or a Fiji-Islander, and set him up there. Or suppose all together, and let them compare notes afterward. Will it appear that they have enjoyed the same prospect? What they will see will be as different as Rome was from heaven or hell, or the last from the Fiji Islands. For aught we know, as strange a man as any of these is always at our elbow.

Why, it takes a sharpshooter to bring down even such trivial game as snipes and woodcocks; he must take very particular aim, and know what he is aiming at. He would stand a very small chance, if he fired at random into the sky, being told that snipes were flying there. And so is it with him that shoots at beauty; though he wait till the sky falls, he will not bag any, if he does not already know its seasons and haunts, and the color of its wing,—if he has not dreamed of it, so that he can *anticipate* it; then, indeed, he flushes it at every step, shoots double and on the wing, with both barrels, even in corn-fields. The sportsman trains himself, dresses, and watches unweariedly, and loads and primes for his particular game. He prays for it, and offers sacrifices, and so he gets it. After due and long preparation, schooling his eye and hand, dreaming awake and asleep, with gun and paddle and boat, he goes out after meadow-hens, which most of his townsmen never saw nor dreamed of, and paddles for miles against a head wind, and wades in water up to his knees, being out all day without his dinner, and *therefore* he gets them. He had them half-way into his bag when he started, and has only to shove them down. The true sportsman can shoot you almost any of his game from his windows: what else has he windows or eyes for? It comes and perches at last on the barrel of his gun; but the rest of the world never see it *with the feathers on.* The geese fly exactly under his zenith, and honk when they get there, and he will keep himself supplied by firing up his chimney; twenty musquash have the refusal of each one of his traps before it is empty. If he lives, and his game spirit increases, heaven and earth shall fail him sooner than game; and when he dies, he will go to more extensive and, perchance, happier hunting-grounds. The fisherman, too, dreams of fish, sees a bobbing cork in his dreams, till he can almost catch them in his sink-spout. I knew a girl who, being sent to pick huckleberries, picked wild gooseberries by the quart, where no one else knew that there were any, because she was accustomed to pick them up-country where she came from. The astronomer knows where to go star-gathering, and sees one clearly in his mind before any have seen it with a glass. The hen scratches and finds her food right under where she stands; but such is not the way with the hawk.

These bright leaves which I have mentioned are not the exception, but the rule; for I believe that all leaves, even grasses and mosses, acquire brighter colors just before their fall. When you come to observe faithfully the changes of each humblest plant, you find that each has, sooner or later, its peculiar autumnal tint; and if you undertake to make a complete list of the bright tints, it will be nearly as long as a catalogue of the plants in your vicinity.

THE SUCCESSION OF FOREST TREES

AN ADDRESS

— ON —

THE SUCCESSION OF FOREST TREES.

Ladies and Gentlemen:

Every man is entitled to come to Cattle-show, even a transcendentalist; and for my part I am more interested in the men than in the cattle. I wish to see once more those old familiar faces, whose names I do not know, which for me represent the Middlesex country, and come as near being indigenous to the soil as a white man can; the men who are not above their business, whose coats are not too black, whose shoes do not shine very much, who never wear gloves to conceal their hands. It is true, there are some queer specimens of humanity attracted to our festival, but all are welcome. I am pretty sure to meet once more that weak-minded and whimsical fellow, generally weak-bodied too, who prefers a crooked stick for a cane; perfectly useless, you would say, only bizarre, fit for a cabinet, like a petrified snake. A ram's horn would be as convenient, and is yet more curiously twisted. He brings that much indulged bit of the country with him, from some town's end or other, and introduces it to Concord groves, as if he had promised it so much sometime. So some, it seems to me, elect their rulers for their crookedness. But I think that a straight stick makes the best cane, and an upright man the best ruler. Or why choose a man to do plain work who is distinguished for his oddity? However, I do not know but you will think that they have committed this mistake who invited me to speak to you to-day.

In my capacity of surveyor, I have often talked with some of you, my employers, at your dinner-tables, after having gone round and round and behind your farming, and ascertained exactly what its limits were. Moreover, taking a surveyor's and a naturalist's liberty, I have been in the habit of going across your lots much oftener than is usual, as many of you, perhaps to your sorrow, are aware. Yet many of you, to my relief, have seemed not to be aware of it; and when I came across you in some out-of-the-way nook of your farms, have inquired,

Transactions of the Middlesex Agricultural Society (1860)

THE SUCCESSION OF FOREST TREES*

Every man is entitled to come to Cattle-Show, even a transcendentalist; and for my part I am more interested in the men than in the cattle. I wish to see once more those old familiar faces, whose names I do not know, which for me represent the Middlesex country, and come as near being indigenous to the soil as a white man can; the men who are not above their business, whose coats are not too black, whose shoes do not shine very much, who never wear gloves to conceal their hands. It is true, there are some queer specimens of humanity attracted to our festival, but all are welcome. I am pretty sure to meet once more that weak-minded and whimsical fellow, generally weak-bodied too, who prefers a crooked stick for a cane; perfectly useless, you would say, only *bizarre*, fit for a cabinet, like a petrified snake. A ram's horn would be as convenient, and is yet more curiously twisted. He brings that much indulged bit of the country with him, from some town's end or other, and introduces it to Concord groves, as if he had promised it so much sometime. So some, it seems to me, elect their rulers for their crookedness. But I think that a straight stick makes the best cane, and an upright man the best ruler. Or why choose a man to do plain work who is distinguished for his oddity? However, I do not know but you will think that they have committed this mistake who invited me to speak to you to-day.

In my capacity of surveyor, I have often talked with some of you, my

*An Address read to the Middlesex Agricultural Society in Concord, September, 1860.

employers, at your dinner-tables, after having gone round and round and behind your farming, and ascertained exactly what its limits were. Moreover, taking a surveyor's and a naturalist's liberty, I have been in the habit of going across your lots much oftener than is usual, as many of you, perhaps to your sorrow, are aware. Yet many of you, to my relief, have seemed not to be aware of it; and, when I came across you in some out-of-the-way nook of your farms, have inquired, with an air of surprise, if I were not lost, since you had never seen me in that part of the town or county before; when, if the truth were known, and it had not been for betraying my secret, I might with more propriety have inquired if *you* were not lost, since I had never seen *you* there before. I have several times shown the proprietor the shortest way out of his wood-lot.

Therefore, it would seem that I have some title to speak to you to-day; and considering what that title is, and the occasion that has called us together, I need offer no apology if I invite your attention, for the few moments that are allotted me, to a purely scientific subject.

At those dinner-tables referred to, I have often been asked, as many of you have been, if I could tell how it happened, that when a pine wood was cut down an oak one commonly sprang up, and *vice versa*. To which I have answered, and now answer, that I can tell,—that it is no mystery to me. As I am not aware that this has been clearly shown by any one, I shall lay the more stress on this point. Let me lead you back into your wood-lots again.

When, hereabouts, a single forest tree or a forest springs up naturally where none of its kind grew before, I do not hesitate to say, though in some quarters still it may sound paradoxical, that it came from a seed. Of the various ways by which trees are *known* to be propagated,—by transplanting, cuttings, and the like,—this is the only supposable one under these circumstances. No such tree has ever been known to spring from anything else. If any one asserts that it sprang from something else, or from nothing, the burden of proof lies with him.

It remains, then, only to show how the seed is transported from where it grows to where it is planted. This is done chiefly by the agency of the wind, water, and animals. The lighter seeds, as those of pines and maples, are transported chiefly by wind and water; the heavier, as acorns and nuts, by animals.

In all the pines, a very thin membrane, in appearance much like an insect's wing, grows over and around the seed, and independent of it, while the latter is being developed within its base. Indeed this is often perfectly developed, though the seed is abortive; nature being, you would say, more sure to provide the means of transporting the seed, than to provide the seed to be transported. In other words, a beautiful thin sack is woven around the seed, with a handle to it such as the wind can take hold of, and it is then committed to the wind, expressly that it may transport the seed and extend the range of the species; and this it does, as effectually as when seeds are sent by mail in a different kind of sack from the Patent Office. There is a patent office at the seat of government of the universe, whose managers are as much interested in the dispersion of seeds as anybody at Washington can be, and their operations are infinitely more extensive and regular.

There is, then, no necessity for supposing that the pines have sprung up from nothing, and I am aware that I am not at all peculiar in asserting that they come from seeds, though the mode of their propagation *by nature* has been but little attended to. They are very extensively raised from the seed in Europe, and are beginning to be here.

When you cut down an oak wood, a pine wood will not *at once* spring up there unless there are, or have been quite recently, seed-bearing pines near enough for the seeds to be blown from them. But, adjacent to a forest of pines, if you prevent other crops from growing there, you will surely have an extension of your pine forest, provided the soil is suitable.

As for the heavy seeds and nuts which are not furnished with wings, the notion is still a very common one that, when the trees which bear these spring up where none of their kind were noticed before, they have come from seeds or other principles spontaneously generated there in an unusual manner, or which have lain dormant in the soil for centuries, or perhaps been called into activity by the heat of a burning. I do not believe these assertions, and I will state some of the ways in which, according to my observation, such forests are planted and raised.

Every one of these seeds, too, will be found to be winged or legged in another fashion. Surely it is not wonderful that cherry trees of all kinds are widely dispersed, since their fruit is well known to be the favorite food of various birds. Many kinds are called bird cherries, and they appropriate many more kinds, which are not so called. Eating cherries is a bird-like employment, and unless we disperse the seeds occasionally, as they do, I shall think that the birds have the best right to them. See how artfully the seed of a cherry is placed in order that a bird may be compelled to transport it,—in the very midst of a tempting pericarp, so that the creature that would devour this must commonly take the stone also into its mouth or bill. If you ever ate a cherry, and did not make two bites of it, you must have perceived it,—right in the centre of the luscious morsel, a large earthy residuum left on the tongue. We thus take into our mouths cherry-stones as big as peas, a dozen at once, for Nature can persuade us to do almost anything when she would compass her ends. Some wild men and children instinctively swallow these, as the birds do when in a hurry, it being the shortest way to get rid of them. Thus, though these seeds are not provided with vegetable wings, Nature has impelled the thrush tribe to take them into their bills and fly away with them; and they are winged in another sense, and more effectually than the seeds of pines, for these are carried even against the wind. The consequence is, that cherry trees grow not only here but there. The same is true of a great many other seeds.

But to come to the observation which suggested these remarks. As I have said, I suspect that I can throw some light on the fact that when hereabouts a dense pine wood is cut down, oaks and other hard woods may at once take its place. I have got only to show that the acorns and nuts, provided they are grown in the neighborhood, are regularly planted in such woods; for I assert that if an oak tree has not grown within ten miles, and man has not carried acorns thither, then an oak wood will not spring up *at once*, when a pine wood is cut down.

Apparently, there were only pines there before. They are cut off, and after a year or two you see oaks and other hard woods springing up there, with scarcely a pine amid them, and the wonder commonly is, how the seed could have lain in the ground so long without decaying. But the truth is, that it has not lain in the ground so long, but is regularly planted each year by various quadrupeds and birds.

In this neighborhood, where oaks and pines are about equally dispersed, if you look through the thickest pine wood, even the seemingly unmixed pitch pine ones, you will commonly detect many little oaks, birches, and other hard woods, sprung from seeds carried into the thicket by squirrels and other animals, and also blown thither, but which are overshadowed and choked by the pines. The denser the evergreen wood, the more likely it is to be well planted with these seeds, because the planters incline to resort with their forage to the closest covert. They also carry it into birch and other woods. This planting is carried on annually, and the oldest seedlings annually die; but when the pines are cleared off, the oaks, having got just the start they want, and now secured favorable conditions, immediately spring up to trees.

The shade of a dense pine wood is more unfavorable to the springing up of pines of the same species than of oaks within it, though the former may come up abundantly when the pines are cut, if there chance to be sound seed in the ground.

But when you cut off a lot of hard wood, very often the little pines mixed with it have a similar start, for the squirrels have carried off the nuts to the pines, and not to the more open wood, and they commonly make pretty clean work of it; and moreover, if the wood was old, the sprouts will be feeble or entirely fail; to say nothing about the soil being, in a measure, exhausted for this kind of crop.

If a pine wood is surrounded by a white oak one chiefly, white oaks may be expected to succeed when the pines are cut. If it is surrounded instead by an edging of shrub oaks, then you will probably have a dense shrub oak thicket.

I have no time to go into details, but will say, in a word, that while the wind is conveying the seeds of pines into hard woods and open lands, the squirrels and other animals are conveying the seeds of oaks and walnuts into the pine woods, and thus a rotation of crops is kept up.

I affirmed this confidently many years ago, and an occasional examination of dense pine woods confirmed me in my opinion. It has long been known to observers that squirrels bury nuts in the ground, but I am not aware that any one has thus accounted for the regular succession of forests.

On the 24th of September, in 1857, as I was paddling down the Assabet, in this town, I saw a red squirrel run along the bank under some herbage, with something large in its mouth. It stopped near the foot of a hemlock, within a couple of rods of me, and, hastily pawing a hole with its fore feet, dropped its booty into it, covered it up, and retreated part way up the trunk of the tree. As I approached the shore to examine the deposit, the squirrel, descending part way, betrayed no little anxiety about its treasure, and made two or three motions to recover it before it finally retreated. Digging there, I found two green pignuts joined together, with the thick husks on, buried about an inch and a half under the reddish soil of decayed hemlock leaves,—just the right depth to plant it. In short, this squirrel was then engaged in accomplishing two objects, to wit, laying up a store of winter food for itself, and planting a hickory wood for all creation. If the squirrel was killed, or neglected its deposit, a hickory would spring up. The nearest hickory tree was twenty rods distant. These nuts were there still just fourteen days later, but were gone when I looked again, November 21st, or six weeks later still.

I have since examined more carefully several dense woods, which are said to be, and are apparently, exclusively pine, and always with the same result. For instance, I walked the same day to a small but very dense and handsome white pine grove, about fifteen rods square, in the east part of this town. The trees are large for Concord, being from ten to twenty inches in diameter, and as exclusively pine as any wood that I know. Indeed, I selected this wood because I thought it the least likely to contain anything else. It stands on an open plain or pasture, except that it adjoins another small pine wood, which has a few little oaks in it, on the southeast side. On every other side, it was at least thirty rods from the nearest woods. Standing on the edge of this grove and looking through it, for it is quite level and free from underwood, for the most part bare, red-carpeted ground, you would have said that there was not a hardwood tree in it, young or old. But on looking carefully along over its floor I discovered, though it was not till my eye had got used to the search, that, alternating with thin ferns, and small blueberry bushes, there was, not merely here and there, but as often as every five feet and with a degree of regularity, a little oak, from three to twelve inches high, and in one place I found a green acorn dropped by the base of a pine.

I confess I was surprised to find my theory so perfectly proved in this case. One of the principal agents in this planting, the red squirrels, were all the while curiously inspecting me, while I was inspecting their plantation. Some of the little oaks had been browsed by cows, which resorted to this wood for shade.

After seven or eight years, the hard woods evidently find such a locality unfavorable to their growth, the pines being allowed to stand. As an evidence of this, I observed a diseased red maple twenty-five feet long, which had been recently prostrated, though it was still covered with green leaves, the only maple in any position in the wood.

But although these oaks almost invariably die if the pines are not cut down, it is probable that they do better for a few years under their shelter than they would anywhere else.

The very extensive and thorough experiments of the English have at length led them to adopt a method of raising oaks almost precisely like this which somewhat earlier had been adopted by Nature and her squirrels here; they have simply rediscovered the value of pines as nurses for oaks. The English experimenters seem, early and generally, to have found out the importance of using trees of some kind as nurse-plants for the young oaks. I quote from Loudon what he describes as "the ultimatum on the subject of planting and sheltering oaks,"—"an abstract of the practice adopted by the government officers in the national forests" of England, prepared by Alexander Milne.

At first some oaks had been planted by themselves, and others mixed with Scotch pines; "but in all cases," says Mr. Milne, "where oaks were planted actually among the pines and surrounded by them [though the soil might be inferior], the oaks were found to be much the best." "For several years past, the plan pursued has been to plant the inclosures with Scotch pines only [a tree very similar to our pitch pine], and when the pines have got to the height of five or six feet, then to put in good strong oak plants of about four or five years' growth among the pines,—not cutting away any pines at first, unless they happen to be so strong and thick as to overshadow the oaks. In about two years it becomes necessary to shred the branches of the pines, to give light and air to the oaks, and in about two or three more years to begin gradually to remove the pines altogether, taking out a certain number each year, so that, at the end of twenty or twenty-five years, not a single Scotch pine shall be left; although, for the first ten or twelve years, the plantation may have appeared to contain nothing else but pine. The advantage of this mode of planting has been found to be that the pines dry and ameliorate the soil, destroying the coarse grass and brambles which frequently choke and injure oaks; and that no mending over is necessary, as scarcely an oak so planted is found to fail."

Thus much the English planters have discovered by patient experiment, and, for aught I know, they have taken out a patent for it; but they appear not to have discovered that it was discovered before, and that they are merely adopting the method of Nature, which she long ago made patent to all. She is all the while planting the oaks amid the pines without our knowledge, and at last, instead of government officers, we send a party of woodchoppers to cut down the pines, and so rescue an oak forest, at which we wonder as if it had dropped from the skies.

As I walk amid hickories, even in August, I hear the sound of green pignuts falling from time to time, cut off by the chickaree over my head. In the fall, I notice on the ground, either within or in the neighborhood of oak woods, on all sides of the town, stout oak twigs three or four inches long, bearing half a dozen empty acorn-cups, which twigs have been gnawed off by squirrels, on both sides of the nuts, in order to make them more portable. The jays scream and the red squirrels scold while you are clubbing and shaking the chestnut trees, for they are there on the same errand, and two of a trade never agree. I frequently see a red or gray squirrel cast down a green chestnut bur, as I am going through the woods, and I used to think, sometimes, that they were cast at me. In fact, they are so busy about it, in the midst of the chestnut season, that you cannot stand long in the woods without hearing one fall. A sportsman told me that he had, the day before,—that was in the middle of October,—seen a green chestnut bur dropped on our great river meadow, fifty rods from the nearest wood, and much further from the nearest chestnut tree, and he could not tell how it came there. Occasionally, when chestnutting in midwinter, I find thirty or forty nuts in a pile, left in its gallery, just under the leaves, by the common wood mouse (*Mus leucopus*).

But especially, in the winter, the extent to which this transportation and planting of nuts is carried on is made apparent by the snow. In almost every wood, you will see where the red or gray squirrels have pawed down through the snow in a hundred places, sometimes two feet deep, and almost always directly to a nut or a pine cone, as directly as if they had started from it and bored upward,—which you and I could not have done. It would be difficult for us to find one before the snow falls. Commonly, no doubt, they had deposited them there in the fall. You wonder if they remember the localities, or discover them by the scent. The red squirrel commonly has its winter abode in the earth under a thicket of evergreens, frequently under a small clump of evergreens in the midst of a deciduous wood. If there are any nut trees which still retain their nuts standing at a distance without the wood, their paths often lead directly to and from them. We therefore need not suppose an oak standing here and there *in* the wood in order to seed it, but if a few stand within twenty or thirty rods of it, it is sufficient.

I think that I may venture to say that every white pine cone that falls to the earth naturally in this town, before opening and losing its seeds, and almost every pitch pine one that falls at all, is cut off by a squirrel, and they begin to pluck them long before they are ripe, so that when the crop of white pine cones is a small one, as it commonly is, they cut off thus almost every one of these before it fairly ripens. I think, moreover, that their design, if I may so speak, in cutting them off green, is, partly, to prevent their opening and losing their seeds, for these are the ones for which they dig through the snow, and the only white pine cones which contain anything then. I have counted in one heap, within a diameter of four feet, the cores of 239 pitch pine cones which had been cut off and stripped by the red squirrel the previous winter.

The nuts thus left on the surface, or buried just beneath it, are placed in the most favorable circumstances for germinating. I have sometimes wondered how those which merely fell on the surface of the earth got planted; but, by the end of December, I find the chestnut of the same year partially mixed with the mould, as it were, under the decaying and mouldy leaves, where there is all the moisture and manure they want, for the nuts fall fast. In a plentiful year, a large proportion of the nuts are thus covered loosely an inch deep, and are, of course, somewhat concealed from squirrels. One winter, when the crop had been abundant, I got, with the aid of a rake, many quarts of these nuts as late as the tenth of January, and though some bought at the store the same day were more than half of them mouldy, I did not find a single mouldy one among these which I picked from under the wet and mouldy leaves, where they had been snowed on once or twice. Nature knows how to pack them best. They were still plump and tender. Apparently, they do not heat there, though wet. In the spring they were all sprouting.

Loudon says that "when the nut [of the common walnut of Europe] is to be preserved through the winter for the purpose of planting in the following spring, it should be laid in a rot-heap, as soon as gathered, with the husk on, and the heap should be turned over frequently in the course of the winter."

Here, again, he is stealing Nature's "thunder." How can a poor mortal do otherwise? for it is she that finds fingers to steal with, and the treasure to be stolen. In the planting of the seeds of most trees, the best gardeners do no more than follow Nature, though they may not know it. Generally, both large and small ones are most sure to germinate, and succeed best, when only beaten into the earth with the back of a spade, and then covered with leaves or straw. These results to which planters have arrived remind us of the experience of Kane and his companions at the north, who, when learning to live in that climate, were surprised to find themselves steadily adopting the customs of the natives, simply becoming Esquimaux. So, when we experiment in planting forests, we find ourselves at last doing as Nature does. Would it not be well to consult with Nature in the outset? for she is the most extensive and experienced planter of us all, not excepting the Dukes of Athol.

In short, they who have not attended particularly to this subject are but little aware to what an extent quadrupeds and birds are employed, especially in the fall, in collecting, and so disseminating and planting, the seeds of trees. It is the almost constant employment of the squirrels at that season, and you rarely meet with one that has not a nut in its mouth, or is not just going to get one. One squirrel-hunter of this town told me that he knew of a walnut tree which bore particularly good nuts, but that on going to gather them one fall, he found that he had been anticipated by a family of a dozen red squirrels. He took out of the tree, which was hollow, one bushel and three pecks by measurement, without the husks, and they supplied him and his family for the winter. It would be easy to multiply instances of this kind. How commonly in the fall you see the cheek-pouches of the striped squirrel distended by a quantity of nuts! This species gets its scientific name, *Tamias*, or the steward, from its habit of storing up nuts and other seeds. Look under a nut tree a month after the nuts have fallen, and see what proportion of sound nuts to the abortive ones and shells you will find ordinarily. They have been already eaten, or dispersed far and wide. The ground looks like a platform before a grocery, where the gossips of the village sit to crack nuts and less savory jokes. You have come, you would say, after the feast was over, and are presented with the shells only.

Occasionally, when threading the woods in the fall, you will hear a sound as if some one had broken a twig, and, looking up, see a jay pecking at an acorn, or you will see a flock of them at once about it, in the top of an oak, and hear them break them off. They then fly to a suitable limb, and placing the acorn under one foot, hammer away at it busily, making a sound like a woodpecker's tapping, looking round from time to time to see if any foe is approaching, and soon reach the meat, and nibble at it, holding up their heads to swallow, while they hold the remainder very firmly with their claws. Nevertheless it often drops to the ground before the bird has done with it. I can confirm what William Bartram wrote to Wilson, the ornithologist, that "the jay is one of the most useful agents in the economy of nature, for disseminating forest trees and other nuciferous and hard-seeded vegetables on which they feed. Their chief employment during the autumnal season is foraging to supply their winter stores. In performing this necessary duty they drop abundance of seed in their flight over fields, hedges, and by fences, where they alight to deposit them in the post-holes, etc. It is remarkable what numbers of young trees rise up in fields and pastures after a wet winter and spring. These birds alone are capable, in a few years' time, to replant all the cleared lands."

I have noticed that squirrels also frequently drop their nuts in open land, which will still further account for the oaks and walnuts which spring up in pastures, for, depend on it, every new tree comes from a seed. When I examine the little oaks, one or two years old, in such places, I invariably find the empty acorn from which they sprung.

So far from the seed having lain dormant in the soil since oaks grew there before, as many believe, it is well known that it is difficult to preserve the vitality of acorns long enough to transport them to Europe; and it is recommended in Loudon's "Arboretum," as the safest course, to sprout them in pots on the voyage. The same authority states that "very few acorns of any species will germinate after having been kept a year," that beech mast "only retains its vital properties one year," and the black walnut "seldom more than six months after it has ripened." I have frequently found that in November almost every acorn left on the ground had sprouted or decayed. What with frost, drouth, moisture, and worms, the greater part are soon destroyed. Yet it is stated by one botanical writer that "acorns that have lain for centuries, on being ploughed up, have soon vegetated."

Mr. George B. Emerson, in his valuable Report on the Trees and Shrubs of this State, says of the pines: "The tenacity of life of the seeds is remarkable. They will remain for many years unchanged in the ground, protected by the coolness and deep shade of the forest above them. But when the forest is removed, and the warmth of the sun admitted, they immediately vegetate." Since he does not tell us on what observation his remark is founded, I must doubt its truth. Besides, the experience of nursery-men makes it the more questionable.

The stories of wheat raised from seed buried with an ancient Egyptian, and of raspberries raised from seed found in the stomach of a man in England, who is supposed to have died sixteen or seventeen hundred years ago, are generally discredited, simply because the evidence is not conclusive.

Several men of science, Dr. Carpenter among them, have used the statement that beach plums sprang up in sand which was dug up forty miles inland in Maine, to prove that the seed had lain there a very long time, and some have inferred that the coast has receded so far. But it seems to me necessary to their argument to show, first, that beach plums grow only on a beach. They are not uncommon here, which is about half that distance from the shore; and I remember a dense patch a few miles north of us, twenty-five miles inland, from which the fruit was annually carried to market. How much further inland they grow, I know not. Dr. Charles T. Jackson speaks of finding "beach plums" (perhaps they were this kind) more than one hundred miles inland in Maine.

It chances that similar objections lie against all the more notorious instances of the kind on record.

Yet I am prepared to believe that some seeds, especially small ones, may retain their vitality for centuries under favorable circumstances. In the spring of 1859, the old Hunt house, so called, in this town, whose chimney bore the date 1703, was taken down. This stood on land which belonged to John Winthrop, the first governor of Massachusetts, and a part of the house was evidently much older than the above date, and belonged to the Winthrop family. For many years I have ransacked this neighborhood for plants, and I consider myself familiar with its productions. Thinking of the seeds which are said to be sometimes dug up at an unusual depth in the earth, and thus to reproduce long extinct plants, it occurred to me last fall that some new or rare plants might have sprung up in the cellar of this house, which had been covered from the light so long. Searching there on the 22nd of September, I found, among other rank weeds, a species of nettle (*Urtica urens*) which I had not found before; dill, which I had not seen growing spontaneously; the Jerusalem oak (*Chenopodium Botrys*), which I had seen wild in but one place; black nightshade (*Solanum nigrum*), which is quite rare hereabouts, and common tobacco, which, though it was often cultivated here in the last century, has for fifty years been an unknown plant in this town, and a few months before this not even I had heard that one man, in the north part of the town, was cultivating a few plants for his own use. I have no doubt that some or all of these plants sprang from seeds which had long been buried under or about that house, and that that tobacco is an additional evidence that the plant was formerly cultivated here. The cellar has been filled up this year, and four of those plants, including the tobacco, are now again extinct in that locality.

It is true, I have shown that the animals consume a great part of the seeds of trees, and so, at least, effectually prevent their becoming trees; but in all these cases, as I have said, the consumer is compelled to be at the same time the disperser and planter, and this is the tax which he pays to Nature. I think it is Linnæus who says that while the swine is rooting for acorns he is planting acorns.

Though I do not believe that a plant will spring up where no seed has been, I have great faith in a seed,—a, to me, equally mysterious origin for it. Convince me that you have a seed there, and I am prepared to expect wonders. I shall even believe that the millennium is at hand, and that the reign of justice is about to commence, when the Patent Office, or Government, begins to distribute, and the people to plant, the seeds of these things.

In the spring of 1857 I planted six seeds sent to me from the Patent Office, and labeled, I think, *Poitrine jaune grosse*, large yellow squash. Two came up, and one bore a squash which weighed 123½ pounds, the other bore four, weighing together 186¼ pounds. Who would have believed that there was 310 pounds of *poitrine jaune grosse* in that corner of my garden? These seeds were the bait I used to catch it, my ferrets which I sent into its burrow, my brace of terriers which unearthed it. A little mysterious hoeing and manuring was all the *abracadabra presto-change* that I used, and lo! true to the label, they found for me 310 pounds of *poitrine jaune grosse* there, where it never was known to be, nor was before. These talismans had perchance sprung from America at first, and returned to it with unabated force. The big squash took a premium at your fair that fall, and I understood that the man who bought it, intended to sell the seeds for ten cents apiece. (Were they not cheap at that?) But I have more hounds of the same breed. I learn that one which I despatched to a distant town, true to its instincts, points to the large yellow squash there, too, where no hound ever found it before, as its ancestors did here and in France.

Other seeds I have which will find other things in that corner of my garden, in like fashion, almost any fruit you wish, every year for ages, until the crop more than fills the whole garden. You have but little more to do than throw up your cap for entertainment these American days. Perfect alchemists I keep who can transmute substances without end, and thus the corner of my garden is an inexhaustible treasure-chest. Here you can dig, not gold, but the value which gold merely represents; and there is no Signor Blitz about it. Yet farmers' sons will stare by the hour to see a juggler draw ribbons from his throat, though he tells them it is all deception. Surely, men love darkness rather than light.

A PLEA FOR
CAPTAIN JOHN BROWN

I.

Lecture by Henry D. Thoreau.*

I TRUST that you will pardon me for being here. I do not wish to force my thoughts upon you, but I feel forced myself. Little as I know of Captain Brown, I would fain do my part to correct the tone and the statements of the newspapers, and of my countrymen generally, respecting his character and actions. It costs us nothing to be just. We can at least express our sympathy with, and admiration of, him and his companions, and that is what I now propose to do.

First, as to his history. I will endeavor to omit, as much as possible, what you have already read. I need not describe his person to you, for probably most of you have seen and will not soon forget him. I am told that his grandfather, John Brown, was an officer in the Revolution; that he himself was born in Connecticut about the beginning of this century, but early went with his father to Ohio. I heard him say that his father was a contractor who furnished beef to the army there, in the war of 1812; that he accompanied him to the camp, and assisted him in that employment, seeing a good deal of military life, more, perhaps, than if he had been a soldier, for he was often present at the councils of the officers. Especially, he learned by experience how armies are supplied and maintained in the field — a work which, he observed, re-

* A Plea for Captain John Brown; read to the citizens of Concord, Mass., Sunday evening, October 30, 1859; also as the Fifth Lecture of the Fraternity Course, in Boston, November 1.

Echoes of Harper's Ferry, edited by James Redpath (Boston, 1860)

A PLEA FOR CAPTAIN JOHN BROWN*

I trust that you will pardon me for being here. I do not wish to force my thoughts upon you, but I feel forced myself. Little as I know of Captain Brown, I would fain do my part to correct the tone and the statements of the newspapers, and of my countrymen generally, respecting his character and actions. It costs us nothing to be just. We can at least express our sympathy with, and admiration of, him and his companions, and that is what I now propose to do.

First, as to his history.

I will endeavor to omit, as much as possible, what you have already read. I need not describe his person to you, for probably most of you have seen and will not soon forget him. I am told that his grandfather, John Brown, was an officer in the Revolution; that he himself was born in Connecticut about the beginning of this century, but early went with his father to Ohio. I heard him say that his father was a contractor who furnished beef to the army there, in the war of 1812; that he accompanied him to the camp, and assisted him in that employment, seeing a good deal of military life, more, perhaps, than if he had been a soldier, for he was often present at the councils of the officers. Especially, he learned by experience how armies are supplied and maintained in the field—a work

*Read to the citizens of Concord, Mass., Sunday Evening, October 30, 1859. Also as the fifth lecture of the Fraternity Course in Boston, November 1; and at Worcester, November 3.

which, he observed, requires at least as much experience and skill as to lead them in battle. He said that few persons had any conception of the cost, even the pecuniary cost, of firing a single bullet in war. He saw enough, at any rate, to disgust him with a military life, indeed to excite in him a great abhorrence of it; so much so, that though he was tempted by the offer of some petty office in the army, when he was about eighteen, he not only declined that, but he also refused to train when warned, and was fined for it. He then resolved that he would never have anything to do with any war, unless it were a war for liberty.

When the troubles in Kansas began, he sent several of his sons thither to strengthen the party of the Free State men, fitting them out with such weapons as he had; telling them that if the troubles should increase, and there should be need of him, he would follow to assist them with his hand and counsel. This, as you all know, he soon after did; and it was through his agency, far more than any other's, that Kansas was made free.

For a part of his life he was a surveyor, and at one time he was engaged in wool-growing, and he went to Europe as an agent about that business. There, as every where, he had his eyes about him, and made many original observations. He said, for instance, that he saw why the soil of England was so rich, and that of Germany (I think it was) so poor, and he thought of writing to some of the crowned heads about it. It was because in England the peasantry live on the soil which they cultivate, but in Germany they are gathered into villages, at night. It is a pity that he did not make a book of his observations.

I should say that he was an old-fashioned man in his respect for the Constitution, and his faith in the permanence of this Union. Slavery he deemed to be wholly opposed to these, and he was its determined foe.

He was by descent and birth a New England farmer, a man of great common sense, deliberate and practical as that class is, and tenfold more so. He was like the best of those who stood at Concord Bridge once, on Lexington Common, and on Bunker Hill, only he was firmer and higher principled than any that I have chanced to hear of as there. It was no abolition lecturer that converted him. Ethan Allen and Stark, with whom he may in some respects be compared, were rangers in a lower and less important field. They could bravely face their country's foes, but he had the courage to face his country herself, when she was in the wrong. A Western writer says, to account for his escape from so many perils, that he was concealed under a "rural exterior;" as if, in that prairie land, a hero should, by good rights, wear a citizen's dress only.

He did not go to the college called Harvard, good old Alma Mater as she is. He was not fed on the pap that is there furnished. As he phrased it, "I know no more of grammar than one of your calves." But he went to the great university of the West, where he sedulously pursued the study of Liberty, for which he had early betrayed a fondness, and having taken many degrees, he finally commenced the public practice of Humanity in Kansas, as you all know. Such were *his humanities*, and not any study of grammar. He would have left a Greek accent slanting the wrong way, and righted up a falling man.

He was one of that class of whom we hear a great deal, but, for the most part, see nothing at all—the Puritans. It would be in vain to kill him. He died lately in the time of Cromwell, but he reappeared here. Why should he not? Some of the Puritan stock are said to have come over and settled in New England. They were a class that did something else than celebrate their forefathers' day, and eat parched corn in remembrance of that time. They were neither Democrats nor Republicans, but men of simple habits, straightforward, prayerful; not thinking much of rulers who did not fear God, not making many compromises, nor seeking after available candidates.

"In his camp," as one has recently written, and as I have myself heard him state, "he permitted no profanity; no man of loose morals was suffered to remain there, unless, indeed, as a prisoner of war. 'I would rather,' said he, 'have the small-pox, yellow fever, and cholera, all together in my camp, than a man without principle. . . . It is a mistake, sir, that our people make, when they think that bullies are the best fighters, or that they are the fit men to oppose these Southerners. Give me men of good principles,—God-fearing men,—men who respect themselves, and with a dozen of them I will oppose any hundred such men as these Buford ruffians.' " He said that if one offered himself to be a soldier under him, who was forward to tell what he could or would do, if he could only get sight of the enemy, he had but little confidence in him.

He was never able to find more than a score or so of recruits whom he would accept, and only about a dozen, among them his sons, in whom he had perfect faith. When he was here, some years ago, he showed to a few a little manuscript book,—his "orderly book" I think he called it,—containing the names of his company in Kansas, and the rules by which they bound themselves; and he stated that several of them had already sealed the contract with their blood. When some one remarked that, with the addition of a chaplain, it would have been a perfect Cromwellian troop, he observed that he would have been glad to add a chaplain to the list, if he could have found one who could fill that office worthily. It is easy enough to find one for the United States army. I believe that he had prayers in his camp morning and evening, nevertheless.

He was a man of Spartan habits, and at sixty was scrupulous about his diet at your table, excusing himself by saying that he must eat sparingly and fare hard, as became a soldier or one who was fitting himself for difficult enterprises, a life of exposure.

A man of rare common sense and directness of speech, as of action; a transcendentalist above all, a man of ideas and principles,—that was what distinguished him. Not yielding to a whim or transient impulse, but carrying out the purpose of a life. I noticed that he did not overstate any thing, but spoke within bounds. I remember, particularly, how, in his speech here, he referred to what his family had suffered in Kansas, without ever giving the least vent to his pent-up fire. It was a volcano with an ordinary chimney-flue. Also referring to the deeds of certain Border Ruffians, he said, rapidly paring away his speech, like an experienced soldier, keeping a reserve of force and meaning, "They had a perfect right to be hung." He was not in the least a rhetorician, was not talking to Buncombe or his constituents any where, had no need to invent any thing, but to tell the simple truth, and communicate his own resolution; therefore he appeared incomparably strong, and eloquence in Congress and elsewhere seemed to me at a discount. It was like the speeches of Cromwell compared with those of an ordinary king.

As for his tact and prudence, I will merely say, that at a time when scarcely a man from the Free States was able to reach Kansas by any direct route, at least without having his arms taken from him, he, carrying what imperfect guns and other weapons he could collect, openly and slowly drove an ox-cart through Missouri, apparently in the capacity of a surveyor, with his surveying compass exposed in it, and so passed unsuspected, and had ample opportunity to learn the designs of the enemy. For some time after his arrival he still followed the same profession. When, for instance, he saw a knot of the ruffians on the prairie, discussing, of course, the single topic which then occupied their minds, he would, perhaps, take his compass and one of his sons, and proceed to run an imaginary line right through the very spot on which that conclave had assembled, and when he came up to them, he would naturally pause and have some talk with them, learning their news, and, at last, all their plans perfectly; and having thus completed his real survey, he would resume his imaginary one, and run on his line till he was out of sight.

When I expressed surprise that he could live in Kansas at all, with a price set upon his head, and so large a number, including the authorities, exasperated against him, he accounted for it by saying, "It is perfectly well understood that I will not be taken." Much of the time for some years he has had to skulk in swamps, suffering from poverty and from sickness, which was the consequence of exposure, befriended only by Indians and a few whites. But though it might be known that he was lurking in a particular swamp, his foes commonly did not care to go in after him. He could even come out into a town where there were more Border Ruffians than Free State men, and transact some business, without delaying long, and yet not be molested; for said he, "No little handful of men were willing to undertake it, and a large body could not be got together in season."

As for his recent failure, we do not know the facts about it. It was evidently far from being a wild and desperate attempt. His enemy, Mr. Vallandigham, is compelled to say, that "it was among the best planned and executed conspiracies that ever failed."

Not to mention his other successes, was it a failure, or did it show a want of good management, to deliver from bondage a dozen human beings, and walk off with them by broad daylight, for weeks if not months, at a leisurely pace, through one State after another, for half the length of the North, conspicuous to all parties, with a price set upon his head, going into a court room on his way and telling what he had done, thus convincing Missouri that it was not profitable to try to hold slaves in his neighborhood?—and this, not because the government menials were lenient, but because they were afraid of him.

Yet he did not attribute his success, foolishly, to "his star," or to any magic. He said, truly, that the reason why such greatly superior numbers quailed before him, was, as one of his prisoners confessed, because they *lacked a cause*—a kind of armor which he and his party never lacked. When the time came, few men were found willing to lay down their lives in defence of what they knew to be wrong; they did not like that this should be their last act in this world.

But to make haste to *his* last act, and its effects.

The newspapers seem to ignore, or perhaps are really ignorant of the fact, that there are at least as many as two or three individuals to a town throughout the North, who think much as the present speaker does about him and his enterprise. I do not hesitate to say that they are an important and growing party. We aspire to be something more than stupid and timid chattels, pretending to read history and our bibles, but desecrating every house and every day we breathe in. Perhaps anxious politicians may prove that only seventeen white men and five negroes were concerned in the late enterprise, but their very anxiety to prove this might suggest to themselves that all is not told. Why do they still dodge the truth? They are so anxious because of a dim consciousness of the fact, which they do not distinctly face, that at least a million of the free inhabitants of the United States would have rejoiced if it had succeeded. They at most only criticise the tactics. Though we wear no crape, the thought of that man's position and probable fate is spoiling many a man's day here at the North for other thinking. If any one who has seen him here can pursue successfully any other train of thought, I do not know what he is made of. If there is any such who gets his usual allowance of sleep, I will warrant him to fatten easily under any circumstances which do not touch his body or purse. I put a piece of paper and a pencil under my pillow, and when I could not sleep, I wrote in the dark.

On the whole, my respect for my fellow-men, except as one may outweigh a million, is not being increased these days. I have noticed the cold-blooded way in which newspaper writers and men generally speak of this event, as if an ordinary malefactor, though one of unusual "pluck,"—as the Governor of Virginia is reported to have said, using the language of the cock-pit, "the gamest man he ever saw,"—had been caught, and were about to be hung. He was not dreaming of his foes when the governor thought he looked so brave. It turns what sweetness I have to gall, to hear, or hear of, the remarks of some of my neighbors. When we heard at first that he was dead, one of my townsmen observed that "he died as the fool dieth;" which, pardon me, for an instant suggested a likeness in him dying to my neighbor living. Others, craven-hearted, said disparagingly, that "he threw his life away," because he resisted the government. Which way have they thrown *their* lives, pray?—Such as would praise a man for attacking singly an ordinary band of thieves or murderers. I hear another ask, Yankee-like, "What will he gain by it?" as if he expected to fill his pockets by this enterprise. Such a one has no idea of gain but in this worldly sense. If it does not lead to a "surprise" party, if he does not get a new pair of boots, or a vote of thanks, it must be a failure. "But he won't gain any thing by it." Well, no, I don't suppose he could get four-and-sixpence a day for being hung, take the year round; but then he stands a chance to save a considerable part of his soul—and *such* a soul!—when *you* do not. No doubt you can get more in your market for a quart of milk than for a quart of blood, but that is not the market that heroes carry their blood to.

Such do not know that like the seed is the fruit, and that, in the moral world, when good seed is planted, good fruit is inevitable, and does not depend on our watering and cultivating; that when you plant, or bury, a hero in his field, a crop of heroes is sure to spring up. This is a seed of such force and vitality, that it does not ask our leave to germinate.

The momentary charge at Balaclava, in obedience to a blundering command, proving what a perfect machine the soldier is, has, properly enough, been celebrated by a poet laureate; but the steady, and for the most part successful charge of this man, for some years, against the legions of Slavery, in obedience to an infinitely higher command, is as much more memorable than that, as an intelligent and conscientious man is superior to a machine. Do you think that that will go unsung?

"Served him right"—"A dangerous man"—"He is undoubtedly insane." So they proceed to live their sane, and wise, and altogether admirable lives, reading their Plutarch a little, but chiefly pausing at that feat of Putnam, who was let down into a wolf's den; and in this wise they nourish themselves for brave and patriotic deeds some time or other. The Tract Society could afford to print that story of Putnam. You might open the district schools with the reading of it, for there is nothing about Slavery or the Church in it; unless it occurs to the reader that some pastors are *wolves* in sheep's clothing. "The American Board of Commissioners for Foreign Missions" even, might dare to protest against *that* wolf. I have heard of boards, and of American boards, but it chances that I never heard of this particular lumber till lately. And yet I hear of Northern men, women, and children, by families, buying a "life membership" in such societies as these;—a life-membership in the grave! You can get buried cheaper than that.

Our foes are in our midst and all about us. There is hardly a house but is divided against itself, for our foe is the all but universal woodenness of both head and heart, the want of vitality in man, which is the effect of our vice; and hence are begotten fear, superstition, bigotry, persecution, and slavery of all kinds. We are mere figure-heads upon a hulk, with livers in the place of hearts. The curse is the worship of idols, which at length changes the worshipper into a stone image himself; and the New Englander is just as much an idolater as the Hindoo. This man was an exception, for he did not set up even a political graven image between him and his God.

A church that can never have done with excommunicating Christ while it exists! Away with your broad and flat churches, and your narrow and tall churches! Take a step forward, and invent a new style of outhouses. Invent a salt that will save you, and defend our nostrils.

The modern Christian is a man who has consented to say all the prayers in the liturgy, provided you will let him go straight to bed and sleep quietly afterward. All his prayers begin with "Now I lay me down to sleep," and he is forever looking forward to the time when he shall go to his "*long* rest." He has consented to perform certain old established charities, too, after a fashion, but he does not wish to hear of any newfangled ones; he doesn't wish to have any supplementary articles added to the contract, to fit it to the present time. He shows the whites of his eyes on the Sabbath, and the blacks all the rest of the week. The evil is not merely a stagnation of blood, but a stagnation of spirit. Many, no doubt, are well disposed, but sluggish by constitution and by habit, and they cannot conceive of a man who is actuated by higher motives than they are. Accordingly they pronounce this man insane, for they know that *they* could never act as he does, as long as they are themselves.

We dream of foreign countries, of other times and races of men, placing them at a distance in history or space; but let some significant event like the present occur in our midst, and we discover, often, this distance and this strangeness between us and our nearest neighbors. *They* are our Austrias, and Chinas, and South Sea Islands. Our crowded society becomes well spaced all at once, clean and handsome to the eye, a city of magnificent distances. We discover why it was that we never got beyond compliments and surfaces with them before; we become aware of as many versts between us and them as there are between a wandering Tartar and a Chinese town. The thoughtful man becomes a hermit in the thoroughfares of the market-place. Impassable seas suddenly find their level between us, or dumb steppes stretch themselves out there. It is the difference of constitution, of intelligence, and faith, and not streams and mountains, that make the true and impassable boundaries between individuals and between states. None but the like-minded can come plenipotentiary to our court.

I read all the newspapers I could get within a week after this event, and I do not remember in them a single expression of sympathy for these men. I have since seen one noble statement, in a Boston paper, not editorial. Some voluminous sheets decided not to print the full report of Brown's words to the exclusion of other matter. It was as if a publisher should reject the manuscript of the New Testament, and print Wilson's last speech. The same journal which contained this pregnant news, was chiefly filled, in parallel columns, with the reports of the political conventions that were being held. But the descent to them was too steep. They should have been spared this contrast, been printed in an extra at least. To turn from the voices and deeds of earnest men to the *cackling* of political conventions! Office seekers and speech-makers, who do not so much as lay an honest egg, but wear their breasts bare upon an egg of chalk! Their great game is the game of straws, or rather that universal aboriginal game of the platter, at which the Indians cried *hub, bub!* Exclude the reports of religious and political conventions, and publish the words of a living man.

But I object not so much to what they have omitted as to what they have inserted. Even the *Liberator* called it "a misguided, wild, and apparently insane . . . effort." As for the herd of newspapers and magazines, I do not chance to know an editor in the country who will deliberately print anything which he knows will ultimately and permanently reduce the number of his subscribers. They do not believe that it would be expedient. How then can they print truth? If we do not say pleasant things, they argue, nobody will attend to us. And so they do like some travelling auctioneers, who sing an obscene song in order to draw a crowd around them. Republican editors, obliged to get their sentences ready for the morning edition, and accustomed to look at every thing by the twilight of politics, express no admiration, nor true sorrow even, but call these men "deluded fanatics"—"mistaken men"—"insane," or "crazed." It suggests what a *sane* set of editors we are blessed with, *not* "mistaken men;" who know very well on which side their bread is buttered, at least.

A man does a brave and humane deed, and at once, on all sides, we hear people and parties declaring, "I didn't do it, nor countenance *him* to do it, in any conceivable way. It can't be fairly inferred from my past career." I, for one, am not interested to hear you define your position. I don't know that I ever was, or ever shall be. I think it is mere egotism, or impertinent at this time. Ye needn't take so much pains to wash your skirts of him. No intelligent man will ever be convinced that he was any creature of yours. He went and came, as he himself informs us, "under the auspices of John Brown and nobody else." The Republican party does not perceive how many his *failure* will make to vote more correctly than they would have them. They have counted the votes of Pennsylvania &. Co., but they have not correctly counted Captain Brown's vote. He has taken the wind out of their sails, the little wind they had, and they may as well lie to and repair.

What though he did not belong to your clique! Though you may not approve of his method or his principles, recognize his magnanimity. Would you not like to claim kindredship with him in that, though in no other thing he is like, or likely, to you? Do you think that you would lose your reputation so? What you lost at the spile, you would gain at the bung.

If they do not mean all this, then they do not speak the truth, and say what they mean. They are simply at their old tricks still.

"It was always conceded to him," *says one who calls him crazy*, "that he was a conscientious man, very modest in his demeanor, apparently inoffensive, until the subject of Slavery was introduced, when he would exhibit a feeling of indignation unparalleled."

The slave-ship is on her way, crowded with its dying victims; new cargoes are being added in mid ocean; a small crew of slaveholders, countenanced by a large body of passengers, is smothering four millions under the hatches, and yet the politician asserts that the only proper way by which deliverance is to be obtained, is by "the quiet diffusion of the sentiments of humanity," without any "outbreak." As if the sentiments of humanity were ever found unaccompanied by its deeds, and you could disperse them, all finished to order, the pure article, as easily as water with a watering-pot, and so lay the dust. What is that that I hear cast overboard? The bodies of the dead that have found deliverance. That is the way we are "diffusing" humanity, and its sentiments with it.

Prominent and influential editors, accustomed to deal with politicians, men of an infinitely lower grade, say, in their ignorance, that he acted "on the principle of revenge." They do not know the man. They must enlarge themselves to conceive of him. I have no doubt that the time will come when they will begin to see him as he was. They have got to conceive of a man of faith and of religious principle, and not a politician or an Indian; of a man who did not wait till he was personally interfered with, or thwarted in some harmless business, before he gave his life to the cause of the oppressed.

If Walker may be considered the representative of the South, I wish I could say that Brown was the representative of the North. He was a superior man. He did not value his bodily life in comparison with ideal things. He did not recognize unjust human laws, but resisted them as he was bid. For once we are lifted out of the trivialness and dust of politics into the region of truth and manhood. No man in America has ever stood up so persistently and effectively for the dignity of human nature, knowing himself for a man, and the equal of any and all governments. In that sense he was the most American of us all. He needed no babbling lawyer, making false issues, to defend him. He was more than a match for all the judges that American voters, or office-holders of whatever grade, can create. He could not have been tried by a jury of his peers, because his peers did not exist. When a man stands up serenely against the condemnation and vengeance of mankind, rising above them literally *by a whole body*,—even though he were of late the vilest murderer, who has settled that matter with himself,—the spectacle is a sublime one,—didn't ye know it, ye Liberators, ye Tribunes, ye Republicans?—and we become criminal in comparison. Do yourselves the honor to recognize him. He needs none of your respect.

As for the Democratic journals, they are not human enough to affect me at all. I do not feel indignation at any thing they may say.

I am aware that I anticipate a little, that he was still, at the last accounts, alive in the hands of his foes; but that being the case, I have all along found myself thinking and speaking of him as physically dead.

I do not believe in erecting statues to those who still live in our hearts, whose bones have not yet crumbled in the earth around us, but I would rather see the statue of Captain Brown in the Massachusetts State-House yard, than that of any other man whom I know. I rejoice that I live in this age—that I am his contemporary.

What a contrast, when we turn to that political party which is so anxiously shuffling him and his plot out of its way, and looking around for some available slaveholder, perhaps, to be its candidate, at least for one who will execute the Fugitive Slave Law, and all those other unjust laws which he took up arms to annul!

Insane! A father and six sons, and one son-in-law, and several more men besides,—as many at least as twelve disciples,—all struck with insanity at once; while the sane tyrant holds with a firmer gripe than ever his four millions of slaves, and a thousand sane editors, his abettors, are saving their country and their bacon! Just as insane were his efforts in Kansas. Ask the tyrant who is his most dangerous foe, the sane man or the insane. Do the thousands who know him best, who have rejoiced at his deeds in Kansas, and have afforded him material aid there, think him insane? Such a use of this word is a mere trope with most who persist in using it, and I have no doubt that many of the rest have already in silence retracted their words.

Read his admirable answers to Mason and others. How they are dwarfed and defeated by the contrast! On the one side, half brutish, half timid questioning; on the other, truth, clear as lightning, crashing into their obscene temples. They are made to stand with Pilate, and Gessler, and the Inquisition. How ineffectual their speech and action! and what a void their silence! They are but helpless tools in this great work. It was no human power that gathered them about this preacher.

What have Massachusetts and the North sent a few *sane* representatives to Congress for, of late years?—to declare with effect what kind of sentiments? All their speeches put together and boiled down,—and probably they themselves will confess it,—do not match for manly directness and force, and for simple truth, the few casual remarks of crazy John Brown, on the floor of the Harper's Ferry engine house;—that man whom you are about to hang, to send to the other world, though not to represent *you* there. No, he was not our representative in any sense. He was too fair a specimen of a man to represent the like of us. Who, then, *were* his constituents? If you read his words understandingly you will find out. In his case there is no idle eloquence, no made, nor maiden speech, no compliments to the oppressor. Truth is his inspirer, and earnestness the polisher of his sentences. He could afford to lose his Sharps' rifles, while he retained his faculty of speech, a Sharps' rifle of infinitely surer and longer range.

And the *New York Herald* reports the conversation "*verbatim*"! It does not know of what undying words it is made the vehicle.

I have no respect for the penetration of any man who can read the report of that conversation, and still call the principal in it insane. It has the ring of a saner sanity than an ordinary discipline and habits of life, than an ordinary organization, secure. Take any sentence of it—"Any questions that I can honorably answer, I will; not otherwise. So far as I am myself concerned, I have told every thing truthfully. I value my word, sir." The few who talk about his vindictive spirit, while they really admire his heroism, have no test by which to detect a noble man, no amalgam to combine with his pure gold. They mix their own dross with it.

It is a relief to turn from these slanders to the testimony of his more truthful, but frightened, jailers and hangmen. Governor Wise speaks far more justly and appreciatingly of him than any Northern editor, or politician, or public personage, that I chance to have heard from. I know that you can afford to hear him again on this subject. He says: "They are themselves mistaken who take him to be a madman. . . . He is cool, collected, and indomitable, and it is but just to him to say, that he was humane to his prisoners. . . . And he inspired me with great trust in his integrity as a man of truth. He is a fanatic, vain and garrulous," (I leave that part to Mr. Wise) "but firm, truthful, and intelligent. His men, too, who survive, are like him. . . . Colonel Washington says that he was the coolest and firmest man he ever saw in defying danger and death. With one son dead by his side, and another shot through, he felt the pulse of his dying son with one hand, and held his rifle with the other, and commanded his men with the utmost composure, encouraging them to be firm, and to sell their lives as dear as they could. Of the three white prisoners, Brown, Stevens, and Coppoc, it was hard to say which was most firm. . . ."

Almost the first Northern men whom the slaveholder has learned to respect!

The testimony of Mr. Vallandigham, though less valuable, is of the same purport, that "it is vain to underrate either the man or his conspiracy. . . . He is the farthest possible remove from the ordinary ruffian, fanatic, or madman."

"All is quiet at Harper's Ferry," say the journals. What is the character of that calm which follows when the law and the slaveholder prevail? I regard this event as a touchstone designed to bring out, with glaring distinctness, the character of this government. We needed to be thus assisted to see it by the light of history. It needed to see itself. When a government puts forth its strength on the side of injustice, as ours to maintain Slavery and kill the liberators of the slave, it reveals itself a merely brute force, or worse, a demoniacal force. It is the head of the Plug Uglies. It is more manifest than ever that tyranny rules. I see this government to be effectually allied with France and Austria in oppressing mankind. There sits a tyrant holding fettered four millions of slaves; here comes their heroic liberator. This most hypocritical and diabolical government looks up from its seat on the gasping four millions, and inquires with an assumption of innocence, "What do you assault me for? Am I not an honest man? Cease agitation on this subject, or I will make a slave of you, too, or else hang you."

We talk about a *representative* government; but what a monster of a government is that where the noblest faculties of the mind, and the *whole* heart, are not *represented*. A semi-human tiger or ox, stalking over the earth, with its heart taken out and the top of its brain shot away. Heroes have fought well on their stumps when their legs were shot off, but I never heard of any good done by such a government as that.

The only government that I recognize,—and it matters not how few are at the head of it, or how small its army,—is that power that establishes justice in the land, never that which establishes injustice. What shall we think of a government to which all the truly brave and just men in the land are enemies, standing between it and those whom it oppresses? A government that pretends to be Christian and crucifies a million Christs every day!

Treason! Where does such treason take its rise? I cannot help thinking of you as you deserve, ye governments. Can you dry up the fountains of thought? High treason, when it is resistance to tyranny here below, has its origin in, and is first committed by the power that makes and forever recreates man. When you have caught and hung all these human rebels, you have accomplished nothing but your own guilt, for you have not struck at the fountain head. You presume to contend with a foe against whom West Point cadets and rifled cannon *point* not. Can all the art of the cannon-founder tempt matter to turn against its maker? Is the form in which the founder thinks he casts it more essential than the constitution of it and of himself?

The United States have a coffle of four millions of slaves. They are determined to keep them in this condition; and Massachusetts is one of the confederated overseers to prevent their escape. Such are not all the inhabitants of Massachusetts, but such are they who rule and are obeyed here. It was Massachusetts, as well as Virginia, that put down this insurrection at Harper's Ferry. She sent the marines there, and she will have to pay the penalty of her sin.

Suppose that there is a society in this State that out of its own purse and magnanimity saves all the fugitive slaves that run to us, and protects our colored fellow-citizens, and leaves the other work to the Government, so-called. Is not that government fast losing its occupation, and becoming contemptible to mankind? If private men are obliged to perform the offices of government, to protect the weak and dispense justice, then the government becomes only a hired man, or clerk, to perform menial or indifferent services. Of course, that is but the shadow of a government whose existence necessitates a Vigilant Committee. What should we think of the oriental Cadi even, behind whom worked in secret a Vigilant Committee? But such is the character of our Northern States generally; each has its Vigilant Committee. And, to a certain extent, these crazy governments recognize and accept this relation. They say, virtually, "We'll be glad to work for you on these terms, only don't make a noise about it." And thus the government, its salary being insured, withdraws into the back shop, taking the constitution with it, and bestows most of its labor on repairing that. When I hear it at work sometimes, as I go by, it reminds me, at best, of those farmers who in winter contrive to turn a penny by following the coopering business. And what kind of spirit is their barrel made to hold? They speculate in stocks, and bore holes in mountains, but they are not competent to lay out even a decent highway. The only *free* road, the Underground Railroad, is owned and managed by the Vigilant Committee. *They* have tunnelled under the whole breadth of the land. Such a government is losing its power and respectability as surely as water runs out of a leaky vessel, and is held by one that can contain it.

I hear many condemn these men because they were so few. When were the good and the brave ever in a majority? Would you have had him wait till that time came?—till you and I came over to him? The very fact that he had no rabble or troop of hirelings about him would alone distinguish him from ordinary heroes. His company was small indeed, because few could be found worthy to pass muster. Each one who there laid down his life for the poor and oppressed, was a picked man, called out of many thousands, if not millions; apparently a man of principle, of rare courage and devoted humanity, ready to sacrifice his life at any moment for the benefit of his fellow man. It may be doubted if there were as many more their equals in these respects in all the country—I speak of his followers only—for their leader, no doubt, scoured the land far and wide, seeking to swell his troop. These alone were ready to step between the oppressor and the oppressed. Surely, they were the very best men you could select to be hung. That was the greatest compliment which this country could pay them. They were ripe for her gallows. She has tried a long time, she has hung a good many, but never found the right one before.

When I think of him, and his six sons, and his son in law,—not to enumerate the others,—enlisted for this fight; proceeding coolly, reverently, humanely to work, for months if not years, sleeping and waking upon it, summering and wintering the thought, without expecting any reward but a good conscience, while almost all America stood ranked on the other side, I say again that it affects me as a sublime spectacle. If he had had any journal advocating "*his cause*," any organ as the phrase is, monotonously and wearisomely playing the same old tune, and then passing round the hat, it would have been fatal to his efficiency. If he had acted in any way so as to be let alone by the government, he might have been suspected. It was the fact that the tyrant must give place to him, or he to the tyrant, that distinguished him from all the reformers of the day that I know.

It was his peculiar doctrine that a man has a perfect right to interfere by force with the slaveholder, in order to rescue the slave. I agree with him. They who are continually shocked by slavery have some right to be shocked by the violent death of the slaveholder, but no others. Such will be more shocked by his life than by his death. I shall not be forward to think him mistaken in his method who quickest succeeds to liberate the slave. I speak for the slave when I say, that I prefer the philanthropy of Captain Brown to that philanthropy which neither shoots me nor liberates me. At any rate, I do not think it is quite sane for one to spend his whole life in talking or writing about this matter, unless he is continuously inspired, and I have not done so. A man may have other affairs to attend to. I do not wish to kill nor to be killed, but I can foresee circumstances in which both these things would be by me unavoidable. We preserve the so-called "peace" of our community by deeds of petty violence every day. Look at the policeman's billy and hand cuffs! Look at the jail! Look at the gallows! Look at the chaplain of the regiment! We are hoping only to live safely on the outskirts of *this* provisional army. So we defend ourselves and our hen roosts, and maintain slavery. I know that the mass of my countrymen think that the only righteous use that can be made of Sharps' rifles and revolvers is to fight duels with them, when we are insulted by other nations, or to hunt Indians, or shoot fugitive slaves with them, or the like. I think that for once the Sharps' rifles and the revolvers were employed in a righteous cause. The tools were in the hands of one who could use them.

The same indignation that is said to have cleared the temple once will clear it again. The question is not about the weapon, but the spirit in which you use it. No man has appeared in America as yet who loved his fellow man so well, and treated him so tenderly. He lived for him. He took up his life and he laid it down for him. What sort of violence is that which is encouraged, not by soldiers but by peaceable citizens, not so much by lay-men as by ministers of the gospel, not so much by the fighting sects as by the Quakers, and not so much by Quaker men as by Quaker women?

This event advertises me that there is such a fact as death—the possibility of a man's dying. It seems as if no man had ever died in America before, for in order to die you must first have lived. I don't believe in the hearses and palls and funerals that they have had. There was no death in the case, because there had been no life; they merely rotted or sloughed off, pretty much as they had rotted or sloughed along. No temple's *vail* was rent, only a hole dug somewhere. Let the dead bury their dead. The best of them fairly ran down like a clock. Franklin—Washington—they were let off without dying; they were merely missing one day. I hear a good many pretend that they are going to die;—or that they have died for aught that I know. Nonsense! I'll defy them to do it. They haven't got life enough in them. They'll deliquesce like fungi, and keep a hundred eulogists mopping the spot where they left off. Only half a dozen or so have died since the world began. Do you think that you are going to die, sir? No! there's no hope of you. You haven't got your lesson yet. You've got to stay after school. We make a needless ado about capital punishment—taking lives, when there is no life to take. *Memento mori!* We don't understand that sublime sentence which some worthy got sculptured on his gravestone once. We've interpreted it in a grovelling and snivelling sense; we've wholly forgotten how to die.

But be sure you do die, nevertheless. Do your work, and finish it. If you know how to begin, you will know when to end.

These men, in teaching us how to die, have at the same time taught us how to live. If this man's acts and words do not create a revival, it will be the severest possible satire on the acts and words that do. It is the best news that America has ever heard. It has already quickened the feeble pulse of the North, and infused more and more generous blood into her veins and heart, than any number of years of what is called commercial and political prosperity could. How many a man who was lately contemplating suicide has now something to live for!

One writer says that Brown's peculiar monomania made him to be "dreaded by the Missourians as a supernatural being." Sure enough, a hero in the midst of us cowards is always so dreaded. He is just that thing. He shows himself superior to nature. He has a spark of divinity in him.

> "Unless above himself he can
> Erect himself, how poor a thing is man!"

Newspaper editors argue also that it is a proof of his *insanity* that he thought he was appointed to do this work which he did—that he did not suspect himself for a moment! They talk as if it were impossible that a man could be "divinely appointed" in these days to do any work whatever; as if vows and religion were out of date as connected with any man's daily work,—as if the agent to abolish Slavery could only be somebody appointed by the President, or by some political party. They talk as if a man's death were a failure, and his continued life, be it of whatever character, were a success.

When I reflect to what a cause this man devoted himself, and how religiously, and then reflect to what cause his judges and all who condemn him so angrily and fluently devote themselves, I see that they are as far apart as the heavens and earth are asunder.

The amount of it is, our "*leading men*" are a harmless kind of folk, and they know *well enough* that *they* were not divinely appointed, but elected by the votes of their party.

Who is it whose safety requires that Captain Brown be hung? Is it indispensable to any Northern man? Is there no resource but to cast these men also to the Minotaur? If you do not wish it say so distinctly. While these things are being done, beauty stands veiled and music is a screeching lie. Think of him—of his rare qualities! such a man as it takes ages to make, and ages to understand; no mock hero, nor the representative of any party. A man such as the sun may not rise upon again in this benighted land. To whose making went the costliest material, the finest adamant; sent to be the redeemer of those in captivity. And the only use to which you can put him is to hang him at the end of a rope! You who pretend to care for Christ crucified, consider what you are about to do to him who offered himself to be the savior of four millions of men.

Any man knows when he is justified, and all the wits in the world cannot enlighten him on that point. The murderer always knows that he is justly punished; but when a government takes the life of a man without the consent of his conscience, it is an audacious government, and is taking a step towards its own dissolution. Is it not possible that an individual may be right and a government wrong? Are laws to be enforced simply because they were made? or declared by any number of men to be good, if they are *not* good? Is there any necessity for a man's being a tool to perform a deed of which his better nature disapproves? Is it the intention of law-makers that *good* men shall be hung ever? Are judges to interpret the law according to the letter, and not the spirit? What right have *you* to enter into a compact with yourself that you *will* do thus or so, against the light within you? Is it for *you* to *make up* your mind—to form any resolution whatever—and not accept the convictions that are forced upon you, and which ever pass your understanding? I do not believe in lawyers, in that mode of attacking or defending a man, because you descend to meet the judge on his own ground, and, in cases of the highest importance, it is of no consequence whether a man breaks a human law or not. Let lawyers decide trivial cases. Business men may arrange that among themselves. If they were the interpreters of the everlasting laws which rightfully bind man, that would be another thing. A counterfeiting law-factory, standing half in a slave land and half in a free! What kind of laws for free men can you expect from that?

I am here to plead his cause with you. I plead not for his life, but for his character—his immortal life; and so it becomes your cause wholly, and is not his in the least. Some eighteen hundred years ago Christ was crucified; this morning, perchance, Captain Brown was hung. These are the two ends of a chain which is not without its links. He is not Old Brown any longer; he is an Angel of Light.

I see now that it was necessary that the bravest and humanest man in all the country should be hung. Perhaps he saw it himself. I *almost fear* that I may yet hear of his deliverance, doubting if a prolonged life, if *any* life, can do as much good as his death.

"Misguided"! "Garrulous"! "Insane"! "Vindictive"! So ye write in your easy chairs, and thus he wounded responds from the floor of the Armory, clear as a cloudless sky, true as the voice of nature is: "No man sent me here; it was my own prompting and that of my Maker. I acknowledge no master in human form."

And in what a sweet and noble strain he proceeds, addressing his captors, who stand over him: "I think, my friends, you are guilty of a great wrong against God and humanity, and it would be perfectly right for any one to interfere with you so far as to free those you wilfully and wickedly hold in bondage."

And referring to his movement: "It is, in my opinion, the greatest service a man can render to God."

"I pity the poor in bondage that have none to help them; that is why I am here; not to gratify any personal animosity, revenge, or vindictive spirit. It is my sympathy with the oppressed and the wronged, that are as good as you, and as precious in the sight of God."

You don't know your testament when you see it.

"I want you to understand that I respect the rights of the poorest and weakest of colored people, oppressed by the slave power, just as much as I do those of the most wealthy and powerful."

"I wish to say, furthermore, that you had better, all you people at the South, prepare yourselves for a settlement of that question, that must come up for settlement sooner than you are prepared for it. The sooner you are prepared the better. You may dispose of me very easily. I am nearly disposed of now; but this question is still to be settled—this negro question, I mean; the end of that is not yet."

I foresee the time when the painter will paint that scene, no longer going to Rome for a subject; the poet will sing it; the historian record it; and, with the Landing of the Pilgrims and the Declaration of Independence, it will be the ornament of some future national gallery, when at least the present form of Slavery shall be no more here. We shall then be at liberty to weep for Captain Brown. Then, and not till then, we will take our revenge.

THE LAST DAYS OF JOHN BROWN

Even the mistake of remaining in the arsenal after the first blow was struck, may prove the key to future success. The tender regard which the dear old man evinced for the lives of the tyrants—and which should have secured him his life—will not be imitated by future insurgents. Slaveholders are as insensible to magnanimity as to justice, and the measure they mete must be meted to them again. My heart is with you.

Very truly, FRED'K DOUGLASS.

In conclusion, Mr. President, I desire to read the manuscript I hold. It was handed to me at Concord, with a note, while on my way here, by one whom all must honor who know him—Henry D. Thoreau. Of a fearless, truthful soul, living near to Nature, with ear attuned to catch her simplest and most subtle thought, and heart willing to interpret them to his eager brain, he often speaks undisguised, in most nervous Saxon, the judgment upon great events which others, either timid or powerless of speech, so long to hear expressed. So it was last fall. Mr. Thoreau's voice was the first which broke the disgraceful silence or hushed the senseless babble with which the grandest deed of our time was met. Herein, Mr. Thoreau gives us some recollections of that eventful period :—

John Brown's career for the last six weeks of his life was meteor-like, flashing through the darkness in which we live. I know of nothing so miraculous in our history.

If any person,. in a lecture or conversation at that time, cited any ancient example of heroïsm, such as Cato or Tell or Winkelried, passing over the recent deeds and words of Brown, it was felt by any intelligent audience of Northern men to be tame and inexcusably far-fetched.

For my own part, I commonly attend more to nature than to man, but any affecting human event may blind our eyes to natural objects. I was so absorbed in him as to be surprised whenever I detected the routine of the natural world surviving still, or met persons going about their affairs indifferent. It appeared strange to me that the 'little dipper' should be still diving quietly in the river, as of yore; and it suggested that this bird might continue to dive here when Concord should be no more.

I felt that he, a prisoner in the midst of his enemies, and under sentence of death, if consulted as to his next step or resource, could answer more wisely than all his countrymen beside. He best understood his position; he contemplated it most calmly. Comparatively, all other men, North and South, were beside themselves. Our thoughts could not revert to any greater or wiser or better man with whom to contrast him, for he, then and there, was above them all. The man this country was about to hang appeared the greatest and best in it.

A portion of a page of *The Liberator* for July 27, 1860. A celebration of John Brown's life had been held at his graveside in North Elba, New York, on July 4, 1860. The organizers asked many people to come, and several of those who could not—including Thomas Wentworth Higginson, James Redpath, Frederick Douglass, and Thoreau—sent testimonials to be read aloud. This fragment shows the end of Douglass's message and the beginning of Thoreau's.

THE LAST DAYS OF JOHN BROWN

John Brown's career for the last six weeks of his life was meteor-like, flashing through the darkness in which we live. I know of nothing so miraculous in our history.

If any person, in a lecture or conversation at that time, cited any ancient example of heroism, such as Cato or Tell or Winkelried, passing over the recent deeds and words of Brown, it was felt by any intelligent audience of Northern men to be tame and inexcusably far-fetched.

For my own part, I commonly attend more to nature than to man, but any affecting human event may blind our eyes to natural objects. I was so absorbed in him as to be surprised whenever I detected the routine of the natural world surviving still, or met persons going about their affairs indifferent. It appeared strange to me that the "little dipper" should be still diving quietly in the river, as of yore; and it suggested that this bird might continue to dive here when Concord should be no more.

I felt that he, a prisoner in the midst of his enemies, and under sentence of death, if consulted as to his next step or resource, could answer more wisely than all his countrymen beside. He best understood his position; he contemplated it most calmly. Comparatively, all other men, North and South, were beside themselves. Our thoughts could not revert to any greater or wiser or better man with whom to contrast him, for he, then and there, was above them all. The man this country was about to hang appeared the greatest and best in it.

Years were not required for a revolution of public opinion; days, nay, hours, produced marked changes in this case. Fifty who were ready to say on going into our meeting in honor of him in Concord, that he ought to be hung, would not say it when they came out. They heard his words read, they saw the earnest faces of the congregation; and perhaps they joined at last in singing the hymn in his praise.

The order of instructors was reversed. I heard that one preacher, who at first was shocked and stood aloof, felt obliged at last, after he was hung, to make him the subject of a sermon, in which, to some extent, he eulogized the man, but said that his act was a failure. An influential class-teacher thought it necessary, after the services, to tell his grown-up pupils, that at first he thought as the preacher did then, but now he thought that John Brown was right. But it was understood that his pupils were as much ahead of the teacher, as he was ahead of the priest; and I know for a certainty, that very little boys at home had already asked their parents, in a tone of surprise, why God did not interfere to save him. In each case, the constituted teachers were only half conscious that they were not *leading*, but being *dragged*, with some loss of time and power.

The more conscientious preachers, the Bible men, they who talk about principle, and doing to others as you would that they should do unto you,—how could they fail to recognize him, by far the greatest preacher of them all, with the Bible in his life and in his acts, the embodiment of principle, who actually carried out the golden rule? All whose moral sense had been aroused, who had a calling from on high to preach, sided with him. What confessions he extracted from the cold and conservative! It is remarkable, but on the whole it is well, that it did not prove the occasion for a new sect of *Brownites* being formed in our midst.

They, whether within the Church or out of it, who adhere to the spirit and let go the letter, and are accordingly called infidel, were as usual foremost to recognize him. Men have been hung in the South before for attempting to rescue slaves, and the North was not much stirred by it. Whence, then, this wonderful difference? We were not so sure of *their* devotion to principle. We made a subtle distinction, forgot human laws, and did homage to an idea. The North, I mean the *living* North, was suddenly all transcendental. It went behind the human law, it went behind the apparent failure, and recognized eternal justice and glory. Commonly, men live according to a formula, and are satisfied if the order of law is observed, but in this instance they, to some extent, returned to original perceptions, and there was a slight revival of old religion. They saw that what was called order was confusion, what was called justice, injustice, and that the best was deemed the worst. This attitude suggested a more intelligent and generous spirit than that which actuated our forefathers, and the possibility, in the course of ages, of a revolution in behalf of another and an oppressed people.

Most Northern men, and a few Southern ones, were wonderfully stirred by Brown's behavior and words. They saw and felt that they were heroic and noble, and that there had been nothing quite equal to them in their kind in this country, or in the recent history of the world. But the minority were unmoved by them. They were only surprised and provoked by the attitude of their neighbors. They saw that Brown was Brave, and that he believed that he had done right, but they did not detect any further peculiarity in him. Not being accustomed to make fine distinctions, or to appreciate magnanimity, they read his letters and speeches as if they read them not. They were not aware when they approached a heroic statement—they did not know when they *burned*. They did not feel that he spoke with authority, and hence they only remembered that the *law* must be executed. They remembered the old formula, but did not hear the new revelation. The man who does not recognize in Brown's words a wisdom and nobleness, and therefore an authority, superior to our laws, is a modern Democrat. This is the test by which to discover him. He is not wilfully but constitutionally blind on this side, and he is consistent with himself. Such has been his past life; no doubt of it. In like manner he has read history and his Bible, and he accepts, or seems to accept, the last only as an established formula, and not because he has been convicted by it. You will not find kindred sentiments in his common-place book, if he has one.

When a noble deed is done, who is likely to appreciate it? They who are noble themselves. I was not surprised that certain of my neighbors spoke of John Brown as an ordinary felon, for who are they? They have either much flesh, or much office, or much coarseness of some kind. They are not etherial natures in any sense. The dark qualities predominate in them. Several of them are decidedly pachydermatous. I say it in sorrow, not in anger. How can a man behold the light, who has no answering inward light? They are true to their *right*, but when they look this way they *see* nothing, they are blind. For the children of the light to contend with them is as if there should be a contest between eagles and owls. Show me a man who feels bitterly toward John Brown, and let me hear what noble verse he can repeat. He'll be as dumb as if his lips were stone.

It is not every man who can be a Christian, even in a very moderate sense, whatever education you give him. It is a matter of constitution and temperament, after all. He may have to be born again many times. I have known many a man who pretended to be a Christian, in whom it was ridiculous, for he had no genius for it. It is not every man who can be a freeman, even.

Editors persevered for a good while in saying that Brown was crazy: but at last they said only that it was "a crazy scheme," and the only evidence brought to prove it was that it cost him his life. I have no doubt that if he had gone with five thousand men, liberated a thousand slaves, killed a hundred or two slaveholders, and had as many more killed on his own side, but not lost his own life, these same editors would have called it by a more respectable name. Yet he has been far more successful than that. He has liberated many thousands of slaves, both North and South. They seem to have known nothing about living or dying for a principle. They all called him crazy then; who calls him crazy now?

All through the excitement occasioned by his remarkable attempt and subsequent behavior, the Massachusetts Legislature, not taking any steps for the defence of her citizens who were likely to be carried to Virginia as witnesses and exposed to the violence of a slaveholding mob, was wholly absorbed in a liquor-agency question, and indulging in poor jokes on the word "extension." Bad spirits occupied their thoughts. I am sure that no statesman up to the occasion could have attended to that question at all at that time,—a very vulgar question to attend to at any time.

When I looked into a liturgy of the Church of England, printed near the end of the last century, in order to find a service applicable to the case of Brown, I found that the only martyr recognized and provided for by it was King Charles the First, an eminent scamp. Of all the inhabitants of England and of the world, he was the only one according to this authority, whom that church had made a martyr and saint of; and for more than a century it had celebrated his martyrdom, so called, by an annual service. What a satire on the Church is that!

Look not to legislatures and churches for your guidance, nor to any soulless, *incorporated* bodies, but to *inspirited* or inspired ones.

What avail all your scholarly accomplishments and learning, compared with wisdom and manhood? To omit his other behavior, see what a work this comparatively unread and unlettered man wrote within six weeks. Where is our professor of *belles lettres* or of logic and rhetoric, who can write so well? He wrote in prison, not a history of the world, like Raleigh, but an American book which I think will live longer than that. I do not know of such words, uttered under such circumstances, and so copiously withal, in Roman or English or any history. What a variety of themes he touched on in that short space! There are words in that letter to his wife, respecting the education of his daughters, which deserve to be framed and hung over every mantelpiece in the land. Compare this earnest wisdom with that of Poor Richard.

The death of Irving, which at any other time would have attracted universal attention, having occurred while these things were transpiring, went almost unobserved. I shall have to read of it in the biography of authors.

Literary gentlemen, editors and critics, think that they know how to write, because they have studied grammar and rhetoric; but they are egregiously mistaken. The *art* of composition is as simple as the discharge of a bullet from a rifle, and its master-pieces imply an infinitely greater force behind them. This unlettered man's speaking and writing are standard English. Some words and phrases deemed vulgarisms and Americanisms before, he has made standard American; such as *"It will pay."* It suggests that the one great rule of composition—and if I were a professor of rhetoric, I should insist on this—is to *speak the truth.* This first, this second, this third; pebbles in your mouth or not. This demands earnestness and manhood chiefly.

We seem to have forgotten that the expression, a *liberal* education, originally meant among the Romans one worthy of *free* men; while the learning of trades and professions by which to get your livelihood merely, was considered worthy of *slaves* only. But taking a hint from the word, I would go a step further and say, that it is not the man of wealth and leisure simply, though devoted to art, or science, or literature, who, in a true sense, is *liberally* educated, but only the earnest and *free* man. In a slaveholding country like this, there can be no such thing as a *liberal* education tolerated by the State; and those scholars of Austria and France who, however learned they may be, are contented under their tyrannies, have received only a *servile* education.

Nothing could his enemies do, but it redounded to his infinite advantage—that is, to the advantage of his cause. They did not hang him at once, but reserved him to preach to them. And then there was another great blunder. They did not hang his four followers with him; that scene was still postponed; and so his victory was prolonged and completed. No theatrical manager could have arranged things so wisely to give effect to his behavior and words. And who, think you, *was* the manager? Who placed the slave woman and her child, whom he stooped to kiss for a symbol, between his prison and the gallows?

We soon saw, as he saw, that he was not to be pardoned or rescued by men. That would have been to disarm him, to restore to him a material weapon, a Sharps' rifle, when he had taken up the sword of the spirit—the sword with which he has really won his greatest and most memorable victories. Now he has not laid aside the sword of the spirit, for he is pure spirit himself, and his sword is pure spirit also.

> "He nothing common did or mean
> Upon that memorable scene,
> Nor called the gods with vulgar spite,
> To vindicate his helpless right;
> But bowed his comely head
> Down as upon a bed."

What a transit was that of his horizontal body alone, but just cut down from the gallows-tree! We read, that at such a time it passed through Philadelphia, and by Saturday night had reached New York. Thus, like a meteor it shot through the Union from the southern regions toward the north! No such freight had the cars borne since they carried him southward alive.

On the day of his translation, I heard, to be sure, that he was *hung*, but I did not know what that meant; I felt no sorrow on that account; but not for a day or two did I even *hear* that he was *dead*, and not after any number of days shall I believe it. Of all the men who were said to be my contemporaries, it seemed to me that John Brown was the only one who *had not died.* I never hear of a man named Brown now,—and I hear of them pretty often,—I never hear of any particularly brave and earnest man, but my first thought is of John Brown, and what relation he may be to him. I meet him at every turn. He is more alive than ever he was. He has earned immortality. He is not confined to North Elba nor to Kansas. He is no longer working in secret. He works in public, and in the clearest light that shines on this land.

WILD APPLES

THE

ATLANTIC MONTHLY.

A MAGAZINE OF LITERATURE, ART, AND POLITICS.

VOL. X.—NOVEMBER, 1862.—NO. LXI.

WILD APPLES.

THE HISTORY OF THE APPLE-TREE.

It is remarkable how closely the history of the Apple-tree is connected with that of man. The geologist tells us that the order of the *Rosaceæ*, which includes the Apple, also the true Grasses, and the *Labiatæ*, or Mints, were introduced only a short time previous to the appearance of man on the globe.

It appears that apples made a part of the food of that unknown primitive people whose traces have lately been found at the bottom of the Swiss lakes, supposed to be older than the foundation of Rome, so old that they had no metallic implements. An entire black and shrivelled Crab-Apple has been recovered from their stores.

Tacitus says of the ancient Germans, that they satisfied their hunger with wild apples (*agrestia poma*) among other things.

Niebuhr observes that "the words for a house, a field, a plough, ploughing, wine, oil, milk, sheep, apples, and others relating to agriculture and the gentler way of life, agree in Latin and Greek, while the Latin words for all objects pertaining to war or the chase are utterly alien from the Greek." Thus the apple-tree may be considered a symbol of peace no less than the olive.

The apple was early so important, and generally distributed, that its name traced to its root in many languages signifies fruit in general. Μῆλον, in Greek, means an apple, also the fruit of other trees, also a sheep and any cattle, and finally riches in general.

The apple-tree has been celebrated by the Hebrews, Greeks, Romans, and Scandinavians. Some have thought that the first human pair were tempted by its fruit. Goddesses are fabled to have contended for it, dragons were set to watch it, and heroes were employed to pluck it.

The tree is mentioned in at least three places in the Old Testament, and its fruit in two or three more. Solomon sings,—"As the apple-tree among the trees of the wood, so is my beloved among the sons." And again,—"Stay me with flagons, comfort me with apples." The noblest part of man's noblest feature is

WILD APPLES

THE HISTORY OF THE APPLE TREE

It is remarkable how closely the history of the apple tree is connected with that of man. The geologist tells us that the order of the *Rosaceae*, which includes the apple, also the true grasses, and the *Labiatae*, or mints, were introduced only a short time previous to the appearance of man on the globe.

It appears that apples made a part of the food of that unknown primitive people whose traces have lately been found at the bottom of the Swiss lakes, supposed to be older than the foundation of Rome, so old that they had no metallic implements. An entire black and shriveled crab-apple has been recovered from their stores.

Tacitus says of the ancient Germans that they satisfied their hunger with wild apples (*agrestia poma*), among other things.

Niebuhr observes that "the words for a house, a field, a plow, plowing, wine, oil, milk, sheep, apples, and others relating to agriculture and the gentler way of life, agree in Latin and Greek, while the Latin words for all objects pertaining to war or the chase are utterly alien from the Greek." Thus the apple tree may be considered a symbol of peace no less than the olive.

The apple was early so important, and generally distributed, that its name traced to its root in many languages signifies fruit in general. Μῆλον, in Greek, means an apple, also the fruit of other trees, also a sheep and any cattle, and finally riches in general.

The apple tree has been celebrated by the Hebrews, Greeks, Romans, and Scandinavians. Some have thought that the first human pair were tempted by its fruit. Goddesses are fabled to have contended for it, dragons were set to watch it, and heroes were employed to pluck it.

The tree is mentioned in at least three places in the Old Testament, and its fruit in two or three more. Solomon sings, "As the apple-tree among the trees of the wood, so is my beloved among the sons." And again, "Stay me with flagons, comfort me with apples." The noblest part of man's noblest feature is named from this fruit, "the apple of the eye."

The apple tree is also mentioned by Homer and Herodotus. Ulysses saw in the glorious garden of Alcinoüs "pears and pomegranates, and apple trees bearing beautiful fruit" (καὶ μηλέαι ἀγλαόκαρποι). And according to Homer, apples were among the fruits which Tantalus could not pluck, the wind ever blowing their boughs away from him. Theophrastus knew and described the apple tree as a botanist.

According to the Prose Edda, "Iduna keeps in a box the apples which the gods, when they feel old age approaching, have only to taste of to become young again. It is in this manner that they will be kept in renovated youth until Ragnarök" (or the destruction of the gods).

I learn from Loudon that "the ancient Welsh bards were rewarded for excelling in song by the token of the apple-spray;" and "in the Highlands of Scotland the apple-tree is the badge of the clan Lamont."

The apple tree (*Pyrus malus*) belongs chiefly to the northern temperate zone. Loudon says that "it grows spontaneously in every part of Europe except the frigid zone, and throughout Western Asia, China, and Japan." We have also two or three varieties of the apple indigenous in North America. The cultivated apple tree was first introduced into this country by the earliest settlers, and is thought to do as well or better here than anywhere else. Probably some of the varieties which are now cultivated were first introduced into Britain by the Romans.

Pliny, adopting the distinction of Theophrastus, says, "Of trees there are some which are altogether wild (*sylvestres*), some more civilized (*urbaniores*)." Theophrastus includes the apple among the last; and, indeed, it is in this sense the most civilized of all trees. It is as harmless as a dove, as beautiful as a rose, and as valuable as flocks and herds. It has been longer cultivated than any other, and so is more humanized; and who knows but, like the dog, it will at length be no longer traceable to its wild original? It migrates with man, like the dog and horse and cow: first, perchance, from Greece to Italy, thence to England, thence to America; and our Western emigrant is still marching steadily toward the setting sun with the seeds of the apple in his pocket, or perhaps a few young trees strapped to his load. At least a million apple trees are thus set farther westward this year than any cultivated ones grew last year. Consider how the Blossom Week, like the Sabbath, is thus annually spreading over the prairies; for when man migrates, he carries with him not only his birds, quadrupeds, insects, vegetables, and his very sward, but his orchard also.

The leaves and tender twigs are an agreeable food to many domestic animals, as the cow, horse, sheep, and goat; and the fruit is sought after by the first, as well as by the hog. Thus there appears to have existed a natural alliance between these animals and this tree from the first. "The fruit of the crab in the forests of France" is said to be "a great resource for the wild boar."

Not only the Indian, but many indigenous insects, birds, and quadrupeds, welcomed the apple tree to these shores. The tent caterpillar saddled her eggs on the very first twig that was formed, and it has since shared her affections with the wild cherry; and the canker-worm also in a measure abandoned the elm to feed on it. As it grew apace, the bluebird, robin, cherry-bird, kingbird, and many more came with haste and built their nests and warbled in its boughs, and so became orchard-birds, and multiplied more than ever. It was an era in the history of their race. The downy woodpecker found such a savory morsel under its bark that he perforated it in a ring quite round the tree, before he left it,—a thing which he had never done before, to my knowledge. It did not take the partridge long to find out how sweet its buds were, and every winter eve she flew, and still flies, from the wood, to pluck them, much to the farmer's sorrow. The rabbit, too, was not slow to learn the taste of its twigs and bark; and when the fruit was ripe, the squirrel half rolled, half carried it to his hole; and even the musquash crept up the bank from the brook at evening, and greedily devoured it, until he had worn a path in the grass there; and when it was frozen and thawed, the crow and the jay were glad to taste it occasionally. The owl crept into the first apple tree that became hollow, and fairly hooted with delight, finding it just the place for him; so, settling down into it, he has remained there ever since.

My theme being the Wild Apple, I will merely glance at some of the seasons in the annual growth of the cultivated apple, and pass on to my special province.

The flowers of the apple are perhaps the most beautiful of any tree's, so copious and so delicious to both sight and scent. The walker is frequently tempted to turn and linger near some more than usually handsome one, whose blossoms are two-thirds expanded. How superior it is in these respects to the pear, whose blossoms are neither colored nor fragrant!

By the middle of July, green apples are so large as to remind us of coddling, and of the autumn. The sward is commonly strewed with little ones which fall still-born, as it were,—Nature thus thinning them for us. The Roman writer Palladius said, "If apples are inclined to fall before their time, a stone placed in a split root will retain them." Some such notion, still surviving, may account for some of the stones which we see placed, to be overgrown, in the forks of trees. They have a saying in Suffolk, England,—

"At Michaelmas time, or a little before,
Half an apple goes to the core."

Early apples begin to be ripe about the first of August; but I think that none of them are so good to eat as some to smell. One is worth more to scent your handkerchief with than any perfume which they sell in the shops. The fragrance of some fruits is not to be forgotten, along with that of flowers. Some gnarly apple which I pick up in the road reminds me by its fragrance of all the wealth of Pomona,—carrying me forward to those days when they will be collected in golden and ruddy heaps in the orchards and about the cider-mills.

A week or two later, as you are going by orchards or gardens, especially in the evenings, you pass through a little region possessed by the fragrance of ripe apples, and thus enjoy them without price, and without robbing anybody.

There is thus about all natural products a certain volatile and ethereal quality which represents their highest value, and which cannot be vulgarized, or bought and sold. No mortal has ever enjoyed the perfect flavor of any fruit, and only the godlike among men begin to taste its ambrosial qualities. For nectar and ambrosia are only those fine flavors of every earthly fruit which our coarse palates fail to perceive,—just as we occupy the heaven of the gods without knowing it. When I see a particularly mean man carrying a load of fair and fragrant early apples to market, I seem to see a contest going on between him and his horse, on the one side, and the apples on the other, and, to my mind, the apples always gain it.

Pliny says that apples are the heaviest of all things, and that the oxen begin to sweat at the mere sight of a load of them. Our driver begins to lose his load the moment he tries to transport them to where they do not belong, that is, to any but the most beautiful. Though he gets out from time to time, and feels of them, and thinks they are all there, I see the stream of their evanescent and celestial qualities going to heaven from his cart, while the pulp and skin and core only are going to market. They are not apples, but pomace. Are not these still Iduna's apples, the taste of which keeps the gods forever young? and think you that they will let Loki or Thjassi carry them off to Jötunheim, while they grow wrinkled and gray? No, for Ragnarök, or the destruction of the gods, is not yet.

There is another thinning of the fruit, commonly near the end of August or in September, when the ground is strewn with windfalls; and this happens especially when high winds occur after rain. In some orchards you may see fully three quarters of the whole crop on the ground, lying in a circular form beneath the trees, yet hard and green, or, if it is a hillside, rolled far down the hill. However, it is an ill wind that blows nobody any good. All the country over, people are busy picking up the windfalls, and this will make them cheap for early apple pies.

In October, the leaves falling, the apples are more distinct on the trees. I saw one year in a neighboring town some trees fuller of fruit than I remember to have ever seen before, small yellow apples hanging over the road. The branches were gracefully drooping with their weight, like a barberry bush, so that the whole tree acquired a new character. Even the topmost branches, instead of standing erect, spread and drooped in all directions; and there were so many poles supporting the lower ones that they looked like pictures of banyan trees. As an old English manuscript says, "The mo appelen the tree bereth the more sche boweth to the folk."

Surely the apple is the noblest of fruits. Let the most beautiful or the swiftest have it. That should be the "going" price of apples.

Between the 5th and 20th of October I see the barrels lie under the trees. And perhaps I talk with one who is selecting some choice barrels to fulfill an order. He turns a specked one over many times before he leaves it out. If I were to tell what is passing in my mind, I should say that every one was specked which he had handled; for he rubs off all the bloom, and those fugacious ethereal qualities leave it. Cool evenings prompt the farmers to make haste, and at length I see only the ladders here and there left leaning against the trees.

It would be well, if we accepted these gifts with more joy and gratitude, and did not think it enough simply to put a fresh load of compost about the tree. Some old English customs are suggestive at least. I find them described chiefly in Brand's "Popular Antiquities." It appears that "on Christmas Eve the farmers and their men in Devonshire take a large bowl of cider, with a toast in it, and carrying it in state to the orchard, they salute the apple-trees with much ceremony, in order to make them bear well the next season." This salutation consists in "throwing some of the cider about the roots of the tree, placing bits of the toast on the branches," and then, "encircling one of the best bearing trees in the orchard, they drink the following toast three several times:—

'Here's to thee, old apple tree.
Whence thou mayst land, and whence thou mayst blow,
And whence thou mayst bear apples enow!
Hats-full! caps-full!
Bushel, bushel, sacks-full!
And my pockets full, too! Hurra!' "

Also what was called "apple-howling" used to be practiced in various counties of England on New Year's Eve. A troop of boys visited the different orchards, and, encircling the apple trees, repeated the following words:—

"Stand fast, root! bear well, top!
Pray God send us a good howling crop:
Every twig, apples big;
Every bough, apples enow!"

"They then shout in chorus, one of the boys accompanying them on a cow's horn. During this ceremony they rap the trees with their sticks." This is called "wassailing" the trees, and is thought by some to be "a relic of the heathen sacrifice to Pomona."

Herrick sings,—

"Wassaile the trees that they may beare
You many a plum and many a peare;
For more or less fruits they will bring
As you so give them wassailing."

Our poets have as yet a better right to sing of cider than of wine; but it behooves them to sing better than English Phillips did, else they will do no credit to their Muse.

THE WILD APPLE

So much for the more civilized apple trees (*urbaniores*, as Pliny calls them). I love better to go through the old orchards of ungrafted apple trees, at what ever season of the year,—so irregularly planted: sometimes two trees standing close together; and the rows so devious that you would think that they not only had grown while the owner was sleeping, but had been set out by him in a somnambulic state. The rows of grafted fruit will never tempt me to wander amid them like these. But I now, alas, speak rather from memory than from any recent experience, such ravages have been made!

Some soils, like a rocky tract called the Easterbrooks Country in my neighborhood, are so suited to the apple, that it will grow faster in them without any care, or if only the ground is broken up once a year, than it will in many places with any amount of care. The owners of this tract allow that the soil is excellent for fruit, but they say that it is so rocky that they have not patience to plow it, and that, together with the distance, is the reason why it is not cultivated. There are, or were recently, extensive orchards there standing without order. Nay, they spring up wild and bear well there in the midst of pines, birches, maples, and oaks. I am often surprised to see rising amid these trees the rounded tops of apple trees glowing with red or yellow fruit, in harmony with the autumnal tints of the forest.

Going up the side of a cliff about the first of November, I saw a vigorous young apple tree, which, planted by birds or cows, had shot up amid the rocks and open woods there, and had now much fruit on it, uninjured by the frosts, when all cultivated apples were gathered. It was a rank, wild growth, with many green leaves on it still, and made an impression of thorniness. The fruit was hard and green, but looked as if it would be palatable in the winter. Some was dangling on the twigs, but more half buried in the wet leaves under the tree, or rolled far down the hill amid the rocks. The owner knows nothing of it. The day was not observed when it first blossomed, nor when it first bore fruit, unless by the chickadee. There was no dancing on the green beneath it in its honor, and now there is no hand to pluck its fruit,—which is only gnawed by squirrels, as I perceive. It has done double duty,—not only borne this crop, but each twig has grown a foot into the air. And this is *such* fruit! bigger than many berries, we must admit, and carried home will be sound and palatable next spring. What care I for Iduna's apples so long as I can get these?

When I go by this shrub thus late and hardy, and see its dangling fruit, I respect the tree, and I am grateful for Nature's bounty, even though I cannot eat it. Here on this rugged and woody hillside has grown an apple tree, not planted by man, no relic of a former orchard, but a natural growth, like the pines and oaks. Most fruits which we prize and use depend entirely on our care. Corn and grain, potatoes, peaches, melons, etc., depend altogether on our planting; but the apple emulates man's independence and enterprise. It is not simply carried, as I have said, but, like him, to some extent, it has migrated to this New World, and is even, here and there, making its way amid the aboriginal trees; just as the ox and dog and horse sometimes run wild and maintain themselves.

Even the sourest and crabbedest apple, growing in the most unfavorable position, suggests such thoughts as these, it is so noble a fruit.

THE CRAB

Nevertheless, *our* wild apple is wild only like myself, perchance, who belong not to the aboriginal race here, but have strayed into the woods from the cultivated stock. Wilder still, as I have said, there grows elsewhere in this country a native and aboriginal crab-apple, *Malus coronaria*, "whose nature has not yet been modified by cultivation." It is found from western New York to Minnesota, and southward. Michaux says that its ordinary height "is fifteen or eighteen feet, but it is sometimes found twenty-five or thirty feet high," and that the large ones "exactly resemble the common apple tree." "The flowers are white mingled with rose color, and are collected in corymbs." They are remarkable for their delicious odor. The fruit, according to him, is about an inch and a half in diameter, and is intensely acid. Yet they make fine sweetmeats and also cider of them. He concludes that "if, on being cultivated, it does not yield new and palatable varieties, it will at least be celebrated for the beauty of its flowers, and for the sweetness of its perfume."

I never saw the crab-apple till May, 1861. I had heard of it through Michaux, but more modern botanists, so far as I know, have not treated it as of any peculiar importance. Thus it was a half-fabulous tree to me. I contemplated a pilgrimage to the "Glades," a portion of Pennsylvania where it was said to grow to perfection. I thought of sending to a nursery for it, but doubted if they had it, or would distinguish it from European varieties. At last I had occasion to go to Minnesota, and on entering Michigan I began to notice from the cars a tree with handsome rose-colored flowers. At first I thought it some variety of thorn; but it was not long before the truth flashed on me, that this was my long-sought crab-apple. It was the prevailing flowering shrub or tree to be seen from the cars at that season of the year,—about the middle of May. But the cars never stopped before one, and so I was launched on the bosom of the Mississippi without having touched one, experiencing the fate of Tantalus. On arriving at St. Anthony's Falls, I was sorry to be told that I was too far north for the crab-apple. Nevertheless I succeeded in finding it about eight miles west of the Falls; touched it and smelled it, and secured a lingering corymb of flowers for my herbarium. This must have been near its northern limit.

HOW THE WILD APPLE GROWS

But though these are indigenous, like the Indians, I doubt whether they are any hardier than those backwoodsmen among the apple trees, which, though descended from cultivated stocks, plant themselves in distant fields and forests, where the soil is favorable to them. I know of no trees which have more difficulties to contend with, and which more sturdily resist their foes. These are the ones whose story we have to tell. It oftentimes reads thus:—

Near the beginning of May, we notice little thickets of apple trees just springing up in the pastures where cattle have been,—as the rocky ones of our Easterbrooks Country, or the top of Nobscot Hill, in Sudbury. One or two of these, perhaps, survive the drought and other accidents,—their very birthplace defending them against the encroaching grass and some other dangers, at first.

In two years' time 't had thus
Reached the level of the rocks,
Admired the stretching world,
Nor feared the wandering flocks.

But at this tender age
Its sufferings began:
There came a browsing ox
And cut it down a span.

This time, perhaps, the ox does not notice it amid the grass; but the next year, when it has grown more stout, he recognizes it for a fellow-emigrant from the old country, the flavor of whose leaves and twigs he well knows; and though at first he pauses to welcome it, and express his surprise, and gets for answer, "The same cause that brought you here brought me," he nevertheless browses it again, reflecting, it may be, that he has some title to it.

Thus cut down annually, it does not despair; but, putting forth two short twigs for every one cut off, it spreads out low along the ground in the hollows or between the rocks, growing more stout and scrubby, until it forms, not a tree as yet, but a little pyramidal, stiff, twiggy mass, almost as solid and impenetrable as a rock. Some of the densest and most impenetrable clumps of bushes that I have ever seen, as well on account of the closeness and stubbornness of their branches as of their thorns, have been these wild apple scrubs. They are more like the scrubby fir and black spruce on which you stand, and sometimes walk, on the tops of mountains, where cold is the demon they contend with, than anything else. No wonder they are prompted to grow thorns at last, to defend themselves against such foes. In their thorniness, however, there is no malice, only some malic acid.

The rocky pastures of the tract I have referred to—for they maintain their ground best in a rocky field—are thickly sprinkled with these little tufts, reminding you often of some rigid gray mosses or lichens, and you see thousands of little trees just springing up between them, with the seed still attached to them.

Being regularly clipped all around each year by the cows, as a hedge with shears, they are often of a perfect conical or pyramidal form, from one to four feet high, and more or less sharp, as if trimmed by the gardener's art. In the pastures on Nobscot Hill and its spurs, they make fine dark shadows when the sun is low. They are also an excellent covert from hawks for many small birds that roost and build in them. Whole flocks perch in them at night, and I have seen three robins' nests in one which was six feet in diameter.

No doubt many of these are already old trees, if you reckon from the day they were planted, but infants still when you consider their development and the long life before them. I counted the annual rings of some which were just one foot high, and as wide as high, and found that they were about twelve years old, but quite sound and thrifty! They were so low that they were unnoticed by the walker, while many of their contemporaries from the nurseries were already bearing considerable crops. But what you gain in time is perhaps in this case, too, lost in power,—that is, in the vigor of the tree. This is their pyramidal state.

The cows continue to browse them thus for twenty years or more, keeping them down and compelling them to spread, until at last they are so broad that they become their own fence, when some interior shoot, which their foes cannot reach, darts upward with joy: for it has not forgotten its high calling, and bears its own peculiar fruit in triumph.

Such are the tactics by which it finally defeats its bovine foes. Now, if you have watched the progress of a particular shrub, you will see that it is no longer a simple pyramid or cone, but that out of its apex there rises a sprig or two, growing more lustily perchance than an orchard-tree, since the plant now devotes the whole of its repressed energy to these upright parts. In a short time these become a small tree, an inverted pyramid resting on the apex of the other, so that the whole has now the form of a vast hour-glass. The spreading bottom, having served its purpose, finally disappears, and the generous tree permits the now harmless cows to come in and stand in its shade, and rub against and redden its trunk, which has grown in spite of them, and even to taste a part of its fruit, and so disperse the seed.

Thus the cows create their own shade and food; and the tree, its hourglass being inverted, lives a second life, as it were.

It is an important question with some nowadays, whether you should trim young apple trees as high as your nose or as high as your eyes. The ox trims them up as high as he can reach, and that is about the right height, I think.

In spite of wandering kine, and other adverse circumstances, that despised shrub, valued only by small birds as a covert and shelter from hawks, has its blossom week at last, and in course of time its harvest, sincere, though small.

By the end of some October, when its leaves have fallen, I frequently see such a central sprig, whose progress I have watched, when I thought it had forgotten its destiny, as I had, bearing its first crop of small green or yellow or rosy fruit, which the cows cannot get at over the bushy and thorny hedge which surrounds it, and I make haste to taste the new and undescribed variety. We have all heard of the numerous varieties of fruit invented by Van Mons and Knight. This is the system of Van Cow, and she has invented far more and more memorable varieties than both of them.

Through what hardships it may attain to bear a sweet fruit! Though somewhat small, it may prove equal, if not superior, in flavor to that which has grown in a garden,—will perchance be all the sweeter and more palatable for the very difficulties it has had to contend with. Who knows but this chance wild fruit, planted by a cow or a bird on some remote and rocky hillside, where it is as yet unobserved by man, may be the choicest of all its kind, and foreign potentates shall hear of it, and royal societies seek to propagate it, though the virtues of the perhaps truly crabbed owner of the soil may never be heard of,—at least, beyond the limits of his village? It was thus the Porter and the Baldwin grew.

Every wild apple shrub excites our expectation thus, somewhat as every wild child. It is, perhaps, a prince in disguise. What a lesson to man! So are human beings, referred to the highest standard, the celestial fruit which they suggest and aspire to bear, browsed on by fate; and only the most persistent and strongest genius defends itself and prevails, sends a tender scion upward at last, and drops its perfect fruit on the ungrateful earth. Poets and philosophers and statesmen thus spring up in the country pastures, and outlast the hosts of unoriginal men.

Such is always the pursuit of knowledge. The celestial fruits, the golden apples of the Hesperides, are ever guarded by a hundred-headed dragon which never sleeps, so that it is an Herculean labor to pluck them.

This is one, and the most remarkable way in which the wild apple is propagated; but commonly it springs up at wide intervals in woods and swamp, and by the sides of roads, as the soil may suit it, and grows with comparative rapidity. Those which grow in dense woods are very tall and slender. I frequently pluck from these trees a perfectly mild and tamed fruit. As Palladius says, "*Et injussu consternitur ubere mali*:" And the ground is strewn with the fruit of an unbidden apple tree.

It is an old notion that, if these wild trees do not bear a valuable fruit of their own, they are the best stocks by which to transmit to posterity the most highly prized qualities of others. However, I am not in search of stocks, but the wild fruit itself, whose fierce gust has suffered no "inteneration." It is not my

"highest plot
To plant the Bergamot."

THE FRUIT, AND ITS FLAVOR

The time for wild apples is the last of October and the first of November. They then get to be palatable, for they ripen late, and they are still perhaps as beautiful as ever. I make a great account of these fruits, which the farmers do not think it worth the while to gather,—wild flavors of the Muse, vivacious and inspiriting. The farmer thinks that he has better in his barrels, but he is mistaken, unless he has a walker's appetite and imagination, neither of which can he have.

Such as grow quite wild, and are left out till the first of November, I presume that the owner does not mean to gather. They belong to children as wild as themselves,—to certain active boys that I know,—to the wild-eyed woman of the fields, to whom nothing comes amiss, who gleans after all the world, and, moreover, to us walkers. We have met with them, and they are ours. These rights, long enough insisted upon, have come to be an institution in some old countries, where they have learned how to live. I hear that "the custom of grippling, which may be called apple-gleaning, is, or was formerly, practiced in Herefordshire. It consists in leaving a few apples, which are called the gripples, on every tree, after the general gathering, for the boys, who go with climbing-poles and bags to collect them."

As for those I speak of, I pluck them as a wild fruit, native to this quarter of the earth,—fruit of old trees that have been dying ever since I was a boy and are not yet dead, frequented only by the woodpecker and the squirrel, deserted now by the owner, who has not faith enough to look under their boughs. From the appearance of the tree-top, at a little distance, you would expect nothing but lichens to drop from it, but your faith is rewarded by finding the ground strewn with spirited fruit,—some of it, perhaps, collected at squirrel-holes, with the marks of their teeth by which they carried them,—some containing a cricket or two silently feeding within, and some, especially in damp days, a shell-less snail. The very sticks and stones lodged in the tree-top might have convinced you of the savoriness of the fruit which has been so eagerly sought after in past years.

I have seen no account of these among the "Fruits and Fruit-Trees of America," though they are more memorable to my taste than the grafted kinds; more racy and wild American flavors do they possess when October and November, when December and January, and perhaps February and March even, have assuaged them somewhat. An old farmer in my neighborhood, who always selects the right word, says that "they have a kind of bow-arrow tang."

Apples for grafting appear to have been selected commonly, not so much for their spirited flavor, as for their mildness, their size, and bearing qualities,—not so much for their beauty, as for their fairness and soundness. Indeed, I have no faith in the selected lists of pomological gentlemen. Their "Favorites" and "None-suches" and "Seek-no-farthers," when I have fruited them, commonly turn out very tame and forgettable. They are eaten with comparatively little zest, and have no real *tang* nor *smack* to them.

What if some of these wildings are acrid and puckery, genuine *verjuice*, do they not still belong to the *Pomaceæ*, which are uniformly innocent and kind to our race? I still begrudge them to the cider-mill. Perhaps they are not fairly ripe yet.

No wonder that these small and high-colored apples are thought to make the best cider. Loudon quotes from the "Herefordshire Report," that "apples of a small size are always, if equal in quality, to be preferred to those of a larger size, in order that the rind and kernel may bear the greatest proportion to the pulp, which affords the weakest and most watery juice." And he says that, "to prove this, Dr. Symonds, of Hereford, about the year 1800, made one hogshead of cider entirely from the rinds and cores of apples, and another from the pulp only, when the first was found of extraordinary strength and flavor, while the latter was sweet and insipid."

Evelyn says that the "Red-strake" was the favorite cider-apple in his day; and he quotes one Dr. Newburg as saying, "In Jersey 't is a general observation, as I hear, that the more of red any apple has in its rind, the more proper it is for this use. Pale-faced apples they exclude as much as may be from their cider-vat." This opinion still prevails.

All apples are good in November. Those which the farmer leaves out as unsalable and unpalatable to those who frequent the markets are choicest fruit to the walker. But it is remarkable that the wild apple, which I praise as so spirited and racy when eaten in the fields or woods, being brought into the house has frequently a harsh and crabbed taste. The Saunterer's Apple not even the saunterer can eat in the house. The palate rejects it there, as it does haws and acorns, and demands a tamed one; for there you miss the November air, which is the sauce it is to be eaten with. Accordingly, when Tityrus, seeing the lengthening shadows, invites Melibœus to go home and pass the night with him, he promises him *mild* apples and soft chestnuts,—*mitia poma, castaneæ molles.* I frequently pluck wild apples of so rich and spicy a flavor that I wonder all orchardists do not get a scion from that tree, and I fail not to bring home my pockets full. But perchance, when I take one out of my desk and taste it in my chamber, I find it unexpectedly crude,—sour enough to set a squirrel's teeth on edge and make a jay scream.

These apples have hung in the wind and frost and rain till they have absorbed the qualities of the weather or season, and thus are highly *seasoned*, and they *pierce* and *sting* and *permeate* us with their spirit. They must be eaten in *season*, accordingly,—that is, out-of-doors.

To appreciate the wild and sharp flavors of these October fruits, it is necessary that you be breathing the sharp October or November air. The outdoor air and exercise which the walker gets give a different tone to his palate, and he craves a fruit which the sedentary would call harsh and crabbed. They must be eaten in the fields, when your system is all aglow with exercise, when the frosty weather nips your fingers, the wind rattles the bare boughs or rustles the few remaining leaves, and the jay is heard screaming around. What is sour in the house a bracing walk makes sweet. Some of these apples might be labeled, "To be eaten in the wind."

Of course no flavors are thrown away; they are intended for the taste that is up to them. Some apples have two distinct flavors, and perhaps one half of them must be eaten in the house, the other outdoors. One Peter Whitney wrote from Northborough in 1782, for the Proceedings of the Boston Academy, describing an apple tree in that town "producing fruit of opposite qualities, part of the same apple being frequently sour and the other sweet;" also some all sour, and others all sweet, and this diversity on all parts of the tree.

There is a wild apple on Nawshawtuct Hill in my town which has to me a peculiarly pleasant bitter tang, not perceived till it is three-quarters tasted. It remains on the tongue. As you eat it, it smells exactly like a squash-bug. It is a sort of triumph to eat and relish it.

I hear that the fruit of a kind of plum tree in Provence is "called *Prunes sibarelles*, because it is impossible to whistle after having eaten them, from their sourness." But perhaps they were only eaten in the house and in summer, and if tried out-of-doors in a stinging atmosphere, who knows but you could whistle an octave higher and clearer?

In the fields only are the sours and bitters of Nature appreciated; just as the woodchopper eats his meal in a sunny glade, in the middle of a winter day, with content, basks in a sunny ray there, and dreams of summer in a degree of cold which, experienced in a chamber, would make a student miserable. They who are at work abroad are not cold, but rather it is they who sit shivering in houses. As with temperatures, so with flavors; as with cold and heat, so with sour and sweet. This natural raciness, the sours and bitters which the diseased palate refuses, are the true condiments.

Let your condiments be in the condition of your senses. To appreciate the flavor of these wild apples requires vigorous and healthy senses, *papillæ* firm and erect on the tongue and palate, not easily flattened and tamed.

From my experience with wild apples, I can understand that there may be reason for a savage's preferring many kinds of food which the civilized man rejects. The former has the palate of an outdoor man. It takes a savage or wild taste to appreciate a wild fruit.

What a healthy out-of-door appetite it takes to relish the apple of life, the apple of the world, then!

"Nor is it every apple I desire,
　　Nor that which pleases every palate best;
'T is not the lasting Deuxan I require,
　　Nor yet the red-checked Greening I request,
Nor that which first beshrewed the name of wife,
Nor that whose beauty caused the golden strife:
No, no! bring me an apple from the tree of life."

So there is one *thought* for the field, another for the house. I would have my thoughts, like wild apples, to be food for walkers, and will not warrant them to be palatable if tasted in the house.

THEIR BEAUTY

Almost all wild apples are handsome. They cannot be too gnarly and crabbed and rusty to look at. The gnarliest will have some redeeming traits even to the eye. You will discover some evening redness dashed or sprinkled on some protuberance or in some cavity. It is rare that the summer lets an apple go without streaking or spotting it on some part of its sphere. It will have some red stains, commemorating the mornings and evenings it has witnessed; some dark and rusty blotches, in memory of the clouds and foggy, mildewy days that have passed over it; and a spacious field of green reflecting the general face of nature,—green even as the fields; or a yellow ground, which implies a milder flavor,—yellow as the harvest, or russet as the hills.

Apples, these I mean, unspeakably fair,—apples not of Discord, but of Concord! Yet not so rare but that the homeliest may have a share. Painted by the frosts, some a uniform clear bright yellow, or red, or crimson, as if their spheres had regularly revolved, and enjoyed the influence of the sun on all sides alike,—some with the faintest pink blush imaginable,—some brindled with deep red streaks like a cow, or with hundreds of fine blood-red rays running regularly from the stem-dimple to the blossom end, like meridional lines, on a straw-colored ground,—some touched with a greenish rust, like a fine lichen, here and there, with crimson blotches or eyes more or less confluent and fiery when wet,—and others gnarly, and freckled or peppered all over on the stem side with fine crimson spots on a white ground, as if accidentally sprinkled from the brush of Him who paints the autumn leaves. Others, again, are sometimes red inside, perfused with a beautiful blush, fairy food, too beautiful to eat,—apple of the Hesperides, apple of the evening sky! But like shells and pebbles on the seashore, they must be seen as they sparkle amid the withering leaves in some dell in the woods, in the autumnal air, or as they lie in the wet grass, and not when they have wilted and faded in the house.

THE NAMING OF THEM

It would be a pleasant pastime to find suitable names for the hundred varieties which go to a single heap at the cider-mill. Would it not tax a man's invention,—no one to be named after a man, and all in the *lingua vernacula*? Who shall stand godfather at the christening of the wild apples? It would exhaust the Latin and Greek languages, if they were used, and make the *lingua vernacula* flag. We should have to call in the sunrise and the sunset, the rainbow and the autumn woods and the wild-flowers, and the woodpecker and the purple finch and the squirrel and the jay and the butterfly, the November traveler and the truant boy, to our aid.

In 1836 there were in the garden of the London Horticultural Society more than fourteen hundred distinct sorts. But here are species which they have not in their catalogue, not to mention the varieties which our crab might yield to cultivation.

Let us enumerate a few of these. I find myself compelled, after all, to give the Latin names of some for the benefit of those who live where English is not spoken,—for they are likely to have a world-wide reputation.

There is, first of all, the Wood Apple (*Malus sylvatica*); the Blue-Jay Apple; the Apple which grows in Dells in the Woods (*sylvestrivallis*), also in Hollows in Pastures (*campestrivallis*); the Apple that grows in an old Cellar-Hole (*Malus cellaris*); the Meadow Apple; the Partridge Apple; the Truant's Apple (*cessatoris*), which no boy will ever go by without knocking off some, however *late* it may be; the Saunterer's Apple,—you must lose yourself before you can find the way to that; the Beauty of the Air (*decus aëris*); December-Eating; the Frozen-Thawed (*gelato-soluta*), good only in that state; the Concord Apple, possibly the same with the *Musketaquidensis*; the Assabet Apple; the Brindled Apple; Wine of New England; the Chickaree Apple; the Green Apple (*Malus viridis*),—this has many synonyms: in an imperfect state, it is the *choleramorbifera aut dysenterifera, puerulis dilectissima*; the Apple which Atalanta stopped to pick up; the Hedge Apple (*Malus sepium*); the Slug Apple (*limacea*); the Railroad Apple, which perhaps came from a core thrown out of the cars; the Apple whose Fruit we tasted in our Youth; our Particular Apple, not to be found in any catalogue; *pedestrium solatium*; also the Apple where hangs the Forgotten Scythe; Iduna's Apples, and the Apples which Loki found in the Wood; and a great many more I have on my list, too numerous to mention,—all of them good. As Bodæus exclaims, referring to the cultivated kinds, and adapting Virgil to his case, so I, adapting Bodæus,—

> "Not if I had a hundred tongues, a hundred mouths,
> An iron voice, could I describe all the forms
> And reckon up all the names of these *wild apples.*"

THE LAST GLEANING

By the middle of November the wild apples have lost some of their brilliancy, and have chiefly fallen. A great part are decayed on the ground, and the sound ones are more palatable than before. The note of the chickadee sounds now more distinct, as you wander amid the old trees, and the autumnal dandelion is half closed and tearful. But still, if you are a skillful gleaner, you may get many a pocketful even of grafted fruit, long after apples are supposed to be gone out-of-doors. I know a Blue Pearmain tree, growing within the edge of a swamp, almost as good as wild. You would not suppose that there was any fruit left there, on the first survey, but you must look according to system. Those which lie exposed are quite brown and rotten now, or perchance a few still show one blooming cheek here and there amid the wet leaves. Nevertheless, with experienced eyes, I explore amid the bare alders and the huckleberry bushes and the withered sedge, and in the crevices of the rocks, which are full of leaves, and pry under the fallen and decaying ferns, which, with apple and alder leaves, thickly strew the ground. For I know that they lie concealed, fallen into hollows long since and covered up by the leaves of the tree itself,—a proper kind of packing. From these lurking-places, anywhere within the circumference of the tree, I draw forth the fruit, all wet and glossy, maybe nibbled by rabbits and hollowed out by crickets, and perhaps with a leaf or two cemented to it (as Curzon an old manuscript from a monastery's mouldy cellar), but still with a rich bloom on it, and at least as ripe and well-kept, if not better than those in barrels, more crisp and lively than they. If these resources fail to yield anything, I have learned to look between the bases of the suckers which spring thickly from some horizontal limb, for now and then one lodges there, or in the very midst of an alder-clump, where they are covered by leaves, safe from cows which may have smelled them out. If I am sharp-set, for I do not refuse the Blue Pearmain, I fill my pockets on each side; and as I retrace my steps in the frosty eve, being perhaps four or five miles from home, I eat one first from this side, and then from that, to keep my balance.

I learn from Topsell's Gesner, whose authority appears to be Albertus, that the following is the way in which the hedgehog collects and carries home his apples. He says,—"His meat is apples, worms, or grapes: when he findeth apples or grapes on the earth, he rolleth himself upon them, until he have filled all his prickles, and then carrieth them home to his den, never bearing above one in his mouth; and if it fortune that one of them fall off by the way, he likewise shaketh off all the residue, and walloweth upon them afresh, until they be all settled upon his back again. So, forth he goeth, making a noise like a cart-wheel; and if he have any young ones in his nest, they pull off his load wherewithal he is loaded, eating thereof what they please, and laying up the residue for the time to come."

THE "FROZEN-THAWED" APPLE

Toward the end of November, though some of the sound ones are yet more mellow and perhaps more edible, they have generally, like the leaves, lost their beauty, and are beginning to freeze. It is finger-cold, and prudent farmers get in their barreled apples, and bring you the apples and cider which they have engaged; for it is time to put them into the cellar. Perhaps a few on the ground show their red cheeks above the early snow, and occasionally some even preserve their color and soundness under the snow throughout the winter. But generally at the beginning of the winter they freeze hard, and soon, though undecayed, acquire the color of a baked apple.

Before the end of December, generally, they experience their first thawing. Those which a month ago were sour, crabbed, and quite unpalatable to the civilized taste, such at least as were frozen while sound, let a warmer sun come to thaw them,—for they are extremely sensitive to its rays,—are found to be filled with a rich, sweet cider, better than any bottled cider that I know of, and with which I am better acquainted than with wine. All apples are good in this state, and your jaws are the cider-press. Others, which have more substance, are a sweet and luscious food,—in my opinion of more worth than the pineapples which are imported from the West Indies. Those which lately even I tasted only to repent of it,—for I am semicivilized,—which the farmer willingly left on the tree, I am now glad to find have the property of hanging on like the leaves of the young oaks. It is a way to keep cider sweet without boiling. Let the frost come to freeze them first, solid as stones, and then the rain or a warm winter day to thaw them, and they will seem to have borrowed a flavor from heaven through the medium of the air in which they hang. Or perchance you find, when you get home, that those which rattled in your pocket have thawed, and the ice is turned to cider. But after the third or fourth freezing and thawing they will not be found so good.

What are the imported half-ripe fruits of the torrid south, to this fruit matured by the cold of the frigid north? These are those crabbed apples with which I cheated my companion, and kept a smooth face that I might tempt him to eat. Now we both greedily fill our pockets with them,—bending to drink the cup and save our lappets from the overflowing juice,—and grow more social with their wine. Was there one that hung so high and sheltered by the tangled branches that our sticks could not dislodge it?

It is a fruit never carried to market, that I am aware of,—quite distinct from the apple of the markets, as from dried apple and cider,—and it is not every winter that produces it in perfection.

The era of the Wild Apple will soon be past. It is a fruit which will probably become extinct in New England. You may still wander through old orchards of native fruit of great extent, which for the most part went to the cider-mill, now all gone to decay. I have heard of an orchard in a distant town, on the side of a hill, where the apples rolled down and lay four feet deep against a wall on the lower side, and this the owner cut down for fear they should be made into cider. Since the temperance reform and the general introduction of grafted fruit, no native apple trees, such as I see everywhere in deserted pastures, and where the woods have grown up around them, are set out. I fear that he who walks over these fields a century hence will not know the pleasure of knocking off wild apples. Ah, poor man, there are many pleasures which he will not know! Notwithstanding the prevalence of the Baldwin and the Porter, I doubt if so extensive orchards are set out today in my town as there were a century ago, when those vast straggling cider-orchards were planted, when men both ate and drank apples, when the pomace-heap was the only nursery, and trees cost nothing but the trouble of setting them out. Men could afford then to stick a tree by every wall-side and let it take its chance. I see nobody planting trees to-day in such out of the way places, along the lonely roads and lanes, and at the bottom of dells in the wood. Now that they have grafted trees, and pay a price for them, they collect them into a plat by their houses, and fence them in,—and the end of it all will be that we shall be compelled to look for our apples in a barrel.

This is "The word of the Lord that came to Joel the son of Pethuel.

"Hear this, ye old men, and give ear, all ye inhabitants of the land! Hath this been in your days, or even in the days of your fathers? . . .

"That which the palmerworm hath left hath the locust eaten; and that which the locust hath left hath the cankerworm eaten; and that which the cankerworm hath left hath the caterpillar eaten.

"Awake, ye drunkards, and weep; and howl, all ye drinkers of wine, because of the new wine; for it is cut off from your mouth.

"For a nation is come up upon my land, strong, and without number, whose teeth are the teeth of a lion, and he hath the cheek teeth of a great lion.

"He hath laid my vine waste, and barked my fig tree: he hath made it clean bare, and cast it away; the branches thereof are made white. . . .

"Be ye ashamed, O ye husbandmen; howl, O ye vinedressers. . . .

"The vine is dried up, and the fig tree languisheth; the pomegranate tree, the palm tree also, and the apple tree, even all the trees of the field, are withered: because joy is withered away from the sons of men."

ANNOTATIONS

BIBLIOGRAPHY

INDEX

ANNOTATIONS

NATURAL HISTORY OF MASSACHUSETTS

In January 1842, both Thoreau's brother, John, and Emerson's young son, Waldo, died, throwing Thoreau into several months of depression and inactivity. In April, in Boston, Emerson came upon a set of scientific reports, each four hundred or five hundred pages long, about the flora and fauna of Massachusetts, and he asked Thoreau to review them for the new transcendentalist journal *The Dial.* Thoreau soon had a draft essay, and in the July 1842 issue of *The Dial* this review appeared. As Robert D. Richardson, Jr., writes: "By one of those little ironies that make life harder to believe than fiction, Thoreau had been writing in his journal on the two days before John [died] about how books of natural history restored one to a sense of health."

3 **Audubon:** John James Audubon (1785–1851), American naturalist, ornithologist, and artist. His five-volume *Ornithological Biography*, published between 1832 and 1839, mixes descriptions of American birds with anecdotes about his life and adventures. Volume 1 (1832) includes descriptions of the magnolia, the cottonwood tree, and the migrations of the ricebird. Volume 2 (1835) has two accounts of a visit to the Florida Keys.

3 **rice-bird:** the bobolink, *Dolichonyx oryzivorus.*

3 **Within the circuit:** Thoreau's own poems, such as this one, appear in his work without quotation marks; poems by other writers appear in quotation marks.

3n ***Reports*:** Each of these was "published agreeably to an Order of the Legislature, by the Commissioners on the Zoölogical and Botanical Survey of the State." They are:

David Humphreys Storer, *Reports on the Fishes, Reptiles, and Birds of Massachusetts* (Boston: Dutton and Wentworth, 1839).

Chester Dewey, *Report on the Herbaceous Flowering Plants of Massachusetts, and on the Quadrupeds of Massachusetts* (Cambridge, Mass.: Folsom, Wells, and Thurston, 1840).

Thaddeus William Harris, *A Report on the Insects of Massachusetts, Injurious to Vegetation* (Cambridge, Mass.: Folsom, Wells, and Thurston, 1841).

Augustus A. Gould, *Report on the Invertebrata of Massachusetts, Comprising the Mollusca, Crustacea, Annelida, and Radiata* (Cambridge, Mass.: Folsom, Wells, and Thurston, 1841).

4 **Johnswort:** Saint-John's-wort. The common variety in New England is *Hypericum perforatum*, an herb with bright-yellow flowers.

4 **mead:** meadow.

4 **fieldfare:** British name of the European thrush *Turdus pilaris*.

4 **hoar:** white with frost.

4 **service-berries:** fruit of the shadbush, or serviceberry, a bush of the genus *Amelanchier* that flowers very early in the spring.

4 **Labrador and East Main:** sites in northern Canada. Labrador is the northeastern coast of what is now Newfoundland. East Main (or Eastmain) is a town on James Bay in northwestern Quebec, the oldest of the Hudson's Bay Company posts.

4 **wots:** knows; is aware.

4 **Great Pine Forest:** or Great Pine Swamp, now Penn Forest in Carbon County, Pennsylvania. It is a site often mentioned by Audubon, who once had a cabin there.

4 **Mohawk:** a river in New York State.

4 **Sing-Sing:** a town on the Hudson River in New York; now Ossining.

4 **Sullivan's Island:** on the north side of the harbor of Charleston, South Carolina. Usually spelled "Sullivans Island."

5 **life-everlasting:** a flower of the genus *Gnaphalium*.

5 **Great Slave Lake:** a three-hundred-mile-long lake in northern Canada that empties into the Mackenzie River.

5 **Esquimaux:** French spelling of "Eskimo."

5 **hyla:** the spring peeper, a small brown tree frog, *Hyla crucifer*.

5 **cupboard:** clock case.

6 **Thales:** Greek philosopher (625?–546? B.C.) who gained fame for his knowledge of astronomy. He is said to have predicted a solar eclipse in 585 B.C.

6 **Linnæus:** Carolus Linnaeus, the Latin pen name of Carl von Linné (1707–1778), Swedish naturalist and creator of the Latin binomial nomenclature by which living things are classified in terms of genus and species.

6 **Russian campaign:** In 1805 and 1806 Napoleon Bonaparte defeated the Russian army in a series of battles.

6 **harvest-fly:** the cicada. In the United States the "dog day harvest-fly" is *Cicada tibicen.*

6 **Anacreon:** Greek lyric poet (570?–485? B.C.) known for short, urbane poems on love and wine. Thoreau translated a group of Anacreon's poems from the Greek, two of them appearing here and the rest in *The Dial*, April 1843.

6 **"We pronounce thee":** Thoreau's version of a poem by Anacreon.

7 **death-watch:** common name of a number of small beetles that bore into old wood and make a clicking sound, supposed to be an omen of death.

7 **snowbird:** the junco, the common snowbird in the United States being *Junco hiemalis.*

8 **Teian poet:** Anacreon, who was born in Teos, a city on the western coast of Asia Minor north of Ephesus. The poem following, "Return of Spring," is Thoreau's version of another poem by Anacreon.

8 **Titan:** the sun.

8 **harrows:** diagonals.

8 **on its beam ends:** tipped on its side.

9 **Nuttall:** Thomas Nuttall (1786–1859) was a botanist and ornithologist who had been the director of the Harvard Botanical Garden and then held the Chair of Natural History at Harvard until replaced by Asa Gray in 1842. Nuttall wrote the standard bird book used during much of the nineteenth century, *A Manual of the Ornithology of the United States and of Canada*, 4 vols. (Cambridge, Mass.: Hilliard and Brown; Boston: Hilliard, Gray, 1832–1834).

9 **Argonautic expedition:** In Greek mythology the Argonauts were heroes who sailed in search of the Golden Fleece.

9 **flight over Parnassus:** figuratively, to rise to poetry or song, Parnassus being the Greek mountain sacred to the Muses.

9 **Goldsmith:** Oliver Goldsmith (1728–1774), English poet, playwright, and novelist. Goldsmith describes the bittern in *A History of the Earth and Animated Nature*, writing that of all the sounds to be heard "by the sedgy sides of unfrequented rivers . . . , there is none so dismally hollow as that which comes from the bittern's croaking voice."

9 **quire:** variant of "choir."

10 **Philip:** Metacomet (1639?–1676), a leader of the Wampanoag Indians, called Philip by the English settlers. In 1662 Metacomet renewed the treaties that his father had made with the settlers. The colonists, however, encroached on native lands, and Metacomet formed a confederation of tribes and led an uprising now known as King Philip's War.

10 **Powhatan:** Algonquian Indian leader (1550?–1618) whose real name was Wa-hun-sen-a-cawh. He was the chief of the Powhatan Confederacy of Algonquian tribes, in what is now Virginia, when the English first settled there in 1607. He was supposed to have been set to kill the Englishman John Smith when his daughter, Pocahontas, intervened and saved Smith's life.

10 **Winthrop:** John Winthrop (1588–1649). With about seven hundred Puritan set-

tlers, Winthrop in 1630 landed in Massachusetts, where he was then the English colonial administrator and first governor of the Massachusetts Bay Colony.

11 **Smith:** John Smith (1579?–1631), English colonizer in North America who in 1607 helped establish Jamestown, Virginia, the first permanent English settlement.

13 **Penobscot:** a Native American tribe formerly dwelling around the Penobscot River in Maine. The Penobscot were the Indians Thoreau actually knew. They used to set up camp along the rivers in Concord and Cambridge, and they were his guides on trips to Maine.

13 **Pilpay:** a collection of ancient Hindu fables drawn from the Pancha Tantra, also known as the *Fables of Bidpai* or the *Book of Kalilah and Dimna.* Thoreau might have known them from the 1819 English translation by the Reverend Wyndham Knatchbull. See also the note for "Veeshnoo Sarma," page 59 of "Paradise (To Be) Regained."

13 **Æsop:** Greek fabulist of the sixth century B.C., to whom are ascribed such fables as "The Fox and the Grapes."

14 **Angler's Souvenir:** a book by William Andrew Chatto (1799–1864), *The Angler's Souvenir* (London: C. Tilt, 1835).

14 **fain:** glad; pleased. Thoreau more often uses the word as an adverb meaning happily or gladly.

14 **"Can such things be":** *Macbeth* III.iv.111–12. Emerson cited the full sentence in *Nature* (1836): "Can such things be, / And overcome us like a summer's cloud, / Without our special wonder?"

14 **seines of flax:** fishnets.

15 **wain:** wagon.

15 **Ararat:** traditionally, the Asian mountain where Noah's ark came to rest after the Flood.

16 **Nahshawtuck:** a hill that sits where the Assabet and Sudbury Rivers join to form the Concord River. Also spelled Nawshawtuck.

16 **Golden Horn:** an inlet off the Bosporus that is the natural harbor of Istanbul.

16 **crate, or jack:** a basket or cage.

17 **cucullo:** firefly; also spelled "cucuyo."

17 **Charon:** in Greek myth the ferryman who carries the shades of the dead over the river Styx. In Roman myth Pluto is the ruler of the underworld.

17 **weight:** pounds.

19 **"winter of *their* discontent":** altering the first line of *Richard III*, "Now is the winter of our discontent."

19 **Baffin's Bay:** a sea passage west of Greenland.

19 **Mackenzie's River:** The Mackenzie River rises in the Canadian Rocky Mountains and flows northwest into the Beaufort Sea.

19 **Minerva:** Roman goddess of handicrafts, arts, and trade. Like the Greek Athena, she embodies the powers of calculation and invention.

19 **Ceres:** goddess of grain and harvest in old Italian mythology, later identified by the Romans with the Greek earth goddess Demeter.

19 **Nereus:** a Greek sea god with shape-shifting powers.
19 **Triton:** a son of Poseidon, human in his upper body and a fish below; often described riding over the sea on sea monsters or horses.
19 **hoar-frost:** white frost formed by the freezing of dew.
20 **creatures of but one law:** Robert D. Richardson, Jr., points out that Thoreau was much influenced by an 1837 reading of Goethe's *Italian Journey.* Goethe had long sought an "original" plant form, one that might have given rise to all other forms. "While walking in the Public Garden of Palermo," Goethe wrote, "it came to me in a flash that in the organ of the plant which we are accustomed to call the *leaf* lies the true Proteus who can hide or reveal himself in all vegetal forms. From first to last, the plant is nothing but leaf." Thoreau expands the idea, claiming that the law governing plants governs *all* kinds of growth, including the growth of crystals.
22 **Bigelow:** Jacob Bigelow (1786–1879), American botanist. Thoreau knew two of Bigelow's books, *American Medical Botany* (Boston: Cummings and Hilliard, 1817–1821) and *Florula Bostoniensis: A Collection of Plants of Boston and Its Environs* . . . . 2nd ed. (Boston: Cummings, Hilliard, & Co., 1824).
22 **demoniacal:** arising from an indwelling spirit, a demon, or genius.
23 **Baconian:** in the style of Francis Bacon (1561–1626), English statesman and philosopher whose method of inquiry was a forerunner of modern empiricism. In scientific study, Bacon wrote, "all depends on keeping the eye steadily fixed upon the facts of nature, and so receiving their images simply as they are; for God forbid that we should give out a dream of our own imagination for a pattern of the world." Thoreau's natural science would keep the first clause, the careful attention to detail, but invert the second, believing that we cannot know the world unless imagination is added to the data that the senses impart. As Emerson says in his essay on transcendentalism, "The senses give us representations of things, but what are the things themselves, they cannot tell."

A WINTER WALK

In May 1843 Thoreau moved from Concord to Staten Island, New York, where he wrote the final draft of this essay. It was first published in the October 1843 issue of *The Dial.* Before it appeared, it was edited considerably by Emerson, and Thoreau apparently accepted the changes. Emerson's journal entry on the essay is often cited: "Henry Thoreau sends me a paper with the old fault of unlimited contradiction. The trick of his rhetoric is soon learned: it consists in substituting for the obvious word and thought its diametrical antagonist. He praises wild mountains and winter forests for their domestic air; snow and ice for their warmth; villagers and wood-choppers for their urbanity, and the wilderness for resembling Rome and Paris. . . . [William Ellery] Channing declared the piece is excellent: but it makes me nervous and wretched to read it, with all its merits." This was, of course, the Emerson whose "Self-Reliance" essay argues eloquently against consistency and in favor of contradiction.

28 **Tartarean:** having to do with Tartarus, the deepest underworld in Greek mythology.

29 **"the sea smokes":** The source for this citation is not known.

30 **fain:** happily; gladly.

31 **gadding:** restless and idle.

32 **"The foodless wilds":** lines 233–34 of "Winter, a Poem," part of *The Seasons* by the Scottish poet James Thomson (1700–1748).

32 **Lapland . . . Spitzbergeners:** a list of northern places and peoples, Lapland being the most northerly part of the Scandinavian Peninsula, Labrador being the northern coast of Newfoundland, Esquimaux (now Eskimo or Inuit) being the original inhabitants of Arctic coastal North America, Knistenaux (more commonly called the Cree) being the original inhabitants of north-central Canada, Dog-Ribs being an Athabascan group of northwest Canada, Novazemblaites and Spitzbergeners being the inhabitants of Arctic islands (Novaya Zemlya, north of Russia, and Spitsbergen, north of Norway).

32 **caddis-worms:** the aquatic larvae of caddis flies or mayflies.

32 **Plicipennes:** obsolete name of the order Trichoptera, the caddis flies.

32 **Seine or Tiber:** rivers in northern France and central Italy, respectively.

33 **Palmyra:** ancient Syrian city in the desert northeast of Damascus destroyed in A.D. 273 and now famous for its ruins.

33 **Hecatompolis:** or Hecatompylos, ancient capital of Parthia, the ruins of which lie in present-day Iran, two hundred miles east of Tehran.

33 **flexure:** bend or curve.

34 **Abu Musa:** Abu Musa al-Ashari, seventh-century Muslim governor and religious teacher from Yemen. Thoreau's source for the citation is not known. Thoreau was living on Staten Island when he wrote this essay, and a letter to Emerson from July 1843 makes it clear that he was homesick for Concord: "My thoughts revert to those dear hills. . . . Others may say, 'Are there not the cities of Asia?' But what are they? Staying at home is the heavenly way."

35 **deal table:** one made of fir or pine.

35 **Alexander:** Alexander the Great (356–323 B.C.), king of Macedonia and conqueror of Asia Minor, Syria, Egypt, Babylonia, and Persia.

37 **Parry or Franklin:** Sir William Edward Parry (1790–1855) and Sir John Franklin (1786–1847), celebrated English Arctic explorers. Thoreau had read both Parry's *Three Voyages for the Discovery of a Northwest Passage from the Atlantic to the Pacific* . . . . 2 vols. (New York: Harper's Family Library, 1841) and Franklin's *Narrative of a Journey to the Shores of the Polar Sea* (Philadelphia: H. C. Carey & I. Lea, 1824).

37 **"the mower whet his scythe":** John Milton, "L'Allegro," line 66 ("the Mower whets his sithe").

38 **cabinet of curiosities:** display of rare and odd items.

38 ***hortus siccus*:** dry garden; a herbarium.

38 **screw or gum:** referring to the method by which naturalists then collected samples of plants.

38 **dreadnaught:** garment made of thick cloth for protection against the weather.

39 **Nootka Sound:** an inlet of the Pacific, on the west coast of Vancouver Island in southwest British Columbia, Canada.

39 **"The snowflakes fall":** *Iliad* XII.278–86.

39 **entablature:** the part of a classical building lying above the columns.

40 **"Drooping the lab'rer ox":** lines 240–42, slightly altered, from Thomson's "Winter." See the note for page 32 above.

41 **"the mansion of the northern bear":** The source for this citation is not known. The "bear" is the constellation Ursa Major, the Big Dipper.

41 **"The full ethereal round":** lines 738–41 of Thomson's "Winter." See the note for page 32 above.

PARADISE (TO BE) REGAINED

This book review, written while Thoreau was living on Staten Island, New York, was first published in the *United States Magazine, and Democratic Review* 13 (November 1843). The text of the first printing differs from the text used here because someone, almost certainly Thoreau, revised the essay before it was reprinted as part of the volume *A Yankee in Canada, with Anti-Slavery and Reform Papers* (1866).

45 **Etzler:** John Adolphus Etzler, a German immigrant who had come to the United States in 1831 as a member of the Mühlhausen Emigration Society. Influenced by Charles Fourier (see below), he spent much of his life writing about and then trying to establish utopian communities, first in Cincinnati and finally in Venezuela. Little is known about him before he emigrated in 1831, and nothing after the failure of his enterprise in Venezuela in 1846.

Etzler was a passionate inventor of large machines such as Thoreau describes. Some were actually built in prototype, though none ever worked very well. By contrast, another German, John Augustus Roebling (1806–1869), who accompanied Etzler to the United States in 1831, went on to design the first-ever suspension bridge (across the Ohio River in Cincinnati) and, finally, the Brooklyn Bridge.

45 **originally published:** in 1833 by Etzler and Reinhold, that is, by Etzler himself, in Pittsburgh, where he was then living and editing a German-language newspaper. The book was perhaps the first technological utopia published in America, and Thoreau's review the first rebuttal.

45 **Fourier:** Charles Fourier (1772–1837), French philosopher and socialist whose writings set out ambitious plans for cooperative living. Fourier imagined reorganizing society by dividing it into communes, or phalanxes, each to number sixteen hundred individuals living in a large communal building surrounded by a collective farm.

Fourier's ideas were introduced into the United States by Albert Brisbane (1809–1890), author of *The Social Destiny of Man* (published in 1840 by C. F. Stollmeyer of Philadelphia, who also published Etzler's later work). For more than a year before Thoreau wrote this review, Horace Greeley's *New-York Tribune* had been publishing a daily column by Brisbane discussing Fourier's doctrines. In 1843 Brisbane and his friends established a Fourierist community in Red Bank, New Jersey, the North American Phalanx. Between 1840 and 1850, in fact, at least forty phalanxes were founded in America, the most famous being Brook Farm (1841–1847) in West Roxbury, Massachusetts.

45 **"Fellow-men!":** As with other citations from Etzler, Thoreau reproduces the sense of the text but silently makes dozens of small changes (about forty in this paragraph alone), as if he were a copy editor working with an unpublished manuscript. Etzler writes that canals will "intersect every-where the land," for example, and Thoreau changes this to "intersect the land everywhere." Most of Thoreau's changes improve or at least standardize Etzler's usage.

46 **ails:** ailments.

46 **Hygeia:** Greek goddess of health.

47 **magnetism, the daguerreotype, electricity:** Great advances in the uses of electricity and magnetism marked the 1830s. Between 1830 and 1831, for example, the British physicist and chemist Michael Faraday (1791–1867) discovered electromagnetic induction, and the American physicist Joseph Henry (1797–1878) made the first powerful electromagnets, the first true "magnetic" telegraph, and one of the first electromagnetic motors.

A daguerreotype is a photograph made on a light-sensitive metallic plate. The method was invented in France in 1837 by Louis Daguerre (1789–1851) and became the first widely practiced form of photography. The earliest images of Thoreau himself, made in 1856, were daguerreotypes.

48 **Hymettus:** a high mountain in Attica, bounding the Athenian plain on the southeast. Its bees produce a flavorful honey from the mountain's aromatic herbs.

48 **Hybla:** an ancient town in Sicily, Hybla Major, on the river Symaethus.

48 **Columella:** Lucius Junius Moderatus Columella, a first-century Roman agricultural writer who, along with other Latin authors (Pliny, Cato, Varro, Palladius), influenced Thoreau's thinking about agriculture. Around 1838 Thoreau had read Columella's *Of Husbandry* in an English translation.

48 ***in extenso*:** at full length; in full.

48 **behoof:** benefit.

49 **" 'life is short, but art is long' ":** an aphorism of Hippocrates (460?–370? B.C.) on the art of healing ("Life is short, the art long, opportunity fleeting, experiment treacherous, judgment difficult"), better known in abbreviated Latin form, *Ars longa, vita brevis.*

49 **"Mechanical System":** *The New World; or, Mechanical System, to Perform the Labours of Man and Beast by Inanimate Powers, That Cost Nothing, for Producing and Preparing the Substances of Life* (Philadelphia: C. F. Stollmeyer, 1841).

50 **chip:** "ship" in the first printing.

50 **careening:** turning a ship on its side for cleaning, caulking, or repairing.

50 ***point d'appui*:** French: point of support; fulcrum; base.

50 **spring and neap tide:** Spring tides are the highest and lowest, occurring at new and full moons; neap tides have the least difference between high and low and occur at the first and third quarters of the moon.

50 ***terrae infirmae*:** unsteady lands, Thoreau's inversion of the standard *terra firma*, firm or solid ground.

51 **terreners:** "dry-landers," Thoreau's neologism to match "mariners."

51 **Green Mountains:** part of the Appalachian range running from southern Quebec through Vermont and into western Massachusetts.

51 **burning-mirrors:** concave mirrors by which the rays of the sun may be concentrated on an object so as to burn it. Legend has it that Archimedes constructed such mirrors to set Roman ships on fire during the siege of Syracuse.

52 **rood:** variant spelling of "rod," a rod being both a unit of linear measure (sixteen and a half feet) and a unit of square measure (the fourth part of an acre), the latter being the sense here.

53 **matting:** fabric woven of coarse material such as hemp, bast, or grass.

53 **as Columbus did:** In his journal for October 11, 1492, Columbus describes seeing, that night, a light in the distance. Columbus's original journal has been lost, but the summary of it made by Bartolomé de Las Casas says that "the Admiral had seen a light at ten in the evening. . . . The light was spotted a couple of times, and it was like a small wax candle being raised and lowered, which struck very few people as being a sign of land, but the Admiral was certain that he was near land." The next day Columbus did in fact make landfall. Thoreau knew the story from Washington Irving's *A History of the Life and Voyages of Christopher Columbus*, 4 vols. (London: J. Murray, 1831).

54 **term-time:** period of gestation.

54 **"tie up the rudder and sleep before the wind":** phrase from a passage in *Christian Morals* by Sir Thomas Browne (1605–1682): "In this virtuous Voyage of thy Life hull not about like the Ark, without the use of Rudder, Mast, or Sail, and bound for no port. . . . Think not that you are Sailing from *Lima* to *Manillia* [sic], when you may fasten up the Rudder, and sleep before the Wind; but expect rough Seas, Flaws, and contrary Blasts."

54 **Manilla:** or Manila, capital city of the Philippines, founded in 1571. To sail from Lima to Manila is to cross the Pacific east to west, carried by the South Equatorial Current, which flows in that direction.

54 **crystal palaces:** In 1840 at Chatsworth (the gardens of the duke of Devonshire), the English gardener and architect Sir Joseph Paxton (1801–1865) built a three-hundred-foot-long conservatory using newly developed techniques for making large sheets of glass. This in turn became the model for the famous Crystal Palace that Paxton built for London's 1851 Great Exhibition, which stood 108 feet high and was at the time the largest building in the world. A replica of it was built in New York in 1853. Thoreau is writing in 1843, so his phrase either refers to Paxton's early conservatory or is a prescient figure of speech.

54 **Fox:** George Fox (1624–1691), English preacher who founded the Society of Friends (the Quakers). When a young man, Fox traveled around England wearing a gray leather outfit (breeches, doublet, and hat), a mode of dress associated with working people and indicating the disdain for fashion typical of religious dissenters.

54 **"glutinated":** glued, as with gluten.

57 **prevalence:** effective power or force; influence.

58 **Μέλλει τὸ θεῖον δ' ἐστι τοιοῦτον φύσει:** Euripides, *Orestes*, line 420. Menelaus has just asked Orestes, "Does not Loxias [Apollo] shield you from these evils?" and Orestes replies with this line: "He delays: such is the nature of the divine." Thoreau alters the Greek punctuation slightly.

59 **Mahometan's heaven:** Heaven in the Qur'an is a place of gardens, running streams, and liquors that intoxicate without intoxicating. The pure are promised beautiful maidens (*houri*) as their consorts. Muslim theologians have stressed the metaphorical and spiritual nature of such images, but Westerners (Edward Gibbon, for example, in his history of Rome) have emphasized their carnality so that, in Thoreau's time, it was known as a heaven of "comfort and pleasure merely."

59 **Veeshnoo Sarma:** or Vishnu-Sarma, the legendary author of the *Hitopadésa*, an ancient collection of Hindu animal fables and proverbial wisdom. In 1842 Thoreau read, and here cites from, an early translation from Sanskrit, *The Hĕĕtōpădēs of Vĕĕshnŏŏ-Sărmā, in a Series of Connected Fables, Interspersed with Moral, Prudential, and Political Maxims* (Bath, U.K.: R. Cruttwell, 1787). In his introduction the translator, Charles Wilkins, notes that the *Hitopadésa* "resembles" what was also known in English as *The Fables of Pilpay.*

60 **Raleigh:** Sir Walter Raleigh (1554–1618), English writer and explorer, prominent at the court of Queen Elizabeth I. Thoreau had lectured on Raleigh before the Concord Lyceum in February 1843. This citation is from Raleigh's *The History of the World*, chap. 1, sec. 11.

KTAADN

Thoreau traveled to Mount Katahdin in Maine at the end of August 1846. He was living at Walden Pond at the time; he finished a draft of this essay before he left the pond the following autumn. In March 1848 he sent it to his friend Horace Greeley, editor of the *New-York Tribune*, who arranged for its publication (in five installments) in John Sartain's *Union Magazine of Literature and Art*, July to November 1848. The version printed here has revisions that Thoreau made in later years when he prepared the manuscript for inclusion in *The Maine Woods*, a posthumous collection published in 1864.

63 **Ktaadn:** now spelled Katahdin; at 5,267 feet, the highest mountain in Maine.

63 **a relative:** George A. Thatcher, the husband of Thoreau's cousin Rebecca Billings.

63 **batteau:** a large, flat-bottomed boat. One that Thoreau measured on a later trip was at its extremities 31 feet long and 5½ feet wide.

64 **Jackson:** Charles T. Jackson (1805–1880) was the brother of Emerson's wife Lydia and of Lucy Jackson Brown, a boarder in the Thoreau home. Thoreau met him at least once, when he lectured at the Concord Lyceum in 1843. Jackson's report of climbing Katahdin is in the *Second Annual Report on the Geology of the Public Lands, Belonging to the Two States of Maine and Massachusetts* (Augusta, Maine: Luther Severance, 1838), pp. 16–19.

64 **two young men:** Edward Everett Hale and William Francis Channing. Hale published an account of the journey in the *Boston Daily Advertiser*, August 15, 1845. Channing was the cousin of Thoreau's friend William Ellery Channing.

64 **Sawyer:** the stock surname of one who runs a sawmill.

64 **riddle:** usually an instrument for cleaning grain, being a large sieve with a perforated bottom that permits grain to pass through but retains the chaff.

66 **"hogging":** bowed; bent.

66 **Charlevoix:** Pierre-François-Xavier de Charlevoix (1682–1761), French Jesuit missionary to Canada and author of *Histoire et description générale de la Nouvelle France* . . . . 3 vols. (Paris: Chez la Veuve Ganeau, 1744).

67 **Abenaki:** the Algonquian-speaking native North Americans, the Penobscot being one of five primary tribes. The Abenaki Confederacy had allied itself with the French in the seventeenth century, and those who converted to Christianity became Roman Catholics.

67 **fish-hawk:** the osprey.

67 **some troops:** a reference to the Aroostook War of 1839–1842. The issue was the boundary between Maine and New Brunswick or, more important, timber rights on disputed land. The Webster-Ashburton Treaty of 1842 established a permanent boundary before any shots were fired, which is why Thoreau says the troops marched "towards Mars' Hill, though not to Mars' *field*."

67 **what the name implies:** The Abenaki word "Passadumkeag" means "where the water goes into the river above the falls."

68 **scions:** the cut shoots or twigs containing buds from a woody plant, used in grafting.

69 **Pomola:** the storm bird of Penobscot tradition, said to live on the summit of Katahdin. Thoreau knew to ask this question because he had read Jackson's *Second Annual Report*, which describes an 1837 ascent of the mountain. Louis Neptune had been Jackson's guide, and Jackson reports that when the party was hit with a snowstorm, "Louis declared that Pomola was angry with us for presuming to measure the height of the mountain, and revenged himself upon us by this storm."

For a full account of Pomola, see Fannie Hardy Eckstorm, "The Katahdin Legends," *Appalachia*, December 1924, pp. 39–52. Eckstorm says that the Indians spell the name "Bumole," "which they pronounce *Bahmolai*." Some say the name is pronounced onomatopoetically, in imitation of thunder.

69 **he had planted letter:** Thoreau's sense is obscure; he may be capturing Neptune's syntax and referring to a custom of leaving messages on mountaintops.

71 **patent hay-scales:** Around 1830 the Vermont farmer Thaddeus Fairbanks (1796–1886) invented a platform scale that could weigh a cartload of hay. The mechanism for balancing the scale lay in a shallow chamber below the platform, which was itself the size of a farmer's cart.

71 **bespoken:** ordered; arranged for.

71 **penetralia:** the innermost parts of a building.

71 **the burning:** the land being cleared by burning it over.

71 **canalés:** percussion caps for a gun with a grooved bore.

72 **to be laid down:** Forest soils are not particularly fertile, but if the trees and brush are burned, the ash provides a few years of fertility; farmers at the time would clear by burning, then take a crop or two of grain, after which the land would be "laid down" to grass.

72 **Province man:** one from the province of New Brunswick, Canada.

72 **Greenleaf's Map of Maine:** Moses Greenleaf (1777–1834), cartographer. Thoreau used his book *A Survey of the State of Maine* (Portland, Maine: Shirley and Hyde, 1829). His map of Maine was published posthumously in 1844.

72 **tow:** the coarse and broken part of flax or hemp, used to stop the charge of powder in a gun and for pressing it close to the shot.

72 **Map of the Public Lands:** a large, sectional map, produced to help resolve land disputes between Maine and Massachusetts. The legend reads, in part: "A Plan of the Public Lands in the State of Maine Surveyed under Instructions from the Commissioners & Agents of the States of Massachusetts and Maine. . . . Copied from the original surveys . . . & corrected by Geo. W. Coffin, Land Agent of the Commonwealth of Massachusetts. . . . 1835. Pendleton's Lithography, Boston. Drawn on stone by J. Eddy." The Concord Free Public Library owns Thoreau's copy of the section showing Mount Katahdin, a portion of which is reproduced in Robert F. Stowell's *A Thoreau Gazetteer* (Princeton, N.J.: Princeton University Press, 1970), p. 15. There are full copies of the map in the Maine State Library, Augusta, and in the Public Record Office, London, England (reference: CO. 700/21).

73 **diet-drink:** medicated liquors; drink prepared with medicinal liquors.

73 **whistler-duck:** the American goldeneye.

73 **pigeon-woodpecker:** the flicker.

73 **bran new:** or "brand-new," said of a manufactured item so new that the brand has not worn off.

76 **"Elegy":** "Elegy Written in a Country Churchyard," poem by Thomas Gray (1716–1771). The phrases and verse that follow come from lines 45–60.

78 **white pine:** *Pinus strobus.* The largest tree in the old-growth forests of New England, the white pine could grow to four hundred years of age and stand two hundred feet high. They were cut as masts for ships and as lumber. No old-growth trees remain in New England.

78*n* **Springer:** John S. Springer, *Forest Life and Forest Trees: Comprising Winter Camp-Life among the Loggers, and Wild-Wood Adventure; with Descriptions of Lumber-*

ing Operations on the Various Rivers of Maine and New Brunswick (New York: Harper & Bros., 1851), pp. 68–71. Springer, born in Maine in 1811, worked in the Maine woods for a decade when a young man, first as a lumberjack, later as a boss hand. At the time he wrote his book, he was a Methodist minister in Massachusetts.

79 **intervale:** a low, level track of land.

79 **Kennebec man:** one from the Kennebec River region, in central Maine.

80 **life-ever-lasting:** wild flowers of the genus *Gnaphalium*.

80 **axe-helves:** ax handles.

81 **Wandering Jew:** Eugène Sue's novel *Le Juif errant* (1844–1845) had recently been translated from the French and published in several American editions.

81 **Criminal Calendar:** an annual product, for example, *The United States Criminal Calendar: or, An Awful Warning to the Youth of America; Being an Account of the Most Horrid Murders, Piracies, Highway Robberies*, compiled from the best authorities by Henry St. Clair (Boston: C. Gaylord, 1835).

81 **Parish's Geography:** Elijah Parish (1762–1825), *A New System of Modern Geography*. There were many editions; for example, Newburyport, Mass.: Thomas and Whipple, 1810.

81 **flash novels:** novels about crime; cheap popular fiction.

82 **Hodge:** James T. Hodge (1816–1871), whose remark cited here comes from a section ("Mr. Hodge's Report") of Jackson's *Second Annual Report,* p. 52. Jackson calls Hodge "my excellent assistant."

82 **buck-beans:** *Menyanthes trifoliata*; also called bog beans.

83 **beer:** made from the young twigs of black spruce.

85 **thole pins:** wooden pegs set in pairs in the gunwales of a boat to serve as an oar-lock.

86 **Argo . . . Symplegades:** In Greek mythology the *Argo* was the boat that Jason and his companions sailed in search of the Golden Fleece. The Symplegades were dangerous rocks guarding the entrance to the Euxine Sea.

86 **"the torrent's smoothness":** from Thomas Campbell (1777–1844), "Gertrude of Wyoming," part III, stanza v, line 4.

87 **boom:** "made by fastening the ends of the trunks of long trees, so as to prevent them from scattering over the lake on the breaking up of the ice" (Springer, *Forest Life and Forest Trees*, p. 159).

87*n* **Abnaquiois:** Abenaki; see the note for page 67 above.

87*n* **No. 10 Relations, for 1647:** *Jesuit Relations. Relation de ce qui s'est passé en la Nouvelle France, en l'années 1633–1672* (Paris: [various publishers], 1633–1672). The Harvard Library owned most of this vast series of reports by Jesuit missionaries in Canada, and Thoreau read everything it had.

88 **Emerson's Address:** a thirty-four-page pamphlet, *An Address Delivered in the Court-House in Concord, Massachusetts, on 1st August, 1844: On the Anniversary of the Emancipation of the Negroes in the British West Indies* (Boston: James Munroe and Company, 1844).

88 ***Liberty party*:** an antislavery party founded in 1840.

88 **Westminster Review:** British quarterly established in 1824 by James Mill and Jeremy Bentham.

88 **History of the Erection of the Monument on the Grave of Myron Holley:** A pamphlet by this title was published in Utica, New York, by H. H. Curtiss in 1844. Holley (1779–1841), from Rochester, New York, was one of the founders of the Liberty Party.

88 **full of the moon:** September 5, 1846.

90 **"Row, brothers":** from "A Canadian Boat Song" by Thomas Moore (1779–1852), an Irish poet who had visited Canada in 1804. Thoreau's "Utawas' tide" alters the original, "Ottawa's tide," the Ottawa being a river flowing into the St. Lawrence at the western tip of Montreal Island.

94 **ferruled:** strengthened by a ring or band.

94 **Michaux:** François André Michaux (1770–1855), French botanist. Thoreau read a three-volume translation of his work *The North American Sylva* (Paris: C. d'Hautel, 1819). All the quotations in this paragraph are from volume 3, pages 166–67.

94*n* **"A steady current":** Springer, *Forest Life and Forest Trees*, p. 64.

95 **"two lines":** about a sixth of an inch. In Michaux's day the Paris line was the twelfth part of a French inch.

99 **Oak Hall:** a Boston clothing store.

100 **Murch Brook:** now called Katahdin Stream.

101 **chivin:** or "chevin," a variety of chub, a river fish of the carp family.

101 **roaches:** In Europe the roach is a small freshwater fish (*Leuciscus rutilus*) of the carp family; in the United States various fish bear the name, including sunfish and chub.

101 **cousin-trout:** In his annotations to Thoreau's journal, Robert Sattelmeyer suggests that "what Thoreau calls alternatively the chivin, the roach, and the cousin trout is probably the modern fall-fish (*Semotilus corporalis*)."

101 **fluviatile:** fluvial.

101 **Proteus:** the shape-shifter of Greek mythology.

101 **Lescarbot:** Marc Lescarbot (1570–1642), French explorer and author of *Histoire de la Nouvelle-France.* Thoreau read the second edition (Paris: Chez Jean-Millot, 1612).

101 **Champdoré . . . de Monts:** early French explorers of the coast of North America, the former being a ship's captain, Pierre Angibault (but called Champdoré), the latter being Pierre du Guast, Sieur de Monts (1560?–1628?).

101 **"qu'en mettant":** "that in putting the boiler on the fire, they had caught enough [fish] for them to eat dinner before the water was hot."

102 **"A quart":** from an anonymous poem, "The Dragon of Wantley," which Thoreau knew from a one-volume edition of Thomas Percy's *Reliques of Ancient English Poetry* (1765). Thoreau changes the original "aqua vitae" to "*arbor*-vitae."

103 **a large slide:** Abol Slide.

104 **Nimrod:** in the Hebrew Bible, a mighty hunter.

104 **Murch Brook:** in fact, Abol Stream ("Abol" being short for "Aboljacknagesic").

106 **Satan's . . . through Chaos:** The reference is to Milton's *Paradise Lost*, which Thoreau begins to cite below.

106 **nipt:** pinched.

106 **bears' dens:** an unlikely assertion, in line with the passage's Miltonic exaggeration.

106 **"nigh founder'd, on he fares":** Milton, *Paradise Lost* II.740–42. Satan, vengeful and proud, is struggling up out of Chaos.

107 **the summit:** Katahdin has two peaks, Baxter (5,267 feet) and South (5,240 feet). Thoreau probably climbed to the saddle between the two, three or four hundred feet below the true summit.

108 **Atlas:** in Greek mythology a Titan condemned by Zeus to support the heavens on his shoulders.

108 **Vulcan:** Roman god of fire and metalworking.

108 **Cyclops:** in Greek mythology one of the three one-eyed Titans who forged thunderbolts for Zeus.

108 **Prometheus:** a Titan who stole fire from Olympus and gave it to humankind, for which Zeus chained him to a rock and sent an eagle to eat his liver, which grew back daily.

108 **Caucasus:** an extensive range of mountains in the northern part of Asia, lying between the Caspian Sea and the Black Sea. From the stories of Prometheus and of the Argonauts, it appears that the Greeks regarded Caucasus as one of the extremities of the earth.

108 **Æschylus:** Greek tragic dramatist (525–456 B.C.). Thoreau's translation of Aeschylus's play *Prometheus Bound* appeared in the January 1843 issue of *The Dial.*

108 **Titanic:** of the Titans; that is, the giants of Greek mythology who sought to rule heaven and were overthrown by the family of Zeus.

109 **"Chaos and ancient Night":** Milton, *Paradise Lost* II.970–74.

110 **"mirror broken":** from J. K. Laski's description of a botanical expedition to Katahdin. In a letter dated October 24, 1847, Thoreau wrote to thank his sister Sophia for clipping the account from the *Bangor Daily Whig & Courier.*

110 **Gazetteer:** *The New England Gazetteer* (1839) by John Hayward (1781–1862). The volume is unpaginated, but the entries are alphabetic, and Thoreau refers to the one for Penobscot County, Maine.

110 **the boundary question:** See the note for Thoreau's mention of "some troops," page 325 above.

110 **Penobscot county:** Hayward's *Gazetteer* was outdated; in 1846 Katahdin lay in Piscataquis County, as it does today.

110 **Murch Brook:** actually Abol Stream.

111 **Robinson Crusoe:** eponymous hero of Daniel Defoe's 1719 novel.

111 **sitz:** a bath in which one sits; a hip bath.

113 **unhandselled:** unused; untested; untried. The *Oxford English Dictionary* gives this sentence as the second of only two examples, the first being from Emerson: "Out of unhandselled savage nature . . . come at last Alfred and Shakespeare."

113 **lea:** open meadow or pasture.

113 **Matter:** Thoreau is playing with the etymological link between "matter" and "mother."

114 **Balboa:** Vasco Núñez de Balboa (1475–1519), Spanish explorer who first saw the Pacific from the Isthmus of Darien (now the Isthmus of Panama).

114 **"When we first came":** from Hodge writing in Jackson's *Second Annual Report*, p. 68.

115*n* **instant:** current.

119 **of the first water:** of the finest quality; the color or luster of a jewel being its water.

120 ***leucisci*:** generic name for freshwater whitefish—chub, dace, carp, minnows, and so on.

120 **Cabot . . . Raleigh:** British explorers or colonizers of North America: John Cabot (1450?–1498?), Bartholomew Gosnold (d. 1607), John Smith (1580?–1631), and Sir Walter Raleigh (1554–1618).

120 **Americus Vespucius:** Latin name of Amerigo Vespucci (1454–1512), Italian explorer of the coast of South America.

120 **New Holland:** Australia.

121 **Fulton:** Robert Fulton (1765–1815) developed the first useful steamboat in 1807 and ran it up the Hudson River from New York to Albany.

CIVIL DISOBEDIENCE

Thoreau's title for this essay changed over the years. A version was first given as a Concord Lyceum lecture on January 26, 1848, under the title "On the Relation of the Individual to the State." When first published the next year in the journal *Aesthetic Papers*, it was called "Resistance to Civil Government." In 1866, four years after Thoreau died, it was reprinted as "Civil Disobedience" in *A Yankee in Canada, with Anti-Slavery and Reform Papers.* We do not know if Thoreau himself changed the title or if his family and publisher did.

The title "Civil Disobedience" is plausibly Thoreau's, because he argues in the essay against William Paley, a British political philosopher whose book *The Principles of Moral and Political Philosophy* has a chapter titled "The Duty of Civil Obedience."

Whatever the later case, with the earlier "Resistance" title Thoreau distinguishes himself from the pacifist abolitionists who called themselves nonresisters (because they opposed resisting injury with injury, evil with evil). In a manuscript essay called "Reform," Thoreau wrote that "after all the peace lectures and non resistance meetings it was never yet learned from them how any of the speakers would conduct in an emergency, because a very important disputant, one Mr. Resistance was not present to offer his arguments." In this essay, Mr. Resistance speaks.

125 **"That government is best":** motto on the title page of a monthly journal, the *United States Magazine, and Democratic Review*, where the sentence reads "The best government is that which governs least." The quotation comes from the introductory essay to the first issue of the journal (October 1837), written by the editor, John Louis O'Sullivan. Thoreau published the third essay in this collection, "Paradise (To Be) Regained," in the *Democratic Review* in 1843.

125 **standing army:** a permanent army maintained in times of peace and war. Before the American Revolution there were two primary complaints against the standing armies that the king maintained in the American colonies. First, the British constitutional tradition held that a peacetime standing army should exist only by consent of the local community (the Declaration of Independence invokes that tradition when it complains that the king had kept armies in the colonies "without the consent of our legislatures"). Second was the question of civil liberties: What was to stop the government from using a standing army to police civilians?

The Revolutionary War was fought by a combination of the Continental army and local militia. After the war, Congress cut the army to fewer than a hundred soldiers, believing that a large standing army was "dangerous to the liberties of a free people."

125 **the present Mexican war:** 1846–1848, between the United States and Mexico. Many abolitionists opposed the war, fearing that territories won from Mexico would become slave states. Though not a "present war" in 1849, when the essay was first published, it had been so when Thoreau was arrested for refusing to pay his poll tax and when he delivered the earliest version of the essay as a lecture.

126 **no-government men:** Nonresisters such as William Lloyd Garrison and Adin Ballou subordinated "human government" to "divine government" and refused to participate in the former. "We recognize but one King and Lawgiver," Garrison wrote. "We are bound by the laws of a kingdom which is not of this world."

Nonresisters would not hold government office, or bring actions at law, or vote, contending that all governments, even democracies, maintain themselves by coercion (jailing those who refuse to pay taxes, for example) and deeming such coercion contrary to the commands of the Gospel.

127 **powder-monkeys:** young soldiers employed to carry gunpowder from the storehouse to the guns.

127 **Navy-Yard:** the U.S. Navy Yard in Boston.

127 **"Not a drum was heard":** from "The Burial of Sir John Moore at Corunna" by Charles Wolfe (1791–1823).

127 ***posse comitatus*:** a group of citizens summoned by a sheriff to aid in law enforcement.

127 **to be "clay," and "stop a hole":** Shakespeare, *Hamlet* V.i.236–37.

128 **"I am too high-born":** Shakespeare, *King John* V.ii.79–82.

128 **Revolution of '75:** The opening battles of the Revolution were fought in Lexington and Concord on April 19, 1775.

128 **a whole country is unjustly overrun:** that is, Mexico.

128 **Paley:** William Paley (1743–1805), British Anglican priest and proponent of theological utilitarianism. Paley's book *The Principles of Moral and Political Philosophy* (1785) was a standard text when Thoreau was a student at Harvard. At home in Concord, the pastor of the First Parish Church read to his parishioners from Paley when they began to stray, Paley's then being a canonical voice of reasonable theology and politics.

In the chapter Thoreau refers to, "The Duty of Submission to Civil Government Explained," Paley sets out "to prove civil obedience to be a moral duty." He considers and rejects the idea that such duty derives from an ancient and enduring social compact, then announces his own proposition: "We assign for the only ground of the subject's obligation, THE WILL OF GOD, AS COLLECTED FROM EXPEDIENCY." The logic that leads to this conclusion he outlines as follows:

> The steps by which the argument proceeds are few and direct.—"It is the will of God that the happiness of human life be promoted:"—this is the first step, and the foundation, not only of this, but of every moral conclusion. "Civil society conduces to that end:"—this is the second proposition. "Civil societies cannot be upheld, unless in each, the interest of the whole society be binding upon every part and member of it:"—this is the third step, and conducts us to the conclusion, namely, that "so long as the interest of the whole society requires it, that is, so long as the established government cannot be resisted or changed without public inconveniency, it is the will of God (which will universally determines our duty) that the established government be obeyed,"—and no longer.
>
> This principle being admitted, the justice of every particular case of resistance is reduced to a computation of the quality of the danger and grievance on the one side, and of the probability and expense of redressing it on the other.

Paley calls his conclusion the "rule of expediency" and says its goal is to augment "the *sum* of public prosperity."

Paley's book was first published in 1785, and the American Revolution was much on his mind, as was the earlier Puritan Revolution. He needs to allow for those events, and thus for fundamental political change, and when he does so, he seemingly supports Thoreau's own position. In particular he admits exceptions to the duty of "submission to civil government":

> It may be as much a duty, at one time, to resist government, as it is, at another, to obey it; to wit, whenever more advantage will . . . accrue to the community, from resistance, than mischief.

But Paley's resistance is not Thoreau's resistance, as becomes apparent when Paley turns to the American Revolution. His defense of civic duty includes the clause "the interest of the whole society [should] be binding upon every part and member of it," and he returns to the point later in discussing "the question of right between Great Britain and her revolted colonies." He argues that colonies should judge their actions with a view toward increasing the prosperity of the whole. "Had [he] been an American," he writes, he would have felt obliged to ask if "the whole happiness of the empire was likely to be promoted" by the Revolution and concludes that it would not. After all, the empire was large and the colonies small and "thinly populated."

Paley elaborates the tension between part and whole by way of colony and empire, but his point applies as well to conflict between individuals and the nation, citizens being urged to judge any impulse toward resistance in terms of "the whole society." In this manner, Paley's utilitarianism provides the moral and theological rationale for majority rule.

This is precisely where an American interested in ongoing revolution parts company. Thoreau was one of many at the time who worried that democracy ran the risk of replacing the despotism of kings with the despotism of the crowd. His scorn of expediency is thus linked to his refusal to submit matters of conscience to majority rule. Paley proposes an obligation of civic duty that allows for change, even for revolution, but he contains both of these with the arithmetic of collective happiness. Thoreau marks the containing strategy and refuses it. In considering civic obligations, Paley looks first to the good of the collective; Thoreau looks first to his conscience. Thoreau, if forced to choose, would rather preserve rectitude than preserve the nation. "This people must cease to hold slaves," he says, "though it cost them their existence as a people."

129 **unjustly wrested a plank:** Thoreau answers Cicero's question "If a fool should snatch a plank from a wreck, shall a wise man wrest it from him if he is able?" *De officiis* III.xxiii.

129 **he that would save his life:** Luke 9:24; Matthew 10:39.

129 **"A drab of state":** Cyril Tourneur (1575?–1626), *The Revenger's Tragedy* IV.iv.72–73. The first line should read: "A drab of State, a cloath, a silver slut."

129 **a hundred thousand merchants:** The Cotton Whigs of Massachusetts, especially those whose income depended on New England cotton mills, preferred to absent themselves from the politics of slavery.

129 **leaven the whole lump:** paraphrase of 1 Corinthians 5:6.

129 **prices-current:** regularly published lists of the prices at which merchandise has recently been sold.

130 **All voting:** Thoreau is here in accord with the no-government nonresisters, who refused to vote. "If *we* cannot occupy a seat in the legislature, or on the bench, neither can we elect *others* to act as our substitutes in any such capacity," wrote William Lloyd Garrison. Thoreau never voted.

130 **a convention . . . at Baltimore:** the 1848 Democratic Party convention, in which delegates remained silent on the question of slavery. Lewis Cass was nominated as the presidential candidate, later to be defeated by the Whig Zachary Taylor.

130 **Odd Fellow:** a member of a secret benevolent society whose U.S. branch was founded in 1819. The object of the order was declared to be "to visit the sick, relieve the distressed, bury the dead, and educate the orphan, to improve and elevate the character of man."

131 **almshouses:** houses for the common residence of the publicly supported paupers of a town. The almshouse in Concord was on the Walden Road between Walden Pond and the center of town.

131 **virile garb:** the toga virilis, or adult clothing, that a Roman boy was permitted to wear upon reaching age fourteen.

131 **substitute:** someone paid to serve in the military in the place of a conscript.

131 **petitioning the State to dissolve the Union:** the followers of William Lloyd Garrison, for example. The motto of Garrison's journal, *The Liberator*, was "No union with slaveholders."

132 **Copernicus:** Nicolaus Copernicus (1473–1543), Polish astronomer who argued that the planets revolve around the sun. His work on the solar system was banned by the Catholic Church, but as he died soon after it was published, he was not excommunicated.

132 **Luther:** Martin Luther (1483–1546), German theologian and leader of the Protestant Reformation. He was excommunicated in 1521 by Pope Leo X as a result of his attacks on the wealth and corruption of the papacy and his contention that salvation depended on faith alone, not on works.

132 **nine shillings:** It is not clear why Thoreau uses this sum. In his own case, the tax he refused to pay was $1.50. A shilling is the twentieth part of a British pound and was worth about 23 cents in Thoreau's time, meaning his tax was equivalent to six shillings.

133 **Constitution is the evil:** The U.S. Constitution, being from the outset a compromise between free and slave states, offered no redress in regard to laws upholding slavery. See Section IV of the Introduction.

133 **majority of one:** an idea that goes back to John Knox (1513?–1572), the founder of Scottish Presbyterianism, who declared that "a man with God is always in the majority."

134 **the State's ambassador:** By South Carolina law, "any free negro, or person of color" coming to the state "on board any vessel, as a cook, steward or mariner" had to be taken from the ship while it was in port and confined "closely in jail" until the ship was ready to leave, at which point the ship's captain had to redeem the prisoner by paying "the expenses of his or her commitment." The law had been passed in 1835 as part of a wave of legislation following the 1831 slave revolt led by Nat Turner, the fear being that any free black entering the state might incite further rebellions.

When the state of Massachusetts found its own black citizens being incarcerated in South Carolina, it tried to challenge the law's constitutionality. No one in the South would help bring a test case, however, and thus in 1844 Massachusetts sent one of its own lawyers south with instructions to commence prosecutions in order to settle the question.

The "State's ambassador" for this task was the former congressman from Concord "Squire" Samuel Hoar (1778–1856). As soon as Hoar arrived in Charleston, the South Carolina legislature passed a resolution censuring him for meddling and expelling him from the state. Before he could be apprised of that order, however, white citizens in Charleston forced him from the city under threat of violence.

The incident was incendiary on both sides. In Massachusetts the legislature resolved that the treatment of Hoar was a plausible cause for war between the states. In Charleston, on the other hand, *The Southern Quarterly Review* declared that "if our rights . . . are to be trampled upon without mercy,—let the sword be raised, and the sooner, perhaps, the struggle comes, the better!"

134 **the prisons of Carolina:** It was black seamen, not Samuel Hoar, who were threatened with imprisonment, Thoreau's point being more figurative: Northern reformers are apt to talk of human rights and litigate in distant cities but not to engage in acts of resistance close to home.

134 **Indian come to plead:** This adds a third issue, after slavery and the Mexican War, to Thoreau's complaint.

135 **the Herodians:** followers of King Herod of Judaea. The Pharisees and the Herodians try to trap Jesus in several Gospel versions of the question of paying taxes to Caesar.

135 **"Show me the tribute-money":** Matthew 22:15–22.

135 **"Render therefore to Cæsar":** Matthew 22:15–22.

136 **Confucius:** Chinese philosopher and political theorist (551–479 B.C.) whose *Analects* contain sayings and dialogues compiled by his disciples. Thoreau's quotations from Confucius are usually his own translations from Jean-Pierre-Guillaume Pauthier's *Confucius et Mencius*, 2 vols. (Paris: Charpentier, 1841).

136 **"If a state is governed":** *The Analects* 8.13.

136 **the State met me in behalf of the Church:** For a discussion of the church tax in Concord, see the Introduction, pp. xxiv–xxvi. It is unlikely that Thoreau was threatened with jail for refusing to pay his tax, "signing off" being a common practice at the time.

136 **another man saw fit to pay it:** This might be more of Thoreau's self-dramatizing, as he would have owed no tax once he signed off. Or perhaps someone paid the tax as a matter of decorum. If so, it might have been Samuel Hoar. In 1843 both Bronson Alcott and Charles Lane were arrested for refusal to pay the poll tax, and Hoar paid the tax for them.

136 **schoolmaster:** Thoreau himself was a schoolmaster at the time he refused the First Parish tax. From 1838 to 1841 he and his brother ran the Concord Academy. They charged their students six dollars per quarter. The ministerial poll tax that Thoreau refused was about eight dollars in 1840.

136 **lyceum:** in New England a cooperative town institution for lectures and debates (the name derives from the gymnasium outside Athens where Aristotle taught philosophy). Thoreau was always active in the Concord Lyceum; in 1842–1843 he was its curator and organized the lecture series.

137 **"Know all men":** Thoreau's statement signing off from First Parish is preserved in the Concord Free Public Library. It reads: "Mr Clerk Concord Jan 6th 1841. I do not wish to be considered a member of the First Parish in this town. Henry D. Thoreau."

137 **poll-tax:** A poll is a head and hence a person. It is also an individual enumerated in a list, and hence the list itself, made up to enumerate taxpayers or voters. A poll tax, or capitation, is one levied at so much per head of the adult population. Such taxes had been a standard source of revenue since colonial days.

137 **six years:** The essay was written in 1848 and published in 1849, meaning Thoreau stopped paying taxes in either 1842 or 1843. The former is more likely, because he was living on Staten Island in 1843 and would not have owed taxes in Concord. In either case, it should be noted that the Mexican War is one of the issues Thoreau says he is protesting, but the war did not start until several years after he stopped paying his taxes.

137 **walls of solid stone:** The jail in question was not a small-town lockup but the Middlesex County Jail, three stories high and built of granite blocks.

139 **shire town:** the town that is the seat of county government. Concord and Cambridge both served as Middlesex County seats.

139 **some one interfered:** probably Thoreau's aunt Maria Thoreau.

140 **huckleberry:** the fruit of a New World shrub of the genus *Gaylussacia*, of which there are several species. The most common in Concord is the black huckleberry, which Thoreau calls *Gaylussacia resinosa* and which is now classified as *G. baccata*. In notes for a lecture on huckleberries, Thoreau writes that the Concord berries ripen in the first half of July, "are thick enough to pick about the twenty-second, at their height about the fifth of August, and last fresh till after the middle of that month." Thoreau was arrested on July 23 or 24, and thus was released just as the berries were "thick enough to pick."

140 **tackled:** harnessed.

140 **"My Prisons":** a reference to *Le mie prigioni* (1832), the memoirs of the Italian patriot Silvio Pellico (1789–1854). Thoreau had read an 1836 English translation.

141 **the course of my dollar:** The tax Thoreau paid would not, in fact, have gone to hire a soldier or buy a musket. Concord's poll tax was not a federal tax but a composite levy for the town, county, and (sometimes) state. Neither the town nor the county provided any financial support for slavery or the war with Mexico, and the state of Massachusetts had passed "personal liberty laws" that forbade the use of state resources to support federal fugitive slave laws.

As Lawrence Rosenwald points out, however, "in linking the slave's government and the poll tax, Thoreau was strictly wrong but broadly and prophetically right." After 1850, whenever a fugitive slave was captured in Massachusetts, events soon demonstrated that there were no clear demarcations between town, county, state, and federal governments. In Boston, city police and state militia would soon be called out to support federal troops enforcing the fugitive slave laws, personal liberty laws notwithstanding.

142 **Mussulman:** a Muslim.

142 **Orpheus:** in Greek mythology the poet whose song had the power to charm even inanimate things.

142 **"We must affect our country":** George Peele (1558?–1598?), *The Battle of Alcazar* II.ii.425–30, inexactly copied. These lines were added after the first printing (1849).

142 **the State will soon:** John Broderick suggests that this is "almost certainly a reference to the possibility that the poll tax would be abolished, and, since the poll tax was the only tax for which Thoreau was liable (except the highway tax, which he paid), he would have no opportunity to demonstrate his patriotism by assessing the actions of the state."

143 **no resting-place without:** a reference to Archimedes (287?–212 B.C.), who supposedly said, "Give me a place to stand and I will move the Earth," meaning that if one had a place to put a fulcrum and a long enough lever, one could lift any weight, no matter how large. A similar image of desired metaphysical mechanics recurs in Thoreau. In *Walden* he imagines finding a *point d'appui* (a base or fulcrum) by getting outside "poetry and philosophy and religion." In "Paradise (To Be) Regained" he asserts that love "can move the globe without a resting-place." Here he argues that true political change requires a total removal from politics.

143 **Webster:** Daniel Webster (1782–1852), famous orator and U.S. senator from Massachusetts whose willingness to compromise with the South in order to save the Union was seen as a betrayal by abolitionists.

143 **the men of '87:** that is, 1787, the year of the Constitutional Convention in Philadelphia.

143 **"I have never made an effort":** taken, slightly altered, from Webster's Senate speech of December 22, 1845, "The Admission of Texas."

143 **"Because it was a part":** The source for this sentence is not known. Webster elaborated the idea in his famous Senate speech of March 7, 1850, "The Constitution and the Union," but that speech was delivered ten months after this essay first appeared in print.

143 **"The manner":** taken, slightly altered, from Webster's Senate speech of August 12, 1848, "Exclusion of Slavery from the Territories."

144 **gird up their loins**: "Let your loins be girded about." Luke 12:35.

144 **Chinese philosopher:** Confucius. See the note for page 136 above. This sentence was added to the text of the first printing (1849).

WALKING

This essay began as an 1851 lecture, "Walking, or the Wild," which grew as Thoreau delivered it over the years until he split it into two lectures, one on walking and one on wildness. These were finally reassembled by Thoreau just before he died, the final essay appearing posthumously in *The Atlantic Monthly* in 1862.

The manuscript page reproduced here is from 1851, as the first sentence implies. It reads: "I feel that I owe my audience an apology for speaking to them tonight on any other subject than the Fugitive Slave Law, on which every man is bound to express a distinct opinion,—but I had prepared myself to speak a word now for *nature*—for absolute freedom & wildness, as compared with a freedom and culture simply civil—to regard man as an inhabitant, or a part and parcel of nature—rather than a member of society. I wish to make an extreme statement, if so I may make an emphatic one—for there are enough champions of civilization—the minister and the school committee—and every one of you will take care of that." The manuscript is in the Houghton Library at Harvard (MS Am278.5, folder 21B).

149 ***sauntering*:** Thoreau takes this false etymology from Samuel Johnson's *A Dictionary of the English Language* (1755), where "to saunter" is derived as follows: "*aller à la sainte terre*, from idle people who roved about the country, and asked charity under pretence of going *à la sainte terre*, to the holy land; or *sans terre*, as having no settled home." Thoreau may have been led to Johnson by Richard Chenevix Trench's *On the Study of Words* (New York: Redfield, 1852), which paraphrases Johnson in the context of a discussion of Crusades to the Holy Land (pp. 86–87). Lexicographers now say that "saunter" is of obscure origin.

150 **Peter the Hermit:** Peter of Amiens (1050–1115), French monk and one of the leading preachers of the Crusades. In 1096 he led the advance division of the first Crusade as far as Asia Minor. Trench's *On the Study of Words* (see the previous note) mentions him just before the discussion of "saunter." When the abolitionist John Brown attacked Harpers Ferry in 1859, the *Chicago Press and Tribune* compared him to Peter the Hermit: the name belongs to the nineteenth century's list of heroic individualists (see the note for "rural exterior," page 359 below).

150 **embalmed hearts:** Nobles who fell during the Crusades, when it was impossible to send a body home, might have their hearts removed, embalmed, and sent home for burial.

150 **Equestrians, Chevaliers, Ritters:** None of these is an actual order of knights; rather, the etymology of each implies men who ride horses.

150 ***Ambulator nascitur, non fit*:** A walker is born, not made. Thoreau alters the Latin proverb *Poeta nascitur, non fit.*

150 **foresters:** officers appointed to watch or maintain a forest.

151 **"When he came to grene wode":** lines 1777–84 of "A Gest of Robyn Hode," the fullest of the early Robin Hood texts. It was first printed around 1530 but probably composed a century earlier.

151 **three-o'clock-in-the-morning courage:** Emerson's *Representative Men* (1850) contains an essay on Napoleon Bonaparte (1769–1821) and quotes him as saying: "As to moral courage, I have rarely met with the two-o'clock-in-the-morning kind: I mean unprepared courage; that which is necessary on an unexpected occasion, and which, in spite of the most unforeseen events, leaves full freedom of

judgment and decision." The source is Napoleon's *Mémorial de Sainte-Hélène* (1823), dictated to Emmanuel de Las Cases.

152 **Wordsworth:** William Wordsworth (1770–1850), English Romantic poet.

153 **mall:** in the nineteenth century, a public walk, both level and shady.

153 **"They planted groves":** Thoreau's source is not known.

153 **"Platanes":** plane trees; in America the plane tree is the sycamore.

153 ***subdiales ambulationes*:** pleasure walks in the open air.

153 **Dahomey:** a kingdom in West Africa, now part of Nigeria. From 1818 to 1858 Dahomey was ruled by King Gezo, who greatly extended the range of his dominions.

154 **quadrivial:** Although "quadrivial" literally means having four roads meeting (as "trivial" means having three roads meeting), Thoreau is inventing a superlative for the common sense of "trivial."

154 ***villa*:** a farm or country house; rightly the root of "village."

154 ***ved*:** Thoreau may be taking the Sanskrit *veda* (knowledge) as a form of "the way."

154 ***vella*:** Thoreau here follows the Roman author Marcus Terentius Varro (116–27 B.C.), who in his book on farming, *De re rustica*, says that the peasants call a farm a *vella* rather than a *villa* because of the connection to *veho*, the verb meaning "to carry." This is not now an accepted etymology.

154 **teaming:** hauling goods with a team (of horses, oxen, and such).

154 ***vellaturam facere*:** See *De re rustica* I.ii.14, where Varro derives "teaming" or "hauling" from *vectura*, cart.

154 ***vilis*:** of small price or value, cheap; common, worthless, vile.

154 ***villain*:** A "villein" is one class of feudal serf, from which "villain" came to mean a brutish peasant.

154 **roadster:** a horse ridden on the road, that is to say, for pleasure or light work rather than for draft.

155 **Menu:** or Manu Vaivasvata, legendary Hindu lawmaker. In 1843 Thoreau selected excerpts for *The Dial* from Sir William Jones's translation of this Sanskrit classic, *Institutes of Hindu Law, or the Ordinances of Menu*, 2 vols. (London: Rivingtons and Cochran, 1825).

155 **Americus Vespucius:** Amerigo Vespucci (1454–1512), Italian explorer of the coast of South America.

155 **Old Marlborough Road:** This road begins about two miles west of Walden Pond and runs southwest toward Marlborough, Massachusetts.

155 **Martial Miles:** a neighbor of Thoreau's whose house was near the Marlborough Road. Elijah Wood and Elisha Dugan were also neighbors.

156 **Quin:** generic Irish name.

156 **guide-boards:** signposts.

156 **Gourgas, Lee, Clark, Darby:** all surnames of Concord families.

156 **Grave:** engrave.

157 **man-traps:** traps formerly set on estates to catch poachers and trespassers. They

have spring-loaded jaws with serrated edges to catch and hold the leg of anyone who steps on the trigger.

158 **settlement of Australia:** Among the initial colonists in Australia were deported felons from England and Ireland.

158 **Tartars:** the Mongolian peoples. Thoreau knew of "the eastern Tartars"—inhabitants of western China—from his 1852 reading of a book by the Christian missionary Évariste Régis Huc, *Recollections of a Journey through Tartary, Thibet, and China, during the Years 1844, 1845, and 1846 . . .* (New York: Appleton & Co., 1852). The citation below is from this book. For a good discussion of Thoreau's knowledge of Asia, see chapter 10 of John Aldrich Christie's *Thoreau as World Traveler.*

158 **Thibet:** variant of Tibet.

158 **Lethean stream:** In Greek mythology Lethe is a river in Hades whose waters induce forgetfulness. The Styx is also a river in Hades, across which the dead must be ferried.

159 **"Than longen folk":** lines 12–13 of the "Prologue" to Chaucer's *Canterbury Tales.* When spring has come, Chaucer writes, "then folk long to go on pilgrimages, and palmers [pilgrims] to seek out foreign shores."

159 **Atlantis:** in antiquity, a legendary sunken island city lying to the west of the known world. The earliest version of the Atlantis legend is found in Plato's *Timaeus.*

159 **Hesperides:** in Greek mythology, celebrated nymphs, "the Western Maidens," whose garden of golden apples lies at the end of the Western world.

159 **Castile and Leon:** two Spanish kingdoms, united under one rule in 1230. Isabella I and Ferdinand V, the sponsors of Columbus's voyages, had succeeded to the throne of Castile and León in 1474.

159 **"And now the sun had stretched":** the last lines of John Milton's "Lycidas" (emphasis added).

159 **Michaux:** Thoreau quotes from François Michaux's *The North American Sylva*, vol. 1, p. 1. See the note for page 94 of "Ktaadn."

159 **Humboldt:** Baron Alexander von Humboldt (1769–1859). He describes the forests of the Amazon in his *Personal Narrative of Travels to the Equinoctial Regions of America during the Years 1799–1804*, 3 vols. (London: H. G. Bohn, 1852).

160 **Guyot:** Arnold Henry Guyot (1807–1884), Swiss-born geographer who taught at Princeton. Thoreau quotes from his book *The Earth and Man: Lectures on Comparative Physical Geography, in Its Relation to the History of Mankind* (Boston: Gould and Lincoln, 1851), pp. 232–33. As Richard J. Schneider has explained, Guyot's book provided a scientific rationale for the ideology of Manifest Destiny.

160 **The younger Michaux:** the same Michaux as above, here differentiated from his father, André Michaux (1746–1802), also a botanist. Thoreau quotes from Michaux's *Voyage à l'ouest des monts Alléghanys* (Paris: Dentu, 1808).

160 **Head:** Sir Francis Bond Head (1793–1875). In February 1852 Thoreau read his book *The Emigrant* (London: J. Murray, 1847); the following citation comes from page 47.

160 **Buffon:** Georges-Louis Leclerc, Comte de Buffon (1707–1788), celebrated French naturalist. Buffon's encyclopedic *Natural History* (published in forty-four volumes beginning in 1749) had famously announced that nature in the Old World was superior to nature in the New. Compared with the Old World lion, for example, the American lion, or puma, not only has no mane, "it is . . . much smaller, weaker, and more cowardly than the real lion." The Americas have no rhinoceroses, no hippopotamuses, no camels, no giraffes. "Elephants belong to the Old Continent and are not found in the New. . . . One cannot even find there any animal that can be compared to the elephant for size or shape." Buffon suspected that the land and climate caused such diminution, claiming that European domestic animals transported to America become smaller as they acclimate. Finally, he claimed that the natives themselves lack vivacity and liveliness of soul. "The savage is feeble and small in his organs of generation; he has neither body hair nor beard, and no ardor for the female of his kind."

Thomas Jefferson dined with Count Buffon while in Paris serving as American minister and, when the conversation turned to the relative degeneracy of the New World, suggested that the diners rise. The Americans each stood over six feet tall, while the Frenchmen averaged just over five. The count was still not convinced, however, and Jefferson later mounted expeditions to send him antlers, bones, and skins in an effort to correct his misconception.

For a full account of Buffon's ideas and the arguments that followed, see Antonello Gerbi's *The Dispute of the New World* (Pittsburgh: University of Pittsburgh Press, 1973). Thoreau knew Buffon through his reading of Joseph Adrien Lelarge de Lignac's *Lettres à un Amériquain sur l'histoire naturelle, générale et particuliere de Monsieur de Buffon* (Hamburg, 1751–1756).

160 **Linnæus:** Carolus Linnaeus, Swedish naturalist. See the note for page 6 of "Natural History of Massachusetts."

161 **"Westward the star of empire":** first line of a poem by George Berkeley (1685–1753), "On the Prospect of Planting Arts and Learning in America." Thoreau substitutes "star" for the original "course." Berkeley was an Anglo-Irish clergyman and philosopher who once traveled to Rhode Island in hopes of establishing a college. Thoreau's source may actually be John Quincy Adams, whose 1802 "Oration at Plymouth" also cites Berkeley and substitutes "star" for "course."

161 **their inheritance:** Under a system of primogeniture, where the eldest son inherits, the younger sons must travel for their fortunes.

161 **panorama:** a painting on a canvas too long to be viewed at once, and so exhibited by being unrolled and made to pass continuously before the viewer. The "panorama of the Mississippi" that Thoreau mentions below was probably the one painted by either Sam Stockwell or John Banvard (1815–1891). At twelve feet high and perhaps five thousand feet long, Banvard's panorama was considered the largest oil painting ever completed. He exhibited it all over the United States and England. Henry Wadsworth Longfellow saw it in Boston in December 1846, just as he was beginning to write *Evangeline*. For more information,

see John Francis McDermott, *The Lost Panoramas of the Mississippi* (Chicago: University of Chicago Press, 1958).

162 **Ehrenbreitstein, Rolandseck, Coblentz:** German cities on the Rhine. Coblentz is also spelled Koblenz.

162 **Nauvoo:** an Illinois town on the Mississippi River. In the early 1840s it was the largest city in the state, ten thousand Mormons having settled there after being driven out of Missouri. In 1846 they were driven farther west, and Nauvoo was abandoned.

162 **Moselle:** river flowing into the Rhine at Koblenz.

162 **Dubuque:** a city on the Mississippi River in northeastern Iowa; also the French-Canadian explorer after whom it is named, Julien Dubuque (1762–1810).

162 **Wenona's Cliff:** Winona, Minnesota, on the Mississippi River, is surrounded by high bluffs.

162 **the Wild:** Thoreau's journal for January 27, 1853, records his reaction to the etymology of this word as given by Trench in *On the Study of Words*, p. 203: "Trench says a wild man is a *willed* man. Well, then, a man of will who does what he wills or wishes, a man of hope and of the future tense, for not only the obstinate is willed, but far more the constant and persevering. The obstinate man, properly speaking, is one who will not. The perseverance of the saints is positive willedness, not a mere passive willingness. The fates are wild, for they *will*; and the Almighty is wild above all."

A recent writer on wilderness, Roderick Nash, agrees on the origins if not the tone: "In the early Teutonic and Norse languages . . . , the root seems to have been 'will' with a descriptive meaning of self-willed, willful, or uncontrollable. From 'willed' came the adjective 'wild' used to convey the idea of being lost, unruly, disordered, or confused." See *Wilderness and the American Mind*, 3rd ed. (New Haven, Conn.: Yale University Press, 1982), p. 1.

162 **Romulus and Remus:** in Greek mythology, twin sons of Mars. Abandoned, they were rescued by a she-wolf, then raised by shepherds. Romulus was the legendary founder of Rome.

162 **Hottentots:** aboriginal South African language group, now known as Khoikhoi.

163 **stolen a march:** gained an advantage; anticipated.

163 **Cumming:** Roualeyn George Gordon-Cumming (1820–1866), Scottish sportsman who lived in South Africa in the 1840s. In December 1850 Thoreau read his account *Five Years of a Hunter's Life in the Far Interior of South Africa*, 2 vols. (New York: Harper & Brothers, 1850). Thoreau refers to vol. 1, p. 218.

163 **"A white man bathing":** from chapter 18, "Tahiti and New Zealand," of Charles Darwin's *Voyage of the "Beagle"* (1839).

163 **"How near to good":** line 296 from a masque, *Love Freed from Ignorance and Folly* (1611), by the English dramatist and poet Ben Jonson (1572–1637).

164 **parterres:** ornamental flower gardens with beds and paths arranged in a pattern.

164 **Dismal Swamp:** the actual one lies on the Virginia–North Carolina border, just southwest of Norfolk.

164 **Burton:** Sir Richard Francis Burton (1821–1890). Thoreau read two of Burton's books: *Personal Narrative of a Pilgrimage to El Medinah and Meccah* (New York: G. P. Putnam & Co., 1856) and *The Lake Region of Central Africa* (New York: Harper & Brothers, 1860). The citation is from the first of these, p. 101.

165 **Tartary:** western China and Tibet. See the note for "Tartars," page 340 above. The citation is from Father Huc's *Recollections of a Journey through Tartary.*

165 ***sanctum sanctorum*:** the holy of holies (often used in reference to the innermost chamber of the old Temple of Jerusalem, where the Ark of the Covenant was kept).

165 **the Reformer:** St. John the Baptist, whose desert food was locusts and wild honey (Matthew 3:3–4).

165 **they sold bark:** as a source of tannic acid, used in tanning hides.

165 **"to work the virgin soil":** from Guyot, *The Earth and Man*, p. 236, as above.

166 **bushwhack:** a short, heavy scythe for cutting bushes.

166 **mallard:** The *Oxford English Dictionary* reports the conjecture that the English "mallard" derives from the Old High German *Madelhart*, which in turn may have been the name for the wild duck in a Germanic beast-epic, now lost. Thoreau's source for the etymological link is not known.

166 **'mid falling dews:** paraphrase of the opening line of "To a Waterfowl" by William Cullen Bryant (1794–1878).

166 **Lake Poets:** the English Romantics, especially Wordsworth and Coleridge.

167 **Augustan . . . Elizabethan age:** figuratively, golden ages or expansive times, both Augustus Caesar (63 B.C.–A.D. 14) in Rome and Elizabeth I (1533–1603) in England having ruled during periods of high cultural achievement.

167 **dragon-tree of the Western Isles:** a huge tree, *Dracaena draco*, of the Canary Islands that yields a resin called dragon's blood. Thoreau read of the great age of the dragon-tree in Alexander von Humboldt's *Views of Nature* (London: H. G. Bohn, 1849), p. 269.

168 **"indicate a faint":** from Robert Hunt, *The Poetry of Science, or Studies of the Physical Phenomena of Nature* (Boston: Gould, Kendall, & Lincoln, 1850), p. 269.

168 **fossil tortoise:** "Although the idea of an elephant standing on the back of a tortoise was often laughed at as an absurdity, Captain Cautley and Dr. Falconer at length discovered in the hills of Asia the remains of a tortoise in a fossil state of such a size that an elephant could easily have performed the feat" (Hunt, *Poetry of Science*, p. 270).

168 **partridge loves peas:** a Wolof proverb, Wolof being the dominant language of those living in the Senegal-Gambia region of western Africa. Thoreau's source for the proverb is not known.

169 **Confucius:** *The Analects* 12.8. See the note for page 136 of "Civil Disobedience." This remark about animal skins is from Pauthier, vol. 1, p. 140.

171 **heating manures:** a reference to the use of the composted manure, warmed by its own decay, that served as the bottom layer of a hotbed for forcing plants in early spring.

171 **Niepce:** In 1826 the French inventor Joseph-Nicéphore Niépce (1765–1833) made the first permanent photographic images using a bitumen-coated plate exposed in a camera obscura. Thoreau's citations come from Hunt, *Poetry of Science*, pp. 133–34. The language belongs to Hunt, not to Niépce.

171 **Cadmus:** In Greek mythology Cadmus brings the initial letters of the alphabet from Phoenicia to Greece.

171 ***Gramática parda*:** *Gramática* means grammar or knowledge, and *parda* means dun colored or brownish gray, but the phrase *gramática parda* means native wit, horse sense, worldly wisdom, instinctive knowledge.

171 **Society for the Diffusion of Useful Knowledge:** Founded in London in 1826, the society's aim was to "impart useful information to all classes of the community, particularly to such as are unable to avail themselves of experienced teachers, or may prefer learning by themselves." It published books, maps, and a journal, *The Penny Magazine* (1832–1845). A Boston Society for the Diffusion of Useful Knowledge was organized in 1828; its first president was Daniel Webster.

172 **more things in heaven and earth:** Shakespeare, *Hamlet* I.v.166.

172 **Chaldean Oracles:** A recent commentary tells us that "the Chaldean Oracles are a collection of abstruse, hexameter verses purported to have been 'handed down by the gods' . . . to a certain Julian the Chaldean and/or his son, Julian the Theurgist, who flourished during the late second century C.E." No full text survives from antiquity, only fragments cited by various ancient authors. Rather than referring to ancient Chaldea, "Chaldean" means metaphorically that the author was adept in magic or was associated with the wisdom of the East. In a modern translation, the line that Thoreau cites reads, in its context: "For there exists a certain Intelligible which you must perceive by the flower of mind. For *if you should* incline your mind toward it and *perceive it as a specific thing, you would not perceive it.*" See Ruth Majercik, *The Chaldean Oracles* (Leiden and New York: E. J. Brill, 1989), especially pp. 48–49. Thoreau's source is not known.

172 **Vishnu Purana:** the best known of the eighteen Puranas, a group of Sanskrit scriptures. Thoreau quotes from *Vishnupurāna. The Vishñu Puráña: A System of Hindu Mythology and Tradition* (London: J. Murray, 1840).

173 **Dante, Bunyan:** Dante Alighieri (1265–1321), author of *The Divine Comedy*, and John Bunyan (1628–1688), author of *The Pilgrim's Progress*, a religious allegory.

173 **Mahomet:** or Muhammad (570?–632), the prophet of Islam. Thoreau's knowledge of Islam came from Washington Irving's *Mahomet and His Successors*, 2 vols. (New York: George P. Putnam, 1850), and from travel narratives such as Burton's *Personal Narrative of a Pilgrimage to El Medinah and Meccah.*

173 **"Gentle breeze":** lines 2–5 of "Ca-Lodin," in Patrick Macgregor, *The Genuine Remains of Ossian, Literally Translated* (London: Smith, Elder & Co., 1841), p. 121. "Loira" is the name of a stream.

Ossian is a legendary Gaelic hero and bard of the third century A.D. In the late eighteenth century the Scottish poet James Macpherson (1736–1796) published *The Poems of Ossian*, which purported to be translations of the ancient bard but which were actually a creative mixture of translations from surviving Gaelic texts and imaginative additions by Macpherson himself. The Ossian that Thoreau knew was not Macpherson's, however, but Patrick Macgregor's later translations from Gaelic.

For a good explanation of the Ossian-Macpherson story, see Fiona Stafford's introduction to *The Poems of Ossian*, ed. Howard Gaskill (Edinburgh: Edinburgh University Press, 1996). In Macpherson's version of Ossian, the poem Thoreau cites is titled "Cath-loda."

173 **moss-trooper:** one who ranges over mosses or bogs; in the seventeenth century a marauder inhabiting the borderlands of England and Scotland.

174 **Spaulding's Farm:** an invented site.

174 **not as in knots and excrescences embayed:** that is, not manifested or made obvious, "embayed" being a poetic way of saying "bathed" or "steeped."

175 **mast:** food, especially acorns, beechnuts, and such.

175 **Shanghai and Cochin-China:** breeds of poultry imported from China.

177 **Elysium:** the paradise of Homeric Greek mythology, lying at the westernmost edge of the world.

SLAVERY IN MASSACHUSETTS

Prompted by the affair of the fugitive slave Anthony Burns (1834–1862), described below, Thoreau first delivered a portion of this essay as a lecture in Framingham, Massachusetts, on July 4, 1854. The entire essay was then published in William Lloyd Garrison's abolitionist newspaper, *The Liberator*, July 21, 1854. At the time, proofs for *Walden* had arrived, but *Walden* itself was not published until August.

181 **meeting of the citizens of Concord:** Emerson and Samuel Hoar called a meeting on June 22, 1854, to condemn the Kansas-Nebraska Act, to urge the repeal of the Fugitive Slave Law, and to begin organizing a new antislavery party. The Republican Party came into being through this and other meetings held that summer in Massachusetts.

181 **destiny of Nebraska:** The Kansas-Nebraska Act had been passed by Congress on May 24, 1854, the same day that the fugitive slave Anthony Burns was arrested in Boston. The act left the question of slavery up to the settlers in Kansas and Nebraska, and thus repealed the Missouri Compromise, which had forbidden slavery in the northern part of the Louisiana Purchase. For a fuller discussion, see Section IV of the Introduction.

181 **citizens of Massachusetts are now in prison:** Abolitionists attacked the Boston Court House, attempting (and failing) to free the fugitive slave Burns. A deputy U.S. marshal, James Batchelder, was killed in the attack, and twelve of the men who led the assault were being held, charged variously with riot, assault, interfering with a federal officer, and murder. Thomas Wentworth Higginson, a friend of Thoreau's, was one of those being held.

181 **their own bridges:** The key event of the 1775 Battle of Concord was the successful defense of the town's North Bridge against the advancing British.

181 **Buttricks, and Davises, and Hosmers:** Major John Buttrick, Captain Isaac Davis, and Abner Hosmer took part in the defense of the North Bridge in the Battle of Concord. Davis and Hosmer were killed.

181 **Lexington Common:** British redcoats met Massachusetts militia on the common early in the morning of April 19, 1775. This was the first battle of the Revolutionary War, followed the same day by the Battle of Concord.

181 **Fugitive Slave Law:** a federal law passed in 1850 that made it much more difficult for fugitive slaves to find refuge in the North. See Section IV of the Introduction.

181 **compromise compact of 1820:** the Missouri Compromise. See Section IV of the Introduction.

182 **full of armed men:** Federal and state troops had secured the Boston Court House after the attempt to free Burns.

182 **Loring:** Edward Greely Loring, Boston judge of probate and U.S. commissioner under the Fugitive Slave Law. Loring had written several articles in defense of that law.

182 **Governor:** Emory Washburn (1800–1877). Washburn, a Whig attorney, and his party were handily defeated in the next election as a consequence of their handling of the Burns affair.

Thoreau's scorn of "the Governor" appears in his 1851 journal entries on the Sims case (see below), and the target then would have been Governor George S. Boutwell (1818–1905). In fact, Thoreau never mentions Boutwell or Washburn by name, and neither man played much of a public role in the fugitive-slave cases. Thus it is the generic term Thoreau intends, for he wants to cast the conflict in terms of morals (there can be no real "governor" without conscience) and in terms of states' rights (the executive officer should act if state and federal laws are at odds).

182 **Simm's:** In April 1851 the fugitive slave Thomas Simms (or Sims) was captured in Boston and sent back to Savannah, Georgia, where he was given a nearly fatal public whipping.

183 **speech to his accomplices:** Five days after Burns was sent back to Virginia, Governor Washburn spoke at a dinner honoring one of the militia units that had helped secure the courthouse.

183 **recent law:** Massachusetts's 1843 "Latimer Law" (named in honor of a fugitive slave, George Latimer). One of a series of Personal Liberty Laws, this statute sought to nullify the federal Fugitive Slave Law of 1793 by making it illegal for the state of Massachusetts to aid in the capture and remanding of slaves.

183 **replevin:** Two lawyers prepared writs of personal replevin in the Burns case. Like a writ of habeas corpus, a writ of replevin is meant to force a hearing to decide if a prisoner is being legally held. Provisions for such writs had been added to the Massachusetts code as part of the Personal Liberty Law of 1837, intended

to help fugitive slaves. These writs had no standing in federal courts, and in this case one of them was denied, the other ignored.

183 **Anthony Burns:** a fugitive slave, arrested in Boston in May and sent back to Virginia on June 2, 1854. See the Introduction, p. xxxiv.

183 **military force of the State:** After the abolitionist assault on the courthouse, the mayor of Boston called out two companies of Massachusetts militia to guard the building. A few days later, when Commissioner Loring remanded Burns, the mayor put the city under martial law. Federal troops were also involved (with the express approval of President Franklin Pierce), and by the time martial law was declared, the state's militia had effectively been federalized.

All these things were illegal under the state's "Latimer Law."

183 **Suttle:** Charles F. Suttle of Alexandria, Virginia, was Burns's master. He had traveled to Boston, had Burns arrested, and took him back to Virginia.

184 **citizen of Massachusetts from being kidnapped:** the "citizen" being Burns. Abolitionists described the remanding of slaves as kidnapping.

184 **rob Mexico:** The United States acquired a great deal of land, including all of California, as a result of the Mexican War (1846–1848). See Section IV of the Introduction.

184 **the 19th of April, 1775:** date of the Battles of Lexington and Concord; the beginning of the American Revolution.

184 **the 12th of April, 1851:** date that the fugitive slave Sims was sent from Boston back to Georgia.

185 **Edward G. God:** a stab at Boston's fugitive-slave commissioner, Edward G. Loring.

185 **Webster:** Daniel Webster (1782–1852), who had supported the compromise of 1850, including the Fugitive Slave Law.

185 **the dirt-bug and its ball:** a dung beetle, such as the American *Phanaeus vindex*, that makes a ball of dung to bury with its egg.

186 **Boxboro:** a small Massachusetts town northwest of Concord.

188 ***Liberator* and *Commonwealth*:** *The Liberator* was William Lloyd Garrison's abolitionist journal; the *Commonwealth* was a Free-Soil paper dedicated to keeping slavery out of the western territories.

188 **time-serving:** obsequiously complying with the humors of men in power.

188 **Mitchell's *Citizen*; Boston *Post*, *Mail*, *Journal*, *Advertiser*, *Courier*, and *Times*; Boston *Herald*:** contemporary newspapers, mostly from Boston. *The Citizen*, published in New York by John Mitchel (1815–1875), addressed itself to the Irish and supported slavery.

188 **groggery:** a tavern.

189 **Do what you will . . . with my wife and children:** an ironic reference to a famous speech by the Unitarian minister Orville Dewey (1794–1882), in which he had announced that he would prefer to see his brother, his son, even himself enslaved than to sacrifice the Union.

189 **expediency:** a key term in William Paley's *Principles of Moral and Political Philos-*

ophy, a standard text that Thoreau read in college. See the note on Paley for page 128 of "Civil Disobedience."

190 **Mammon:** the god or personification of riches and worldliness. Luke 16:13: "No servant can serve two masters. . . . You cannot serve God and mammon."

190 **Seventh Day:** Quaker term for Sunday. The earlier version of this, in Thoreau's journal for June 16, 1854, reads: "Your countrymen . . . steadily worship mammon—and on the seventh day curse God with a tintamarre from one end of the *Union* to the other."

190 **tintamar:** a confused noise; an uproar.

192 **scoriæ:** plural of "scoria": dross; cinder; slag.

192 **villa:** Andrew Jackson Downing's 1841 book, *A Treatise on the Theory and Practice of Landscape Gardening*, initiated a mid-nineteenth-century fad in the building of villas. The term meant not a large country house but a simple woodland or lakeside cottage, such as Thoreau built at Walden Pond.

192 **Court street:** site of the state courthouse where Burns was imprisoned.

193 **white water-lily:** Burns was sent back to Virginia on June 2, 1854; Thoreau spoke on July 4. His journal for June 16 includes this entry: "*Nymphæa odorata.* Again I scent the white water-lily, and a season I had waited for is arrived."

193 ***Nymphæa Douglasii*:** an invented variant on the scientific name of the water lily. Thoreau's target is either Stephen Douglas (1813–1861), Democratic senator from Illinois, or Frederick Douglass (1817–1895), the abolitionist and former slave, whose slave narrative had been published in 1845.

Senator Douglas was instrumental in passing the Compromise of 1850, a package of bills that included the Fugitive Slave Law. He also presented the Kansas-Nebraska Act. Later, in the 1858 presidential campaign, he famously debated Abraham Lincoln.

Frederick Douglass was a compromiser to some abolitionists, because he was willing to work with the Constitution, reading it for its promise of freedom, not for its acceptance of slavery.

In the first printing of Thoreau's essay, published by William Lloyd Garrison in *The Liberator*, the phrase reads "*Nymphæa Douglassii*," making Douglass the target. This makes some sense, because both Thoreau and Garrison questioned the authority of the Constitution (at the July 4 antislavery rally where Thoreau first read the essay, Garrison had read out the pro-slavery clauses in the Constitution, and then burned the document).

The first book publication of the essay, in *A Yankee in Canada, with Anti-Slavery and Reform Papers* (1866), also prints the phrase as "*Nymphæa Douglassii.*"

Later editions print the phrase as "*Nymphæa Douglasii,*" which to my mind makes more sense, because Stephen Douglas's willingness to compromise was the issue of the day.

LIFE WITHOUT PRINCIPLE

A version of this essay was first given as a lecture in December 1854. Thoreau delivered it (under various titles, typically "What Shall It Profit a Man?") seven or eight more times over the next six years. It was finally published with the present title as one of the group of essays Thoreau prepared just before his death, appearing posthumously in *The Atlantic Monthly*, October 1863.

197 **superficies:** outer surfaces.

197 **go to law for my meat:** press me for my substance (the metaphoric "meat" here being that of a nut or a shellfish).

198 **making a minute:** writing a note.

198 **bank-wall:** a retaining wall to control erosion.

199 **Dexter:** Timothy Dexter (1747–1806), a rich merchant and self-proclaimed "Lord" from Newburyport, Massachusetts, was a study in pretentiousness and eccentricity.

199 **Chancery:** a Court of Chancery, which settled matters of debt or equity.

199 **pipe of wine:** a cask; a wine measure of about one hundred gallons. In the seventeenth and eighteenth centuries the poet laureate annually received a cask of wine from the king.

200 **cord-wood:** A cord of firewood is 128 cubic feet, usually stacked 4 feet by 4 feet by 8 feet.

200 **tunnel a mountain:** In 1848 a firm was hired—for two million dollars—to tunnel through Hoosac Mountain in northeastern Massachusetts. Supposed to take five years, the project lasted eleven and cost fourteen million dollars.

201 **mess of pottage:** In Genesis 25:32–34, Esau sells his birthright to Jacob for "bread and pottage of lentils."

201 **"Greatness doth not":** from a fable found in *The Hĕĕtōpădēs of Vĕĕshnŏŏ-Sărmā.* See the note for page 59 of "Paradise (To Be) Regained."

202 **rush to California:** Gold was discovered in central California in January 1848, and the gold rush began the following spring.

202 **Mahomet:** See the note for page 173 of "Walking."

202 **upon a tree:** an allusion to Judas Iscariot's suicide after his betrayal of Jesus, Matthew 27:5.

203 **muck-rake:** allusion to John Bunyan's *The Pilgrim's Progress* in which a man "that could look no way but downward" thus fails to see an offer to trade his muck rake for a celestial crown.

203 **Howitt:** William Howitt (1792–1879), English poet and travel writer. In October 1855 Thoreau read his book *Land, Labor, and Gold; or, Two Years in Victoria; with Visits to Sydney and Van Diemen's Land*, 2 vols. (Boston: Ticknor and Fields, 1855). Thoreau's citations below are from vol. 1, p. 21.

203 **Australian gold-diggings:** The Australian gold rush began in New South Wales in 1851. Ballarat and Bendigo are cities in southeastern Australia founded during the gold rush.

204 **cradles:** troughs on rockers in which gold-bearing dirt is shaken in water to separate and collect the gold.

204 **toms:** stationary troughs for washing gold from gravel.

205 **Isthmus of Darien:** the Isthmus of Panama. The *New-York Daily Tribune*, September 29, 1859, reported the story Thoreau comments on in this paragraph.

205 **New Granada:** old name of Colombia.

205 ***guacas*:** tombs or funeral mounds.

205 **Boca del Toro:** an inlet on the east coast of Panama.

205 **Burker:** one who murders by suffocation in order to sell the body for dissection. The word derives from a notorious criminal, William Burke (1792–1829), who was executed for this crime in Edinburgh.

205 ***illuminati*:** enlightened ones.

206 **Kane:** Elisha Kent Kane (1820–1857), American physician and explorer who joined an expedition to the Arctic, 1850–1851, that went in search of Sir John Franklin (1786–1847). Franklin, also an Arctic explorer, had last been heard from in the summer of 1845; the remains of his expedition were not found until 1859. The Masons (or Freemasons) are an international fraternal order.

206 **D. D.s:** Doctors of Divinity; ministers.

207 **Kossuth:** Lajos Kossuth (1802–1894), Hungarian patriot who tried unsuccessfully to establish an independent Hungarian republic in the late 1840s. He traveled and lectured in the United States, 1851–1852, stopping in Concord on May 11, 1852. Emerson introduced him on that occasion, so when Thoreau says that speeches for Kossuth expressed a "want of thought," he is sparring with his friend.

207 **Kossuth hat:** As Bradley Dean has explained, this was a black felt hat with the left side of the brim fastened to the crown and ornamented with a feather. John Nicholas Genin (1819–1878) owned a hat store in New York City in 1852 and had a warehouse full of dusty old black felt hats that he had been unable to sell. After modifying these hats to look similar to the hat Kossuth wore, Genin slipped aboard Kossuth's ship soon after it arrived in New York and distributed several of these hats to Kossuth's followers. When Kossuth and his cohorts were paraded through the city, "the arbiters of high fashion decreed that these 'Kossuth hats' were 'all the go,' " and a fad was born that eventually generated an estimated half-million dollars.

207 **serve two masters:** Luke 16:13: "No servant can serve two masters. . . . You cannot serve God and mammon."

207 **sporules:** spores.

207 ***thallus*:** young shoot or twig; a plant body not yet differentiated into stem, root, or leaf.

208 **live and move:** Acts 17:28.

208 **Tartars, Huns:** invading peoples, the Tartars being Turkic and Mongolian peoples who entered eastern Europe in the Middle Ages, and the Huns being nomads who invaded Europe in the fourth and fifth centuries A.D.

208 **"I look down":** from "Carric, a Poem," in Patrick Macgregor, *The Genuine Remains of Ossian, Literally Translated* (London: Smith, Elder & Co., 1841), p. 160. Thoreau silently drops four lines. "Lodin" in the Ossian poems is sometimes identified with the Norse god Odin. In James Macpherson's eighteenth-century edition of the Ossian material, the poem is titled "Carric-Thura," and Lodin is called Loda. See the note for "Gentle breeze," page 173 of "Walking."

208 **lumber:** to burden uselessly; to encumber.

208 **hypæthral:** open to the sky.

209 ***sanctum sanctorum*:** See the note for page 165 of "Walking."

209 **coggy:** fitted with cogs, as a machine.

209 **Parnassian:** of Mount Parnassus, home of the Muses.

209 **macadamized:** paved. John McAdam (1756–1836) invented a way to make a road by putting down layers of broken stone topped with stone dust.

210 **asphaltum:** asphalt.

210 **fane:** a temple, church, holy place.

210 **Pompeii:** ancient Italian city southeast of Naples, destroyed by an eruption of Mount Vesuvius in A.D. 79. The ruins were discovered in 1748.

210 **"*ne quid res*-PRIVATA":** from Marcus Tullius Cicero, *Orations* (Boston, 1831), "Oratio pro Milone," lines 26–70. Cicero actually writes *respublica*, which Thoreau changes to '*res*-PRIVATA'." The Latin *res publica* means the public thing.

211 **quarter troops:** The paragraph recalls the Declaration of Independence, whose list of complaints against King George includes his "imposing Taxes on us without our Consent" and "quartering large Bodies of Armed Troops among us."

211 **Jonathans:** colloquial name for Americans.

211 **Irish question:** the question of Irish independence from Great Britain, and of relations between Catholics and Protestants, these perennial problems having been exacerbated by the potato famine of the 1840s and the economic changes brought on by the Industrial Revolution.

211 **natures are subdued:** Shakespeare, Sonnet 111, lines 6–7: "My nature is subdu'd / To what it works in, like the dyer's hand."

211 **knee-buckles:** breeches fastened at the knee with a small buckle. Small-clothes are close-fitting breeches fastened at the knee, but with buttons instead of a buckle. Both were fashionable during the late eighteenth century.

211 **cabinet of curiosities:** a display of rare and odd items.

211 **Decker:** Thomas Dekker (1570?–1632?), English dramatist. The remark about Christ comes from a play, *The Honest Whore*, by Dekker and Thomas Middleton (1570?–1627), act I, scene 13, line 777.

211 **Transalpine:** situated beyond the Alps, especially from Rome.

211 **Numas, Lycurguses, and Solons:** legendary lawgivers of the ancient world, Numa Pompilius in seventh-century Rome, Lycurgus in ninth-century Sparta, and Solon in sixth-century Athens.

212 **vessel:** On July 19, 1850, the ship *Elizabeth*, carrying Margaret Fuller-Ossoli, her husband, and their infant child from Leghorn (Livorno), Italy, wrecked off Fire

Island, New York. Thoreau traveled to the scene from Concord in hopes of retrieving the Ossolis' bodies and effects, though he came home with little more than a button from one of their coats, scavengers having picked the beaches clean in the five days it took Thoreau to arrive.

212 **bitters:** medicines, usually alcoholic, used to sharpen appetite, stimulate digestion, expel intestinal worms, and so on. The oils of both juniper berries and bitter almonds were possible ingredients.

212 **Herndon:** William Lewis Herndon (1813–1857), American naval officer. In 1851–1852 he was one leader of a party sent to explore the Amazon and its Peruvian tributaries. He was a co-author of *Exploration of the Valley of the Amazon* (Washington, D.C.: R. Armstrong, 1853–1854); Thoreau quotes from vol. 1, p. 251. Herndon was from Virginia and suggests in his book that Southern planters might "remove their slaves to [Brazil, and] cultivate its lands."

213 **Po:** the largest river in Italy.

213 **Fort Independence:** the army garrison in Boston Harbor.

213 ***infra*-human:** beneath the human.

213 **into quarters:** Thoreau refers to the proliferation of parties after the Compromise of 1850 began to undermine the old opposition between Whigs and Democrats.

214 **life . . . a forgetting:** allusion to William Wordsworth's "Ode: Intimations of Immortality," lines 59ff.

214 ***eu*peptics:** those with *good* digestion.

AUTUMNAL TINTS

This essay, begun in 1857, was first delivered as a lecture in February 1859. Thoreau would illustrate the talk with specimen autumn leaves mounted on white cardboard. When he sent a final text to *The Atlantic Monthly*, he gave instructions for them to print exactly the outline of a large scarlet oak leaf, as reproduced on page 216. *The Atlantic Monthly* eventually printed "Autumnal Tints" in October 1862, five months after Thoreau died.

217 **Thomson:** James Thomson (1700–1748), Scottish poet. Thoreau cites from *The Seasons,* "Autumn," lines 948–52 and 1051.

217 **"Imbrown":** embrown; that is, make brown or darken.

218 **physiologist:** William Carpenter (1813–1885), British naturalist. Thoreau paraphrases Carpenter's remarks on the death of leaves. See *Vegetable Physiology and Botany* (London: Wm. S. Orr and Co., 1854), p. 199.

218 **pellicle:** skin.

218 **"parenchyma":** Carpenter, *Vegetable Physiology*, p. 307. The parenchyma are the thin-walled cells forming the primary tissue of leaves.

219 **brakes:** ferns.

220 **selvages:** the edges of a fabric woven so that it will not fray. Thoreau uses the word more aptly in *Walden*: "The trees have ample room to expand on the water

side, and each sends forth its most vigorous branch in that direction. There Nature has woven a natural selvage."

220 **timothy:** a grass of the genus *Phleum*, in this case probably *P. alpinum*, widely cultivated for hay. The name derives from Timothy Hanson, an eighteenth-century American farmer who dispersed the seed.

220 **culm:** the stem of a grass or similar plant.

220 ***lacca*, from *lac*, lake:** Lake is a pigment made from vegetable matter. Poke is a source of red lake, thus its genus name.

221 **pipes:** See the note for page 199 of "Life without Principle."

221 **ensanguined:** stained as if with blood.

221 **andropogons:** a large genus of grasses. The Greek roots mean "man + beard," the male flowers having plumose beards. There are about twenty-five species in the United States, where they are also known as broom grasses or broom sedge.

222 **upland haying:** In Thoreau's day, the ecologist David R. Foster writes, "the term 'meadow' had a specific and quite restricted meaning, referring to the grassy and uncultivated lowland areas bordering rivers and similar sites of low, moist vegetation. Fields on the uplands might consist of cultivated grains, scraggly pastures of chewed and matted grasses, thistles and shrubs, or 'mowings' covered with imported English grasses" (*Thoreau's Country*, pp. 47–48).

222 **horse-raking:** A horse rake is a large, horse-drawn rake.

222 **whetting of my scythe:** an allusion to John Milton, "L'Allegro" ("the Mower whets his sithe").

222 **August . . . commencements:** Nineteenth-century college commencements were held toward the end of August; Thoreau's from Harvard, for example, was August 30, 1837.

222 **guide-board:** signpost.

223 **congeners:** others belonging to the same taxonomic genus.

225 ***rubric*:** both *rubrum*, the species name of the red maple, and "rubric" (meaning a name or title) share a Latin root (*ruber*, red), the latter because the titles of laws were once written in red.

225 **Michaux:** François Michaux, *North American Sylva.* See the note for page 94 of "Ktaadn."

226 **tithing-men:** in early New England, town officers elected to police the general morals.

227 ***ulmarium*:** a plantation or nursery of elms.

227 **blasted:** dried or blighted. "Pig-corn" is corn grown for animal feed; "cob-meal" is made from corncobs ground down.

228 ***Lycopodium lucidulum*:** a species of club moss.

228 **Aaron's rod:** a magic staff. In the Bible, Aaron's rod variously turns into a serpent (Exodus 7:10), turns the waters of Egypt to blood (Exodus 7:14–24), and sprouts buds, blossoms, and ripe almonds (Numbers 17:8).

228 **Assabet:** river just north of Concord that joins with the Sudbury River to form the Concord River.

229 **knee:** in shipbuilding, a piece of timber with an angular bend, used to secure the beams of a ship to its sides.

229 **Charon:** in Greek mythology the ferryman who carries the shades of the dead over the river Styx. "Charon's boat" is also the name of a boat-shaped leaf (*cymbifolius*).

229 **coppers:** boilers or kettles.

230 **discounting:** One dictionary Thoreau used, John Walker's *Critical Pronouncing Dictionary* (1823), defines "to discount" as "to count, to pay back again."

230 **sulphur:** It is not clear why one might haggle over "sulphur." Farmers in Thoreau's day carted muck from swamps and low meadows to improve their upland soils. Perhaps a smell of sulfur was a sign of good muck. Or perhaps this is a reference to the fact that farmers spread gypsum, calcium sulfate, as a fertilizer, gypsum being widely used as ballast in ships.

230 **weeds:** widows' weeds, or mourning clothes.

231 **Mount Auburn:** The 1830s saw the beginnings of the "rural cemetery movement," the planting of "gardens for the dead." Mount Auburn, the first important landscaped cemetery, was established in Cambridge, Massachusetts, in 1831. Greenwood Cemetery, in Brooklyn, New York, soon followed.

231 **huckleberry-bird:** the field or rush sparrow. Thoreau called it *Fringilla juncorum,* following Thomas Nuttall; the current scientific name is *Spizella pusilla.*

232 **make some odds:** make a difference.

232 **paper-stainers:** makers of wallpaper.

232 **Naples yellow . . . Tyrian purple:** prepared pigments, Naples yellow being a light yellow based on antimoniate lead, Prussian blue a royal blue based on ferrocyanide of iron, raw Sienna a yellow-brown ocherous earth from Italy, burnt Umber a red-brown ocherous earth from Umbria, Gamboge a transparent yellow derived from plant resin, and Tyrian purple a crimson derived from the juices of various shellfish. This last supposedly came from the Mediterranean city of Tyre and was the most celebrated purple dye of the ancient world.

233 **cabinet-keepers:** keepers of cabinets of curiosities. See the note for page 211 of "Life without Principle."

233 **Nabobs, Begums, and Chobdars:** In India, a nabob was a provincial governor under the Mogul Empire and, figuratively, someone fond of luxury; begums were princesses or ranking ladies; chobdars were a superior class of footmen.

233 **costs no powder:** no gunpowder; that is, for firing ceremonial guns.

233 **liberty-pole:** a flagstaff set up in honor of liberty, usually topped with a liberty cap.

233 **cornwallis:** a muster of soldiers in masquerade commemorating the end of the Revolutionary War, the British general Charles Cornwallis having surrendered on October 19, 1781.

234 **shaking of props:** a reference to a gambling game popular in Boston in the 1850s. Props was a kind of dice game using small white seashells that were shaken in the hand and then thrown on a table.

234 **fluviatile egg-pop:** fluvial eggnog.

234 **ivy *never sere*:** allusion to Milton, "Lycidas," line 2.

234 **C——:** Concord (in Thoreau's journal draft of the passage, October 18, 1858). It was *The Atlantic Monthly*'s editorial policy to employ this anonymous form for all proper nouns used, as here, in an unflattering context.

235 **spiritual communication:** Crackings or knockings were believed to signify the presence of a spirit. In a letter to his sister Sophia on July 13, 1852, Thoreau refers to "idiots inspired by the cracking of a restless board, humbly asking, 'Please, Spirit, if you cannot answer by knocks, answer by tips of the table'!!!!!!"

235 **"Wrought in a sad sincerity":** from Emerson's poem "The Problem." Thoreau has changed the italicized words. The original refers to the architects of Christian churches and reads: "They builded better than they knew;— / The conscious stone to beauty grew."

235 **twelve species:** Thoreau owned Asa Gray's *Manual of the Botany of the Northern United States* (Boston: J. Munroe, 1848), which lists eighteen species of oak. The twelve local species Thoreau had likely seen are the scrub oak (*Quercus ilicifolia*), the black oak (*velutina*, then called *tinctoria*), the chestnut oak (*prinus*), the dwarf chinquapin oak (*prinoides*), the scarlet oak (*coccinea*), the shingle oak (*imbricaria*), the mossy-cup or bur oak (*macrocarpa*), the pin oak (*palustris*), the red oak (*rubra*), the swamp white oak (*bicolor*, then called *prinus discolor*), the white oak (*alba*), and the willow oak (*phellos*).

236 **arrow-headed character:** cuneiform script such as that used in ancient Sumerian, Assyrian, and Persian writing.

236 **Rosetta Stone:** the famous tablet bearing inscriptions in Greek, Egyptian hieroglyphic, and demotic scripts. It provided the key to deciphering hieroglyphics.

236 **embayed:** a poetic way of saying "bathed" or "steeped." Thoreau seems to intend a pun as well: the eye is bathed, but also held as if in a bay.

237 **friths:** firths, long narrow inlets of the sea.

237 **Dionysius:** Thoreau's journal entry for July 29, 1857, includes this: "Loudon in his 'Arboretum,' vol. iv, page 2038, says, 'Dionysius the geographer compares the form of the Morea in the Levant, the ancient Peloponnesus, to the leaf of this tree [the Oriental plane]; and Pliny makes the same remark in allusion to its numerous bays." Dionysius is probably Dionysius Periegetes (fourth century A.D.), the author of a geographical poem, *Oikumenes Periegesis.*

237 **Pliny:** Pliny the Elder (23–79), a celebrated Roman naturalist.

237 **Morea:** the Peloponnesus, the peninsula forming the southern portion of Greece.

237 **Oriental plane tree:** *Platanus orientalis*; the related American species is the sycamore or buttonwood, *P. occidentalis.*

237 **filibusters:** adventurers who engage in a private military action in a foreign country. In Thoreau's day the famous examples were Narciso López, who led an expedition against Cuba (1850–1851), and William Walker, who led expeditions against the Mexican state of Sonora (1853–1854) and against Nicaragua (1855–1858).

237 **New-found Island:** probably meant generically, though the Canadian province of Newfoundland contains many islands.
237 **Celebes:** an island of central Indonesia, first visited by Europeans in 1512.
238 **cliff:** Lee's cliff, about a mile and a half southwest of Walden Pond. Pine Hill straddles the Concord-Lincoln town line, two miles from Lee's cliff.
239 **Methuselah:** the biblical patriarch, said to have lived 969 years.
239 **China-aster:** *Callistephus chinensis.*
239 **Isle of Orleans:** an island near Quebec, Canada, in the St. Lawrence River.
240 **Hudson's Bay:** an inland sea of east-central Canada.
241 ***Juncaceae* and *Gramineae*:** at the time, the family names of the rushes and the grasses, respectively.
241 **Brocken spectre:** ghostly reflection. Specifically, an optical phenomenon named from the Brocken, a mountain of the Harz range in Germany, where it had been frequently observed. It consists of the shadow of the observer cast at sunrise or sunset in apparently gigantic size upon the mist or fog around the mountain summit.
241 **Swedenborg:** Emanuel Swedenborg (1688–1772), Swedish scientist and mystical theologian (and one of the figures in Emerson's *Representative Men*).
241 **meadow-hen:** the Virginia rail, *Rallus limicola.*
242 **have the refusal:** may choose to accept or refuse.

THE SUCCESSION OF FOREST TREES

Thoreau's journals show that he began to focus on the problem of seed dispersal early in 1856. His observations culminated in this, his most scientific work, initially delivered as a lecture on September 20, 1860. It was first printed in the *New-York Weekly Tribune*, October 6, 1860, and soon thereafter in the *Transactions of the Middlesex Agricultural Society* for 1860.

A major event in the previous year had been the publication of Charles Darwin's *On the Origin of Species*, a copy of which arrived in Concord on January 1, 1860. The book sharpened the debate between those who believed in "special creation" (new species being placed in the world by God) and those who believed in the "developmental principle" or "descent with modification." Thoreau found the latter argument more persuasive, as this essay shows. As Robert D. Richardson, Jr., writes, in his intellectual biography of Thoreau, "Darwin's concluding chapter repeats his conviction . . . that 'we are as yet profoundly ignorant of the many occasional means of transport' of species from one place to another. The dispersion of seeds, then, was a topic that needed attention. . . . The more Thoreau could show about plants springing from other plants via seeds transported from one place to another, the less tenable the theory of special creation becomes."

245 **Cattle-Show:** the county fair or, more formally, the Exhibition of the Middlesex Agricultural Society. In 1860 the event included plowing matches with teams of

horses and exhibitions of horses, fowl, swine, carts and wagons, boots and shoes, fruit, vegetables, butter, and needlework.

245 **cabinet:** that is, cabinet of curiosities for the display of rare and odd items.

247 **Patent Office:** At the time the U.S. Patent Office distributed packets of seed by mail (the squash seeds, for example, that Thoreau speaks of at the end of the essay).

248 **pericarp:** the wall of a ripened seed or fruit.

249 **pignuts:** seeds of the broom hickory, *Carya glabra.*

251 **Loudon:** John Claudius Loudon (1783–1843), Scottish landscape gardener and horticulturalist. In July 1857 Thoreau's journals begin referring to Loudon's encyclopedic work *Arboretum et fruticetum Britannicum; or, The Trees and Shrubs of Britain*, 2nd ed., 8 vols. (London: J. C. Loudon, 1844). The citations he gives here are from volume 3 of that work.

252 **chickaree:** popular name of the American red squirrel, *Tamiasciurus hudsonicus.*

252 ***Mus leucopus*:** now *Peromyscus leucopus*, the white-footed mouse.

253 **"when the nut":** from volume 3 of Loudon's *Arboretum et fruticetum.*

253 **rot-heap:** compost pile.

253 **Kane:** Elisha Kent Kane (1820–1857), American physician and Arctic explorer. In February 1854 Thoreau had read Kane's book *The U.S. Grinnell Expedition in Search of Sir John Franklin: A Personal Narrative* (New York: Harper & Brothers, 1853).

254 **Dukes of Athol:** James, duke of Atholl, and his son John had estates at Dunkeld and Atholl in northern Scotland. They planted first thousands and then millions of larch trees on rocky ground. Thoreau knew of them from several sources, primarily Loudon's *Arboretum et fruticetum*, but also George Emerson's *A Report on the Trees and Shrubs Growing Naturally in the Forests of Massachusetts* (Boston: Dutton and Wentworth, 1846) and John S. Springer's *Forest Life and Forest Trees: Comprising Winter Camp-Life among the Loggers, and Wild-Wood Adventure; with Descriptions of Lumbering Operations on the Various Rivers of Maine and New Brunswick* (New York: Harper & Brothers, 1851).

254 ***Tamias*:** The Greek root, ταμεια, means housekeeper or housewife, and related words mean steward or storeroom.

254 **Bartram:** William Bartram (1739–1823), American naturalist who wrote *Travels through North and South Carolina* (1791).

254 **Wilson:** Alexander Wilson (1766–1813), American ornithologist. Thoreau cites Bartram's remarks on the jay from Wilson's *American Ornithology* (Philadelphia: Bradford & Inskeep, 1808), vol. 1, pp. 16–17.

255 **"nuciferous":** bearing or producing nuts.

255 **"very few acorns":** from volume 3 of Loudon's *Arboretum et fruticetum.*

255 **beech mast:** beechnuts used as animal food.

255 **"acorns that have lain":** The source for this citation is not known.

255 **Emerson:** George B. Emerson (1797–1881), educator and naturalist. Thoreau cites from Emerson's *Report on the Trees and Shrubs*, p. 54.

255 **ancient Egyptian:** Both this and the story of the raspberry seeds come from William Carpenter, *Vegetable Physiology and Botany* (London: Wm. S. Orr and Co., 1854), p. 291.

256 **Carpenter:** William Carpenter (1813–1885). See the note for page 218 of "Autumnal Tints." The source is Carpenter's *Vegetable Physiology*, p. 290.

256 **Jackson:** Charles T. Jackson (1805–1880) wrote a series of annual reports on the geology of Maine. Thoreau's source here is Jackson's *Third Report* (1839). See the note for page 64 of "Ktaadn."

256 ***Urtica urens*:** the small stinging nettle, a European plant. Thoreau's account of finding these plants is in his journal for the mentioned date, September 22, 1857.

256 ***Chenopodium Botrys*:** a species of goosefoot or pigweed, commonly called both Jerusalem oak and feather geranium. It is a garden plant brought from Europe.

256 ***Solanum nigrum*:** also called common nightshade. It is an import from Europe.

257 **Linnæus:** See the note for page 6 of "Natural History of Massachusetts."

258 **Blitz:** Signor Blitz (1810–1877), a professional magician, was an accomplished ventriloquist, juggler, and bird handler.

A PLEA FOR CAPTAIN JOHN BROWN

On October 16, 1859, John Brown and twenty-one men attacked the federal arsenal at Harpers Ferry, Virginia (now West Virginia). Brown seems to have hoped to incite a slave insurrection and start a guerrilla war against the South.

News of the raid reached Concord on October 19. Brown was well known in town, having visited early in 1857 and again in May 1859, lecturing both times about the Free-Soil fight against slavery in the Kansas Territory (see Section IV of the Introduction).

Thoreau delivered this plea at the Concord Town Hall on October 30. Many of his neighbors thought it a bad idea for Thoreau to speak, but he insisted. Walter Harding, in his biography of Thoreau, writes: "Since he was a citizen of Concord, the selectmen could not deny him the use of the Town Hall, but they did refuse to ring the town bell to announce the meeting, so Thoreau rang it himself. The hall was filled. . . . Edward Emerson thought Thoreau read his paper 'as if it burned him' and noted that 'many of those who came to scoff remained to pray.' "

The speech was published the next year in James Redpath's anthology *Echoes of Harper's Ferry* (Boston: Thayer and Eldridge, 1860).

261 **fain:** happily; gladly.

261 **his grandfather:** Brown's paternal grandfather joined the Continental army but was probably not "an officer," as he died of dysentery a few weeks after enlisting.

261 **born:** in West Torrington, Connecticut, May 9, 1800.

261 **to Ohio:** In 1805 the Browns moved to Hudson, Ohio, southwest of Cleveland.

262 **troubles in Kansas:** A civil war had broken out in Kansas over the question of whether the territory would be Free-Soil or slaveholding. See the note for "des-

tiny of Nebraska," page 181 of "Slavery in Massachusetts," and see Section IV of the Introduction.

262 **Kansas was made free:** Thoreau's past tense may refer to the fact that the Free State party had gained control of Kansas in the election of October 1857; Kansas did not actually enact a constitution prohibiting slavery until it entered the Union in January 1861.

262 **Germany:** Brown traveled to Europe in 1849 in hopes of selling wool in England; the trip included a visit to Hamburg.

262 **Ethan Allen and Stark:** heroes of the American Revolution. In what is now Vermont, Allen (1738–1789) organized a volunteer militia, the Green Mountain Boys, who helped capture Fort Ticonderoga from the British (1775). General John Stark (1728–1822) defeated the British at Bennington, Vermont (1777).

263 **"rural exterior":** from an article in the *Chicago Press and Tribune* as reprinted in the *New-York Daily Tribune*, October 24, 1859.

263 **Cromwell:** Oliver Cromwell (1599–1658), who ruled England (1653–1658) after the Puritan Revolution.

263 **parched corn in remembrance:** An apocryphal story had it that during the summer of 1623 the Pilgrims had so little corn that they were forced to ration five kernels per person per day until the harvest. It had become the custom in Thoreau's time for a Forefathers' Day dinner to include five symbolic parched corn kernels on each plate in remembrance of the colonists' privations and perseverance.

263 **"In his camp":** Thoreau's source is James Redpath, who met Brown in Kansas shortly after the Pottawatomie massacre. Redpath, a journalist and would-be hagiographer, published his memoir of the meeting in the Boston *Atlas and Daily Bee* on the Monday before Thoreau's speech. The sketch later appeared in his 1860 book *Public Life of Capt. John Brown.*

263 **" 'Buford ruffians' ":** In the spring of 1856 a battalion of about four hundred armed Southerners, led by Jefferson Buford, entered the Kansas Territory prepared to fight the Free State settlers. Their banners read THE SUPREMACY OF THE WHITE RACE and ALABAMA FOR KANSAS—NORTH OF 36°30'.

264 **Cromwellian troop:** Of his troops during the Puritan Revolution Cromwell said, "We can only resist the superior training of the King's soldiers, by enlisting godly men."

264 **Border Ruffians:** pro-slavery settlers in the Kansas Territory, active along the Missouri-Kansas border.

264 **talking to Buncombe:** giving an empty or insincere speech. Buncombe is a county in North Carolina whose congressman in the 1820s had supposedly said that he was obligated to give a dull speech "for Buncombe."

264 **run an imaginary line:** This event supposedly happened in the spring of 1856 near Pottawatomie, Kansas, Brown and his son Salmon having disguised themselves as government surveyors to spy on a company of Georgians.

265 **price set upon his head:** After Brown had led a raid into Missouri in December

1858, President James Buchanan offered a reward of $250 for his capture; the state of Missouri offered $3,000. Brown and Thoreau would have had this exchange the following spring, when Brown was in Concord and stayed in the Thoreau household.

265 **Vallandigham:** Representative Clement L. Vallandigham (1820–1871), a conservative Democrat from Ohio. He arrived in Harpers Ferry the day after Brown was captured and participated in the interrogation, suspecting a conspiracy involving men from Ohio. The remarks Thoreau cites are from a letter to the editor of an Ohio newspaper Vallandigham wrote, October 22, 1859, describing his time in Harpers Ferry.

265 **deliver from bondage a dozen:** In December 1858 Brown and his men moved from southeastern Kansas into Missouri and attacked the homes of two planters, liberating eleven slaves. He and his party then moved eastward until they reached Detroit, where the slaves embarked for Canada.

266 **Governor of Virginia:** Henry A. Wise (1806–1876). Thoreau probably knew of his remarks from the report in the *New-York Tribune*, October 22, 1859.

267 **"surprise" party:** at the time, a party where a group of people, without invitation, brought food and gifts to a friend's house.

267 **four-and-sixpence:** a proverbial figure indicating the trifling sum for which the greedy might debase themselves.

267 **Balaclava:** During the Crimean War (1853–1856), the British won a battle at Balaklava, but not before Russian artillery had cut down more than five hundred men. Alfred, Lord Tennyson (1809–1892), the poet laureate, glorified the battle in his poem "The Charge of the Light Brigade."

267 **"insane":** Brown's lawyer tried to enter an insanity plea at his trial, but Brown rejected the attempt, calling it "a miserable artifice." After Brown's sentencing, a group of friends and relations tried to get the governor of Virginia to commute the death sentence, claiming that Brown was subject to a hereditary insanity. As Thoreau indicates, the newspapers were full of speculations about the state of his mind (*The Weekly Sentinel*, of Portage, Ohio, for example, proclaimed that Brown's backers were responsible for the crime, "not Brown, for he is mad"). Despite all this, and despite the fact that Brown could be stubborn and wildly single-minded, there is no evidence that he was insane in any modern sense of the word. For a good discussion of the topic, see Stephen Oates's biography, *To Purge This Land with Blood*, pp. 324–34.

267 **Plutarch:** Greek essayist (46?–120?), whose *Parallel Lives* presented exemplary biographies.

267 **Putnam:** Israel Putnam (1718–1790), a fabled general in the Revolutionary War who, when a boy, was supposed to have captured a wolf in its den.

267 **Tract Society:** The New England Tract Society, founded in Massachusetts in 1814, was dedicated to publishing and disseminating Christian literature. It became the American Tract Society in 1823.

267 **"American Board of Commissioners for Foreign Missions":** the first American

foreign missionary society, established in 1810 by New England Congregationalists.

268 **salt:** Various kinds of "salt" (sulfur, usually) were used to deodorize outhouses.

269 **Wilson:** Republican senator Henry Wilson (1812–1875) of Massachusetts, a Free-Soiler who knew Brown but did not support his actions.

269 **egg of chalk:** such as may be put into the nest to encourage a hen to lay.

269 **game of straws . . . game of the platter:** games of chance. Thoreau's "Indian Notebooks," now in the Pierpont Morgan Library in New York, contain several references to these. See especially volume 11, page 129, the entry for which Thoreau drew from Louis Hennepin, *Description de la Louisiane* (Paris: Sebastian Huré, 1683), p. 46.

269 ***Liberator*:** William Lloyd Garrison's abolitionist newspaper.

270 **spile:** a wooden faucet.

270 **bung:** the hole in a cask through which it is filled.

271 **Walker:** William Walker (1824–1860), an adventurer from Tennessee. In 1853 he led an armed invasion of Baja California; in 1855 revolutionaries in Nicaragua enlisted his help, and he was briefly that country's president. Alternatively, Thoreau might mean Robert J. Walker (1801–1869), pro-slavery governor of the Kansas Territory in 1857–1858.

272 **Mason:** Senator James M. Mason (1798–1871) of Virginia. He arrived at Harpers Ferry on the day after Brown was captured.

272 **Pilate:** Roman governor who interrogated Jesus, then ordered his crucifixion.

272 **Gessler:** legendary fourteenth-century Austrian despot. See the note for William Tell, page 283 of "The Last Days of John Brown."

272 **Sharps' rifles:** long-range cartridge rifles designed by Christian Sharps; those manufactured in the mid-1850s later came to be called John Browns or Beecher's Bibles.

273 **"Any questions":** Brown and the surviving raiders were captured on the morning of October 18, a day and a half after the raid began. That afternoon a contingent of officials and reporters interrogated the imprisoned Brown, who lay wounded on a pile of bedding in one of the armory buildings. The interview lasted three hours and was reported in several newspapers. Thoreau read the version in the *New York Herald*, October 21, 1859. Here he cites Brown's response to a question from Virginia senator Mason, "How many are engaged with you in this movement?" Brown had already asserted that he would answer questions about himself "but not about others."

273 **Wise:** Henry A. Wise, governor of Virginia.

273 **"Colonel Washington":** Brown's men rounded up several hostages the night of the raid on Harpers Ferry, one of them being Colonel Lewis W. Washington, a local planter and the great-grandnephew of President George Washington.

273 **"Stevens":** Aaron D. Stevens, a guerrilla fighter and brawler whom Brown had first met in Nebraska in 1856.

273 **"Coppoc":** Edwin Coppoc, a twenty-four-year-old Quaker from Iowa, had joined Brown a year before the raid.

274 **Plug Uglies:** ruffians or rowdies, especially, at the time, those who practiced politics by intimidation.

274 **France and Austria:** In 1859 these countries were subject to autocratic rule, France under Napoleon III (1808–1873) and Austria under Emperor Franz Joseph (1830–1916).

274 **Treason:** Brown was charged with murder, conspiring to start a slave revolt, and treason against the state of Virginia. As Stephen Oates has noted, treason was an odd charge, because Brown "was not a citizen of that state and owed it no allegiance."

274 **cannon-founder:** one who casts the metal for cannons.

274 **coffle:** a group chained together in a line, said especially of slaves.

275 **Massachusetts . . . sent the marines:** On the first day of fighting at Harpers Ferry, President James Buchanan ordered three artillery companies and ninety U.S. Marines to the town. These were federal troops and thus supported by all the states in the Union.

275 **Vigilant Committee:** Following passage of the Fugitive Slave Law, Northern abolitionists organized vigilance committees to engage in acts of resistance. In Boston such committees were organized by the reformer Samuel Gridley Howe (1801–1876) and the minister Theodore Parker (1810–1860), both of whom were later among the small group—the "Secret Six"—who knew in advance of Brown's planned raid.

275 **Cadi:** in Muslim countries, a judge or magistrate.

277 ***Memento mori*:** remember to die; that is, that all must die.

278 **"dreaded by the Missourians":** Thoreau's source is the same as for "rural exterior," page 359 above.

278 **"Unless above himself":** from stanza 12 of "Epistle to the Lady Margaret, Countess of Cumberland," by Samuel Daniel (1562?–1619).

278 **Minotaur:** in Greek mythology a monster who devours humans.

280 **"No man sent me here":** This and the following quotations come from the *New York Herald* report of the interrogation of Brown cited above. Here, for example, Brown replies to Representative Vallandigham's question, "Who sent you here?" Thoreau drops part of the answer, which reads in full: "No man sent me here; it was my own prompting and that of my Maker, or that of the devil, whichever you please to ascribe it to. I acknowledge no master in human form."

280 **our revenge:** During the civil war in Kansas, one Martin White shot and killed Brown's son Frederick. Several years later Brown and his men stumbled upon White at his cabin in Missouri. Despite his companions' urgings, Brown refused to kill White. He later told a friend: "People mistake my objects. I would not hurt one hair on [White's] head. . . . I do not harbour the feelings of revenge. *I act from a principle.* My aim and object is to restore human rights." Brown's mention of "revenge" during the Harpers Ferry interrogation may have set Thoreau thinking of this story. Whether it did or not, the import is that true revenge is the triumph of principle.

THE LAST DAYS OF JOHN BROWN

Thoreau was invited to speak at a memorial for Brown, July 4, 1860, in North Elba, New York; he could not make the journey but sent this piece to be read. It was published later that month in *The Liberator*, July 27, 1860.

283 **six weeks:** from the raid on Harpers Ferry, October 16, to Brown's hanging, December 2, 1859.

283 **Cato:** Marcus Porcius Cato, called Cato the Younger (95–46 B.C.), Roman politician and opponent of Julius Caesar. After Caesar's decisive victory in North Africa, Cato first saw his comrades safely out of Utica, then calmly committed suicide. Thoreau was much interested in the school of the Stoics, for whom Cato was a kind of patron saint.

283 **Tell:** According to tradition, William Tell insulted the fourteenth-century Austrian despot Gessler, who then demanded that Tell shoot an arrow through the apple on the head of Tell's son. Tell's triumphs over Gessler are part of the legendary history of the origin of the Swiss Confederation.

283 **Winkelried:** Arnold Winkelried (d. 1386), legendary hero of the Battle of Sempach, in which the Swiss Confederation defended itself against the Habsburgs. Winkelried is supposed to have died drawing the fire of enemy spears toward himself so as to open a gap in the Habsburg phalanx. In the nineteenth century he became an example of the individual who sacrifices himself for the common good.

283 **"little dipper":** Thoreau's name for various small diving birds, usually the pied-billed grebe, sometimes the horned grebe.

284 **class-teacher:** Sunday-school teacher.

284 **golden rule:** Brown repeatedly said that he based his actions on the Golden Rule and the Declaration of Independence. At his sentencing he said to the court: "I see a book kissed which I suppose to be the Bible, or at least the New Testament, which teaches me that all things whatsoever I would that men should do to me, I should do to them."

285 **modern Democrat:** that is, one belonging to the Democratic Party, which presumed Brown's raid was a plot of the Republican Party and were demanding congressional investigations. Brown himself belonged to neither party, as the Republicans were quick to point out.

285 **office:** excrement.

285 **pachydermatous:** thick-skinned.

286 **her citizens . . . to Virginia:** It had been reported that the governor of Virginia was trying to have Franklin B. Sanborn (1831–1917), Samuel Gridley Howe (1801–1876), and others arrested and extradited.

286 **"extension":** The word can mean a permission for sale of alcoholic drinks until a later time than is usual (an allowed but unusual evening of drinking being an "extension night").

286 **Charles the First:** The king of England from 1625 to 1649, Charles was tried for treason and beheaded in 1649.

287 **Raleigh:** Sir Walter Raleigh (1554–1618) was imprisoned in the Tower of London for thirteen years, during which time he wrote *History of the World* (1614). See also the note for page 60 of "Paradise (To Be) Regained."

287 **American book:** In the time between his capture and his execution, Brown wrote scores of letters, many of which were printed in the newspapers.

287 **to his wife:** In a letter written on November 16, 1859, from the jail in Charleston, Virginia, Brown urges that his children be educated first in practical matters and "the common business of life": "The music of the broom, wash-tub, needle, spindle, loom, axe, scythe, hoe, flail, etc., should first be learned at all events, and that of the piano, etc., afterwards."

287 **Poor Richard:** Benjamin Franklin's *Poor Richard's Almanack*, published annually from 1732 to 1757, contains conventional wise sayings.

287 **Irving:** The writer Washington Irving (b. 1783) died on November 28, 1859.

287 ***"It will pay"*:** The source for this remark is not known.

287 **pebbles in your mouth:** The Greek orator Demosthenes (384–322 B.C.) supposedly overcame his stammer by practicing speeches with pebbles in his mouth.

288 **slave woman:** a widespread but apocryphal story. Brown went from his jail cell to the hanging ground surrounded by soldiers and with his hands tied. In *The Life and Letters of John Brown* (1885), Franklin B. Sanborn writes that before leaving the jail John Brown was asked "if he desired the presence of a clergyman to give him 'the consolations of religion.' Brown . . . said . . . that he did not recognize as Christians any slaveholders or defenders of slavery, lay or clerical; adding that . . . if he had his choice he would rather be followed to his 'public murder,' as he termed his execution, by 'barefooted, barelegged, ragged slave children and their old gray-headed mother,' than such clergymen." Sanborn adds that from these words "arose the legend that on his way to the gallows he took up a little slave-child, kissed it, and gave it back to its mother's arms."

288 **"He nothing common did":** "An Horatian Ode upon Cromwell's Return from Ireland," by Andrew Marvell (1621–1678), lines 57–64. Thoreau silently drops two lines.

288 **transit:** passage; in astronomy the passage of a heavenly body across the meridian of any place or the passage of a celestial body across the sun's disk (as "the transit of Venus").

288 **his translation:** his conversion from a mortal into an immortal; his removal to heaven without death.

288 **North Elba:** In 1849 Brown moved his family to a farm in North Elba, New York. He is buried on the site.

288 **working in secret:** Brown's actions in Kansas were always "secret missions," and the few Northerners to whom he had revealed his Harpers Ferry plans were known as the Secret Six.

WILD APPLES

This essay was first given as a lecture before the Concord Lyceum in February 1860. It was published posthumously in *The Atlantic Monthly*, November 1862.

291 **geologist:** Louis Agassiz (1807–1873), Swiss-born naturalist then at Harvard, though Thoreau's source is actually Hugh Miller's book *The Testimony of the Rocks; or, Geology in Its Bearing on the Two Theologies, Natural and Revealed . . .* (Boston: Gould and Lincoln, 1857). Miller elaborates on a remark by Agassiz.

291 ***Rosaceae*:** rose family.

291 **Tacitus:** Cornelius Tacitus (55?–120?), Roman historian. Thoreau's source is a three-volume edition of Tacitus, *Cornelii Taciti opera ex recensione io* (Boston: Wells and Lily, 1817).

291 **Niebuhr:** Barthold Georg Niebuhr (1776–1831), German classical historian. Thoreau's source for the following citation is Niebuhr's *The History of Rome* (Philadelphia: Thomas Wardel, 1835), p. 64.

292 **"As the apple-tree":** Song of Solomon 2:3 and 2:5. For "Stay me with flagons, comfort me with apples," the Revised Standard Version reads "Sustain me with raisins, refresh me with apples."

292 **Herodotus:** Greek historian of the fifth century B.C.

292 **"pears and pomegranates":** Homer, *The Odyssey* VII.117. Alcinoüs is the legendary king of the Phaeacians.

292 **Tantalus:** in Greek mythology a favorite of the gods until he was caught deceiving them, whereupon he was condemned to hang from a tree in the underworld, thirsty and hungry. Under the tree lay a pool of water, but if Tantalus stooped to drink, the pool dried up. Ripe fruit hung above him, but if he reached for it, the wind lifted the branches away. Homer describes these tortures in *The Odyssey* XI.582–92.

292 **Theophrastus:** (372?–287 B.C.), Greek philosopher. A student of Aristotle, he wrote on many topics, including natural history.

292 **Prose Edda:** a collection of ancient Scandinavian myths and legends, recorded around 1220 by the Icelandic aristocrat Snorri Sturluson.

292 **Iduna:** in Scandinavian mythology the goddess of spring, "The Rejuvenating One." She tended the garden where the Apples of Immortality grew.

292 **Ragnarök:** In Icelandic the gods are called *reginn*, which means organizing powers. *Ragna-* is the possessive plural of this word. The suffix *-rök* means marvels, fate, doom, and *ragnarök* thus means the gods' wonders or the gods' fate/doom. *Rök*, however, later became confused with *røkkr*, twilight, and thus the word took on a sense such as Thoreau offers.

292 **Loudon:** John Claudius Loudon (1783–1843). Here and below Thoreau cites from the second volume of his *Arboretum et fruticetum*. See the note for page 251 of "The Succession of Forest Trees."

292 **Pliny:** Pliny the Elder (23–79), celebrated Roman naturalist. Thoreau owned,

and cites from, Pliny's *Historiae mundi*, 3 vols. ([Geneva]: Apud Jacobum Storer, 1593).

293 **our Western emigrant:** probably a reference to John Chapman (1774–1845), also known as Johnny Appleseed, who is supposed to have dispersed apple seeds throughout the Ohio River valley.

293 **"The fruit of the crab":** The source for this citation is not known.

293 **canker-worm:** name of certain caterpillars destructive to apple (and other) trees. In the United States, for example, the spring cankerworm is *Paleacrita vernata*.

293 **cherry-bird:** the cedar waxwing, *Bombycilla cedrorum*. The kingbird is a flycatcher such as *Tyrannus tyrannus*.

294 **coddling:** stewing; boiling gently.

294 **Palladius:** Rutilius Taurus Aemilianus Palladius (fourth or fifth century A.D.), Roman author of *De re rustica*, parts of which Thoreau read in an anthology of Latin agricultural writing, *Scriptores rei rusticae* (Heidelberg: Hier. Commelini, 1595).

294 **"Michaelmas":** the feast of St. Michael, celebrated September 29; hence, colloquially, autumn. Thoreau's source for this couplet is not known.

294 **Pomona:** the ancient Roman goddess of fruit trees.

295 **apples are the heaviest:** in Pliny, *Historiae mundi*, book 13, chap. 55.

295 **pomace:** the pulp of apples, both before and after being pressed. The root is the Latin *pomum*, apple.

295 **Loki:** in Scandinavian mythology the mischief maker who, at the behest of the giant Thjassi, lures the keeper of the Apples of Immortality, Iduna, out of Asgard (the home of the gods) and into Jotunheim (the realm of giants). As a result of this transgression, the gods begin to age, until Loki repairs the damage.

295 **"The mo appelen":** The source for this citation is not known.

295 **bloom:** the powdery coating sometimes found on the skin of fresh fruit.

295 **fugacious:** fleeing; volatile.

296 **Brand:** John Brand (1744–1806), English antiquary and topographer. Thoreau's journals for the spring of 1860 record his reading Brand's *Observations on Popular Antiquities: Chiefly Illustrating the Origin of Our Vulgar Customs, Ceremonies, and Superstition*, 2 vols. (London: F. C. and J. Rivington, 1813). Bradley Dean points out that the following citations (from "on Christmas Eve" to "Hurra!") are from the second volume of Loudon's *Arboretum et fruticetum*. Loudon bases them on the "Notes to Twelfth Day" in the first volume of Brand's *Popular Antiquities*. The last word of the poem reads "Huzza" in the original, not "Hurra."

296 **toast:** in the old sense of bread browned at the fire and put in wine or some other drink. "In state" means done publicly, with ceremony and pomp.

296 **several:** in the sense of "different"; we would say, "three different times."

296 **"Stand fast":** The source for this citation is not known.

296 **Herrick:** Robert Herrick (1591–1674), English lyric poet. Thoreau quotes a four-line poem, "Another," from a series of Christmas poems by Herrick. The last line should read "As you doe give . . . ," not "so give." Brand cites the same poem in the "Twelfth Day" section of *Popular Antiquities*.

296 **"Wassaile":** The *Oxford English Dictionary* gives this 1648 verse by Herrick as the earliest use of the verb "to wassail," meaning "to drink to (fruit-trees, cattle) in wassail [that is, in salutation], in order to ensure their thriving."

297 **cider . . . wine:** Fermented cider was then common; wine was not.

297 **English Phillips:** John Philips or Phillips (1676–1709), English poet whose most ambitious work was *Cyder*, an imitation of Virgil's *Georgics*.

297 **ungrafted:** Cultivated varieties of apple do not breed true from seed and so are grown by grafting cuttings or scions.

297 **Easterbrooks Country:** a twelve-hundred-acre tract of largely uncultivated land lying about a mile and a half north of Concord. Thoreau identifies it as one of two such tracts in the Concord area, the other being Walden Woods.

298 **Michaux:** All citations in this paragraph come from François André Michaux's *North American Sylva*, vol. 2, pp. 67–68. See the note for page 94 of "Ktaadn."

298 **sweetmeats:** fruits preserved with sugar. Michaux writes that crab apples "make very fine sweet meats . . . , by the addition of a large quantity of sugar."

299 **"Glades":** In his comments on the crab apple, Michaux writes: "It abounds, above all, in the *Glades*, which is the name given to a tract 15 or 18 miles wide, on the summit of the Alleghenies, along the road from Philadelphia to Pittsburgh."

299 **St. Anthony's Falls:** in Minneapolis, the head of navigation on the Mississippi River.

299 **herbarium:** collection of dried plants.

299 **Nobscot Hill:** on the Framingham-Sudbury line, ten miles southwest of Concord.

300 **malic acid:** found in a range of unripe fruit, including apples, cherries, and tomatoes.

302 **Van Mons and Knight:** European horticulturists Jean-Baptiste Van Mons (1765–1842) in Belgium and Thomas Andrew Knight (1759–1838) in England. Each published books on the cultivation of fruit trees.

302 **Porter, Baldwin:** varieties of apple.

302 **Hesperides:** in Greek mythology the nymphs who guarded, with the dragon Ladon, the golden apples that had been Hera's wedding gift from the goddess Earth. One of the tasks imposed on Hercules by Eurystheus was to bring him some of this golden fruit.

303 **"*Et injussu*":** Thoreau's exact source is not known, though Palladius wrote only one book, an agricultural treatise usually called *De re rustica*, parts of which Thoreau knew from an anthology of Latin agricultural writing. See the note for Palladius, page 366 above.

303 **"inteneration":** the act of making soft or tender.

303 **"highest plot":** lines 31–32 of "An Horatian Ode upon Cromwell's Return from Ireland," by Andrew Marvell (1621–1678), a poem that Thoreau also cites on page 288 of "The Last Days of John Brown." The bergamot is an old and popular variety of pear.

303 **"the custom of grippling":** from Loudon, as above.

304 **"Fruits and Fruit-Trees":** generically, but also referring to A. J. Downing's *The Fruits and Fruit Trees of America* (New York: Wiley and Putnam, 1845).

304 **pomological:** involved in pomology, the cultivation of fruit trees.

304 ***verjuice*:** "green-juice," the acid liquor expressed from crab apples, unripe grapes, and such, used in sauces, ragouts, and the like.

304 ***Pomaceæ*:** the apple family.

304 **"apples of a small size":** from Loudon, as above.

304 **Evelyn:** John Evelyn (1620–1706). Thoreau cites from Evelyn's *Sylva; or, A Discourse of Forest-Trees and the Propagation of Timber in His Majesties Dominions* . . . . 3rd ed. (London: Printed for John Martyn, printer to the Royal Society, 1679).

305 **Tityrus:** Virgil's first "Eclogue" is a dialogue between two shepherds, Tityrus and Meliboeus, the first still on his land, the second dispossessed and going into exile. In the final stanza of the poem Tityrus invites his exiled friend to pause for the night and share his apples, chestnuts, and cheese.

305 **"producing fruit":** Whitney's report was in the first volume (1785) of the *Memoirs of the American Academy of Arts and Sciences.* Northborough, Massachusetts, lies about twenty miles southwest of Concord.

306 **Nawshawtuct Hill:** just west of the confluence of the Assabet and Sudbury Rivers; also called Lee's Hill.

306 **squash-bug:** a dark-brown ill-smelling insect, *Anasa tristis*; the young feed on beans, melons, squash, and such.

306 **"*Prunes sibarelles*":** from Loudon, as above. The phrase is not a Latin binomial. The French *prunes* means plums; *sibarelles* is not a word in French (or Latin, or Spanish . . .), though apparently related to the Latin *sibilare*, to whistle. Provence is a region in the south of France.

306 ***papillæ*:** taste buds.

306 **"Nor is it every":** The source for this citation is not known.

306 **"Deuxan":** This and "Greening" are varieties of apple.

306 **"beshrewed":** cursed.

306 **"golden strife":** In Greek mythology the goddess of discord, Eris, threw a golden apple bearing the inscription "For the fairest" into an assembly of the gods. Aphrodite, Hera, and Pallas contended for it; the ensuing strife ended in the Trojan War.

307 **meridional lines:** north-south lines of meridian (on the globe).

308 ***lingua vernacula*:** native language; local dialect.

308 **fourteen hundred:** from Loudon, as above.

308 **Wood Apple:** The names are Thoreau's inventions, the Latin echoing the English. *Musketaquidensis* alludes to the Native American name of the Concord River, the Musketaquid (Meadow) River. "Chickaree" is another name for the red squirrel. *Choleramorbifera aut dysenterifera, puerulis dilectissima* means "cholera morbus and dysentery, loved by young boys," which is to say, stomach troubles attractive to youth. In Greek mythology Atalanta is a virgin huntress;

she promised to marry the man who could win a footrace with her and finally lost to Hippomenes, who distracted her with three golden apples given to him by Aphrodite.

309 **Bodæus:** Thoreau's edition of Theophrastus contained commentary in Latin by Johannes Bodaeus, which includes the poem that Thoreau "adapts" below. Bodaeus's poem is itself adapted from Virgil's *Georgics* (II.42–44), and the final word in Bodaeus's version is *pomorum* (fruits), which Thoreau changes to "wild apples."

309 **Blue Pearmain:** a variety of apple.

309 **Curzon:** Robert Curzon (1810–1873), who tells of finding such manuscripts in *Visits to Monasteries in the Levant* (New York: George P. Putnam, 1849).

310 **Topsell's Gesner:** Edward Topsell (1572–1625) and Konrad Gesner (1516–1565). Gesner was a Swiss naturalist whose *Historiae animalium* (1551–1587) attempted to describe and systematize all known animals. Topsell's *The Historie of Foure-Footed Beasts and Serpents . . .* (London: W. Iagard, 1607) was translated from Gesner's work. Thoreau read Topsell in February 1860.

310 **Albertus:** Albertus Magnus (1193–1280), German theologian known for his wide interest in natural science.

311 **lappets:** parts of a garment that hang loose; flaps.

311 **temperance reform:** Because fermented cider was the wine of the day, both it and the planting of apple trees were targets of the temperance movement.

312 **pomace-heap:** the pulp discarded after making cider.

312 **plat:** piece of land set off.

312 **"The word of the Lord":** Joel 1:1–12. A prophet of the fourth century B.C., Joel had witnessed a ravishing locust plague and called on the people to repent.

312 **"palmerworm":** a hairy caterpillar injurious to vegetation. In this case the word translates the Hebrew *gazam*, the root of which means "to cut off." The Revised Standard Bible renders these lines as: "What the cutting locust left, / the swarming locust has eaten. / What the swarming locust left, / the hopping locust has eaten, / and what the hopping locust left, / the destroying locust has eaten."

BIBLIOGRAPHY

The literature on Thoreau being vast, I list here only those works that were useful to me in assembling this volume. For anyone just beginning to work on Thoreau, I recommend three sources, each listed below: Richardson's *Henry Thoreau*, Harding's *The Days of Henry Thoreau*, and the essays that accompany the Norton Critical Edition of *Walden*. If one had each of these in hand, and followed each to its sources and antecedents, one would be deep into the work that has been done on Thoreau.

Angelo, Ray. *Botanical Index to the Journal of Henry David Thoreau.* Salt Lake City: Peregrine Smith, 1984. This index is also available on the World Wide Web at: http://www.herbaria.harvard.edu/~rangelo/BotIndex/WebIntro.html

Broderick, John C. "Thoreau, Alcott, and the Poll Tax." *Studies in Philology* 53 (1956): 612–26.

Buell, Lawrence. *Literary Transcendentalism.* Ithaca, N.Y.: Cornell University Press, 1973.

Cavell, Stanley. *The Senses of Walden.* Expanded ed. San Francisco: North Point Press, 1981.

Christie, John Aldrich. *Thoreau as World Traveler.* New York: Columbia University Press, 1965.

Cooley, Henry Scofield. *A Study of Slavery in New Jersey.* Baltimore: Johns Hopkins Press, 1896.

Dean, Bradley P. "Reconstructions of Thoreau's Early 'Life without Principle' Lectures." In *Studies in the American Renaissance*, edited by Joel Myerson. Charlottesville: University Press of Virginia, 1987, pp. 285–364. An updated version of this text is available at the Web site: http://www.walden.org/thoreau

Emerson, Ralph Waldo. "Address on Emancipation in the British West Indies." In *Miscellanies.* Vol. 11 of *The Works of Ralph Waldo Emerson.* Boston: Houghton Mifflin, 1883, pp. 131–75.

Etzler, J. A. *The Collected Works of John Adolphus Etzler.* Facsimile reproductions with an introduction by Joel Nydahl. Delmar, N.Y.: Scholars' Facsimiles & Reprints, 1977.

Foster, David R. *Thoreau's Country.* Cambridge, Mass.: Harvard University Press, 1999.

Franklin, John Hope. "Slavery and the Constitution." In *Encyclopedia of the American Constitution.* New York: Macmillan, 1986, pp. 1688–95.

Gray, Asa. *Manual of the Botany of the Northern United States.* 2nd ed. New York: George P. Putnam & Co., 1856.

Harding, Walter. *The Days of Henry Thoreau.* New York: Alfred A. Knopf, 1965.

Huber, J. Parker. *The Wildest Country: A Guide to Thoreau's Maine.* Boston: Appalachian Mountain Club, 1981.

Lynd, Staughton, and Alice Lynd, eds. *Nonviolence in America: A Documentary History.* Indianapolis: Bobbs-Merrill, 1966.

Moldenhauer, Joseph J. Introduction to *The Illustrated Maine Woods.* Princeton, N.J.: Princeton University Press, 1974, pp. xi–xxii.

"Mr. Hoar's Mission." *The Southern Quarterly Review* 14 (April 1845): 455–78.

Nasr, Seyyed Hossein. *Knowledge and the Sacred.* Albany, N.Y.: State University of New York Press, 1989.

Oates, Stephen B. *To Purge This Land with Blood: A Biography of John Brown.* 2nd ed. Amherst: University of Massachusetts Press, 1984.

Ostrander, G. M. "Emerson, Thoreau, and John Brown." *Mississippi Valley Historical Review* 39 (1953): 713–26.

Packer, Barbara L. "The Transcendentalists." In *Prose Writing, 1820–1865*, edited by Sacvan Bercovitch. Vol. 2 of *The Cambridge History of American Literature.* New York: Cambridge University Press, 1995, pp. 329–604.

Paley, William. *The Principles of Moral and Political Philosophy.* Boston: Richardson and Lord, 1825.

Redpath, James. *The Public Life of Capt. John Brown.* Boston: Thayer and Eldridge, 1860.

———, ed. *Echoes of Harper's Ferry.* Boston: Thayer and Eldridge, 1860.

Richardson, Robert D., Jr. *Henry Thoreau: A Life of the Mind.* Berkeley: University of California Press, 1986.

Rosenwald, Lawrence. "The Theory, Practice, and Influence of Thoreau's 'Civil Disobedience.' " In William E. Cain, ed., *A Historical Guide to Henry David Thoreau* (New York: Oxford University Press, 2000), pp. 153–79.

Sanborn, Franklin B., ed. *The Life and Letters of John Brown, Liberator of Kansas, and Martyr of Virginia.* Boston: Roberts Brothers, 1885. Reprint, New York: Negro Universities Press, 1969.

Sattelmeyer, Robert. *Thoreau's Reading.* Princeton, N.J.: Princeton University Press, 1988.

Scheidenhelm, Richard, ed. *The Response to John Brown.* Belmont, Calif.: Wadsworth, 1972.

Schneider, Richard J. "'Climate Does Thus React on Man': Wilderness and Geographic Determinism in Thoreau's 'Walking.'" In *Thoreau's Sense of Place*, edited by Richard J. Schneider (Iowa City, Iowa: University of Iowa Press, 2000), pp. 44–60.

Sweet, John Wood. "The Liberal Dilemma and the Demise of the Town Church: Ezra Ripley's Pastorate in Concord, 1778–1841." *Proceedings of the Massachusetts Historical Society* 104 (1992): 73–109.

Thoreau, Henry D. *Faith in a Seed.* Edited by Bradley P. Dean. Washington, D.C.: Island Press, 1993.

———. "Huckleberries." In *The Natural History Essays.* Edited by Robert Sattelmeyer. Salt Lake City: Peregrine Smith, 1980, pp. 211–62.

———. *The Maine Woods.* Edited by Joseph J. Moldenhauer. Princeton, N.J.: Princeton University Press, 1972.

———. *The Moon.* Boston: Houghton Mifflin, 1927.

———. *Reform Papers.* Edited by Wendell Glick. Princeton, N.J.: Princeton University Press, 1973.

———. *Thoreau in the Mountains.* Edited by William Howarth. New York: Farrar, Straus and Giroux, 1982.

———. *Thoreau on Birds.* Edited by Francis H. Allen. Boston: Beacon Press, 1993.

———. *Walden and Resistance to Civil Government.* Edited by William Rossi. 2nd ed. A Norton Critical Edition. New York: W. W. Norton, 1992.

———. *Wild Fruits.* Edited by Bradley P. Dean. New York: W. W. Norton, 2000.

———. *The Writings of Henry David Thoreau.* 20 vols. Boston: Houghton Mifflin, 1906.

———. *A Year in Thoreau's Journal: 1851.* Edited by H. Daniel Peck. New York: Penguin, 1993.

Von Frank, Albert J. *The Trials of Anthony Burns: Freedom and Slavery in Emerson's Boston.* Cambridge, Mass.: Harvard University Press, 1998.

Warren, Robert Penn. *John Brown: The Making of a Martyr.* New York: Payson & Clarke, 1929.

INDEX

Page numbers in *italics* refer to illustrations.